The Devil and the Land of the Holy Cross

Witchcraft, Slavery, and Popular Religion
in Colonial Brazil

LLILAS Translations from Latin America Series

The Devil and the Land of the Holy Cross
Witchcraft, Slavery, and Popular Religion in Colonial Brazil

Laura de Mello e Souza

**Translated from the Portuguese by
Diane Grosklaus Whitty**

 University of Texas Press, Austin
Teresa Lozano Long Institute of Latin American Studies

This translation was made possible in part by a subsidy from the Vitae Foundation, São Paulo, Brazil.

Originally published in 1986 as *O diabo e a terra de Santa Cruz: Feitiçaria e religiosidade popular no Brasil colonial*. São Paulo: Companhia Das Letras / Editora Schwarcz Ltda. Copyright © 1986, Laura de Mello e Souza.

Translation copyright © 2003 by the University of Texas Press
All rights reserved
Printed in the United States of America

First University of Texas Press Edition, 2003
Second paperback printing, 2008

Requests for permission to reproduce material from this work should be sent to Permissions, University of Texas Press, P.O. Box 7819, Austin, Texas 78713-7819.
www.utexas.edu/utpress/about/bpermission.html

∞ The paper used in this book meets the minimum requirements of ANSI/NISO Z39.48–1992 (R1997) (Permanence of Paper).

Library of Congress Cataloging-in-Publication Data

Souza, Laura de Mello e.
   [Diabo e a Terra de Santa Cruz. English]
   The Devil and the land of the holy cross : witchcraft, slavery, and popular religion in colonial Brazil / Laura de Mello e Souza ; translated from the Portuguese by Diane Grosklaus Whitty. — 1st University of Texas Press ed.
      p. cm. — (LLILAS Translations from Latin America Series)
   Includes bibliographical references and index.
   ISBN 978-0-292-70236-3 (pbk. : alk. paper)
      1. Witchcraft—Brazil—History—16th century. 2. Witchcraft—Brazil—History— 17th century. 3. Witchcraft—Brazil—History—18th century. 4. Brazil—Religious life and customs. I. Title. II. Series.

BF1584.B7S6813 2003
133.4'0981—dc22
                                                                                    2003059904

For my parents
and for Maurício

*The day that the captain-major Pedro Álvares Cabral raised the cross
. . . was the third of May, when we celebrate the creation of the Holy
Cross on which Christ Our Redeemer died for us, and for this reason
he named the land that he had discovered Santa Cruz, and by this
name it was known for many years. However, inasmuch as the devil,
with the sign of the cross, lost all dominion that he had over men, and
feared losing as well the great share that he had over those of this land,
he endeavored that the first name be forgotten and the name of Brazil
remain, because of a wood so called, fiery red in color, with which they
dye cloths, rather than that of the divine wood, which gave color and
virtue to all the sacraments of the Church.*
        —Friar Vicente do Salvador, *História do Brasil* (1627)

Contents

Preface to the English Edition

Published now for the first time in English, this book was originally written in 1985 as my dissertation, for which I received a doctorate in history from the Universidade de São Paulo in May 1986. The first Brazilian edition came out in December 1986; although the book has been reprinted seven times to date, its content has never been altered. It can thus be said that in 2003 *The Devil and the Land of the Holy Cross* enters its eighteenth year of existence true to its original conceptualization.

I conceived this book at a moment when works addressing sorcery and related phenomena were much fewer than they are today and thoughts on the topic were much less sophisticated. Three studies were then regarded as notable classics: Robert Mandrou's *Magistrats et sorciers en France au XVIIe siècle* (1968), Carlo Ginzburg's *I Benandanti* (1966; tr. *The Night Battles,* 1983), and Keith Thomas's *Religion and the Decline of Magic* (1980). Remarkable progress has been made since then in studies on sorcery and magical practices. Two of the most important books devoted to the topic date from 1989 and 1997: *Storia notturna* (1989; tr. *Ecstasies: Deciphering the Witches' Sabbath,* 1991) by Carlo Ginzburg and *Thinking with the Devil* by Stuart Clark (1997). The topic has been debated at a number of international conferences, in Copenhagen (1987), Budapest (1988), Saint-Cloud, France (1992), and Budapest once again (1999). Published proceedings provide an idea of the vigor of current scholarship and the interest elicited by the topic. Further evidence of recent attention to the theme was Brian Levack's extensive collection of major writings of the past few decades: *Articles on Witchcraft, Magic and Demonology: A Twelve-Volume Anthology of Scholarly Articles* (1992).

This same interest has been expressed with ever greater attention to specific contexts, pointing up regional singularities in what are now England, France, Germany, and Portugal. Examples include *Witches and Neighbours*

(1996) by Robin Briggs; *Sorcières, justice et société aux 16ᵉ et 17ᵉ siècles* (1987) by Robert Muchembled; *Witchcraft Persecutions in Bavaria* (English tr. 1997 [*Hexenverfolgung in Bayern*, 1987]) by Wolfgang Behringer; *O imaginário da magia* (1987) by Francisco Bethencourt; and *Bruxaria e superstição num país sem caça às bruxas* (1997) by José Pedro de Mattos Paiva. Meanwhile, one of the most thought-provoking books ever written on sorcery appeared in the United States in 1982: *Entertaining Satan* by John Putnam Demos, which investigated witchcraft in New England. Demos excluded the Salem trials, which had been analyzed from various angles since the publication of Paul Boyer and Stephen Nissenbaum's classic *Salem Possessed* (1974); although this work had already come out before I finished my research, I only learned of it after 1986.

In their approaches to witchcraft and sorcery, all of the aforementioned studies fit the European mold, including an identification, on the one hand, with the doctrine of demonology and, on the other, with popular practices that tend to involve demonic intervention or collective rituals (the witches' sabbat). But a large volume of scholarship also focuses on the magical and religious practices of non-European peoples, particularly those living in the Americas, who were systematically "demonized" by mission work and by the Catholic Church's repressive actions in general. In this field, considerable progress has come through vertical studies aimed at elucidating the nature of "autochthonous" practices and their surrounding "thought systems"— for example, the work of Alfredo López Austin, most especially *The Human Body and Ideology* (English tr., 1988 [*Cuerpo humano e ideología*, 1980]), and that of Linda Schele, above all *Maya Cosmos* (1993), co-authored by David Freidel and Joy Parker.

I would also like to draw attention to another line of scholarship, concerned with relationships between distinct cultural universes and how these universes came to intermingle and fertilize each other. Relativizing and reworking such polemic concepts as syncretism, acculturation, transculturation, and "cultural hybridity," this line of research is more horizontal than vertical, consonant with the belief that phenomena are better understood when studied in relationship than alone. In this regard, Serge Gruzinski's *La colonisation de l'imaginaire* (1988; tr. *The Conquest of Mexico*, 1993) is a landmark work in which the author launches the theory that Westernization is a kind of "First-World-ization." It also introduces the concept of cultural hybridity, further developed in a number of later works. Among studies on relationships between the Meso-American and European cultural universes, two other noteworthy analyses should be mentioned: Inga Clendinnen's magnificent *Ambivalent Conquests* (1991) and Fernando Cervantes's *The Devil in the New World* (1994). Sabine McCormack has made valuable contributions with regard to the Andean world, especially in *Religion in the Andes* (1991).

The late 1980s and 1990s also witnessed substantial progress in Brazilian scholarship. *Trópico dos pecados* (1989) and *A heresia dos índios* (1995) by

Ronaldo Vainfas refined the application of Inquisition sources to the analysis of culture. The first work affords a clearer picture of the part played by magical-religious phenomena in daily life, where they were often confused with breaches of morality. The second book offers one of the finest Brazilian analyses of cultural circularity and casts light on an important episode in indigenous millennialism that took place in Bahia's Recôncavo region in the second half of the sixteenth century and was demonized by Jesuit indoctrination. In 1992 Luiz Mott brilliantly probed the boundaries between the sacred and the profane, between holiness and diabolic possession, in his seminal case study of Afro-Brazilian religious syncretism, *Rosa Egipcíaca: Uma santa africana no Brasil colonial*. In another vital contribution, Mott examined the construction of Afro-Brazilian religiosity in "O calundu angola de Luzia Pinta" (1994), an article that engages in a dialog with excerpts from *The Devil and the Land of the Holy Cross* and adds to what I have written here. The same can be said about "Magia Jeje na Bahia: A invasão do calundu do Pasto da Cachoeira" by João José Reis (1988) and "Metrópole das mandingas," Daniela Calainho's doctoral dissertation (defended at the Universidade Federal Fluminense in 2001). Calainho's work portrays the thriving world of black magic and sorcery in Lisbon, capital of the empire— a world linked to the Portuguese colony in America.

In the field of anthropology but following the vein of historical approaches that explore relations between cultural universes, mention must be made of Eduardo Viveiros de Castro's fine essay "O mármore e a murta: Sobre a inconstância da alma selvagem" (1992). Two more recent contributions have made significant progress in analyzing Catholic indoctrination and the dialog between Jesuits and native Brazilians: Cristina Pompa's doctoral dissertation, "Religião como tradução: Missionários, tupis e tapuias no Brasil colonial" (defended at the Universidade Estadual de Campinas in 2001), and Adone Agnolin's research on Tupi-language catechisms used in Portuguese America during the sixteenth and seventeenth centuries (currently in progress as part of postdoctorate work in social history at the Universidade de São Paulo).

I offer this bibliographic preamble in the hopes of illustrating what an impossible task it would be to bring this book up to date by incorporating the vast and important scholarship produced in the nearly twenty years separating this English translation from the first Brazilian printing. It would mean writing another book and pondering issues other than my earlier concerns. In some senses, I feel I accomplished this task in 1993 with *Inferno Atlântico: Demonologia e colonização,* where, with the new bibliography in mind, I revisited topics first addressed in my doctoral dissertation. *The Devil and the Land of the Holy Cross* is a study of sorcery, magical practices, and popular religiosity in colonial Brazil based on empirical evidence and my own reflections. But I also think the book stands as witness to a certain era and to the mental atmosphere prevailing in Brazil's universities during the mid-1980s; the dark days of the military dictatorship were waning and the quest was on for new (or at least renewed) directions, following quite specific intellectual traditions, above all the works of Gilberto Freyre and Sérgio Buarque de Holanda. I would not like to betray or obscure the historical context of this book, for better or for worse. Nor would I wish to cleanse the text of an enthusiasm and abundance of adjectives that now at times may sound a bit much to me. For these reasons I have left the book as it was first conceived, written, and accepted for publication.

The Devil and the Land of the Holy Cross endeavors to understand the phenomenon of sorcery from the perspective of its tangled relations with culture and religion, with daily practices, and with a memory spun over the centuries, when time and again the region now called Brazil was viewed negatively. It is not a specific study of sorcery but rather of the meaning sorcery may acquire in a setting of unique historical relations, woven from the extremely varied cultural traditions of three continents: Europe, America, and Africa. While my debt to major European historians and anthropologists may be obvious (Edward Evans-Pritchard, Jacques Le Goff, Emmanuel Le Roy Ladurie, Carlo Ginzburg, Jean Delumeau), my greatest debt is to Sérgio Buarque de Holanda, Gilberto Freyre, and Roger Bastide, the most Brazilian of the French masters.

These acknowledgments would not be complete were I not to express my gratitude to my U.S. and British colleagues who saw merit in this work and in one way or another contributed to its publication in the United States: Sandra Lauderdale Graham and Richard Graham, Stuart Schwartz, Alida Metcalf, John Russell-Wood, and Susan Deans-Smith. I am particularly grateful to the University of Texas Press and to Virginia Hagerty (for her incomparable efficiency) at the Teresa Lozano Long Institute of Latin American Studies, jointly responsible for publication of this book. Finally, I record here my sincere thanks to Diane Grosklaus Whitty, skilled and dedicated translator, for whom perfection is an obsessively pursued goal.

—Laura de Mello e Souza
São Paulo, 2003

Preface to the First Edition

In recent years, some of the major works in historiography have focused on sorcery and witchcraft, a topic appertaining as well to the history of mentalities and to what has become known as the history of culture. Yet so far the subject of sorcery in Brazil during the sixteenth, seventeenth, and eighteenth centuries has prompted no research. This is not because we lack sources. Magical practices and sorcery caused concern both to the colony's civil authorities and to ecclesiastical authorities as well. Visitations to Brazil by the Holy Office verified alleged charges and then sent them on to Portugal for judgment by the Inquisition's tribunal.

When I first thought about making at least some headway in filling this gap, I had in mind a study on sorcery during colonial days, based on the trials of accused Brazilians. This endeavor would broaden the studies I had been developing on socially dispossessed strata and the articulation of power apparatuses in colonial Brazil. When I was working on my master's thesis ("Desclassificados do ouro"), my attention was called to the notable presence of sorceresses and sorcerers among the poor, marginalized population of Minas Gerais, whose everyday practices—often permeated with magic and witchcraft—were portrayed by the Ecclesiastical Inquiries (Devassas Eclesiásticas). At that time I believed that the sorcery practiced by these poor individuals—free, slave, and freed—displayed primarily African elements. They were the targets of reproach not only from the powerful but also from common people, who by condemning their peers sought to identify themselves with the ruling strata and introjected their ideology. The repression of African magic forestalled possible expressions of a unique culture belonging to black people and, more seriously yet, to slaves, which represented a grave threat to the reigning order.

As I delved deeper into specific works, however, I realized that many of the cases contained in the Devassas, which I had been reading as evidence of the survival of African practices, in fact involved a substratum common to European sorcery. Of course there were basic differences; the colony was not witness to the huge waves of diabolic possession that occurred in France's seventeenth-century convents or that were experienced by the inhabitants of Salem, New England (now Massachusetts). Still, sorcery figured markedly in colonists' daily lives, something that became more evident as I progressed in reading my sources. Of the forty-seven total offenses investigated during the Visitation to Grão-Pará alone (1763–69), twenty-one entailed sorcery and nine, curative magic. On the one hand, colonial sorcery was closely related to the colonists' urgent daily needs and aimed at solving concrete problems. On the other, it revealed a great proximity to the population's living religion, and magical prescriptions often took the form of prayers addressed to God, Jesus, the saints, and the Virgin.

A new issue thus emerged: the singularity of the colonial population's living religion, riddled with folkloric European reminiscences while it gradually acquired new tones through the cultural contributions of black and indigenous peoples. Brilliant and sophisticated analyses such as those of Le Goff (on popular medieval culture); Ladurie (on the daily life of the Cathars); Ginzburg (on popular culture and religiosity in the Early Modern age); and Delumeau (on the religious question during the same period) all led me to a growing conviction that I would not make much progress on this topic if I did not expand my concerns. I also needed to take into consideration the limits of Christianization within popular sectors—limits that have caused certain scholars to embrace the notion of the "imperfect Christianization" of western Europe's masses.

The nature of the colonial population itself impelled new theoretical concerns, once more changing the direction of my study. These people's singularity stemmed from the coexistence and interpenetration of populations from different places of origin and of different creeds. A diversity of cultural traditions thus flowed into sorcery and popular religiosity. Accounting for this complexity means understanding it as the place where multiple cultural levels intersected and were reconfigured, as agents in a long process of syncretization.

Colonial sorcery and religiosity thus became associated with the very formation of the colony as such. To detect how and by what means this process transpired, it would be necessary to return to the sixteenth century, when the European colonizer's imagination had been alternately dominated by both paradisiacal and infernal visions of the colony. Paradise was primarily associated with the new land's nature and its economic universe, while hell always pertained to its men: indigenous peoples, blacks, and, soon after, settlers. Between the two a third possibility insinuated itself: purgatory. Errors committed in the metropolis were purged in the colony through banishment, while deviant settlers, heretics, and sorcerers were in turn branded with a double stigma, living as they were in a land particularly prone to the propagation of evil. This is the route I follow in chapter 1, "The New World between God and the Devil," where I endeavor to combine ethnological procedures with a historical approach.

Next a more in-depth exploration of the nature of colonial religiosity was necessary. As the process of colonization moved forward, syncretism intensified. Initially, elements of magic and popular religiosity common to Portugal predominated, as clearly registered during the sixteenth-century Visitation; the sorcery then described was notably European in tone, and expressions of Amerindian religiosity had not as yet become exactly syncretic or were so only within a restricted realm. In the seventeenth and eighteenth centuries, the development of the colonizing process fostered greater interpenetration of European, African, and Amerindian religiosity. While Tridentine Europe strove to refine religion and "cleanse" it of folkloric survivals, European colonization of the tropics spurred syncretism. During the eighteenth century—despite catechizing efforts or perhaps because of them—antagonistic processes unfolded on both sides of the colonial system. This is the subject of chapter 2, "Popular Religiosity in the Colony." These first two chapters, which paint a broad backdrop essential to understanding the sorcery and magical practices, constitute part I, "A Wealth of Impieties: The Colony's Lot."

Part II, "Sorcery, Magical Practices, and Daily Life," is divided into four chapters that describe these practices in greater detail, taking something of an archaeological approach and relating them to daily life: survival, drudgery, fights, conflicts, hatred, love, the yearning to communicate with the other world, and the hope for revelations from the Beyond. The chapters are entitled "Material Survival," "The Onset of Conflict," "Maintaining Bonds of Affection," and "Communicating with the Supernatural."

The final part of the book, "Culture, Imagination, and Everyday Life," analyzes the intersection of distinct cultural levels and demonstrates how they diverge while at the same time merging to construct a common object: the stereotype of sorcery—a crossroads where popular concepts are subjugated to elite concepts while in turn penetrating them. This overlapping of discourses was not easy; the ensuing traumas and violence left painful marks on the course of human lives. The final two chapters, "Intertwined Discourses" and "Remarkable Stories: Where Their Roads Led," are an attempt to cover this subject.

The path that led from the European sabbat to the colonial *calundu* was long and wide; it stretched over three centuries and encompassed the mightiest economic centers. The object of my study thus dictated a limited period of focus and regional boundaries—if it is possible to speak of drawing boundaries when trying to cover such a broad geographical area. The present study deals with sorcery, magical practices, and popular religiosity in colonial Brazil during the sixteenth, seventeenth, and eighteenth centuries and covers the regions of Bahia, Pernambuco, Paraíba, Grão-Pará, Maranhão, Minas Gerais, and Rio de Janeiro. All but the last two areas received Visitations by the Holy Office, proving once again that "impurities of faith" and colonization went hand in hand. Since these Visitations took place from the sixteenth to eighteenth centuries, my sources also contributed to delineating the study's chronological framework.

Finally, two things need to be said about my archival research. It was essentially based on records of Visitations, ecclesiastical inquiries, and trials of accused Brazilians found in the National Archives at Lisbon's Torre do Tombo. To state that I read all Brazilian trials involving sorcery would be less than truthful and put me at risk of being contradicted by any researcher who has ever worked in this archive (where the classification system is still quite faulty, at least in terms of documentation on the Inquisition). In view of this, I consulted the largest number of trials possible within given constraints. Many must still be lying in wait for new researchers—which is not only an exciting thought but reinforces the idea that there is neither definitive history nor definitive research. Moreover, it is of some consolation to remember that the great Antonio José Saraiva, author of perhaps the most brilliant study ever written on the Portuguese Inquisition (*Inquisição e cristãos-novos*), believed that the researcher grappling with the inquisitorial documentation in the Torre do Tombo was condemned to "fishing with a hook."

Acknowledgments

I would like to thank the Fundação de Amparo à Pesquisa (FAPESP) for the grant I received for work on my doctoral dissertation between 1982 and 1984, including plane fare to Portugal. There I was able to carry out my archival research thanks to a grant endowed by the Fundação Calouste Gulbenkian, to whom I likewise extend my gratitude.

Once again, I owe special thanks to Fernando A. Novais, who agreed to serve as my dissertation advisor and accompanied this work through all stages.

In Portugal and in Brazil, I benefited from the help and collaboration of numerous friends, students, colleagues, and former professors. I would like to acknowledge my gratitude to the *conservadoras* of the Arquivo Nacional da Torre do Tombo, especially Maria do Carmo Farinha and Manuela Nunes. I am also grateful to the colleagues and friends who read excerpts of the manuscript and/or contributed suggestions or bibliographic sources: Leila Mezan Algranti, Edgard Carone, Hilário Franco, Jr., Sílvia H. Lara, Luiz Mott, Carlos Roberto Figueiredo Nogueira, Mary del Priore, Janice Theodoro da Silva, and Ronaldo Vainfas. For her constant encouragement and generosity in referring me to certain documents, I am particularly indebted to Professor Anita Novinsky. During part of my research, I enjoyed the assistance of the students José Augusto dos Santos Felipe, Kátia Gerab, Márcia Fonseca de Mendonça Lima, and Maria Angélica de Campos Resende.

Finally, my thanks go to the friends and relatives who offered me their emotional support and helped with the demands of daily life: Yvonne Cunha Rego, Caio Cesar Boschi, Regina von Christian, my parents, and Maurício, my husband.

Translator's Note

It has been my privilege to provide English readers with a translation of *O diabo e a terra de Santa Cruz,* a work remarkable both for its scholarship and for the richness of Laura de Mello e Souza's prose. In my approach to this task, I have sought not to lend Laura my own voice but to craft an English rendition of hers. Translation is a series of roads taken or not taken, and I hope I have kept readers on the truest path.

In this short note I would like to shed some light on my methods and offer glimpses into what has on occasion been lost—or even added—along the way, with the intent of achieving a balance between readability for foreign eyes and fidelity to content and style.

A great number of quotations in the book were extracted from Inquisition trial records and Devassas, written mostly in seventeenth- to eighteenth-century Portuguese. Transcribed by hand and unedited, these originals were rife with run-on sentences, repetitious vocabulary, and perplexing pronouns that in some places leave the reader with a furrowed brow. After consultation with the author, I omitted a few expressions of quite obscure meaning (e.g., *alho íngreme*), in our judgment without harming the text. Where a particular transcript excerpt was so obscure as to be potentially misleading, I at times inserted punctuation, rendered tense usage consistent within a passage, broke sentences into shorter units, or made other minor changes to reduce ambiguities (e.g., replacing a pronoun with a proper name). Yet it would be a deception to provide absolute clarity in a translation when it is not to be found in the original, so the reader will still encounter traces of mystery. Indeed, my goal was never to revise the transcripts but, by adhering closely to their original structure, to preserve much of their flavor and impact.

Two final comments on these and other quotations from pre–nineteenth century Portuguese: every effort has been made to avoid anachronistic use of vocabulary, while modern English spelling has been employed throughout.

Another of the particular challenges in translating this book was the number of quotations that had traveled into Portuguese through one or sometimes two other languages. Where published English-language versions of these works were available to me (and when the corresponding citations could be located), these were used. For the most part this likewise applies to works originally authored in Portuguese, as indicated in the notes.

In the endeavor to reproduce a text in a different language and culture, the singularity of a term in the source language at times forces us to admit that we are dwelling in a foreign universe. Definitions of terms that I judged best left in Portuguese are found in the glossary. For example, the semantics of skin color is a complex question in Brazil, where people are not only "black" or "white" but may also be *cafuzo, pardo, mulato, mulato claro, criolo, moreno, cabra, sarará, caboclo,* and so on. Moreover, the meanings assigned to these words have differed over time. I chose to translate only three such terms: *negro* and *preto,* both of which were rendered throughout the text as "black," and *branco* or white. All other designations related to skin color were kept in Portuguese and loosely defined in the glossary.

Military nomenclature from colonial Brazil is another complex case. But since the precise significance of these terms was only incidental to the text at hand, they were either translated literally or maintained in Portuguese, followed by a rough approximation in English.

One term deserves special note. *Feitiçaria,* which can be translated as either "sorcery" or "witchcraft," has been rendered as "sorcery" (and *feiticeiro/ a* as "sorcerer/ess"). The only exceptions occur where standard English usage prefers a form of the word "witch" (e.g., Horace's witch and the Salem witchcraft trials). Weighing in this choice were the author's own thoughts on the distinction between witchcraft and sorcery, which she addresses in the introductory pages of part II.

Finally, while the book has undergone no revision since its 1986 publication in Brazil, century references have been updated to account for the intervening advent of the new millennium.

While I of course bear ultimate responsibility for the hits or misses of this translation, I would like to acknowledge the valuable assistance of many others. First and foremost, I am grateful to Laura de Mello e Souza, with whom I have enjoyed a rewarding working relationship for some years. As always, the author was indefatigable in her willingness to help untangle obscure passages, track down meanings dimmed by time, or unravel yet another doubt.

Special thanks are owed to Professor Luiz Mott and Professor Francis Dutra, colleagues of the author, who generously offered their assistance with certain terms and translations. Others who kindly responded to my or Laura's requests for clarifications within their areas of expertise include Auxiliomar Ugarte, Luciano Raposo de Almeida Figueiredo, Márcia Moisés Ribeiro, and Neri de Almeida Souza.

Last, I could have neither begun nor ended this project without the encouragement, indulgence, and culinary support of my husband-cum-proofreader, Michael R. Whitty. While Lynx watched over my shoulder, Michael watched over my body and soul. My deepest thanks.

—Diane Grosklaus Whitty

PART I

A Wealth of Impieties:
The Colony's Lot

One hundred and four people will be appearing today, most of them having come from Brazil, a land rich in diamonds and impieties.
                    —José Saramago, *Memorial do convento*

CHAPTER 1

The New World between God and the Devil

That unripe side of earth . . .
—John Donne, "To the Countess of Huntingdon"

From Imaginary Voyages to Real Voyages

The discovery of America was perhaps the most amazing feat in the history of humanity. It opened the doors to a new time, different from all others—or "like to no other," as Bartolomé de Las Casas wrote. It joined the known worlds of Africa and Asia to a new part of the globe, as men "discovered the totality of which they are a part."[1] The novelty of the discovery was not, however, immediately understood. In the Caribbean Islands a restless Christopher Columbus searched for the signs of Asia that would assure him he had reached the land of the Great Khan. Calling the indigenous peoples he encountered "Indians," Columbus struggled to link what he saw to the travel narratives of Juan de Monte Corvino, Giovanni da Pian Carpino, Marco Polo, and so many other medieval explorers who from the thirteenth through the end of the fourteenth century had taken advantage of the Pax Mongolica to journey throughout Asia and the Indian Ocean region.[2] This new information brought with it and fertilized a whole imaginary universe. European eyes sought confirmation of what they already knew, leery of recognizing the Other.[3] At a time when hearing meant more than *seeing,* the eyes first saw what they *had heard said,* and everything they saw was filtered through reports of fantastic voyages, of far-off lands and monstrous beings who inhabited the ends of the known world.[4] Perhaps with some trauma, the evidence of these new things gradually crept into the age-old patrimony of the European imagination, destroying dreams and fantasies and finding echo in other signs of the world's disenchantment. In 1820 Giacomo Leopardi pointed his accusing finger at what he felt was a lamentable trend.[5] As a European, he was lost in this inability to recognize the Other, that is, the new universe emerging around the American image. Three hundred years had gone by, time enough for the mental projections of sixteenth-century Europeans to stretch into the newly discovered continent, encountering the imaginary universe of peoples from other cultures and ultimately merging with them. The colonizing process would see the weaving of an American colonial imagination, while other Europeans, not just Leopardi, would not realize it.

Although it was singular—that is, colonial—the New World would owe much to elements of the European imagination, under whose sign it was born. Heavily influenced by extensive reading of works like Sir John Mandeville's *Book of Marvels* and Cardinal Pierre d'Ailly's *Imago Mundi,* Columbus saw India in America. Shackled to the medieval universe, he *saw* in order to write narratives that would in turn be *heard*.[6] In Columbus, medieval thought commingled with the intrepid adventurer of a new age—the age of navigation and discovery—just as the habit of *hearing* was allied to that of *seeing,* in a kind of premonition of the baroque's characteristic visual primacy.[7] Columbus was overcome by the "vertigo of curiosity" that was to contaminate so many others after him, from the Portuguese chroniclers to Hans Staden, Anthony Knivet, and Jean de Léry. Placed "at the service of the discovery of the world," the eye gained precedence over the other senses, seizing and imprisoning the rare, the strange, and the unique, just as these had captured medieval attention earlier. Reorchestrated, the senses gave birth to new travel narratives, this time early modern.[8]

Yet before Columbus had written his letters and his journal, and even before medieval explorers had reached Mongolian Asia and told of their actual travels using a narrative structure in which the imaginary element still played a central role, imaginary voyages enjoyed immense popularity in the Christian West. Among the most interesting of these were the complex travel narratives and visions of the Carolingian period.[9] In the twelfth century, the marvelous acquired new strength and began melding with geographical descriptions of a world unknown or little known to Europeans. The legend of Alexander, for example, popularized the marvels of India, the flower-women, and other exotic beings that the Crusades had made more familiar to medieval man.[10] Around the same time, another growing legend was that of Prester John, a Christian sovereign of the East (about whom more will be said later on). Fantastic voyages beyond the known world, like the *Vision of Tungdal, Navigation of St. Brendan, Purgatory of St. Patrick,* and *Le livre d'Alexandre* were "remarkably disseminated in the Iberian area throughout all of the fifteenth century and in part during the sixteenth." Of these, *A vida de Santo Amaro* is notable for its richness of invention and particularly because it told of a maritime adventure that reached a number of desert islands.[11] So from early on, travel narratives linked fantasy and reality, blurring the borders between real and imaginary. Fictitious adventures like those of St. Patrick contained elements drawn from the earthly world, while real adventures like those of Marco Polo were interlaced with fantastic accounts and implausible situations that the merchant had heard from someone and believed he had actually experienced himself.[12]

Mandeville's *Travels* is a good example of this blending of the imaginary and the real. Written in French, probably in Liège in the mid-fourteenth century, these narratives are authored by an imaginary Sir John of Mandeville. Based on geographical texts and encyclopedias like Vicent of Beauvais's, this compilation was published several times in Latin and in a number of European languages as well. The first of the two-part work offers an itinerary of the Holy Land (a "sort of pilgrim's tourist guide," in the words of Carlo Ginzburg), while the second describes a trip to the East that encompasses far-off islands and reaches India and Cathay (China). It ends with the description of the Earthly Paradise and of the islands surrounding the mythical kingdom of Prester John. Although both parts are presented as direct testimonies, there is a difference between them: "the first abounds in precise and documented observations, [whereas] the second is mostly imaginary."[13]

What was people's vision of earth in the fourteenth century? They believed in the existence of the equator, the tropics, five climatic zones, three continents, three seas, and twelve winds. Northern Europe and the Atlantic Ocean were already part of an imaginary geography and were described in almost fictional form; arctic peoples lived in darkness in the cold north, while the sea held countless mysterious islands. Talk about Africa included the Maghrib and Egypt; hypotheses were fashioned about the sources of the Nile, said to lie within India (in turn believed to be connected to Africa, enclosing the Indian Ocean) or in the upper part of the Niger. Immensely fascinating to the European imagination, Asia enclosed the Earthly Paradise, sealed off by high mountains, an iron curtain, and hordes of monstrous animals. To the north lay the legendary country of Gog and Magog, inhabited by the tribes of Israel cast out by Alexander. Stretching over the middle was the kingdom of Prester John, descendant of the wise men and relentless enemy of the Mohammedans. The first mention of this kingdom—of major importance in the European imagination—comes from Otto of Freising (1145), twenty years before Prester John was supposed to have written his letter to Alexander III, Manuel Comnenus, and Frederick Barbarossa. To the south lay India, location of the Christian community of St. Thomas, according to legend narratives. Beyond the Indian Ocean was the country of antipodes, antinomic world *par excellence*, inhabited by monstrous beings: dog-headed apes, Cyclops, troglodytes, headless beings, ant-men. . . .[14]

For centuries, the Indian Ocean had constituted the mental realm that incarnated the medieval West's exoticism (or need for it), "the place where its dreams freed themselves from repression."[15] For Le Goff, the fear of unveiling this world was like the fear of unveiling one's own dreams. One of the basic components of the Indian dream was wealth—islands overflowing with pearls, precious wood, spices, lengths of silk—which linked the dream with the need for greater trade and the acquisition of new markets to supplement Europe's. The expansion of trade thus constituted the infrastructure of these oneiric projections or at least a part of them.[16] The other side of the Indian dream was the fantastic exuberance of nature, of people, of animals, some of which were monstrous. For Europeans, this was a way of compensating for their own deprived and limited world. From a sexual perspective, it was the fascination with difference: cannibalism, nudism, sexual freedom, eroticism, polygamy, incest.[17]

All of these themes, analyzed by Le Goff in relation to the Indian Ocean, are present in the discovery of America. As Europeans gained ever-greater familiarity with the Indian Ocean, where the travels of medieval explorers had figured importantly, these countries of legend and these monstrous peoples were pushed farther away, into peripheral regions as yet untouched by Westerners. Claude Sutto shows that Gog and Magog became inhabitants of northern Russia. Prester John shifted from Central Asia to Ethiopia. Medieval man had first placed Ethiopia in Meridional India, in Le Goff's opinion symbolizing the union of the queen of Sheba and Alexander, and no longer her union with Solomon. By the fifteenth century, the Portuguese already saw Ethiopia as part of Africa. Ever more often, reports depicted Asia in strictly human dimensions.[18]

From this perspective, it would seem justifiable that once the Indian Ocean had become known and its fantastic universe demystified, the Atlantic would begin playing an analogous role in the fifteenth-century European imagination: it was the last stronghold of monstrous peoples, of an Earthly Paradise, of the Kingdom of Prester John, and perhaps—as Friar Vicente do Salvador stated—of the kingdom of the devil himself, who here would engage in bloody battle against the cross and its knights.[19] The marvelous would be forever fated to occupy the fringes of the world known to the West, and the American colonial world would thus be its last frontier.

The legend of Prester John is enlightening for two reasons. First, it is a model illustration of the notion that a geographical migration took place within the European imagination when unknown lands were finally revealed. Second, it is closely related to Portuguese navigation and to the discoveries. Sérgio Buarque de Holanda believes that the long-standing legend of the Eastern Christian potentate was diluted and simplified by the Portuguese, who had little inclination for fantastic daydreams. He does, however, recognize that this navigating people played an important role in the "demand for the fabulous country of Prester John."[20] In 1487, when Afonso de Paiva and Pero da Covilhã left Portugal charged with discovering an overland route to the Indies, they carried with them Dom João II's instructions concerning reconnaissance of Prester John's land. As Buarque de Holanda has stated, the legend was already over a century old by then and did not benefit much from the Portuguese imagination. Yet Brazil's greatest historian does not focus on the fact that by incorporating this legend the Portuguese inscribed it within the genesis of their enterprise of world discovery. In the imagination of the Portuguese sailors who left with Vasco da Gama or with Pedro

Álvares Cabral, how great was their expectation that they would at long last touch the legendary lands of the Christian king?

It was also Sérgio Buarque de Holanda who pointed out this shift of the Earthly Paradise to the Atlantic universe, transferred from the distant reaches of Asia and Africa and in its new habitat associated with quite ancient Celtic traditions.[21] It was a slow process. In the tenth century the Earthly Paradise was to be found in the middle of the ocean. It subsequently traveled first northward then westward, accompanying the progress of geographical knowledge, "until disappearing in the late sixteenth century, though it did not fade from the popular imagination before the eighteenth century."[22]

As the European imagination accumulated legends, relocated them spatially, and remolded them, it also came to encompass the archipelago of the Brazil islands, possibly a transformation of the island of São Brandão. From 1351 to 1508, this land went by myriad designations: Brazi, Bracir, Brasil, Brasill, Brazil, Brazile, Brazille, Brazill, Bracil, Braçil, Braçill, Bersill, Braxil, Braxili, Braxill, Braxyilli, Bresilge.[23] In 1367 Pizigano's letter listed the three islands of Bracir, which would from that time on be registered on most maritime charts, with their position unchanged: "the southernmost of the islands we find indicated within the Azores group, approximately at the latitude of Cape Saint Vincent; the second lies NW of Cape Finisterre, at the latitude of Brittany; the third, to the W and not very far off the coast of Ireland."[24]

Friar Vicente do Salvador most likely was unaware that the name "Brazil" had appeared on medieval maps, and it seems to me that he was the first to associate this title with the reddish dyewood. But it is curious to note that when he did so he offered a very complicated explanation of a religious bent, alluding to the struggle between good and evil, between heaven (kingdom of God) and hell (kingdom of the devil). Moreover, he associated "this immature portion of Earth" with the realm of demoniac possessions, unburdening upon the nascent colony the full weight of the European imagination, where the devil had played a major role since at least the eleventh century. If an identification with infernal regions is visible in Friar Vicente's text, less evident is the association between the fruit of a concrete voyage—to wit, the discovery of Brazil—and the many imaginary voyages that Europeans had been undertaking for centuries, though one connection is just as legitimate as the other. Brazil, colony of Portugal, was thus born under the sign of the demon and the projections of the Western imagination. But in this excerpt from Friar Vicente, infernal dominion was not the only possibility. The first move, made by Pedro Álvares, had been toward heaven, to which the colony was meant to be coupled—had Lucifer's successful efforts not turned it all into a lost cause. The text of Brazil's first historian is remarkable precisely because it takes into account the complexity underlying these two possibilities: seeing the colony as the dominion of God (i.e., as paradise) or of the devil (i.e., as hell). For Friar Vicente, the devil came out on top: Brazil was the name that stuck, and the monk laments that the other appellation fell into oblivion, for it was much more virtuous and consonant with the coura-geous Portuguese people's goal of saving souls.

Taking quite a different stance, Antonio de Santa Maria Jaboatão, an-other friar, saw the discovery of Brazil as supernatural and miraculous. For many years, God had kept the existence of this expansive region hidden and had finally unveiled it to human eyes so that heaven might gather "bountiful profits" from this treasure. Not only is that which occurs supernaturally and miraculously to be deemed wonderful, but so too is that which "occurs natu-rally, outside the normal order of things," as was the case with the discovery of Brazil—which was therefore miraculous and supernatural.[25] For Jaboatão, the supernatural was a positive force in the case of Brazil's discovery; it had been a divine act, and it was God, through His unfathomable designs, who led men to this land. The discovery of Brazil revealed and reinforced the existence of God: a divine miracle—such was the revelation of the Portu-guese colony in America.

The formulations of these two clerics, separated from the event they inter-preted by a greater or lesser number of years—in the case of Jaboatão, by two and a half centuries—lead us to think about the constancy of the mental universe, less permeable to change than are economic and social structures. The age of the discoveries was characterized by religious zeal; as is well known, the discoverer of America himself was seriously thinking about using Ameri-can gold in a Crusade against the Infidel. For Columbus, it can be said there were three kinds of reasons for navigating the seas: the human, the divine, and the natural.[26] As components of the mental universe, they were never isolated from each other but maintained a constant and contradictory rela-tionship: in the divine sphere, God does not exist without the devil; in the world of nature, there is no Earthly Paradise without hell; among human beings, virtue and sin alternate.

The maritime venture thus played itself out under the heavy influence of the European imagination, both positive and negative currents of thought. The golden age of European utopias was tightly linked to the great discover-ies and travel accounts, "embellished by the imagination." They produced culture shock and led to comparisons with, and questionings of, the prevail-ing social structures.[27] André Thevet and most especially Jean de Léry made their influence felt in the construction of the myth of the noble savage, and edenizing tendencies find resonance in many of the chronicles and treatises written on Brazil; Pero de Magalhães Gandavo, among others, was consid-ered a propagandist of Portuguese colonization of the tropics.[28] But even the rosiest interpretations spoke of risk, danger, and death. Thevet himself calls attention to the other side of expansion—the fear of the ocean sea, of mael-stroms, of Adamastor giants: ". . . abandoned at the whim and mercy of the most uncertain, least merciful, and least safe of all elements, with small wooden ships, fragile and dilapidated *(from which one can almost always expect death more than life)* to navigate their way toward the Antarctic pole, which had never been discovered nor was even known to the ancients."[29]

Léry and his companions even started to believe they would be eternal prisoners of the sea: "Indeed, since we had been tossing and afloat on the sea almost four months without putting into port, it had often occurred to us that we were in exile out there, and it seemed as though we would never escape it."[30] Gandavo's tantalizing prognoses saw a tragic reversal in the accounts of shipwrecked Portuguese, a curious literary genre that flourished during the sixteenth and seventeenth centuries. "We have nothing but ships swallowed by the waves; crews wasted by disease; extreme suffering by women, the aged, children; lean gains for the more fortunate, who may perhaps manage to survive one journey but will die on the next."[31] Viewing overseas expansion as the "petty eagerness of greed and oppression," the authors of these accounts in effect denounced the ideological instrumentalization of elements of the imagination, which was grounded on the justification of "spreading the faith and the empire."

Once discovered, Brazil was to occupy a position in the European imagination analogous to that previously held by the far-off mysterious lands that, once known and penetrated, had lost their enchantment. With the advent of slavery, this imagination would be remolded and restructured while still maintaining deep European roots. As a modified extension of the European imagination, Brazil also became an extension of the metropolis with the advance of the colonizing process. Everything that existed there existed here, but in a singular, colonial form. Once again, it was the highly astute Friar Vicente who perceived this similarity within difference: "Does wheat flour come from Portugal? That of this land suffices. Wine? A most mild one is made from sugar and for those who like it strong, by boiling it for two days, it leaves one drunk like grape wine. Oil? It is made from palm-tree coconuts. Cloth? Cotton is made with less effort than it takes to make linen or wool there. . . . Almonds? They too can be replaced with cashews, *et sic de ceteris*."[32] "This Brazil is now another Portugal," Fernão Cardim was to write, shortly thereafter adding its differences: a much more temperate climate, much rarer diseases, but less comfort in dwelling and in dress.[33] This was an early perception of being-and-nonbeing, which would intensify in the eighteenth century. America was much more a child of Europe than Asia or Africa had ever been. But "it was Europe, and at the same time, non-Europe; it was the geographical, physical, and soon the political antithesis of Europe."[34] Good and evil, heaven and hell, which in Europe (the metropolis) ended up reaching equilibrium, could here (the colony) more than anywhere else tend toward polarization. In terms of nature, the idea that the New World was an extension of Europe—and thus the place where the myths of an Earthly Paradise would be realized—tended to triumph; almost always, nature was edenized. But when it came to a distinct kind of humanity, painted black by the African slave and brown by indigenous peoples, difference won out. The human world was infernalized to an extent never before dreamed by all of European teratology—an imaginary place of Western visions of an inviable humanity. Clouds of insects, gigantic snakes, and intense heat all aroused great perplexity, but the cannibalism and lassitude of indigenous peoples, the sorcery and noisy music of blacks, the mixing of the races, and, last, the colonists' desire for autonomy engendered repudiation.

Nature: The Predominance of the Edenic Vision

Western expansion was twofold in nature. On the one hand, new lands were incorporated and made subject to the temporal power of European monarchs. On the other, new flocks were gathered for religion and for the pope.[35] Of all the fruits that the newly discovered land could yield up, to Pero Vaz de Caminha it seemed the finest would be the salvation of indigenous peoples. "And this should be the principal seed that Your Highness should sow," the scribe of Calicut took the liberty to advise, writing quite naturally. In Caminha's text, spreading the Catholic faith appears to be the monarch's great desire: "to do what Your Highness so desires, that is, *expand our holy faith!*"[36] Nearly fifty years later, Dom João III reiterated the Christianizing goals of the Portuguese monarchy: "The principal thing that compelled me to command that said lands of Brazil be peopled was so that its folk be converted to our holy Catholic faith," he wrote to Tomé de Souza in 1548.[37] It has become a commonplace to state that religion furnished the ideological means for justifying the conquest and colonization of America, masking and camouflaging the atrocities committed in the name of faith. This was undeniably true. But if so much has been said about the relations between infrastructure and superstructure, almost no efforts have been made to dissect the complex world of religiosity. It never hurts to remember that the close of the Middle Ages and dawning of the Early Modern age were typified by a deep, zealous, angst-filled religiosity.[38] Therefore, while material objectives were not minor, Christianizing was indeed an integral part of Portugal's colonizing program for the New World. Moreover, it was an important part, given the weight of religion in the lives of sixteenth-century people.

The Portuguese were sincerely convinced of their missionary role. "Other men, by divine institution, are only obliged to be Catholic: the Portuguese man is obliged to be Catholic and to be apostolic. Other Christians are obliged to believe in their faith: the Portuguese man is obliged to believe and moreover to propagate it," said António Vieira one century and a half after discovery. The example of missionary zeal came from above, from the king: "All kings are of God, made by man: the king of Portugal is of God and made by God and for this he is more His," said Vieira. But the example also came from God Himself above, who had elected the Portuguese from among other peoples, in a kind of repetition of the history of Israel.[39]

The question of faith was not separate from the issue of the overseas enterprise: the faith would be spread, but lands would be colonized as well. Portuguese caravels were vessels of God, and missionaries and soldiers sailed in them together, for "not only are the missionaries apostles, but so too are the soldiers and captains, as all go in search of heathens to bring them to the light of faith and to the congregation of the Church."[40] In the first quarter of the eighteenth century, Sebastião da Rocha Pitta would continue to explain the discovery of Brazil theologically. Here the land was uncultivated and its inhabitants were barbarians "when general Pedro Álvares Cabral discovered it," "joyous to be the first who found an unknown region of so many heathens (where our monarchs had that which they sought, to expand our Catholic faith, which was their purpose in ordering the plowing of the seas with so many armadas)." Expansion of the faith, colonization, and strengthening of monarchical power always appear in conjunction. Dom João III "devoted his Catholic zeal to the enterprise, among the lands as well as the souls of Brazil, and he achieved both victories, gathering as many lambs into the fold of the universal pastor as subjects under the rule of his dominion." In lines almost identical to Vieira's, Rocha Pitta wrote that the monarch sent "captains and missionaries together" to the Portuguese colonies.[41]

Friar Vicente do Salvador justified the colonizing endeavor on the basis of religion. Among the products raised in the colony were bread and wine, required for the holy sacraments. "If you say to me that a land that has no wheat bread and grape wine for mass cannot sustain itself, I will agree, for this divine sacrament is our true sustenance; but for this purpose that which grows in this same Brazil, in São Vicente and the fields of São Paulo, suffices."[42] Colonial nature was thus enfolded into the sphere of the sacred.

Gandavo proposed to engage colonists in the exploitation of maritime riches until mines of precious metal could be discovered inland. He said that in addition to exploiting this wealth, it was important to bring indigenous peoples from the *sertão* [Brazilian backlands], for when "placed before the light and knowledge of our Holy Catholic Faith," their souls would be saved.[43] It was up to the settler to discover the land's riches and also to enrich the heavens, converting souls. There seems to have been a flow of reciprocity, a kind of balancing of accounts: Providence's benevolence, affording the discovery of silver and gold, should be repaid in souls. By the same token, the more souls that were sent to heaven, the more benevolent the Creator would feel toward the colonists.

According to Father Simão de Vasconcellos, divine attention was first directed toward Europe, Asia, and Africa, where humanity, the Earthly Paradise, and the patriarchs had been placed. The other part of the world, "no less agreeable," had lain bereft of paradise, patriarchs, the divine presence, the light of faith, and salvation for 6,691 years. At the end of this period, "the order was given for this new and hidden world to appear"; the Portuguese were made God's arm and charged with spreading the faith to these new parts.[44] Once more, here is the idea that God provided for everything, determining that the Portuguese should discover lands in order to colonize and Christianize them—again, the idea of a "kingdom of God by Portugal."

It was thus a generalized idea, particularly among clerics, that the discovery of Brazil had been a divine action and that God had chosen the Portuguese from among all peoples. Furthermore, as masters of the new colony, the Portuguese had the duty to make it produce material wealth by exploiting nature and spiritual wealth by recovering souls for the divine legacy.

The discovery of Brazil—a divine action—unveiled to the Portuguese the paradisiacal nature that so many would liken to the Earthly Paradise. Within the storehouse of their imagination, they searched for elements of identification with the new land. Associating fertility, lush vegetation, and the pleasant climate with the traditional descriptions of the Earthly Paradise made this faraway, unknown land seem closer and more familiar to the Europeans. The divine presence could be felt in nature as well; elevated to the divine sphere, this nature once more reinforced the presence of God in the universe.

This is what Rocha Pitta, Thevet, Léry, and others have to say. In a famous passage, Rocha Pitta describes the passion-fruit flower and associates it with Christ's passion: "mysterious creation of nature, which from the same parts that composed the flower shaped the instruments of the holy passion."[45] Awed by the beauty of a certain bird, possibly from the parrot family, Thevet wrote: "Thou shalt know not how to deny praise to He who is the artisan of such a lovely work."[46] In an admirable passage, Léry, an author of greater skill, tries to show that the diversification of the natural world is proof of the grandeur of God's divine work. During the year he spent involved in the French effort to establish a religious colony in Brazil—known as French Antarctica—Léry says he observed trees, fruits, and animals wholly unlike those found in Europe. Each time he recalled the image of that new world, "the serenity of the air, the diversity of the animals, the variety of the birds, the beauty of the trees and the plants, the excellence of the fruits, and, in short, the riches that adorn this land of Brazil," he remembered the cry of the Prophet in Psalm 104:

O Seigneur Dieu que tes oeuvres divers
Sont merveilleux par le monde univers
O que tu as tout fait par grand sagesse!
Bref, la terre est pleine de ta largesse.

Fortunate were the peoples dwelling there, he concluded—but with this caveat: "if they know the author and creator of all these things."[47]

Thevet's stance is more straightforward: the beauty and perfection of the natural world refer us to God, again proving His existence. What other craftsman could fashion such a perfect work? Léry goes further: the beauty of the New World reinforces the existence of God not simply because it is beautiful but indeed because it is different. In this context, the specific lends evidence to the varied and the multiple found within divine will and action. God thus exists, for He makes what is beautiful and makes what is different. Léry's position of course reflects the Calvinist notion that the world was created for the glory of God. Incorporating these ideas, he read the colonial world through a religious prism in which Catholics and Protestants ended up converging.

If the European imagination shifted its projections to the New World and if spreading the Christian faith and colonization went hand in hand, it was no surprise that the discoverer of America would be its first "edenizer" as well.[48] As a Soldier of Christ, Columbus was concerned with the salvation of souls. In order to justify the need for Christianization, the New World's "indigenous" peoples had to be denigrated—and by denigrating them, slavery was justified. Columbus therefore inaugurated the double-edged movement that would last for centuries in American lands: the edenization of nature and the denigration of men—barbarians, animals, demons. This tendency to associate the men of the colony with animals or demons would later be accentuated; but in Columbus there is an inarguable display of ceaseless interest in examining nature and a disinterest in the men who reaped its benefits. "Here and in all the island, the trees are green and the plants and grasses as well, as in the month of April in Andalusia. The singing of the small birds is such that it would seem that a man would never willingly leave this place. The flocks of parrots darken the sun. Birds great and small are of so many kinds and so different from ours that it is a wonder," the discoverer was to write.[49]

Ever since his first voyage, based on analogies between what he saw before him and what he had read in authors like Mandeville, Columbus would endeavor to prove that he had reached the environs of the Earthly Paradise.[50] Like him, countless authors would make repeated reference to the presence of paradise in American lands, in the literal or figurative sense.[51] Friar Vicente do Salvador stopped short of expressing the idea that paradise lay there, but he did unreservedly state that "Brazil has a greater abundance of provisions than all lands that there are in the world, for in it are found the provisions of all the others."[52] With these words he echoed the man who had first written about Brazil: Pero Vaz de Caminha. Making no reference to the Earthly Paradise, focused much more on describing people than landscapes, Caminha said this new land was "so generous that, desiring to profit of it, everything shall grow in it, by virtue of the waters it hath." The potential utility of this discovery was of greater import than fanciful deliriums. In contrast to Columbus, the Portuguese were incapable of dreaming, Sérgio Buarque de Holanda was to state. How did the earth look to Caminha? "Very flat, very lovely," "very big," "very fine climate, fresh and temperate."[53] For Rocha Pitta, on the other hand, Brazil was not just the best part of the New World— "a most vast region, a fortunate land upon whose surface all is harvest, within whose center all are treasures, along whose mountains and coasts all is aroma," a remarkable country where a lavish nature surrenders fertile production for the "affluence of the monarchy and the benefit of the world"— rather, it was the Earthly Paradise itself.[54] It is well worth citing the passage where he defends this position, for it lists all the paradisiacal features there-after to be repeated ad infinitum (in Brazil's national anthem as well):

> In no other region does the sky appear so serene, nor does the dawn awaken more lovely; in no other hemisphere does the sun have such golden rays, nor such radiant nocturnal reflections; the stars are the gentlest, and appear always joyful; the horizons, be the sun rising or be it dying, are always clear; the waters, drawn from springs in the fields or from aqueducts within settlements, are the purest; *Brazil is, in short, the earthly paradise discovered,* where the greatest rivers are born and flow; a wholesome climate prevails; gentle stars have influence, and the gentlest zephyrs breathe, although, since it lies beneath the torrid zone, Aristotle, Pliny, and Cicero would doubt and consider it uninhabitable.[55]

Jaboatão was to reiterate many of the edenizing features enumerated by Rocha Pitta. Brazil—"remarkable, delicious, and rich portion of the great America"—had for a long time remained "hidden from the news of human discourse." For this reason it was called the fourth part of the world, though it deserved the title of first. Healthy air, fresh breezes, a mild climate, fertile earth, all cloistered by two precious keys: one of silver, demarcating its southern part; the other of gold, defining its northern. Alluding to the Prata and Amazonas rivers, which delimited Brazil's lands, the author thus sought to liken Brazil to the Earthly Paradise. The beauty of this perspective—the natural world—reinforced the idea of an Earthly Paradise: "Peaked mountains" and "extensive valleys" filled with lush, fruitful trees, covered with "pomes at any season of the year"; joyous, multihued flowers, growing "with no more care for their raising than that of nature, and of time," capturing one's eye and stimulating one's sense of smell; birds that both "entertained the eye with the variety and sheen of their feathers" and "satisfied the taste with their tantalizing and appetizing meat," in addition to delighting people with their sweet songs—in short, a New World, where the Creator sought to repair some of the Old World's imperfections. "A new world at last, and such an accommodating place for man to live that not much censure would be deserved by whoever wanted to plant the Earthly Paradise in it, or at least to describe it with the excellencies and privileges of an earthly Paradise."[56]

As can be seen, Jaboatão did not go so far as to affirm that the Earthly Paradise lay in Brazil, perhaps leery that his work would meet the same fate as that of the priest Simão de Vasconcellos.[57] Still, even though somewhat timidly, Jaboatão insinuates this analogy in more than one passage. Citing an unnamed author, he exalts the qualities of Pernambuco—the most "flowering, fertile, and rich" of the captaincies. "Its climate is a *second* Paradise," he adds, leaving aside (and for others) the question of the initial paradise.[58]

Knivet, a sixteenth-century Englishman who sailed with Thomas Cavendish, left some interesting images of Eldorado that reveal what a strong influence the European imagination wielded in views of the New World.

Like Gandavo and Gabriel Soares, Knivet beheld the Resplendent Mountains: "We came into a fair Country, and we saw a great glistening Mountain before us, *ten days before we could come to it,* for when we came into the plain Country, and were out of the Mountains, the Sun began to come to his height, we were not able to travel against it, by the reason of the glistening that dazzled our eyes." Knivet was convinced they were in the vicinity of the Potosí, which was the case whenever gold and precious gems were found: "We came to many Mountains, where we found good store of gold, and many precious stones; when we came into this Country, we thought we had been in the Province of Peru."[59]

Pero de Magalhães Gandavo and Ambrósio Fernandes Brandão were advocates of the edenizing line. What is interesting about them, however, is that they lent new hues to this edenization, reiterating the notion that the edenic character is restructured and transformed during the process of colonization. Nature is prodigious, generous, friendly—so long as transformed by humans. These humans may even be the poor expropriated fellows from the metropolis or banished undesirables, for nature, with its bountiful positive features, is greater than human pettiness. For these two authors, who wrote in 1576 and 1618, respectively, colonization became an indispensable prerequisite to the edenization of nature.

The images Gandavo uses to describe the Province of Santa Cruz are those commonly found in European descriptions of Earthly Paradises. The land is "very delicious and fresh," all "cloaked in very tall and thick trees, wetted by the waters of many and very precious streams of which all the land has an abundant part, where the verdure always remains with that moderation of spring that April and May offer us here." Unlike the situation in Europe, plants do not suffer in the winter, for Providence has provided a perfect nature, rich, moreover, in precious gems and metals.[60]

Yet in very few passages is nature dissociated from humans. The province is "better for the life of man than each of the others in America."[61] In Gandavo's view, the colony's edenic potential favors and facilitates human labor. For this reason all who cannot find opportunities in Portugal should seek the new land; the colony serves to "correct" the metropolis's ills. In the new land, "no poor walk from door to door begging as in this Kingdom [Portugal]"; and "all those who live in poverty in these kingdoms should not doubt in choosing it for their shelter."[62]

Underscoring the quality of the New World's climate, the fresh winds, the symmetry in length of days and nights, Ambrósio Fernandes Brandão adds his voice to the edenic chorus. "There is no lack of authors who want to affirm that the earthly paradise is located in these parts," he states.[63] Even the Elysian Fields so celebrated by the Europeans fell far short of the Brazilian land; like "the fabulous paradise of the scurrilous Maphamedes," these fields were no more than "deceits." Here, on the contrary, ran actual rivers of milk and honey—the wild honey found in abundance in the forests, the excellent butter taken from cows, goats, and sheep.[64] Brandão thus incorporates edenization, an important element of the European imagination, but offers a new reading of it. Paradise is here, where exuberant nature (native honey gushing forth) joins with systematic work (livestock, milk, butter). The happy marriage of nature and labor, initiated by colonization, made Brazil superior to Europe, Asia, or Africa. "The land is ready to have done on it all the husbandry of the world, for its great fertility, excellent climate, good skies, the willingness of its temperament, healthy air, and another thousand features assembled on it." Docile birds, most excellent fish, crabs, and shellfish abounded here within hand's reach—"countless eggs, marvelous fruit," "various types of legumes," provisions, and "other infinities of wholesome things."[65]

It was a bountiful nature but one already transformed by the colonizing effort. As in Gandavo, these efforts are attenuated by the presence of slaves (a propagandizing tool?); but in Brandão more than in *Tratado da terra do Brasil,* the Europeans' work in the tropics was eased by the conveniences of a wild nature (plentiful fish and game).

The colonizing, re-edenizing process was thus superimposed on the already edenic nature of the discovered land, which revived images of the Earthly Paradise in the European imagination. When Brandão listed the six essential riches of Brazil, the only native ones he included were timber and brazilwood (in two differentiated categories). All the others—sugar, trade, cotton, crops, and cattle—presuppose the colonizing endeavor. "Of all these things, the principal fiber and substance of the land's wealth is sugar-raising," Brandão was to conclude, placing prime emphasis on the most typically colonial of the colonial products.[66] Is there any room for doubt?

Jaboatão, as seen earlier, likewise embraced the idea of an Earthly Paradise. In an enigmatic text, he shows the other side of the coin. Rich with its infinite treasures of metals, precious gems, and valuable *drogas* [tropical products such as cloves, pepper, and sarsaparilla], Brazil enriched the rest of the world with the fruit of its womb, "yielding itself up." But like the viper that nourishes ungrateful offspring and harvests death and destruction, the colony would ultimately suffer; colonial assets, "who does not know it, were, are, and always will be the reason for this same ruin, *and for the ruin of its own native sons.*"[67] Viewed within the whole of Jaboatão's work, this passage might even seem a lapse, a pessimistic outburst by the historian of the Seraphic Order. His meaning is clear: the colonists do not reap the benefits of colonization, which bear fruit elsewhere: in Europe. In the first place, this negative tone clashes with the author's positive formulations, where Brazil is always cast as having a great destiny to fulfill, favored as it is by the Creator's generosity. In the second place, what is Jaboatão's interest in pointing out the defects in the colonial system, since he showed himself to be an enthusiast of the Marquês de Pombal, the true ruler of Portugal (he even dedicated some flattering *décimas* to this illustrious minister of Dom José I)?[68]

Even if this mystery cannot be deciphered, one can draw inferences from the passage. In writings on the New World—whether by European authors or by colonial authors, who belonged to the elite or shared its culture and therefore let themselves be influenced by projections of the European imagination—edenization rarely reigns supreme or absolute. The specter that haunts it, sometimes more timidly, sometimes more resolutely, is the denigrating view of America, one that seeks to reinforce its negative aspects.

Negative readings of the New World—works by its so-called detractors—multiplied, especially in the eighteenth century. In a notable book, the Italian historian Antonello Gerbi followed the reverse trail of Sérgio Buarque de Holanda. From Juan Ginés de Sepúlveda to G. W. F. Hegel, he studied the polemics on America, focusing more on the negative than the positive current, however. During the second half of the eighteenth century, when Jaboatão was writing *Novo orbe,* these polemics reached one of their most heated moments.[69]

Edenic formulations were projected on America, erecting a bridge that drew the New World closer to the Old, made it part of its imagination, and filled the space formerly occupied by far-off lands that had gradually been unveiled. In a way, edenizing America meant forging a kind of camaraderie with it, a complicity grounded in the imaginary world. Something was found here that had somehow already been conceived; people saw what they wanted to see and what they had heard said.

Yet as the new continent's unique features began to emerge, edenization was threatened: novel plants, strong winds, heavy rains, but above all, the most peculiar people and animals—*others,* different from the Europeans.[70]

It must be made clear that there was no orderly sequence between one tendency and the other, between edenization and detraction. Even the great edenizers of nature did not refrain from more or less pejorative observations about the New World. Though the tendency toward edenization predominated in their case, it did not enjoy exclusivity.

To gain a better understanding of this other side of edenization—detracting and even infernalizing (as will be seen later)—I believe it is worthwhile to remember Erwin Panofsky's analysis of the paintings of Piero di Cosimo, a Florentine artist born in the mid-fifteenth century. A recluse who refused to eat hot meals and nourished himself on hard-boiled eggs, di Cosimo devoted a series of pictures to mythological motifs. Panofsky views these as an expression of the "hard primitivism" of classical origin.[71] Idealizing the world's primal condition, "soft primitivism" is in keeping with a religious concept of life—it is the time when Eve spun and Adam wove; "hard primitivism," on the other hand, is associated with materialism.

From Panofsky's lesson, it can be understood that the Italian Renaissance presupposed two possibilities: revival of the myth of the Golden Age and, simultaneously, the negation of this myth. There could thus be no pure and simple idealization of nature; ever since the classic era, its opposite had always been taken into account.

In a way, Jean Delumeau returned to this issue in *Le péché et la peur.* In his opinion, the Renaissance was more pessimistic than optimistic. "Francesco

Pico della Mirandola and Guillaume Postel were a minority," says Delumeau. And in another passage: "Sadness and Renaissance: these two terms would seem mutually exclusive, yet they were often close traveling companions."[72] To back up his position, Delumeau borrows a passage from Eugenio Garin, who says it is not hard to find—and sometimes in a single author—"on the one hand, the signs of the Anti-Christ and the imminent cataclysm; on the other hand, the Golden Age."[73]

The Renaissance was enigmatic and contradictory, and its contemporaries were aware of this ambiguity. "Everything . . . has been mixed and tangled up, the loftiest with the lowest, *Hell with Heaven,* the best with the worst," Guillaume Budé was to lament.[74] Consequently, it is not surprising that heaven and hell would also intermingle in stories of America and that even the most edenizing of authors would find themselves caught up in detraction.[75]

Gandavo, an edenizer *par excellence* and propagandist of the new land, deemed the place delightful and temperate albeit subject to deadly winds. "This wind from the land is very dangerous and unwholesome," he stated, "and if it aims to stay a few days, many people die, both Portuguese as well as the Indians of the land." Positive and negative qualities alternate in the same paragraph: "The land itself is weary and neglected; in it one finds the men somewhat weak and wanting in the strength that they possess here in this Kingdom, because of the heat and the provisions that they use here; this is when people are new to the land, but after a time they grow accustomed, and so solid and so hale and hearty as if this land were their very native country."[76]

The negative aspects of both the climate and the land itself even influenced the animals. Gandavo deliberately avoided discoursing about them, but nevertheless did so in one paragraph, where he endeavored to justify their existence and endow them with a certain inevitability:

> There are many other poisonous animals and creatures in this Province, *with which I do not deal,* of which there are so many in such abundance that it would be a very long story to name them all here and specifically deal with the nature of each one, there being, as I say, an infinity of them in these parts, where, because of the temperament of the land and of the climates that rule it, these could not but exist. Because as the winds that originate from this same land become infected with the rottenness of the grasses, woods, and swamps, [these creatures] produce themselves, many and most venomous, under the influence of the sun that contributes to this [and are] scattered about all the land, and for this reason grow and are found in maritime areas, and throughout the *sertão,* infinite in the way I say.[77]

Writing his *Tratado* around 1584—thus making him one of Brazil's first chroniclers—the priest Fernão Cardim realized that the same climate that stimulates development of fine animals brings the proliferation of repulsive beings. In his words: "It seems that this climate induces venom, for the infinite snakes that there are, as well as the many scorpions, spiders, and other filthy creatures, and the lizards are so many that they cover the walls of the houses and their openings." And then the counterpoint: "Just as this climate induces venom, it likewise seems to induce beauty in the birds, and as the entire land is filled with woods and groves of trees, so is it filled with handsome birds, of all kinds of colors."[78]

Unlike other authors, Cardim detected fleas and lice solely among the indigenous peoples and blacks. In compensation, "there is no want of cockroaches, moths, wasps, flies, and mosquitoes of so many kinds and so cruel, and venomous, so that when they bite a person the hand is swollen for three or four days." They primarily afflicted members of the kingdom, since the insects were hungry for the blood running "fresh and sweet" thanks to the food from Portugal.[79] Knivet tells of crab-lice. His group walked through mountainous lands so infested with these bugs that to get them off their skin and be rid of them, they had to take dry straw from the ground and scorch themselves, "as you would singe hogs."[80]

A great admirer of Brazilian birds, Léry would prove more moderate in regard to quadrupeds. But, ethnologist *avant la lettre,* he introduced them as *different,* unique. "Concerning the four-footed animals, I will say first of all that in general and without exception there is not a single one in that land of Brazil in America that is in all respects exactly like any of ours."[81] In *Historia natural de Chile,* two centuries later, Father Giovanni Ignazio Molina was to state that American nature was not inferior but, rather, different.[82]

The Jesuits who were in Brazil from the late sixteenth century to the early seventeenth were wholly oblivious to the question of the New World's singularity. In the Luso-Brazilian tradition, they were the greatest representatives of miscomprehension of the colonial universe. More than the animal and vegetable world, people were the prime target of Jesuit ill-will. But creatures, plants, and lands also received their quota of detraction.

The land of the colony was very poor and wretched: "Nothing is to be gained from it" because its inhabitants were likewise very pitiable, Manuel da Nóbrega wrote to the superior general of the Society of Jesus, Father Diogo Láinez. "Here there is no wheat, nor wine, nor oil, nor vinegar, nor meats, save by miracle," he went on in disappointment. "Whatever is found in this land, which is fish, and roots, no matter how much may be had, we shall not cease to be poor, and even this we do not have." In addition to being scarce, the food that was available was "very weak" and the work to be done in the colony "much greater."[83]

Besides being poor and not highly fertile (the native food was "weak"), the land was swarming with "an immense number of vermin, namely, *bichos de pé* [chigoes], and much smaller than those [in Portugal], with which all are covered," according to Father Jerônimo Rodrigues. "Fleas such as one cannot believe, save one has lived with them, as we have lived with them for these two years, in summer as in winter, for much of the day we spent killing fleas."[84] The fleas were "the perdition" of the priests' drawers and shirts, which were soiled all over with bloodstains. One night, says Father Jerônimo, he swatted four hundred and fifty fleas to death in his bed, not counting those that fled. "And here came the Father to say that we would not take ill, because of the many bleedings the fleas were giving us," our narrator goes on, "but I, to the contrary, said that they take the good blood, leaving the bad." The legions of fleas were due to the "infinity of dogs" and because the indigenous people urinated wherever they happened to be.

As if fleas were not enough, a cricket plague destroyed books and clothing. Although they killed "a great multitude every day," it was easy to reach out and grab forty to fifty; there was no end to them. Faithful to the habit of tallying insects, Father Jerônimo once counted five hundred crickets.[85]

And the cockroaches? What "there was, one could not believe, for the altar, the table, the food, and everything was covered with them. And every day the father took a large number of them in his hood, and every day with traps we caught thousands and they always seemed to grow."[86]

Already in the sixteenth century, the contours of the polemic on America were being outlined: a humid, inferior continent, thick with inferior animals like insects and reptiles. In the mid-eighteenth century Georges-Henri Leclerc de Buffon was to state: "Let us then see why such large reptiles, such fat insects, such small quadrupeds, and such cold men exist in this new world. The reason is the quality of the land, the state of the sky, the degree of heat and humidity, the location and elevation of the mountains, the quantity of running or still waters, the expanse of the forests, and above all the raw state in which nature is found."[87]

At the time the New World was discovered, Isabel of Castille appeared troubled and worried by the information from the Admiral of the Ocean Sea. He explained to her that because of the quantity of rainfall the earth was made rotten and kept tree roots from penetrating deep into the soil. "In this land where trees do not take root," the queen said, "little truth and less steadfastness will there be in the men."[88] A humid climate, inferior animals, weak people with no will—this is an association the Portuguese chroniclers did not make in the sixteenth century. Once again it is Buffon who systematizes the negative data on America, in his concern with explaining the reasons for the inferiority of animal species on this continent. It was sparsely populated, and most of the people lived as animals, "leaving nature in its raw state and neglecting the land." Uncultivated, the land became cold and unable to reproduce active cultures, like the embryos of the great quadrupeds, which in order to grow and multiply require "all the warmth, all the activity that the sun can give the beloved land." For the opposite reason, what proliferated were reptiles, insects, and "all species of animals that crawl in the mud, whose blood is of water, and which multiply in putridity."[89] In the eloquent words of Gerbi, America was fated to be the "prolific humid mother of cruel tiny animals, barren of noble beasts."[90] In America, the majestic lion of the old continent would be reduced to pitiful dimensions; here the king of the animals was a maneless coward.[91] In 1768 Cornelius De Pauw would take Buffon's observations to their ultimate consequences: American nature, like American people, was decadent and decaying. "It is without a doubt a great and awful sight," he stated, "to see one-half of this globe so forsaken by nature, so that all in it is defiled, or monstrous."[92]

Humanity: The Predominance of Demonization

The inhabitants of far-off lands, which were fantastic realms to European eyes, constituted another humanity—fantastic as well, and monstrous.[93] As the great discoveries took place, these peoples migrated from India to Ethiopia, to Scandinavia, and, finally, to America. In the precarious medieval world, it became necessary to name the unknown and make it incarnate in order to contain fear within bearable limits—monsters described by religion (Satan); monsters described in the world of beasts (unicorns, dragons, ant lions, mermaids, and so on); individual human monsters (crippled people, fiends); and monsters that inhabited the ends of the earth, resembling normal people (i.e., western Europeans) but bearing monstrous hereditary traits.

Classic authors like Ctesias and Pliny were references for the Latin teratologists (Solinus, Macrobius, St. Augustine, Isidore of Seville, Rabanus Maurus), all incorporated by authors of the early Middle Ages. In the late Middle Ages, it had been St. Augustine who had established certain concepts about monsters—monsters had something to *demonstrate*. Isidore of Seville was to return to St. Augustine, classifying monsters in four large families: individual monsters, monstrous races, fictitious monsters, and human-beast monsters. This classificatory labor represented the Westerner's desire and effort to "affirm his own normality, comparing it point by point with the deformity of imaginary races."[94] In the thirteenth century, Thomas of Cantimpré compiled a list of monsters drawn from a number of earlier writings—a list that the largest medieval encyclopedia, Vicent of Beauvais's *Speculum,* would include in its entirety. Realizing their pedagogical value, medieval moralists made ample recourse to monsters, bestowing upon them a moral meaning and social dimension; the monstrousness of monsters was somehow depleted by their internalization.[95]

As a reader of Cardinal d'Ailly's *Imago Mundi,* Columbus believed in monsters. The cardinal wrote of peoples "whose customs had fallen away from human nature," of "anthropophagic wild men with horrible, misshapen features, at the two extreme regions of the Earth . . . : it is difficult to ascertain whether these beings are men or beasts."[96] Columbus thought that as he moved inland he would encounter one-eyed humans and others with snouts like dogs. On January 8, 1492, he saw three mermaids leap out of the sea and was disappointed, for they were not as beautiful as he had imagined. In the direction of the setting sun, he wrote to Santángel, people were born with tails.[97] Perhaps he would sign below François de Belleforest's words: "The present time is more monstrous than it is natural."[98]

In two of the most popular forms of "escapist literature," monsters played a central role: travel books and knightly romances. "Monstrous races—giant monopodes, or with enormous ears, or with their faces on their chests— had had a place in descriptions of Africa and Asia from ancient times, and still could be found in Renaissance cosmography."[99] In the seventeenth century, Francisco Correia's account of the wreck of *Nossa Senhora da Candelária* ("which, coming from the coast of Guinea in the year of 1693, a heavy storm caused to come aground on the Ilha Incógnita") told of monsters and exotic animals. On the island there were apes "eight palms tall and with teeth the size of four fingers"; snakes as "thick as a small wine cask of eight *almudes* [roughly 65 gallons]"; marine women who would leave the waters swiftly and climb uphill, ladies of "all perfection down to the waist, as lovely as can be" but made ugly by huge ears that "dropped below their shoulders" and rose half a palm above their heads when lifted. From their waists down, they were covered with scales, "and their feet were shaped like a she-goat's, with fins along their legs." Near Tenerife, the author also saw "a marine man of such horrendous features that he looked like the devil himself."[100]

Many of the chroniclers writing of Brazil in the sixteenth century referred to sea monsters. Knivet saw "a great thing come out of the water with great scales on the back, with great ugly claws and a long tail." It advanced on him, opened its mouth, and "thrust out a long tongue like a Harping-Iron."[101] Gabriel Soares made reference to the many marine men in the Recôncavo region, known as *upupiara* by indigenous peoples. These creatures swept *jangadas* [fishing rafts with one sail] and people to the bottom, drowning them in the sea. The tide would later return them "bitten on their mouth, on their nostrils, and on their nature [genitals]."[102] The author himself claims he lost a number of slaves this way.

Gandavo's writing is rich in details. A monster had been killed in the captaincy of São Vicente in 1564, and he set himself the task of penning a faithful account of the event, "even though in many parts of the world news has already been heard of it." In the middle of the night, an indigenous woman had spotted the monster "moving about with unusual steps, swaying back and forth, and roaring now and again." He was crossing a low area near the sea and was so ugly "that he could only be the devil." "He was fifteen palms long and covered by hair all over his body, and on his snout he had some very large threads, like a mustachio." The boy who killed it, by the name of Baltazar Ferreira, went about "as if terrified, without saying anything for a great time." In the language of the land, that being was called a *hipupiára.*[103]

In the eighteenth century, the fear of sea monsters still persisted, now in the form of a "boy of three or four years" who was the color of heathens, with thick, misshapen features, "his head covered with few hairs"; he was most agile in the art of dodging shots taken at him. Jaboatão recounts an episode involving these sea boys and a native Brazilian manning a canoe. The Indian, "with the first sight he had of the beast, fell to the bottom of the boat with a great cry, tightly shutting his eyes and his teeth, so that for all the medicine that they gave him in the town, there was none for his life, which only lasted him, in the state in which he fell, four and twenty hours."[104] His companions in the canoe, black men from Guinea, were neither afraid nor upset by the sight.

Disseminated throughout the world—as Gandavo himself stated—the legend of the marine man acquires indigenous tones in Gandavo and in Gabriel Soares and combines its characteristics with European ones (as, for example, in Knivet's narrative). Similarly to what occurred with the Earthly Paradise, the European imagination's projections of monstrous humanities and animals migrated to America. Perhaps relatives of the centuries-old European dragon were the serpents with "most large and frightful wings" of which Gandavo had heard tell.[105] The immense lizard "covered with whitish scales as sharp and rough as oyster shells" that approached Léry and his companions to stare at them with its sparkling eyes no doubt had its European counterparts as well. "It has occurred to me since, in accord with the opinion of those who say that the lizard takes delight in the human face, that this one had taken as much pleasure in looking at us as we had felt fear in gazing upon it," Léry wrote.[106]

In Europe, monsters remained in vogue through the seventeenth century. Protestant preachers like Martin Luther and Philipp Melanchthon used them generously in their preaching, following the example of the medieval moralists; at a time of religious reformation, they associated heresy with monstrousness.[107] Folk ballads sang of monsters. Crowds rushed to public squares to see the Siamese twins Lazarus and John Baptist Coloredo, who were exhibited all across Europe between 1637 and 1642.[108] People discussed whether hermaphrodites could marry, if both heads of Siamese twins should be baptized, and so on.[109] Even Pierre de Ronsard wrote verses about monsters.[110] Once a commonplace part of everyday life, the monster entered a process of demonization starting in the fifteenth century. It shifted to a separate part of the world, compacted with the devil, and fell out of harmony. As the world rejected ambiguities at the close of the Middle Ages, the monster lost its position as an integral part of creation and became instead a freak.[111]

But sixteenth- and seventeenth-century Europe's fascination with the monster was concentrated on a specific type: individual human monsters. To the other monsters—the beastly ones, the "geographical" ones that inhabited the ends of the earth, those described by religion (Satan)—the Europeans added the concept of the Wild Man. Through the discoveries, monsters thus did not cede their place to wild folk but joined them.[112]

Fifteenth-century cosmographers believed the new lands would be inhabited by monsters, but Columbus found only the Wild Man—to his surprise, well shaped and well built, of "incontestable human character," belying longstanding legends and suggesting the "essential unity of humankind."[113]

Like monsters, the Wild Man was not a new theme but had roots in the ancient world. He was the antithesis of the knight·and contrasted the Christian ideal with instinctive life in a pure state. In the Middle Ages, what held sway was an ambivalent attitude of fear and envy toward the Wild Man; he threatened society but was exuberant, sexually active, and led a free existence in the forests.[114] His spiritual traits were seen as negative, while his physical gifts were considered positive.[115] The medieval Wild Man lent many of his characteristics to the people of the New World. Until the mid-sixteenth century, when he was portrayed in processions, at parties, at masquerades, and in solemn representations as well, he was melded with authentic aborigines from the American jungles. For Gerbi, William Shakespeare's Caliban is the "greatest poetic representation of one of these lascivious, ignorant men."[116] But even before Caliban, Naturmenschen appeared in medieval legend, theater, and literature, especially in northern Europe.[117]

For François Gagnon, this monstrous humanity expressed geographic marginality, reflecting a concentric representation of the world; the Wild Man, however, expressed sociological marginality, constituting a hierarchical representation of the world.[118] The Amerindian could fit in with either representation: in terms of geographical distance, he was the monster; in terms of his nakedness and natural life, he was the Wild Man.

These two representations coexisted, as Gagnon shows. Over time, however, that of the Wild Man eventually prevailed, although his monster side was never totally forgotten. Monstrousness was tightly linked to the geographical unknown, demolished by the experience of navigation and discoveries. The Wild Man, however, did not depend on the unknown but rather on Christian society's hierarchical representation. The image justified the colonial enterprise as an effort to bring culture and religion to those who had none, and so it endured as long as the colonial system did.

By the seventeenth century the need was felt to make the indigenous peoples of Brazil part of the Old World's mental universe. Interestingly, this was achieved precisely through recourse to their geographic marginality. Friar Vicente, citing Dom Diogo de Avalos, provides an interpretation for their origin, which he then immediately discards; it is nevertheless worth mentioning because it fits in perfectly with the notion of geographically marginal humanities. Dom Diogo, in *Miscellanea Austral,* said that

> in the Altamira mountains in Spain, there was a *barbarian people* that was regularly at war with the Spaniards and that *ate human flesh,* with whom the Spaniards grew wrathful and so they joined together their forces and took this people to battle in Andalusia, where they laid waste to them and killed many. The few that remained, not being able to sustain themselves on the land, abandoned it and embarked for wherever fortune would lead them, and thus found themselves on the Ilhas Afortunadas, now called the *Canaries;* touched land at the islands of *Cape Verde;* and made port in *Brazil.* Two brothers were made chiefs of this people, one called Tupi and the other Guarani; the latter, leaving Tupi to people Brazil, went to Paraguay with his folk and peopled Peru.[119]

In this remarkable passage, the European imagination conjoins two migrations: that of the Earthly Paradise to the Atlantic (Ilhas Afortunadas) and that of geographical "marginalities" (wild folk and cannibals) to the same region! By all indications, from the close of the sixteenth century the European imagination thus saw unknown lands and monstrous humanities as converging in Brazil.

Friar Vicente says that Dom Diogo de Avalos's opinion was not correct because it was unfounded: "What is correct is that this people came from elsewhere; from whence, however, it is not known, for even among them there are no writings, nor has any ancient author written about them."[120]

In a brief passage, Rocha Pitta bears witness to the fact that in the early eighteenth century theories on the Eastern origin of indigenous peoples were already well known; here again appears the need to connect this other humanity to the many humanities that had populated the European imagination during the time when communication between West and East had been interrupted. "I will leave aside the controversy on the origin of the first inhabitants that passed through this region, and from whence they came, whether from Troy, from Phoenicia, from Carthage, from Judaea, from the creators of the Tower of Babel, or whether from Ophir, because on this point the arguments of the authors have no more strength than a few feeble conjectures," he says.[121]

European perceptions of indigenous Americans took three different forms: they were seen as another humanity, as animals, and as demons. These perceptions follow no chronological order—indigenous groups were not *first* perceived as another humanity and *then* as animals—but may even be present during the same period. Regarding Brazil, the European imagination restructured itself in response to its observation of the American difference. Commentaries on these people were almost always derogatory. Merged with the Wild Man, the almost likable European monsters gained a much more animal-like and devilish form in the colony than in the hegemonic centers.

For the purposes of analysis, it can be said that at the first level the European saw *another humanity* in the Amerindian. One of the sixteenth century's main edenizers of the colony, Gandavo, wrote much about the "multitude of barbarian heathens that nature sowed throughout all this land of Brazil." He emphasized their negative traits: they threaten the settlers' safety; with weapons in hand, they combat "all human nations" (among which they of course are not included); they do not pronounce the *f, l,* and *r* and therefore have no "faith," "law," or "Rex"; "they live as beasts, without numbers, or weights, or measures." "This is a very bold people," he wrote further on, incapable of friendship, with no belief in the soul, vengeful. "Most inhuman and cruel," pitiless, "most dishonest and given to sensuality," they engaged in vices "as if they had within them no human reason."[122] How could one colonize such a paradisiacal land with people who behaved as irrational beings—or, in other words, behaved as if they were not human? Brazil only failed to flourish more robustly because of the indigenous slaves "that rose up and fled to their lands and flee every day: and if these Indians were not so runaway and inconstant, Brazil's wealth would know no comparison," Gandavo was to state.[123] It does not seem to be overstating things to affirm that when he edenized nature and made propaganda in favor of colonization, Gandavo felt himself obliged to vilify everyone who was born in the new land, going so far as to question their humanity. At the same time, he drew the rough draft of a justification for slavery: "There are many slaves from Guinea as well: these are surer than the Indians of the land because they never run away, nor do they have anywhere to run to."[124] In *História da Província de Santa Cruz,* Gandavo would again question the indigenous peoples' human condition, adding his thoughts on their disdain for work. "They all live very idly, with no thoughts other than eating, drinking, and killing people, and for this they grow very fat. . . . They are most inconstant and changeable."[125] It would be difficult, if not impossible, to advance the colonizing enterprise with people so unqualified for systematic work.

Gaspar Barleus and André Thevet—both Europeans involved in colonizing experiences different from Portugal's—display quite different perceptions of indigenous peoples. Describing the Amerindians' way of adorning themselves, Barleus blasts away with a value judgment: "In short, they take remarkable delight in sordid and fetid barbarism."[126] Difference is thus perceived and immediately condemned. Thevet, however, vacillates more, undecided. The indigenous are a "vulgar herd"[127]—and "coarse"[128]—but, credulous and manipulated by their prophets, they are to be pitied—"ces pauvres gens [these miserable people]," he says in compassion.[129] They have no faith, law, or religion, nor civility, but live as "irrational beasts," as nature made them. Yet they are "marvelously strange."[130] The way Thevet perceives this difference brings to mind the medieval imagination, where Americans are not what Europeans—based on the medieval concept of the Wild Man—had imagined them to be. "However, many have the mad opinion that these people we call Wild Men, because they live in forests and in fields almost like brute animals, are also covered by hair all over their bodies, like a bear, a deer, a lion, and they even paint them like this in their rich pictures; finally, to describe a Wild Man, they assign him an abundance of hair, from his toes to his head, as an inseparable feature, like the blackness of a raven, which is totally false," says Thevet, backed by experience. Those who made such assertions did so without ever having seen an American Indian. "As to myself," he goes on, "I know and I can state it with certainty because that was what I saw." Reality was not like that: "To the contrary, the Wild Men both from Eastern India as well as from our America leave their mother's womb as pretty and smooth as the children of our Europe."[131] The indigenous man has no hair; he is beardless; he is inferior—so would the detractors of America state in the next century, overlooking the adult male's habit of depilation, common among the Indians and reported by Thevet himself, among others.

Knivet is one of the few Europeans who set down unfavorable thoughts on European behavior in America, and he of course did so in the context of the hegemonic countries' dispute over control of the overseas colonies.[132] He writes of Portuguese inhumanity and urges the indigenous peoples to stand against them. Thus he displays the other side of Amerindian antihumanity: European antihumanity. "Notwithstanding all these fearful inconveniences [leopards, lions, crocodiles, *surucucus* (bushmasters, the largest venomous snake in the New World)], we chose rather to fall into the paws of a Lion, and the claws of the Serpent, than into the bloody hands of the Portuguese." Knivet incites the indigenous peoples against the Portuguese, showing them how the colonizers do not recognize them as human beings; instead they enslave them, brand them with an iron like dogs, flog them, and inflict torture on them as if they were not flesh and blood.[133] The Englishman said he would rather "stand at the Heathen mercy of savage Man-eaters, than at the bloody cruelty of Christian Portuguese."[134]

One feature of the Amerindians' alleged antihuman humanity was routine daily violence. At the hands of this menacing humanity, Europeans lived with the risks of being struck by arrows or being eaten.

Jaboatão offers us remarkable cinematographic descriptions of massacres by indigenous peoples. In Ilhéus, he tells us, Tapuia Gueréns shot arrows through the family of Sergeant-Major Bartolomeu Lopes da Franca, comprising himself, his wife, and five children, and "all who were supping around the table were found dead." The slaves fell dead in the fields, and only the fifth child survived, for he was studying in town; he would inherit nothing but sorrow, for the estate was lost in the slaughter.[135] The "tyranny" of the indigenous people was also unleashed against the sugar plantation of Captain-Major Antonio de Couros Carneiro, a Knight in the Order of Christ, even though the place was well guarded by people and weapons. They fell upon the *engenho* before midday with "their frightening roar," beating their arches and "using their arrows on the unwatchful, unwary family." Inside the houses, the servants cried out in terror: "Heathens, heathens!" One of the captain's daughters, Dona Isabel de Góis, was saying her rosary when she was surprised by the commotion. She ran to the rooms of one of her brothers; but they caught her in a "cloud of arrows," and she fell before the whole family, invoking the name of Jesus, asking for confession, straightening "her skirts with her hands, for the modesty of her feet," covering her face with a kerchief, raising her hands to heaven, and offering herself in martyrdom—an involuntary victim sacrificed to the hatred of the Holy Catholic Faith. She died, pierced by more than twenty arrows. Her mother hid in the millstream, and though "almost frozen to death," she was found alive. In the inner rooms, in the fields, all over, lay the dead. Luiz de Freitas, a child who had gone out to hunt wild pigs, was found "shot through from head to feet with more than seventy arrows."[136] During the attack on the home of Francisco de Sá Menezes, who was sick in bed, indigenous peoples killed a small child of his, carried in the arms of its wet nurse, in the patio. Both were "pierced and covered with arrows."[137] It was also in Bahia that another indigenous attack took place, this time against the home of Francisco de Araújo de Brum, "a single man who a short while before had finished his Studies of Philosophy in the city." One morning he had sent his armed men and slaves to do the outside work and had stayed at home alone, with only the house servants. He was strolling about his grounds when a troop of heathens surrounded his house, keeping him from going back inside. The licentiate "took off running" toward the nearby river, thinking that once in the water he could dodge the enemy's arrows. "But as his luck would have it, the tide was out, and huge mud holes slowed his steps; as he fled death on land, he drank it in the mire and clouds of arrows, with which he was covered. . . ."[138]

Reference to the risk of being eaten is found in many of the pages written by Jesuits. "Next year, if the *negros* [i.e., indigenous peoples] do not eat us, I shall write you in greater detail of everything, if it so serveth God," Father Azpilcueta Navarro wrote to the Brothers of Coimbra in a letter dated 1553.[139] Preparing to enter the *sertões*—"a treasure of souls"—Nóbrega expressed to the provincial of Portugal his fear of indigenous cannibalism. Before departing, he wanted to leave work on the boys' houses "well advanced," for there lay "the basis of the Society, if by chance they should kill and eat every one of us that goes."[140] Knivet left an impressive account of the execution and ingestion of a Portuguese man by indigenous peoples. First they killed the man by striking him on the nape of the neck; next they removed his skin with the "tooth of a Conie [capybara]," aided by fire, until, using their hands, all the skin of the body could be detached. The head was cut off and handed over to the executioner, while the innards were given to the women. The body was carved up joint by joint, and the parts were distributed. The next day the women boiled every joint in a "great pot of water," and the whole group made a huge kettle of soup.[141]

Jaboatão blames the continual indigenous wars on this appetite for human flesh. He conveys the affable testimony delivered by an old Potiguar woman, who on her deathbed dreamt of her favorite delicacy. She had already received "all the medicine of the soul" and seemed in fine spiritual disposition, inclined toward the Catholic faith. Taking pity on the old woman's weakness, the priest in attendance decided to "offer her some courage for her body as well" and inquired whether she wanted a little sugar or something else tasty from overseas. "Oh, my grandson," the old woman replied, "I desire nothing of life, everything bothers me now; only one thing could take this want of appetite from me. If I now had the tiny hand of a Tapuia boy, young and very tender, and I could suck those wee bones, then it seems I would gather some strength, but I, poor me, no longer have anyone to hunt me one down by arrow!"[142]

This antihuman humanity also manifested itself in the state of sin in which the natives of the land dwelled, in the eyes of the European Catholics. One of the main sources of records on the wicked lives of the people of Portuguese America was of course the Jesuit letters. In these the colony was the place of sin *par excellence;* sin was so widespread that many priests came to doubt the regenerative power of faith. "I have stayed here solely for a want of priests and the need to awaken people in this land who were and are in the slumber of sin, Christians in name only, immersed in malevolence, mixed up in fights, publicly involved in veneries and foul matters, all of which have caused me frailty and little faith and hope of being able to gather fruit," Father Azpilcueta Navarro wrote from Bahia.[143]

What were their sins? Vices of the flesh (incest at the top of the list, in addition to polygamy and concubinage), nudity, sloth, covetousness, paganism, cannibalism. "In the vice of the flesh, they are filthy," Father Jerônimo Rodrigues reported of the Carijó. There were many women for one man: nieces, stepdaughters, granddaughters; "and some take their own daughters as wives." It was even more appalling that there were many men for one woman, and husbands letting "their wives go where and with whom they please."[144] In the words of conservative historian Paulo Prado, this was an "unformed, tumultuous" society.[145]

Sloth was another pillar of Prado's explanation (he was an assiduous reader of the Jesuits and the Visitations of the Holy Office). He considered them "the laziest people one could find, because from morning till night, and their whole lives, they have no occupation whatsoever: all they do is fetch something to eat, lie about in hammocks." These people are "effeminate, alien to any kind of work."[146] The Englishman Knivet called them "a kind of lazy people, that care not for any thing, but will lie all day lazing in their houses, and never go abroad but for their victuals."[147]

Covetousness was also on the roll of sins, this time involving white people first and foremost—and demonstrating how the colony indeed encouraged transgression. The account of Brother Antonio Rodrigues, who like St. Ignatius had first been a soldier, is quite enlightening in this regard. Rodrigues left Seville in 1523 with 1,800 men, in search of precious metal. He reached the Prata River and saw many of his companions perish in the fangs of wild cougars. Then came hunger—and next the Indians. "Our Lady seeks to punish our covetousness and sins, which soldiers regularly commit." Hunger thus is seen as a punishment for the atrocities committed: cannibalism, the eating of feces, immoderation of various types, blasphemy, false witness, "unjust justice." "There the officials in charge would say: 'Better they die, for there will not be gold enough for so many.'" This is a curious account, where the Europeans are ferocious and the indigenous people kindly: "We found some heathens called 'Timbos,' of which there are many. They do not eat human flesh, but rather keep away from this. They are very merciful, for we were languishing and our teeth and lips black, resembling more dead men than alive; they carried us in their arms and gave us food to eat and healed us with so much love and charity, that Our Lord must be praised, seeing so much natural piety in people divorced from faith, who with such gentleness and love treated foreign people that they did not know."[148]

This was a peculiar humanity, antihuman, rather monstrous, different, sinful. Were they really human? Could they be converted and receive the Holy Word?[149] Following the tradition of Giambattista Vico, Abbot

Ferdinando Galiani believed that the indigenous people of California were not humans but "the most witted, most cunning, and most able of the monkeys."[150] Even though he recognized human traits in the American Indians, William Robertson could not help but classify them as a "melancholy animal" in his *History of America*.[151] For Immanuel Kant, some American races represented the lowest echelon of humanity.[152]

Assertions of this kind carry with them a long history of detraction. Sérgio Buarque de Holanda pointed out that during the first century of conquest the Spanish who visited the Indies "tended to see the Indians either as *nobres salvajes* [noble savages] or as *perros cochinos* [filthy mongrels]." Documents show that the second tendency gained the upper hand in Brazil, as its oldest missionaries got closer to Sepúlveda than to Las Casas.[153]

The comparison with animals appears as early as Caminha's letter: indigenous groups were a "bestial people of little knowledge," incapable of understanding Cabral's gracious gesture. Nevertheless, they were clean, of sound health, and therefore good animals: "They are like birds, or wild animals, for whom the air makes better feathers and better hair than on tame ones." Hence the wholesomeness, fleshiness, and beauty of their bodies.[154]

In 1555 Father José de Anchieta, the "gentle evangelizer of our jungles," practically compared himself to a veterinarian. Serving as a doctor and bleeder, he describes his treatment of indigenous people's illnesses: "laying on plasters, raising sternums, and other arts of horse doctors *that were necessary for those brutes, namely, for the Indians.*"[155]

But it was Nóbrega who most debated the animality of Brazil's indigenous people. In his letters as well as in his *Diálogo sobre a conversão do gentio,* he repeats the same ideas. "The Jesuit always harps on the same string . . . and ever more openly so as the years go by."[156] The indigenous people "are dogs in their eating and killing of each other, and are pigs in their vices and behavior." This famous passage goes on to say that the priests would arrive from Portugal thinking they would convert "all of Brazil in one hour," whereas it took more than a year to convert one single Indian—such was "their brutishness and bestiality."[157]

Nóbrega's experience with indigenous people soon undermined his hopes regarding the magnitude of conversion and moved him to consider what "little could be done," since this "was a kind of people more like wild beasts than rational people." Inarguably rational, the Christian settlers also were close to animality; they gave the Jesuits "little help" and "much trouble" and with their lifestyles demonstrated "scandal" and "poor example" to the native Brazilians.[158] The idea of an inviable humanity, first ascribed to the indigenous peoples, would gradually come to permeate the colony's entire population and become associated with the colonial condition itself. The mixing of the races would be one of the factors responsible for this "contagion."[159] In addressing the topic, Gaspar Barleus compared this mixture to semiferocity: "By whites and Negroes mixing among themselves, brown skins are born, the blackness *corrected* by a lighter coloring." The Spanish called this type *mulatos* and the Romans, hybrids: "namely, produced from unlike parents, *like the Demibeasts, born of the fierce and of the tame.*"[160]

Returning to Nóbrega, his letter of May 8, 1558, offers a summary of his ideas on indigenous peoples. From the time of the Discovery, indigenous peoples had harmed many Christians, taking from them ships, plantations, and ranches and mistreating without distinction both those who were cruel to them and those who were kind. "And they are so cruel and *bestial* that they kill those who never did them any harm, clerics, friars, and women of such fine appearance that *brutish animals* would find themselves content with them and do them no harm." In this colony, the valiant Portuguese—the most feared among all nations—were despised by the indigenous groups; they suffered at the hands of and subjected themselves "to the most vile and wretched heathens in the world." It was therefore necessary to make the indigenous groups conform to a political order with an authoritarian structure, where there was room enough for slavery. "By subjugating heathens, many improper ways of obtaining slaves and many scruples shall cease, for men shall have legitimate slaves, taken in a just war." Only this would keep the *"infernal mouth* from eating as many Christians as were lost on boats and ships along the entire coast," Nóbrega went on to say, indicating the third level of European thought on the indigenous people of America: Indians as demons.[161]

Other Jesuits would follow Nóbrega's and Anchieta's footsteps in perceiving the Brazilian natives as animals. "In eating human flesh, they are worse than *dogs,*" stated Father Jerônimo Rodrigues.[162] But the Ignatians were not the only ones to view the heathens as closer to animals than to human society. The indigenous people's excessive cruelty repudiates the human condition, stated Gandavo in *História da Província de Santa Cruz.* Not only do they kill all those who are not of their *flock,* but they eat them as well, "for this purpose making use of such *diabolical* cruelties that they even exceed the *brutish animals,* who have no reason."[163] The Aimoré—a handful of whom are enough to destroy much land—have no fixed house or place where they can be found, "but walk like *lions and tigers* through the forests," said Friar Vicente do Salvador.[164] *"Human tigers"* is also the term Friar Gaspar applies to the Guaitacá in the region of Rio de Janeiro.[165]

Like Robertson's Indian, Barleus's is a melancholy animal: "The heathens in the *sertão* and all those who preserve their native customs are more like *beasts* in their cruelty than like men. They are most hungry for vengeance and for human blood, foolhardy and eager for hand-to-hand combat and for battles," the historian of Dutch Brazil wrote.[166] Black-haired, threatening in appearance, ferocious of eye, the Tapuia "rarely lose to *beasts* in the speed of their running." Cannibals, they terrorized "the other barbarians and the Portuguese with their renown for cruelty." In their hostilities they were animal-like as well; they proved to be "bloodthirsty, beyond that permitted by humanity or hatred."[167] Jaboatão calls the Indians a people "notable for the barbarism of their customs and for the *ferocity* of their nature." A little further on he associates them with animals: "A region [Brazil] so inhabited by human individuals, as by *fierce animals,* many of the latter as harmful as the former are inhuman; wild Indians, as brutish as these same irrational beings, and even appearing more irrational than these same brutes." Jaboatão justified this assertion that indigenous people were more irrational than animals based on their cannibalism; no animal eats a member of its own species, and the indigenous people not only eat other Indians but eat ones that are close to them, relatives and friends.[168]

In colonial times, it was mainly the writings of Thevet and Léry that provided a positive counterpoint to the image of a mean, animal-like savage. In *La cosmographie universalle,* Thevet states that the Wild Men "are not such brutes that nature has not given them intelligence to speak of natural things," and they were thus able to talk about the salty water of the sea and the composition of the land.[169] They also had a notion of good and evil, Thevet affirms two pages later. Léry goes further in his perception of the Other. Even though they were barbaric and cruel with their enemies, their savageness does not prevent these nations from taking into careful consideration "that which is said to them in a reasonable manner."[170] Contrary to what was believed in Europe, the bodies of the Tupinambá were "neither monstrous nor extraordinary" when compared to those of the Europeans.[171]

But sympathetic portrayals did not thrive among the Portuguese, who, as Silva Dias and Buarque de Holanda observed, avoided the myth of the noble savage, leaning instead toward the idea of the "perro cochino [filthy mongrel]."[172] Writing in the eighteenth century, the Jesuit priest André João Antonil saw the black slave as an animal: "There are years in which, because of the *great mortality of slaves, horses, mares, and steers* or the small cane yield, plantation owners cannot wholly fulfill that which they promised," he stated, making no distinction between people and farm animals.[173]

The European perception of America's inviable humanity took a third form: demonization. Friar Vicente said the devil had lost his control over Europe (Christianized throughout the late Middle Ages) and had victoriously set up camp on the other half of the earth, in America, more specifically—as expressed in the text of my epigraph—in Brazil. The devil's hellishness had even colored the colony's name. For Friar Vicente, "Brazil" brings to mind the red flames of hell. Here the demon had been victorious, at least during the first stage of the struggle: the name of Santa Cruz had fallen into oblivion, and the designation championed by Satan won out. By spreading Christianity, the Portuguese sought to diminish the devil's hordes of followers; after all, hell was in Brazil.[174] As the activities of the Soldiers of Christ progressed, two categories came into existence: "Indian Indians," subjugated to the devil, and "converted Indians," subjugated to God.[175] But the colony remained "Brazil," bearing forever in its name the infernal stigma that had marked its birth.

The Indians are a people of the devil, the Jesuits affirmed repeatedly. "I do not even know a better sign of hell than to see a multitude of them, when they drink, because for this purpose they invite people from far away, and especially when they have . . . some flesh to eat that they bring on a wood grate," Father Luís da Grã wrote to St. Ignatius of Loyola.[176] They were demons not only in their eating habits but also in their manner of dwelling and dressing.

> Each of these houses has two or three holes with no doors or locks: inside them live easily one hundred or two hundred people, each couple in its grouping, with no separation at all, and they live in one part and the other, with a great breadth in the middle, and all are as in a community, and upon entering the house one sees everyone that is in it, because all are in view of each other, with no separation or division. And since there are many people, they usually have fire day and night, summer and winter, *because the fire is their clothing, and they are most miserable without fire. The house seems an inferno or labyrinth; some sing, others cry, others eat, others make flour and wines, etc., and the entire house burns with fires.*[177]

Lord of the colonial lands, as Friar Vicente argues in my epigraph, the devil would not blithely hand his people over to the enemy; with each new step that evangelization took, he raged, demonizing nature and insinuating himself into daily life. A torrential stream could be inhabited by demons, Father Jerônimo Rodrigues speculates. Traveling from Paranaguá to Porto de Dom Rodrigo, he encountered a São Francisco River "so agitated that it seemed demons were visibly moving about there, which boiled in leaps toward the heavens, which caused astonishment."[178] Along the entire course of their trip, the devil tried to make trouble. Failing to do so, "he put himself inside a whale, and so fiercely did he follow us in the wake of the canoe that he vexed us immensely." First coming closer, then moving away, the bedeviled whale terrified the priests. "I, however, when I saw it so close and that it brought before it a heavy sea, threw it a small Agnus Dei." Only then did the whale (devil) go away.[179]

At the Carijó mission, when the Ignatians were preparing to celebrate the first masses "and take possession, on the part of God, of people that he had held in his power for so many thousands of years," Satan made his strength felt. It was a peaceful day, sunny and "serene." But when the priests were fixing the altar in preparation for the mass scheduled for the next day, "the damned one could not bear it, and ordering a tempest of lightning, thunder, wind, and rain, it seems that the demons were visibly about, and that indeed they were showing how they felt about our coming, and it was so great that, as well covered and well protected as our church was, the adornment and frontlet were made wet, and the image of Our Lady went from the altar to the ground, it seemed as if to see whether it could break the glass, and it was not even enough that the priest covered the altar with hides." The devil's malice did not stop there, however. The next day during mass thousands of flies covered the altar and the priest—"it was an astounding thing." The finger of the devil was no doubt in both events: "And from that day on, in the two years we were there, never again were there such flies nor such tempests."[180] The struggle raged throughout the colony. "In this place we had many battles with the demon and even now we have them," Father Pero Correia had written years before from São Vicente.[181]

It was basically in relation to the supernatural that the people of the colony paid tribute to the devil and confirmed their character as diabolical humanity. Assailed by fantastic illusions, the poor Indians—says Thevet—went about in terror, afraid of the dark and carrying fire with them when they went out at night. These illusions could not be explained by reasoning, for the indigenous peoples were deprived of true reason; they could only be explained by the Evil One's relentless persecution of those who do not know God.[182] Led into error by the Evil One, incapable of discernment because they did not possess reason, the indigenous people became more deeply mired in the error of idolatry, adoring the devil through his ministers, the *pajés*, "people of evil life, who have devoted themselves to serving the devil in order to receive his neighbors."[183] When Léry describes an indigenous ceremony led by the *pajés*—which he confesses enthralled him—he associates it with the thing that most haunted the imagination of Europe's seventeenth-century populations: the witches' sabbat.[184] Festive, damned, threatening—in the words of Michel de Certeau—the world of the Beyond "re-appears, exiled, at the ends of the universe, at the far edges of the colonial enterprise." In the New World, the missionary-explorer would serve as his exorcist colleague served on the other side of the Atlantic. "Unfortunately, travel literature has not yet been systematically studied as a tremendous complement to and displacement of demonology. And yet the same structures are to be found in both."[185]

Observed in the colonists' habits and daily lives, confirmed in their magical practices and sorcery, the demonization of colonial people spread from the Indian—its first object—to the slave, eventually reaching the other members of the colony. To evade harsh punishment, the black slaves resorted to "diabolic arts."[186] In the early eighteenth century, fearing slave rebellions and sensing uprising all around, the Count of Assumar, governor of Minas Gerais, saw nature itself goaded by the climate of rebellion in Minas, nerve center of the eighteenth-century Portuguese colonial economy. Everything was cold in that captaincy, save vice, which was always inflamed. "The land seems to exhale disturbances; the water breathes out riots; the gold rings out insults; the air parades liberty about; the clouds vomit impertinence; the stars inspire disorder; the climate is the tomb of peace and birthplace of revolt; nature is restless inside itself and, mutinous there within, like *hell*," the governor stated.[187] Restless and rebellious, the Minas settlers and the inordinate numbers of slaves stirred nature itself to revolt. The possibility of its inhabitants gaining consciousness of their colonial condition underscored Brazil's status as an immense inferno, where not even nature escaped—a nature that by itself, in isolation, was edenic.

Catechizing efforts combined with the "normatizing" measures of colonial authorities and church dignitaries and with the actions of the Holy Office, all for the purpose of homogenizing the diabolical, animal-like, inviable humanity of colonial Brazil. It was their duty to "correct the body of Brazil," part its people from the devil, and draw them unto Christ,[188] pacifying them.[189] In his *Carta de doação* (Donatary Charter) to Pero Lopes, written in 1535—even before the Jesuits arrived—Dom João III asserted that the colony's idolaters and infidels should be brought into the Catholic faith with a view to populating and making good use of this land, punishing heretics, sodomites, and perjurers with the death penalty and handing down the verdict and order of execution "without appeal or grievance."[190] The royal power itself was ahead of the church in the task of restraining the devil's legions and converting hell into paradise, even if earthly.

Was hell a destiny? On July 23, 1763, Domingos Marinho, native of Vila Rica, confessed to the Inquisition that because he was suffering from "some infirmities," he had summoned the *curandeira* [healer] Maria Cardosa and her 16-year-old godson Antonio, both of them freed blacks. They said a number of prayers while rubbing over his body first a small white stone and then a razor with a skein of cotton tied to it. They also prayed to the Most Holy Trinity, to St. Domingos, and to St. Francis, speaking "in their tongue." Domingos Marinho had repented—or at least said he had. At the end of his confession, he declared: "This Minas is quite infected by the Demon."[191] Frightened, Domingos was speaking with the voice of the Inquisition, of the powers-that-be. He lived in Minas Gerais, which unquestionably synthesized the eighteenth-century colony.[192] Twenty-six years later, the Inconfidência Mineira would demonstrate with blood—always blood—how the Indian-beast and the Indian-devil had merged in the damned body of the colonist in quest of a consciousness of the colonial condition. And the colony would remain a hell because of the inner demons it fortunately contained.

The Colony and Colonization: A Purgatory Come True

In his *Divine Comedy,* Dante Alighieri indelibly fixed the image of purgatory, even vesting it with a geographical existence: it was a mountain where souls paid for their sins, purging themselves and awaiting the salvation that Final Judgment might possibly bring. But before it became embodied in Dante's mountain, purgatory traveled a long path, constructed out of deliberations, dreams, and projections of the European imagination melded with age-old traditions originating in the ancient world. Elements of high culture and popular culture interlaced in the weaving of this purgatory. Between 1150 and 1250 popular beliefs thrived, finding their way into the elites' sermons, coloring hagiographies, and even lending traditions to the elite formulation of purgatory. Although it was part of this process, the popular imagination never ceased to be viewed as threatening, as something that should be resisted. The councils that institutionalized purgatory—Second

Lyons (1274), Florence (1438), and Trent (1563)—tended to keep all the rich imagination regarding purgatory outside the dogmas and truths of faith, accentuating the gap between popular culture and high culture.[193]

Purgatory eased the terrible tension of having one's fate inexorably bound to the two extreme possibilities represented by hell and by paradise. It was an opportunity that unfolded before Christians, allowing for correction of errors and forgiveness of sins. This came to figure so importantly in the Christian mentality that a special saint was assigned to hear the pleas and prayers offered in name of those sent there: St. Luthgard.

The nascent Early Modern age found itself grappling with notions of a "world turned upside down," a sign of the Renaissance's pessimistic current of thought mentioned earlier. Madness was one of the favorite objects of such discourses, as Michel Foucault has shown. Countless critical essays have celebrated it: Desiderius Erasmus's *Praise of Folly*; Miguel de Cervantes's *Don Quixote*; Francisco Gómez de Quevedo's *La hora de todos . . .*; Baltasar Gracián's *Criticón*; Tomaso Garzoni's *L'ospidale de' pazzi incurabili*; and Sebastian Brandt's *The Ship of Fools (Narrenschiff)*.[194]

As an object of the imagination, the ship of fools emerged during the Renaissance, "a strange 'drunken boat' that glides along the calm rivers of the Rhineland and the Flemish canals."[195] A literary piece inspired by the old cycle of the Argonauts, at that time the ship was revived in a series of creative works, including Brandt's *Narrenschiff*. "Fashion favored the composition of these Ships, whose crew of imaginary heroes, ethical models, or social types embarked on a great symbolic voyage which would bring them, if not fortune, then at least the figure of their destiny or their truth."[196] Unlike so many other imaginary ships, the *Narrenschiff* really existed, carrying its load of fools from one place to another. In Germany, it was common practice to entrust the mad to boatmen, who would take them away.

Places of pilgrimage and places of passage (crossroads) as well as markets were other locations where the mad were taken; perhaps these ships of fools were boats on pilgrimage.[197] Abandoned at such spots, "lost," through their absence these lunatics purified the places from whence they had come. But their exile was not merely a socially useful measure or one that guarded citizens' safety; it approached a rite and joined the roster of other ritual exiles.

The role of water and its relation to madness is fundamental in the European oneiric universe. While transporting them far away, the water purifies the mad. Furthermore, navigation abandons individuals to the uncertainty of their fate. "Each of us is in the hands of his own destiny; every embarkation is, potentially, the last. It is for the other world that the madman sets sail in his fools' boat; it is from the other world that he comes when he disembarks."[198] Imprisoned on a ship, "the madman is delivered to the river with its thousand arms, the sea with its thousand roads, to that great uncertainty external to everything. He is a prisoner in the midst of what is the freest, the openest of routes: bound fast at the infinite crossroads. He is the Passenger *par excellence:* that is, the prisoner of the passage. . . . He has his truth and his homeland only in that fruitless expanse between two countries that cannot belong to him."[199]

In the late sixteenth century, already one hundred years after the discovery of America, the judge-demonologist Pierre De Lancre "sees in the sea the origin of the demoniacal leanings of an entire people: the hazardous labor of ships, dependence on the stars, hereditary secrets, estrangement from women—the very image of the great, turbulent plain itself makes man lose faith in God and all his attachment to his home; he is then in the hands of the Devil, in the sea of Satan's ruses."[200]

Like De Lancre, Luíz Vaz de Camões would contrast the productive chores of agricultural labor with the fortuitousness and unpredictability of maritime adventure. This is the tone of the old man of Restelo's speech, which Antonio Sérgio, a liberal historian of the early twentieth century, would posit as representing two national policies: one of *rootedness* (Dom Dinis) and one of *flux* (Dom Henrique)—where unfortunately, according to this historian, the latter got the upper hand.[201]

This concurrence between De Lancre and Camões is not incidental. De Lancre judged crimes of sorcery, a serious offense in the sixteenth and seventeenth centuries. Camões sang the feats of overseas expansion and meditated on the destiny of the Portuguese people, worried about the inconstancy of colonial activities. The fickle sea carried brave sailors far away, making them "prisoners of passage," or passengers *par excellence,* as Foucault saw them. The sea also carried away Portugal's damned children, those who had to a greater or lesser degree breached the laws of the kingdom or the laws of God. And so it purged the metropolis of its evils; the overseas possessions were the "dungeon of its delinquents."[202]

In the late fifteenth century overseas expansion thus impelled a merger vital to the history of European culture; it articulated and recombined European formulations on purgatory, on the purifying role of maritime crossings, and on banishment as purification—all different manifestations of a great rite of passage.

Once discovered, the colonial world catalyzed access to purgatory; with gold from America, Columbus wanted to save sinful souls and take them to paradise.[203] From the very outset, in the European imagination the overseas world was thus associated with the region where the price of sin was paid, the "third place" about which Martin Luther would speak critically.

In 1602 Manuel Godinho Cardoso had written an account of a shipwreck involving the *Santiago* that had taken place some twenty years earlier. In his moving description, the shipwrecked people squeezed onto a reef, crowding one on top of another, waiting for boats and rafts to come to their rescue. As the tide rose, those who did not know how to swim drowned, "and those who knew how drowned as well, avoiding death a little longer, however." Searching the waves for the boat that would save them, with water up to their chests, many spent the whole night "in a perpetual scream because of the coldness of the water and unbearable pain. No voices could be heard other than sighs, moans, and great laments."[204] This description no doubt evokes the sufferings of souls on the mountain of purgatory. Purgatory and the purgation could begin with the crossing that led to the world of the overseas colonies, perpetually haunted by the terror of monsters, extraordinary accidents, and death due to disease. Enduring dreadful suffering, pervading the vessels with a fetid odor, one-fourth and even one-third of the voyagers died during the crossing, victims of scurvy, veritable scourge of the seas, the "cruel and ugly disease" to which Camões refers.[205]

Writing about the truce that had just been signed by the Spanish and Dutch, Friar Vicente denounced its ephemeral character and, highly perceptive once again, laid bare the colonial system's deep structures. "*New wars*" were to be expected "*in these overseas parts, for these are always the ones to pay for our sins* and for those of others as well," he stated.[206] The colonies were thus fated to serve as an immense purgatory for the sins of the Old World.

America's detractors almost always viewed it as purgatory. Knivet was not exactly a detractor, but neither did he edenize nature. Far from his native land, naked, living in discomfort, Cavendish's colleague pondered the reasons that had led him to abandon the certain for the uncertain: "I sat down remembering my self in what state I was, and thinking what I had been, I began to *curse the time that ever I heard the name of the Sea,* and grieved to think how fond I was to forsake my natural Country where I wanted nothing: then was I out of all hope either to see Country or Christian again."[207] Food was scarce; and when some was found, the men would gorge themselves till "they lay all vomiting that they were not able to stand."[208] At the tip of South America, the Englishman suffered from cold. "Our men [froze], and many of them lost their toes, as I myself for one, for in one night that I lay moist of my feet, I lost three of my toes on one of my feet, and four of the tops of the other foot."[209] Some men lost both feet, while others lost their noses, like the blacksmith Harris. Whether reality or imagination, this was a dreadful place where terrible things happened, for which men often were to blame owing to their sins. In the River Plate region, the soldier Antonio Rodrigues and his companions indulged in all types of immoderation, unleashing divine wrath: "Clearly it can be seen that Our Lord permitted so much evil because of our sins," the Jesuit soldier would state. "Now I wish I were twenty years old and could live a long life, to go with some priests of our Society, for I have more experience in this land, and to spend my energy and life teaching these people."[210] This land invited sin and, at the same time, was the place where it could be purged.

The New World was hell primarily because of its different humanity, animal-like and diabolical, and it was purgatory primarily because of its colonial condition. Opposite it stood Europe: the metropolis, place of culture, land of Christians. In Europe, heaven was therefore closer, and the divine word clearer and more intelligible. In the colony, everything was hazy and blurred. "The words that in those parts seemed clear here become obscure to me; I know not if it is from living among people who are always eating each other and walk about covered in human blood," Father Azpilcueta Navarro stated, thus localizing the truth of faith and its negation on one and the other side of the colonial system.[211] It was up to the European metropolis to redeem the Americans from the world of perdition and sin where they dwelled and to correct it. Catechizing was the way to fulfill the metropolis's salvational duty; but should it prove insufficient, the natives of the land should be removed from the sinful place in which they were immersed. The colony would always be a danger; and the Jesuit *colégio,* imbedded in it, appeared to be an oasis of salvation. Nóbrega was the astute formulator of the following position: "In this land, Father, we have before us a great number of heathens, and a great want of laborers. All possible means of attaining them should be embraced, and the Society perpetuated in these parts, *to remedy such perdition of souls.* And if it is dangerous to raise them here, because there are more opportunities for not maintaining one's chastity after they are grown, *send them to Europe before this time,* both the mestizos and the children of heathens, and from there send as many young students as possible to study here in *our Schools, because in these there is not as much danger."*[212]

In the face of so much sinfulness, there was no sure remedy other than strictness and punishment. Nóbrega accused the bishop of Bahia of excessive compromise, inappropriate for the huge purgatory that the colony was. "The Bishop has other ways of proceeding, through which I believe sins will not be removed and people will be robbed of as much money as they can earn, and the earth will be destroyed. His clergy absolve as many paramours as there are, and the [bishop] and his preacher, who is the visitor, give them such preaching that they sin and raise themselves up, *leaving the way to heaven very wide for them, and Our Lord Christ says that it is narrow."*[213]

It is once more the astute Jesuit who perceives the colony's double role as purgatory: rooting out sin and purifying souls while also guaranteeing the continuity of the production of wealth by a purified—that is, a standardized—population. If no money is earned, the land is destroyed; the colony becomes meaningless if it does not produce wealth, for this is its primary function. One must suffer, producing bread by the sweat of one's brow; this is our role in the valley of tears that is earthly life. Nothing is accomplished without effort, for the way to heaven is narrow.

One and a half centuries later, another clever Jesuit would complete Nóbrega's thoughts. Referring to the process of cleaning and purifying sugarcane, Antonil stated that the prime objective was to use every last drop of the liquid. "In this fashion, there is no loss of one single drop of that sweet liqueur, which costs so much blood, sweat, and tears to gather."[214] Purifying sugar—the seventeenth-century colony's finest product—was a task befitting the colonial purgatory; in purifying the product, souls were purified.

But this purification was neither random nor unconditional. The best sugar is the sugar that spends more time purifying. "If it is purified hastily, it will yield little." The better the cane, the less time it takes to purify. The purifying process yields not only clean, pure white sugar; it also yields dark sugar, brown sugar. And, contradiction of contradictions, it is dark, dirty clay that permits production of clean white sugar. "It should be no cause for admiration that the clay, which is by nature filthy, is the instrument that purifies sugar through its washings, as if reminding us of our own clay, and of the tears with which once filthy souls are purified and whitened."[215] The transparency of this analogy between the purgatory of souls and the purgatory of sugar leaves not a shadow of doubt: homogenizing the population through catechizing efforts and producing profitable goods for the foreign market were the two great purging roles of the colonial purgatory; they should be accomplished at all costs, mixing blood, sweat, and tears as well as—paradoxically—dismissing the sweetness and not weighing the hardships implied in achieving this greater task.

In the theological justification of the colonial system, Brazil is once again a purgatory-colony. Here Portuguese Christians faced the question of enslaving their fellow human beings; and in this ultimate of contradictions, the church figured importantly by devising and disseminating a theology that justified slavery. Eduardo Hoornaert offers a brilliant analysis of Vieira's role in this regard; the Jesuit "compared Africa to hell, where the Negro was a slave in body and in soul; Brazil, to purgatory, where the Negro was freed in his soul by baptism; and death, to the entrance into heaven." Brazil was a kind of transition place between the land of slavery and of sin (Africa) and heaven, the place of final liberation. In Vieira's view, the path to heaven was the solution for the slave, and slavery was a kind of *pedagogy.*[216]

Although Hoornaert's reading offers one possible explanation, to me it seems incomplete. Perhaps the best formulation is to be found in Antonil, who wrote some years later. Boasting a more modern mentality, adapted to nascent capitalism, and aware of the role of productive labor, the Italian Jesuit had a more accurate understanding of the colonial system's structure. "Brazil is hell for the Negroes, purgatory for the whites, and paradise for the *mulatos* and *mulatas,*" he stated in an outstanding synthesis.[217] Contrary to Vieira's explanation—where the slave has a way out, through death—the universe of the colonial system affords the slave no possible way out. Hell is not only the African continent, submerged in sin; hell is the place from which there is no escape ever, not even through death: the infernal fire burns eternally. In an effort to solve the impasse created by this irreversibility, Europeans conceived of a third place: the mountain of purgatory, where souls would suffer till Judgment Day, when they could then earn their right to enter heaven. In the sixteenth century, purgatory was a reality, a hope for the Christian.

Slavery was thus the metropolis's necessary hell within the colony. No redemption was possible; without slaves, the colonial world would capsize. Offering the slave a way out through salvation was an ideological artifice embraced by Vieira, among others. In a more modern author, like Antonil, who was more concerned with economic issues, this artifice would become transparent. The colony was truly the black people's hell.

For whites, the system afforded a range of possibilities. As the ruling stratum, they dealt the cards within the colonial system and formed the link between the damned land of the colony and the metropolis—which, if it was not paradise (and sometimes it actually was), at least was closer to heaven.[218] Colonial purgatory was an option for those white people who were burdens, misfits, or undesirables in the metropolis. Even when life in the colonies implied extreme hardship, it still left open the possibility of eventually returning to life as an inhabitant of the metropolis. Banishment was the supreme mechanism by means of which Portuguese whites could purge their sins in the colony-purgatory.

And paradise? It excluded the colonial system, which was the negation of paradise that had to be avoided. The colony was paradise only for *mulatos*— people who did not live in infernalized captivity, who had escaped from it and turned against it, often refusing to perform systematic labor, inventing instead a new state of being through their mixing of bloods and their singular lifestyle. Their existence was a major testing ground for suppression of the system, and Antonil grasped that paradise would be theirs, even if, in the early days of the eighteenth century, this was merely a possibility.

From its birth, and even before that, the colony had been the purgatory of banished whites. As tradition has it—and it matters little whether this is fact or fiction—at least one exiled man had lived in Brazil prior to its discovery: the legendary João Ramalho, who supposedly arrived around 1490.[219] In various passages, Caminha mentions the exiled men who came over with Cabral's squadron: Afonso Ribeiro, manservant to Dom João Telo, sent by the captain to "go among [the indigenous peoples] and learn their lifestyle and habits";[220] and another two, unnamed (would one of them have been Afonso Ribeiro himself?), who were to be left in the discovered land to learn the indigenous language, thus becoming interpreters.[221] Convinced of their roles, they set off on the long path of purgatory, taking communion with their departing companions.[222] On May 2, as the squadron set sail for Calicut, they stayed behind on the beach, crying.[223]

Banishment, a little-studied topic, has inspired equivocated interpretations.[224] It has even contributed to the development of deterministic, pessimistic, and covertly racist analyses like that of Paulo Prado, who endeavors to attribute a hapless Brazilian history to the fact that "all the filthy scum of the old civilizations" ended up there.[225] Colonized by a people "already infected with the germ of decadence," the Brazilian colony heightened the moral degeneration; the only ones to escape this "overseas degeneration" would be those "ethnic groups segregated and cleansed by an appropriate mixing of bloods"—whatever he may mean by "appropriate mixing of bloods."[226] In a literal reading of colonial chroniclers, Prado thus perpetuated the image of an inviable colonial humanity, where banishment provided one of the chief reasons for this disqualification. Biased as it was, Prado's viewpoint nevertheless comprehended the hell-purgatory-paradise complex cemented together by the colonial system: "The transplanted Portuguese man thought of nothing but the overseas homeland: Brazil was banishment or purgatory."[227]

As a ritual exile, banishment was part of age-old traditions present in the European imagination; in the Early Modern age, the colonial system endowed it with a new meaning. The act of cleansing was still the crux of the matter but now in a new context, articulating metropolis and colonial world. Medieval passengers on the ship of fools, the Portuguese lepers were now deported to Cape Verde, where they would supposedly be cured by eating turtles and washing themselves in their blood.[228]

Throughout the colonial period, the tendency was to purge one's sins and serve out more serious sentences not where an infraction had been committed but elsewhere. The misappropriation of tobacco in Brazil was punished by banishment to Angola.[229] Those accused of offenses and then tried and convicted by the Inquisition's tribunal in Portugal often served out their sentences in Brazil or were sent to Angola or other places in Africa. The relation between the specific offense and the place where cleansing occurred varied during the colonial period. A preliminary examination reveals that in the seventeenth century those accused of sorcery were sent primarily to Brazil; in the following century, however, Portuguese sorcerers began serving their sentences on the Atlantic islands or, more and more often, in Portugal's *coutos*. Coincidentally, it was during the eighteenth century that the colonial system was being rethought.[230]

Defined in relation to the colonial system, purgatory had a geographical, spatial existence as well. "The most depraved and perverse persons in the Kingdom" were exiled to Brazil, and that was how it had to be. But to keep this people from disintegrating into an inviable humanity, it would be necessary to "people [Brazil] with better persons than so far have come to it."[231]

Jaboatão chronicles the disorder reigning in Espírito Santo during the early colonization, to which bad government and "excesses in customs" both contributed. "In those early days, there came to these parts, save some noble persons of distinction, unruly peoples, some for their crimes, some banished, and thus they lived, as disorderly men, given over to all kind of vices." It did not take long for purgation to come. "*Disorders of nature* always bring punishment from Heaven," and this came in the form of the war the heathens fought against the white settlers.[232]

Gandavo's whole line of argument is centered round the idea that the metropolis must be purged of its evils through colonization, which should serve to attract—thus the edenization of nature—dispossessed peoples. Responding to Alviano's allegation that "Brazil was settled first by banished persons," Brandônio goes a bit further: in the colonial purgatory, the evil nature of metropolitan people is corrected. In Brandônio's words: "Thou shalt know that these men, who firstly came to people Brazil, in a short while, given the largesse of the land, were made wealthy, and with their wealth rid themselves of their evil natures, to which the necessities and poverty they suffered in the Kingdom had compelled them. And the children of these people, already enthroned with this same wealth and rule over the land, cast off their old skin, like snakes, in all ways displaying the most honorable behavior."[233] Being the place of cleansing, the colony attenuated sins as the colonizing process advanced. The greater the harmony between the activities undertaken and the interests of the metropolis, the faster this purging would progress. The laborious efforts of the good settlers thus widened their path to heaven—barred to black slaves.

Born into a capitalist nation, João Maurício de Nassau had a lucid perception (not always found among the Portuguese) of the colony's role as purgatory and as the dungeon of delinquents. He typified Brazil as "a fertile land and fortunate country." But he added: "Without settlers, these lands can neither be of use to the Society nor capable of forestalling enemy incursions. If in this manner the proposition cannot be achieved, I would wish that the prisons of Amsterdam be opened and that the galley slaves be sent here, so that, tilling the earth with their spades, they may correct their wickedness, wash away their prior infamy through honest sweat, and return to the Republic not harmful but useful."[234] Purging sins and cleansing Europe, the colony would make it possible to transform an onus into something useful. This reversal would be possible, however, only through great effort—"*honest* sweat"—where the qualifier serves, along with the edenic vision, to alleviate the harshness of the labor.[235]

Brazil—Earthly Paradise owing to its nature and hell owing to the peculiar humanity it sheltered—was purgatory owing to its relationship to the metropolis. The damned could reach heaven through honest effort, daily labor, and subjugation to the will of the metropolis. The colonial system perpetuated purgation; it cast undesirable elements to the colony, promising them Eden (as in Gandavo's propagandistic discourse) and initiating their purification with the ritual exile represented by the crossing of the Atlantic. Once in Brazilian lands, the settlers dreamed of the distant metropolis and saw their stay in the New World as temporary; the promised paradise had been transformed into purgatory.

For the white settlers, heaven was their return to the metropolis; for the black slaves, salvation through faith. So long as the colonial system was in force, for both groups purgatory could metamorphose into hell: for whites, if they refused systematic labor and embraced confrontation with the metropolis—that is, revolt; for blacks, if they cloistered themselves within their own cultural universe, living in *quilombos*, turning their backs on Christianization and on endorsement of the colonizers' cultural and political values, killing off masters, and seeking their freedom. Escaping hell, or even purgatory, meant breaking free of the colonial condition. For whites, it meant no longer exhausting themselves in the daily toil that brought glory to the metropolis, purifying sugar and sins. For blacks, it meant no longer being slaves, becoming citizens instead. Under the colonial system, blacks would always live in hell, and whites in purgatory. Antonil was crystalline in his formulation.

Hell and purgatory could be confused, as was the case in Europe. Describing the countless forms of torture afflicting souls in purgatory, Le Goff defined the "third place" as a hell of a specific duration. Through "honest effort," the white settlers could to some extent control the length of their suffering. The slaves, captives until death, were fated to suffer eternally; for them, not even purgatory was possible.

Within this being and not being, nothing defined the condition of a great purgatory better than the condition of being a colony. For this reason, as long as it lasted, there would always be a purgatory at the heart of the colonial system.

An edenic nature, a demonized humanity, and a colony viewed as purgatory were the mental formulations with which the Old World cloaked Brazil during the first three centuries of its existence. Within these notions, centuries-old European myths and traditions blended with the cultural universe of Amerindians and Africans. Monsters, Wild Men, indigenous people, black slaves, exiles, and settlers who bore the thousand faces of the scorned, the inhabitants of colonial Brazil frightened Europeans, who were unable to grasp their singularity. These hybrid, multifaceted, and early modern beings could relate to the supernatural only in a syncretic fashion.

CHAPTER 2

Popular Religiosity in the Colony

It is unacceptable that systems of ideas like religion—which have played such tremendous roles down through history and into which people of all times have poured their life's energy—are no more than the stuff of illusions.
—Émile Durkheim, *Formes élémentaires de la vie religieuse*

Overview

Brazil was subject to the jurisdiction of the bishopric of Funchal for over half a century and in the subsequent one hundred years had only one bishopric, Bahia. This meant that Catholicism in the colony was first organized by the Jesuits.[1] Under the Padroado, an institution predating discovery, the Portuguese Crown was the patron of Catholic missions and ecclesiastical institutions in Africa, in Asia, and later in Brazil.[2] It was the Padroado that encouraged and supported missionaries in colonial lands, moving ahead of the Roman Catholic Church to occupy a void.[3] When Bahia's bishopric was created in 1551, the Council of Trent was already under way (1545–63). But while the council in some ways represented the triumph of southern Christianity, it did not place the overseas world at the top of its immediate agenda.[4] Not even a single prelate from the colonies attended the sessions, which were focused on Europe.[5] It was only in the seventeenth century that Rome began concerning itself with the evangelization of the colonial world at a time when it was also endeavoring to restrict the scope of the Padroado's actions, creating the Congregation of the Propaganda Fide (also known as the Congregation for the Propagation of the Faith) in 1622.[6]

Based on these facts, the historiography of colonial religiosity has sought to account for its singular characteristics. The fluid nature of ecclesiastical organizations is seen to have left room for the activities of plantation chaplains, who gravitated around the sugar planters. Paying little attention to the state's role but underscoring the role of families within the colonization process, Gilberto Freyre includes in his interpretation what he calls "family Catholicism, with the chaplain subordinated to the paterfamilias."[7] Religiosity was thus subordinated to the amalgamating and organizational strength of the *engenhos,* as part of the Mansion–Slave Quarters–Chapel triad. Its greatest singularity was familism, which accounts for the markedly affective attitude and greater intimacy with Catholic symbology that is so characteristically Brazilian. Freyre's recognition of this facet of Brazilian religiosity is brilliant, and we will return to it later. His explanation, however, relegates indigenous manifestations to the shadowy forests and African manifestations to the insalubrity of the slave quarters.

Mixing white, indigenous, and black blood, it is as if Brazilians had been "condemned" to syncretism because Brazil was not then Roman Catholic: the colony had only one bishopric in one hundred years; there were none of the pastoral visits recommended by Trent (the latter in fact would only be enforced in Brazil in the nineteenth century); and the Constituições Primeiras do Arcebispado da Bahia (1707) represented the sole ecclesiastical legislation of the first colonial period.[8] Moreover, the monarchy, a temporal power, meddled in religious affairs through the Padroado and based evangelization more on reasons of state than on reasons of the soul. The result was a church that countenanced slavery, indispensable to colonial exploitation. What made Brazilian Christianity unique therefore lay in this mixing of the races, in its nonconcentric relation to Rome, and in the eternal conflict of condoning slavery as a facet of the colonial system—forging a Christianity marked by the stigma of nonbrotherhood.[9]

Freyre sees religious familism as filling the void left by Trent's disregard for the colony during its first century of existence. Hoornaert, offering a more complex explanation, attributes unquestionably great weight to the fluid nature of the ecclesiastical structure during the colony's early days. He even states that until 1750 Brazil was characterized by a medieval spirituality that colored popular religiosity and was evinced in the organization of *confrarias* [brotherhoods].[10] What seems to go unnoticed is the basic characteristic of Brazilian religiosity back then—precisely its singularly *colonial* character. White, black, and indigenous, it recast diverse spiritualities into an absolutely singular yet simultaneously multifaceted whole.

If it had been tied to the church of Trent back in the sixteenth century, would colonial Brazil's religiosity have been any different? Today we know how long it actually took to establish Trent uniformity within Europe itself. Through the sixteenth century parishes failed to gain any true importance in the religious lives of European populations, much to the despair of the archbishop of Milan, Carlo Borromeo (1564–84). The archbishop sought to transform dioceses into "well-organized armies, which have their generals, colonels, and captains," like St. Ignatius adopting the military organizational model as the parameter that would lend homogeneity to this people's multifaceted religiosity.[11] During the seventeenth century, two different religions cohabited within European Christianity—that of theologians and that of believers—despite the elites' intensified efforts to crush archaic cultural features that had for centuries survived in the heart of these Christianized masses. The magical conception of the world was found in all social classes, common to "gentlemen and to the bourgeois, to village men and to rural men.

Empirical knowledge was shared by all, and Galileo's physics only spoke to a minority of sages."[12] A famous example that intrigued Lucien Febvre and Robert Mandrou was Jean Bodin, author of both *Six livres de la republique* and *De la démonomanie,* proof that he was not unaware of his contemporary universe of popular and peasant beliefs.[13] The Reformed Church and absolutism would eventually shape the elites in cultural terms, but they would not homogenize the entire population. In the eighteenth century the peasant world still believed it was thanks to the devil's influence that the allied armies succeeded—as apparent in *Mémoires,* by Jamerey-Duval, a man of the common people who became librarian for the emperor in Vienna.[14]

The violent actions committed under Trent for the purpose of establishing a more uniform faith and ridding religion of its archaic remnants would only achieve any effect in the seventeenth century and be more acutely felt in the eighteenth. Undertaking systematic pastoral visits, eighteenth-century bishops "discovered a rural people that often did not know the basic elements of Christianity."[15] In 1617, in Folleville, Picardy, St. Vincent de Paul realized the local curé did not even know the words of absolution.[16] This was perhaps more serious than the bare-legged priests in medieval Brittany who celebrated mass using chalices made from horns.[17] Preaching in Lower Brittany in 1610, Michel le Nobletz learned of "delusions and superstitions that brought tears to his eyes."[18] In 1680 the statutes of the Angers diocese stated that the Christians encountered during pastoral visits "seemed so little instructed in the mysteries of our Religion as if they had always inhabited savage countries unknown to the entire world. They knew nothing of the Trinity, nor of the incarnation of Jesus Christ."[19] Between 1565 and 1690, thirty-two episcopal orders, council decisions, and synod statutes were directed against superstition in France.[20] Around the same time, religious heterodoxy in England coexisted with theoretical uniformity, since the Reformation had failed to do away with popular skepticism. This is what Keith Thomas has termed "religious unorthodoxy."[21]

It should therefore cause no surprise that priests in the colony did not know the correct order of the members of the Holy Trinity, or the proper way to cross themselves, or whether Christ would come again or not.[22] In classifying the colony's syncretic religious practices as "gross deviations" or "deformed religiosity,"[23] contemporary historians are reproducing Trent's astonishment over what was deemed an "imperfect Christianization," which also found itself the target of acrid adversaries in the form of Protestant preachers: the "startling of Christian conscience,"[24] the "promotion of the Christianizing will,"[25] and the desire to "depaganize" were common to both Reformations.[26] "Yet supposedly they all bear the name Christian, are baptized, and receive the holy sacrament, even though they do not know the Lord's Prayer, the Creed, or the Ten Commandments," an indignant Luther was to state in the preface to his *Small Catechism.* "As a result they live like simple cattle, or irrational pigs."[27]

Based on recent studies, it is known to what degree early modern European religiosity was heavily imbued with paganism and how much violence accompanied Catholic and Protestant efforts to separate Christianity from paganism. The Christianity practiced in people's daily lives was characterized by a profound ignorance of dogma and by participation in the liturgy detached from any understanding of what either the sacraments or mass itself meant.[28] Accustomed to a magical universe, people could barely distinguish between the natural and the supernatural, the visible and the invisible, part and whole, the image and what it represented.[29] For the most part, what Trent's catechizing efforts achieved was at best the rote learning of a few religious rudiments, not always fully understood and even then forgotten within a few years.[30] In this sense, fifteenth-century Portuguese religiosity was no aberration within the European context; permeated with paganism, it was the "complex fusion of beliefs and practices, in theory baptized Christianity but in practice quite remote from it," of which A. H. de Oliveira Marques wrote.[31] For this author, "hidden behind the façade of Christianity, [this religiosity] lent names of saints and Catholic feasts to the forces of nature and to pagan devotions."[32]

At the same time, the exaggerated penchant for masses and processions known in Brazilian scholarship as "religious externalism" was not so uniquely Portuguese—as many authors have posited[33]—but European instead. This religiosity was imbued with magic belief, more inclined to images than to what they represented, to external aspects more than to the spiritual. Nuno Álvares Pereira would usually attend mass twice every day and three times on Sundays and fast thrice weekly.[34] When the seventeenth century brought a strong Catholic reaction, bent on cleansing spirituality, European externalism faded away, while in the colony it would linger on for reasons specific to the unique construction of colonial religiosity, as will later be seen. In any case, explaining this externalism as the "fruit of the spiritual childishness of ignorant people who do not explore beyond the simplest evidence of faith" is first and foremost an error that reveals ignorance about the features of popular Christianity in the West.[35]

The Jesuits Jorge Benci and André João Antonil, members of the same generation, would remain faithful to the inglorious Trent crusade.

Let the parish priests not think that they fulfill their obligation by merely asking the slaves about Lent at the time of release from obligation, whether they know the Prayers and the Commandments of the Law of God; and seeing that they know them, or, *better stated, that they recite them (for many recite them but know not what they are reciting),* without any further doctrine, they give them the Sacraments. This certainly is not the manner in which these ignorant people should be indoctrinated; because we have not reached the point where slaves may say how many are the members of the Most Holy Trinity and recite a Credo and the Commandments and other Prayers; *but it is necessary that they understand what*

they say, perceive the mysteries in which they shall believe, and compre-
hend well the precepts they shall keep. And it is up to the parish priest to
explain these things to them and make them comprehensible in such a
manner that the slaves understand them.

Benci's words here suggest that Trent was not at such a remove from the
colony, contrary to what historians like Hoornaert contend. These clerics
also said it was necessary to be patient with these "ignorant and uncultured"
people and to illustrate preaching with examples. "If they are taught but
once, they will not profit of it; but by teaching them one time and then again,
explaining and then explaining once more, then shall it be watered and reaped,
even on the hardest stones, namely, the most ignorant of souls."[36]
Priests should thus arm themselves with patience and perseverance in order to supplant the slaves' imperfect Catholicism, says Benci. Antonil, on the
other hand, blames the disregard of neglectful masters for flaws in their captives' Catholicism. They kept them unbaptized and occupied with labor rather
than letting them attend mass on Holy Days—in short, as St. Paul said, "being Christians and neglecting their slaves, they are acting worse than if they
were infidels." Even baptized blacks "do not know who their creator is,
what they shall believe, what laws they shall keep, how they shall supplicate
to God, for what purpose Christians go to church, why they reverence the
consecrated host, what they shall say to the priest when they kneel and speak
into his ears, whether they have a soul, whether it dies, and where it goes
when it leaves the body." Yet these "imperfections" were not the result of
the slaves' inability to comprehend, says Antonil, more lucid than many contemporary historians. The captives were fully capable of knowing their
master's name, the number of manioc holes they should plant in a day, how
much sugarcane must be cut, "and other things pertinent to the regular service of their masters." Furthermore, they were capable of asking for pardon
when they erred and of pleading for clemency. Why then should they not be
capable of learning to confess, to say the rosary, to recite the Ten Commandments? "It is all for want of teaching," the Jesuit responded.[37]
Antonil was perhaps one of the first to realize how important it was, in
terms of social and ideological control, to let syncretic expressions bloom.
"To wholly deny them their merrymaking, which is their sole relief from
captivity, is to wish them disconsolate and melancholic, with little life and
health. *Thus, the masters should not wonder at their creation of kings,* their
singing and dancing honestly for some hours on some days of the year, and
their amusing themselves innocently in the afternoon after having in the
morning fulfilled the feasts of Our Lady of the Rosary, of St. Benedict, and of
the plantation chapel's saint," Antonil said.[38] In recognizing the legitimacy
of the cult of St. Benedict, this Jesuit was ahead of Rome. St. Benedict the
Moor had died in 1569; soon afterward he was deemed a thaumaturge and
because of his color became the protector of blacks. His veneration, however, remained outside Roman orthodoxy and was only authorized by the

church in 1743. "These facts suggest that the worship of black saints or Virgins was initially imposed upon the Africans from the outside, as a step toward their Christianization, and that the white masters regarded it as a means of social control to promote subservience in their slaves."[39]

A slave-based colony was thus fated to religious syncretism.[40] Perhaps first sanctioned by the ruling stratum, the slaves' Afro-Catholic syncretism was a reality that ended up merging with the maintenance of "primitive" African religious rites and myths. St. Benedict was worshipped, but so was Ogum; and *atabaque* drums were beaten in the colony's *calundus*. Within the social structures imposed upon them, and through religion, blacks endeavored to find niches where they could develop their religious expressions in integrated fashion.[41] Dragged from their native villages, the slaves could not re-create in Brazil the ecological environment where their divinities had taken form. Nevertheless, they rebuilt it within their new milieu, anchored in the mythic system of their origins. "Like a living creature," Bastide stated, African religion slyly "secreted its own shell."[42]

The living African religion practiced by black slaves in Brazil thus came to differentiate itself from their ancestors' religion. Indeed, not all the slaves came from one same place; nor did they belong to one culture. Gêgê, Anago, Yoruba, Malê, and many others all brought their own unique contribution, reconfigured in response to the needs and realities of a new life, where an African quasi-syncretism was superimposed on an Afro-Catholic syncretism. Why ask for women's fertility, if they would bear infant slaves in the land of captivity? How could the gods be supplicated to provide good harvests if farming benefited the whites and its fruits went for foreign trade rather than for subsistence? "Better to pray for drought or for epidemics that would destroy the plantations, because for the slave a bountiful harvest simply meant more work, more weariness, more hardship."[43] The first winnowing within the heart of African religion would put aside divinities that protected agriculture, emphasizing instead those related to war (Ogum), justice (Xangô), and vengeance (Exu).[44]

Rife with paganisms and "imperfections" in the colony, as seen above, European-born Catholicism would continue to mingle with elements foreign to it, often multifaceted, like transmigrated African religion itself. As early as its first century of existence, the colony would witness a proliferation of syncretic Santidades on its soil, a mixture of indigenous and Catholic practices. The most famous of these was reported by the Holy Office's First Visitation to Brazil. Fernão Cabral de Taíde, owner of the Jaguaripe *engenho*, allowed the indigenous peoples on his lands to hold a syncretic service where center stage was occupied by a woman named Santa Maria and by a man who appeared either as "Santinho" (little saint) or as "Filho de Santa Maria" (the son of St. Mary). The worshippers had a temple containing idols that they worshiped. Some testimonies allude to a pope who lived in the *sertão*, who "had been left after Noah's flood and had escaped by hiding in the eye of a palm tree."[45] Followers of the Santidade said "that they had come to amend the law of Christians."[46] During their ceremonies, they "gave shouts and cries that could be heard from afar,"[47] "mocking and imitating the customs and ceremonies that were usual in the churches of Christians, but with everything imitated in their heathen and unfitting manner."[48] This Santa Maria—also known as "Mother of God"—would baptize neophytes, all with the permission of Fernão Cabral and his wife, Dona Margarida. The owner of Jaguaripe himself was in the habit of going into the temple and kneeling before the idols. According to one witness, he was a good Christian, and it seemed "that he did this so as to win over the heathens."[49] Fernão Cabral can thus be seen as a precursor in the manipulation of syncretism as a form of social control. When Governor Manuel Teles ordered the destruction of the Jaguaripe Santidade, Cabral told his emissary "that he was risking grave danger because the Indians would kill him" and refused to provide the back-up personnel requested by the governor.[50]

Fernão Cabral was right to keep all the indigenous people on his plantation under his watchful eye. Indications are that after a certain Silvestre, of indigenous blood, had learned Santidade practices at Jaguaripe, he meandered about the captaincy, teaching these precepts to other native groups. These indigenous people would "rise up with him in the fields, practicing the ceremonies of said erroneous theology, in which they said that this was the time when they had their God and their true saints *and that they, the Indians, would become masters of the whites and the whites their slaves,* and that whoever did not believe this erroneous theology of theirs, which they called Santidade, would be turned into fish and birds."[51]

The Jewish influence that still existed in Portugal would also persist and grow in the colony. Gilberto Freyre provides a remarkable description of a fifteenth-century procession based on a document from that time:

First we see the procession being organized inside the church: gilt banners and ensigns, dancers, apostles, emperors, devils, saints, *rabbis, jostling one another and falling into line.* Soldiers with the flat part of their swords taking care of the stragglers. *Up in front, a group performing the "judinga," a Jewish dance. The rabbi carrying the Torah.* Then, after all this seriousness, a clown making faces. An enormous serpent of painted cloth upon a wooden framework, with a number of men underneath. Blacksmiths. Carpenters. A dance by gypsies. Another by Moors. St. Peter. Stonemasons carrying little toy-like castles in their hands. Fisherwomen and fishwives dancing and singing. Ferrymen with the image of St. Christopher. Shepherds. Monkeys. St. John surrounded by shoemakers. The Temptation depicted by a dancing woman, swinging her hips. St. George, protector of the army, on horseback and acclaimed in opposition to St. Iago, protector of the Spaniards. *Abraham. Judith. David.* Bacchus seated on a hogshead. A semi-nude Venus. Our Lady on a little donkey. The Christ Child. St.

George. St. Sebastian naked and surrounded by ruffians pretending they will fire at him. Monks. Nuns. Upraised crosses. Sacred hymns. His Majesty. Gentry.[52]

For a long time, Jews and Christians had lived together in relative harmony on Portuguese soil. Many Christians had consciously or unconsciously adopted Jewish practices; the Old Testament circulated almost freely during the fifteenth century and part of the sixteenth; Christian and Jewish feasts intermingled, because many of the former were part of Jewish tradition. As is well known, when the Inquisition was installed in Portugal, the subsequent persecution of the Jews prompted mass emigration, giving birth to an entire Portuguese colony of Jewish extraction in Amsterdam. Emigration to the East would become unfeasible as of 1560, when Goa inaugurated a tribunal of the Holy Office (the only one in the Portuguese colonial world). From then on, Brazil, alongside the Netherlands, would become the safest refuge for Jews and *conversos*.[53]

It would, however, be wrong to state that the Jews and New Christians who set down roots in Brazil continued to practice the Jewish faith fervently. They joined the clergy and became stewards at almshouses and members of religious brotherhoods.[54] Among those arrested by the Inquisition between 1619 and 1644, the rate of Jewish religiosity was low.[55] Everything thus suggests that elements of Judaism became blended into the set of syncretic practices that made up the colony's popular religiosity, constituting one of its many facets.[56] Yet this process was not simple. Just as the Africans worshipped Catholic saints and *orixás,* reshaping their old religion to the reality of the new land, very often the New Christians also straddled the fence between two faiths. "He does not accept Catholicism, he does not take part in the Judaism from which he has been distant for almost ten generations. He is considered a Jew by the Christians and a Christian by the Jews. . . . Internally, he is a divided man."[57]

Catholic, black, indigenous, and Jewish traits thus mixed together in the colony, forming a syncretic, singularly colonial religion. To a certain extent, the history of the Christianization of the West was repeated here. "A whole network of institutions and practices, some of them doubtless very old, made up the warp of a religious life that unfolded on the fringes of Christian worship."[58] In Brazil syncretism was tolerated and encouraged when necessary, keeping it within possible limits. In Europe folk expressions were incorporated into official religion with a view to satisfying the needs of popular piety. This was the case, for example, with the institution of the feast of All Saints, which incorporated the cult of the dead.[59] But the incorporation of popular or syncretic elements did not come about by mere osmosis.[60] In the colony, the cases of African religiosity and of the New Christian division cited above serve well to illustrate a climate of *tension.* Incorporated traits carried with them a world of meanings. Assimilation and selections were not arbitrary, as demonstrated in Bastide's fine analysis showing how the importance of the *orixás* was reshaped in the colony. Moreover, they were not permanent or definitive.[61] The whole set of myriad pagan, African, indigenous, Catholic, and Jewish traditions cannot be viewed as remnants or as *survivals,* however, for they were still a *living* part of these people's daily lives.[62] It is within this tension between the multiple and singular, between the transitory and persisting, that the colony's popular religiosity should be understood and its syncretism inscribed.[63]

Despite some acute perceptions regarding the use of syncretism as a form of social and ideological control—recall the cases of Fernão Cabral de Taíde and of Antonil—condemnation and horror of syncretism almost always prevailed within the culture of the elites. Back in the sixteenth century the Franciscan Bernardino de Sahagún offered his reflections on the Christianization of Mexico, where syncretism was very strong. He showed the missionaries how paganism remained hidden behind a Christian setting "and that there was a danger of syncretism."[64] The Holy Office's Visitations revealed a tremendous intolerance of syncretic practices, particularly in the sixteenth and seventeenth centuries and less so in the second half of the eighteenth. The same was true of the tribunal at Lisbon when trials were initiated in the colony and the accused were then sent there to be judged. Municipal authorities often found themselves dealing with the popular dramatic representations known as *congadas* and *reisados.*[65] In his *Compêndio narrativo do peregrino da América* (Narrative Compendium of the Pilgrim of America), Nuno Marques Pereira vehemently condemned those "who go in mask, with indecent dances, at the head of processions, and particularly where the Most Holy Sacrament goes," suggesting greater repression of "such pernicious outrages."[66] The singularity of Catholic religion as practiced in the colony—the worshipping of saints, the exaggerated number of chapels, the theatrical aspect of religion, which was called "religious ignorance" as well as "externalism"—scandalized the foreign travelers passing through Brazil.[67] These voyagers, particularly the Anglo-Saxons and Protestants, said the Brazilians of color were "distorting Christianity and turning it into a mixture of burlesque and immorality."[68]

Dogmas and Symbols: Uncertainties and Irreverence

The joyful masses sponsored by sixteenth-century Jesuits—where indigenous peoples "would play and sing" frolicking music "in their manner" to the sound of maracas, berimbaus, and bamboo sticks—seem to have stirred moments of similar religious euphoria: the eighteenth-century baroque festivals of Minas Gerais that became known as the Triunfo Eucarístico (Eucharistic Triumph) and Áureo Trono Episcopal (Golden Episcopal Throne).[69] The festive processions that Nuno Marques Pereira's pilgrim commented on in horror also illustrate the joyful side of the colony's religiosity. But the latter was not constructed solely of colors, rhythms, and sounds. Through its visits to the Brazilian colony, the Tribunal of the Holy Office was responsible for a good share of the tears shed, for the dread, for the fear of persecution. The documentation left by these appalling incursions exposes secrets of daily life along with doubts, uncertainties, anger, and discord that the official religion was unable to settle. The general tone varies from skepticism to a desire to believe, from materialism to reverence for the supernatural forces, and it is almost always tinged with characteristically colonial syncretism. I will endeavor to show, however, that there is no complete uniformity in the signs of religiosity found in Visitations, ecclesiastical inquests, and inquisitorial trials—the three basic types of sources I have used here. Consistencies can be noted over three centuries, but alternations, substitutions, and the disappearance of traits can be detected as well.

"There come the devils of the Inquisition," exclaimed the New Christian merchant João Batista in the home of the archdeacon of the Salvador See, the same year that the Visitor Heitor Furtado de Mendonça began his inquisitorial journey through the colony's lands.[70] From north to south, the actions of Holy Office personnel were feared. In 1646, writing from Rio de Janeiro to the inquisitors of Lisbon, the Reverend Antonio de Maris Loureiro reported that inhabitants of the captaincy had stoned an inquisitor, forcing him to seek refuge in a church.[71] The anti-inquisitorial tradition of southern Brazil dated back to the sixteenth century. The irate words of one *mameluco* [of white and indigenous blood] adventurer are well known: reprimanded by Father Anchieta for his heathen practices and threatened with the Inquisition by the Jesuit, the *bandeirante* [adventurer in search of precious metals, Indians to be taken into slavery, or runaway slaves] "replied that he would pierce two inquisitions with arrows."[72]

This wrath against the Inquisition was not a product solely of the fear instilled by its horrendous practices, known to all, which were constant companions of frightened imaginations. It also reflected the ill-will, discontent, and popular irritation with official religion. In this sense members of the clergy were also a target. In 1595 the notary public of Filipéia de Nossa Senhora das Neves (now located in Paraíba), Francisco Lopes—a New Christian and *mameluco*!—confessed before the Board (Mesa) that he had grown annoyed at the Society of Jesus priests residing in the towns and said "in anger that if it depended on clerics and friars the world would be lost."[73] He felt that priests lied and preached a religion that did not speak to people's concerns. The shoemaker Baltazar Leal, an inhabitant of Bahia, argued about the resurrection of Jesus with the student João da Costa; he said Christ had not died and that if the priests said the opposite, they did so "to convince us that Christ Our Lord had died, but that he had not died."[74]

Why were there dignitaries in the church? Maria Gonçalves Cajada, the famous Arde-lhe-o-rabo ["Butt-That-Burns"] of the First Visitation, deaconess of the colonial sorceresses, "had said that if the bishop had a miter, she had a miter as well, and that if the bishop preached from the pulpit, she too preached, from a chair."[75]

The anticlerical beliefs of the Bahian ropemaker Isidoro da Silva won greater attention from the Holy Office, which saw heresy in them. Isidoro was from the Recôncavo region of Bahia; he had been born in Santo Amaro and resided in Madre de Deus, on the island of Cações, where he lived "from his fishing." Unmarried, a baptized and confirmed Christian, he had been accused four times of concubinage since 1725, when he was about thirty-five. Once jailed, he complained about the other prisoners' unruliness and violence, which he claimed had left him "weak in Reason"; it was then that he professed heretical postulates. In 1729 he appeared before the Lisbon Inquisition, where he was further questioned. He petitioned the recall of witnesses and protested that he had always been a good Christian. On May 15, 1732, he was put on the rack and given "all the torment to which he had been judged, in which more than a quarter of an hour would be spent," while the poor man cried out that, "for the love of God, they should release him and have compassion on him." Immediately thereafter the verdict was given: like some heretics condemned by the church, Isidoro demonstrated that he felt that

> God had asked for tithes to provide for loafers, who were the clergy, and that the sacraments were useless and a deceptive thing, and that there was no need for confessors because he, the Defendant, made his own confession with a mere act of contrition, and that the boys, and other people, who died without baptism went to heaven, and that men did not have in them the power to say I baptize you, and only God could baptize, and not the clergy, and if they did so, it was so that they would have an office by which they earned money without working, and also the sacraments of Baptism and Penance were merely ceremonies, and the words said during them were fantastical.

Judged an offender *de levi,* he appeared in a public auto-da-fé on July 6, 1732, at the Convent of São Domingos Church in Lisbon, in the presence of Dom João V, the princes, and the inquisitors. From there he was sent to serve a three-year period of exile in the bishopric of Miranda, far from the Recôncavo and the island of Cações.[76]

Isidoro's beliefs are similar to those of the miller Menocchio, whose inquisitorial trial has been brilliantly analyzed by Carlo Ginzburg in *The Cheese and the Worms.* Like his fellow believer, the ropemaker preached the simplification of religion (e.g., there is no need for confessors, an act of contrition is enough); the abolishment of the sacraments (ceremonies composed of fantastical words, "goods" exploited by the clergy as a tool of oppression); and the belief in God alone and in His powers (only He can baptize). Despite features clearly also found in Anabaptists, Ginzburg detected in Menocchio a representative of "an autonomous current of peasant radicalism, which the upheaval of the Reformation had helped to bring forth, but which was much older."[77] In Isidoro—who was probably white, since the trial records make no mention of mixed blood or black roots—any possible peasant past traceable to Europe (that is, to Portugal) was quite remote, for his father, a *lavrador* [farmer], was also from the Recôncavo region. Calvinism, on the other hand, was not quite so far away; it had been about one hundred years since the Dutch had left the Recôncavo.

Angered outbursts against the sale of Holy Crusade bulls and other types of papal bulls should be understood as popular expressions not necessarily linked to Calvinism. In 1595 Luís Mendes stated that the Crusade bulls "only came to take money."[78] Brás Fernandes, at seventy-one an elderly New Christian and *meirinho* [bailiff] for the town of Igaraçu, said that "those bulls were passed around to collect money and gather some alms."[79] Simão Pires Tavares, living on the *fazenda* of Guararapes, twenty-seven years old in 1594, doubted that the papal bulls could absolve and save Christians; he also scorned the power of rosaries and of indulgences granted by pontiffs. "They could hold no value for the soul," he insisted, perhaps seeking a religion with a more purified spirituality. He stated to a number of people that "the offerings that are given to the clergy in church for the rites were not to the benefit of their souls, and that not even God would do good for their souls because of said offerings, further stating that offerings to the clergy had little benefit, because with their singing, souls would not go to glory."[80]

A conversation that took place at Duarte Dias's sugar plantation around 1590 is a good example of how far indulgences had fallen into discredit by the end of the century, perhaps still under the influence of the Protestant preaching that Trent had as yet failed to revert, with the council quite recent and not yet a part of colonial life. The conversation took place between the sugar master Manuel Pires and two *lavradores,* Estêvão Cordeiro (who was part New Christian) and Álvaro Barbalho. Estêvão Cordeiro said that "in Rome the women walked about with their breasts uncovered and that the holy priests granted indulgences to the men who slept with [these women] carnally, with the intent of thus diverting these men from committing the abominable sin."[81] Protestant and Jewish influences thus joined with the discredit into which Rome and the entire ecclesiastical hierarchy had fallen among Catholics.

Extremely commonplace in the colony were discussions of clerical celibacy, of the superiority of the clerics' state over that of laypeople, and other analogous issues that appear under the title "order of the wedded being better than that of the clergy." A good share of those interested in this subject did not even know it was a matter falling within the jurisdiction of the Holy Office and therefore subject to its sanctions.[82] After all, matrimony brought pleasures and joy and should be as respected by God as divine service. Had God not made people to be happy? For the colonists at least, happiness was their aspiration. Gaspar Dias Matado, known as Barqueiro ["Boatman"], believed that "a good married man does as much service to God *in his bed and home* as a priest who celebrates mass at the altar."[83] God had created the religious order as well as the conjugal order. "The state of a wedded person was matrimony, which God had made and ordained," reasoned Beatriz Mendes, daughter of farmers and wife of a carpenter. She concluded: "The other states and orders that exist in the world were made and ordained by the male saints and female saints, and the friars and nuns did no better than the wedded, who lived just as God commanded."[84] Unchaste clerics who ran after women would be better off married, stated the oxcart driver Bastião Pires Abrigueiro. He longingly recalled the time when he himself had been married, when he had led a good and contented life. That is why he professed words that were condemnable from the perspective of the Inquisition.[85] Diogo Carneiro, a sugarcane worker in Itamaracá, was unaware that it was a sin to acclaim the benefits of wedlock. "He said that God had made the order of matrimony first, and that the order of those who were happily married and who did what God commanded was as good as that of priests, or better, and that he said this for the purpose of speaking about some priests who said whatever they wanted and slandered other men." He realized his error only when the edicts of the Holy Office were posted.[86]

This discredit into which members of the clergy had fallen was perhaps further kindled by the substantial number of priests notorious for their wicked ways. Such clerics were numerous in eighteenth-century Minas Gerais and were constantly involved in brawls, deflowerings, concubinage, abductions, gambling, drinking sprees, and irreverence toward the faithful.[87] The priest Manuel de Morais, of São Paulo, "was 'relaxed' [handed over to civil authorities] in the auto of 1642, charged with being a Calvinist heretic and with marrying, while a priest, a woman of the same sect." He was incarcerated, sentenced to wear a *sanbenito* [penitential habit] for the rest of his life, and permanently defrocked—extremely severe penalties for such a minor offense compared with those of other clerics in the colony.[88] In the auto-da-fé held on August 8, 1683, in the Terreiro do Paço, in the center of Lisbon, Antonio de Vasconcellos was found guilty "of saying masses, taking confession, and administering the Most Holy Sacrament of the Eucharist although he was not a priest, nor did he have holy orders." Originally from the island of Madeira, he lived in Salvador, State of Brazil. As part of his punishment, he was prohibited from taking orders "for the purpose of being a priest" and sentenced to floggings as well as six years in the galleys.[89] Friar Luís de Nazaré was convicted privately, not in a public auto-da-fé; early in the second quarter of the eighteenth century, he had committed all species of follies in the city of Bahia, performing superstitious cures and false exorcisms and taking advantage of women.[90] A little before that, Father José de Souza de Azevedo, cleric of São Pedro, was condemned to banishment outside of Lisbon for three years for the offenses committed in that city: resorting to superstitious objects and words in exorcisms "and making the devil come into his presence in the form of a tortoise, having a pact with him."[91] Like the Bahian priest, he received his sentence privately. For members of the clergy, the Inquisition avoided the public embarrassment of an auto-da-fé.

The colonists were often skeptical of the clergy (from the lowest to the highest dignitaries of the church), fearful of and angry at the long arm of the Inquisition, which stretched out to hunt them down in the distant colony—what did they think about the Creation, about God, about Jesus, about the mystery of the Holy Trinity?

Around 1617 a member of the Order of Carmo had said that "when God removed man's rib to create Eve, a dog had come along and eaten it, and that God had made woman from that which issued from the hind part of the dog, and so God had made woman from the hind end of a dog and not from man's rib."[92] A first reading of this passage appears to express irreverence toward the Creation, a sexist belittling of the figure of woman. It would be fitting that woman—sinful, infidel, traitor by nature—should issue forth from the dog's anus, as if she were excrement. This explanation would be consonant with Delumeau's thesis, which analyzes antifeminism as a component of the fear of women characteristic of the Early Modern age.[93] But what may also be implicit in this excerpt is a carnivalization of the Creation, which is not necessarily derogatory but brings to mind popular medieval traditions where obscenity played an important role. Present in religious festivities—lewd dances, vulgar songs, pantomimes loaded with erotic symbology—these traditions were also found in sixteenth-century poetry about the land of Cockaigne. Even more rife with buffoonery, these poems were transported to the context of the New World, as in *Begola contra la Bizaria:*

He's big and fat like a big millstone . . .
Manna flows from his hind end
When he spits, he spits marzipan
And he has fish instead of fleas on his head.[94]

If in testimonies like that of Isidoro, the Bahian ropemaker, God is the central object of popular beliefs,[95] He can also be the one mainly to blame for the hardships of daily life and, consequently, the object of doubt and questioning. The difficulties of life in the colony inspired reproach and bitterness. The New Christian André Gomes renounced God several times in just one day and extended his wrath to the entire colonial population. He also said that "for this reason the people of this Brazil had much cunning and guile because they were people who had been banished from the kingdom owing to their wicked deeds."[96] They were a godless people or a people for whom one god was not enough. For a heterogeneous population like that of the colony, there had to be many gods. "There were more gods than one, because there was the God of the Christians and another of the Moors, and another of the heathens," stated Lázaro Aranha at the time of the First Visitation to Bahia.[97]

Behind this apparent sacrilege perhaps lay an actual desire to humanize God and draw Him closer. Troubled by heavy rainfalls, many colonists complained of God's negligence—that He was relieving Himself at their cost.

Such was the case of Violante Fernandes, a gypsy in her forties and widow of a gypsy blacksmith who had been banished from Portugal for mule theft. Vexed by the rains, she said that "God pissed on her and wanted her to drown." Before the Visitation Board, she attempted to amend the offensive words by stating that she knew that "God does not piss, for this is something of man and not of God."[98] As in a game of telephone, the gypsy Tareja Roiz had heard from the gypsy Argelina that the gypsy Maria Fernandes had said "that she was weighed down by God, because it rained so much."[99] Likewise endowing God with human features, the gypsy—always the gypsies!—Apolônia Bustamante, upon walking "through rains and mud and landslides," had declared "with vexations and labors, . . . blessed be the prick of my lord Jesus Christ who now pisses upon me." Originally from Évora, from whence she had been banished for thievery, and wrestling with blasphemy and marital strife, Apolônia provides an accounting of her insults: she had done so "ten or twelve times, thereabouts," "in Portugal and Castela, and it seems to her in this captaincy as well."[100] This pissing, phallic, penis-equipped God of the sixteenth-century Visitations still had much to do with Europe's medieval religiosity, where it was so hard to distinguish Christian from pagan practices. At the same time, this God was well over a century removed from the distant, unattainable God of the Jansenists.[101]

For the overwhelming majority of the colony's inhabitants, disease and the forces and snares of nature appeared indomitable and tenacious. For this precise reason, faith displayed traditional and archaic contours, with the desire for material goods and concrete advantages assuming great importance, as if faith worked like a kind of barter contract. "'St. Anne, if thou save me, I shall become a monk,' Luther had sworn in the midst of a storm on his way back from Erfurt. This was the kind of prayer that the Reformer would reject shortly thereafter but that was practiced by the majority of the Christian world," writes Delumeau.[102]

In the colony, things were no different. Cecília Fernandes, seventy, married to a pottery worker from the captaincy of Pernambuco, had said in rage that "there was no God in the world if God did not take revenge on those against whom she asked for revenge." Violante Pacheca, a New Christian, forty-four, had had a falling out with her husband and, "vexed, had said that God would not be God if He did not avenge her against her husband and a woman because of whom she had been beaten by him."[103] A *mameluca* married to a fisherman, Domingas Gonçalves, thirty, had suffered from a horrible toothache at the time of her last pregnancy. Given her state, they did not pull her tooth, and the pain would not go away. One night, "inside her chamber, she went before a crucifix and said that a God who did not take that pain from her was not God."[104] A *mameluco* son of Jerônimo de Albuquerque, by the name of Salvador, had fought with his slaves and said that "he did not believe in God if they did not do such and such for him." Fighting with the merchant João de Paz, on João Eanes Street, "likewise with anger and vexation, he had said he did not believe in God if he did not pay him."[105] Manuel de Figueiredo, a 21-year-old student of Grammatics, became somewhat deranged because he had been "tied up naked, with his shirt raised to his upper chest," and cruelly flogged by three people, while none of the witnesses came to his aid. "With impatience," he renounced God and Our Lady.[106] Martim Álvares, a 30-year-old native of Biscaia, also found himself faced with unexplained violence. He lived in Itaparica and was seized by Gaspar de Azevedo, who tied his hands behind his back and treated him very badly, though he did not deserve it. Covered with bruises, he "had gone out of his head . . . under the force of passion, and seeing that none of the white people came to aid him, he had said in a loud voice, in desperation, five or six times, that he renounced God and Our Lady the Virgin Mary, and St. Peter and St. Paul, and all of the saints of the Court of the Heavens, and the Priest who had baptized him," continuing to blaspheme for about four hours.[107] Why were Manuel de Figueiredo and Martim Álvares arrested? The documentation does not tell us. It is certain, however, that colonial life's ever-present violence fostered disbelief in dogmas.

Afflicted by an interminable disease, with sharp pains constantly traveling from his back to his chest "and many times to his heart," despairing that he would ever regain sound health, the tonsured cleric Dionísio de Affonseca, twenty-six, born in Vila da Vigia, lost hope in God and doubted divine justice. "Tearing his nails into his head and pulling his own hair," he asked the devils to take him and for God to bury him in hell, "because he despaired of His Mercy." He was perplexed by the fact that God would punish "some for a single fault" and not punish "others who had committed countless faults"; many of the former would be lost, while the latter would be saved by making an act of contrition at the hour of their death. For these reasons, "he held God sometimes as unjust, and at the very least wondered whether he was just or unjust."[108]

It is curious that none of the colonists who were discontent with their lot and who renounced and doubted God went to the extremes of two Portuguese condemned by the Inquisition in the seventeenth century. João Fernandes, a tailor from the region of Covilhã, had said that "he owed nothing to God Our Lord because, being able to make him rich, He had made him poor, and giving many goods to others, to him He had given only labor, and *that if he reached God, he would have at Him with a knife.*" Like Dionísio, he doubted divine justice. But whereas the cleric delved into metaphysical considerations, the tailor went straight to the point: if God was the Creator to be adored, why had He created social inequality? The boatman Luís Roiz, thirty years old (twenty years younger than the tailor), stated that he "owed nothing to God, and if this same Lord did not provide him with food to eat, *he would remove His bowels with a knife,* and indeed with this knife he made a mark on an image of this same Lord, and if He did not give him the money, *he would drown Him in the Tagus.*"[109] Without calling into question the existence of God, the two blaspheming Portuguese—who appeared in the same auto-da-fé, on June 21, 1671—doubted His justice because they were poor and barely able to survive. The only difference in their cases was the degree of violence: Luís Roiz's was greater, expressed in an aggression against the image of God. This confrontation with God was perhaps an early modern feature; the intermediation of the medieval saints (who established a relation between the believer and God while at the same time serving to protect the Supreme Being from the occasional wrath of the faithful) had lost its efficacy.[110]

Jesus, Son of God, was also the target of people's discontent. "I put on Christ much shit, and on the host much shit, and on the Virgin Mary much shit" was the response of the licentiate Filipe Tomás de Miranda when asked how things were going for him.[111] The New Christian Simão Pires Tavares, in addition to doubting the power of the clergy, "said shit on the school of Jesus, and the same filth on Jesus." He also made a habit of swearing by the bowels and marrow of Jesus.[112] People imagined a human Jesus—like the pissing God—complete with intestines, who procreated like any other man. Losing at gambling, the sailor Antonio Nunes, thirty, "had sworn twice by the son of Jesus Christ."[113] But supernatural assistance was also expected of Him. The Jew Duarte Roiz, upon watching the Maundy Thursday procession pass by the door of his jail, ridiculed the other prisoners' conformity to their situation, asking "alms for the love of God Our Lord Jesus Christ." "If it is Our Lord Jesus Christ who goes by there, why does he not remove us from jail?" he asked.[114]

Christ was also disrespected through the symbols representing him: images and crucifixes. In an atmosphere that recalls joyful medieval religiosity, two New Christians—the licentiate Filipe Tomás mentioned earlier and the peddler Luís Álvares—amused themselves by making observations on the image of Jesus that had passed by in the Procession of the Steps. Without kneeling, "taunting with great laughter," the licentiate had said: "What a bad face Christ has!" "What a shit beard He has!" Luís Alvares added. "Very shitty indeed," agreed Filipe Tomás.[115]

Irreverence toward the crucifix was one of the most common infractions in the colony, above all during the first two centuries. Almost invariably, the accused were Jews and New Christians. Luís Vaz de Paiva and his nephew, both New Christians, stole a crucifix from the small chapel of Nossa Senhora da Ajuda and walked about the streets with it, frightening people at night. When someone would open the door of his home, the two men would stick in just their arms, bearing the crucifix. They carried it to gambling houses and said, "Make it cheaper for this man."[116] A 38-year-old white man by the name of Isidro, allegedly a Jew and probably from Vila de Cametá, had a round face, full body, and braided hair; he was accused before the Board of the Visitation to Grão-Pará of tying a crucifix to a guava tree and lashing it.[117] Diogo Castanho, single, was another New Christian; he forced the crucifix to participate in his sexual activities. "When he had carnal knowledge of one of his Negro women he would shove a crucifix beneath her."[118]

In the records of the First Visitation to Pernambuco, one of the names that appears most often is that of the merchant João Nunes, accused of constantly having "a crucifix in view of a filthy pot where he relieved himself"[119] and of having "in his chamber" a crucifix upon which he urinated, saying, "Here, wash Thyself."[120] He had even poisoned to death a mason who had witnessed this heinous crime.[121] However, the testimony of the licentiate Diogo do Couto casts doubt on the manner in which João Nunes really relieved himself. Diogo do Couto was best situated to speak about the case, for he had ordered the arrest of both the mason and João Nunes. He in part negates the charges against the merchant, stating, among other things, that he had no knowledge that João Nunes had relieved himself on a crucifix. To be perfectly honest, the licentiate affirmed, there was a crucifix at the merchant's house, relatively close to the place that served as his chamber pot but not in the same room. Diogo do Couto further clarifies that the only reason he had ordered João Nunes's arrest was adultery.[122]

True or false? It is pointless to wonder. Stories of this kind were fashioned collectively, with each imagination contributing to the construction of a semilegendary tale marked by the presence of centuries-old archetypes that ridiculed symbols, inverted them, denied them, and perhaps sought to create a desacralizing antiorder.

Acts of irreverence against crucifixes are a part of ancient stereotypes, ascribed to various marginal or marginalized social categories down through time. Spitting on the crucifix, dragging it about the house, and trampling it underfoot or urinating on it were offenses ascribed to the Templars in the fourteenth century, part of the monumental process through which Philip the Fair destroyed this order and all its power.[123]

Very often there was an underlying reality, not always imputed to Jews, however. Besides the Templars, the Cathars were accused of repudiating the cross. "It is worthless; it is a sign of evil," said Arnaud Vital, a Cathar shoemaker living in Montaillou in the early fourteenth century. Bélibaste, the venerable mayor, frothed with hatred at the wooden crosses scattered over the countryside: "If I could, I would chop them down with an ax; I would use them as wood to boil the pots," said the holy man.[124] The sign of the cross was hated as well, and Pierre Authié proposed to Pastor Pierre Maury a formula by which he could fool the Christians when entering the church, without betraying his intimate, secret faith (the Inquisition was greatly feared at that time): "In the summer, Pierre, you can (with the pretext of crossing yourself) swat the flies away from your face; in so doing, you can also say: here is my forehead and here is my beard; here one ear and here the other."[125] Considering how the Cathars ridiculed the sign of the cross, there is no escaping comparisons. Diogo Soares, a New Christian and son of a woman who reportedly had died on the gallows, taught a black man to cross himself in this way: "placing his hand on his forehead he said ox, and placing his hand on his chest he said rope, and placing his hand on his left shoulder he said knife, and placing his hand on his right shoulder he said horse, then bowing his head he said, Amen, Jesus." Diogo Soares and his brother, Fernão Soares, a sugar planter in Pernambuco, burst into laughter.[126]

In the eighteenth century, in the old kingdom of Congo, the Antonian movement—a reconfigured, wholly Africanized form of Christianity—was exhorted by their prophetess Kimpa Vita (or Dona Beatriz) not to worship the cross "because it was the instrument of the death of Christ."[127]

Eduardo Hoornaert analyzes the symbolism of the cross as the embodiment of metropolitan power and colonization, where Jesus represents a white aristocrat who suffers as a hero and not as a poor man. "In Brazil, Jesus is not born in a manger but rather in a cradle of gold; he does not belong to the slaves' quarters but rather to the plantation house."[128] Whatever the validity of this commentary, it is interesting to note that the black slaves rarely rebelled against the representation of Jesus on the cross. Rather, it was members of the middle classes or the economic elite themselves who would do so, despite their social position and power, letting a popular substratum of superstitious practices and heretical beliefs rooted in the Old World erupt. To the contrary, the black slaves, who assimilated Christianity as befit their needs and the rules of their logic, had a tendency to use images and crucifixes in their syncretic rites, as did indigenous peoples. In the sixteenth-century Congo, Georges Balandier observed the use of crucifixes in fertility rites and in the magical protection of houses and of individuals.[129] In twentieth-century *catimbós* in Paraíba, a wooden cross was essential. "It must be inside a wash basin or on the towel or underneath a taboret."[130]

As to acts of sacrilege involving the crucifix, I believe a more plausible explanation would follow the lines of Ginzburg's interpretation of Menocchio's heretical syncretism. Under the impact of the religious upheavals of the fifteenth and sixteenth centuries, popular and heretical beliefs blossomed. In their effort to eradicate these beliefs, the two Reformations focused their attention on them and in a way assured their perpetuity.[131]

Irreverence toward saints and the Virgin was also part of ancient traditions common to peoples of western Europe. But first in Portugal and later in the colony they acquired singular features that came to distinguish them substantially from their counterparts in other regions of Europe. In the Old World, affective forms of popular religiosity tended to disappear in the late eighteenth century or at least became much more restricted. They were to last longer in the colony, still present at the time of the empire, as Gilberto Freyre points out in *Casa Grande e Senzala*. Within popular religiosity, this emotional component, or affectivization, is more clearly visible in the cult of the Virgin and, above all, of the saints. In an ambiguous movement (as popular culture is ambiguous), affectivization and detraction often approach each other: the saint who is worshipped and adored, with whom confidentialities are shared, is also the saint who, in the religious economics of the barter system, may be hurled into a corner, cursed, and abhorred in outbursts of anger or dissatisfaction.

In practice since the twelfth century, the Marian cult saw a period of renewed vigor in the fifteenth: Our Lady of Mercy, of Grace, of Good Succor, of the Rosary (whose veneration owed much to Alain de La Roche, a Dominican from Brittany), of the Immaculate Conception.[132] The reformers would later grow annoyed by this proliferation of representations of the Virgin. In *Apologie pour Hérodote,* Henri Estienne wondered which of these many Virgins was truly the mother of God.[133]

According to Hoornaert, the first Marian images in Brazil were miracle-makers or mediums. One example was Nossa Senhora da Graça, the famous image that Caramuru found in Bahia in 1530, in honor of which Paraguaçu had a chapel built.[134] Next came warrior images, patronesses of victories over Indians and heretics. Nossa Senhora da Vitória brought triumph over the Indians and the French in Bahia,[135] while Nossa Senhora dos Prazeres guaranteed the 1656 victory over the Dutch.[136]

Worshipping the Virgin in churches, chapels, processions, and brotherhoods and syncretizing her as colonization progressed (e.g., the black slaves' extremely popular Nossa Senhora do Rosário, highly revered in eighteenth-century Minas Gerais), Brazilian colonists carnivalized and disrespected Mary in their daily religion. Manuel Dias was a cleric who presided over services at the main cathedral in Pernambuco. One day he was seen in front of the church's chapel to Nossa Senhora do Rosário, with his leg raised and emitting "a great fart before the lovely image of the Virgin that is on the altar."[137] Reprimanded by Rodrigo Soares, the assisting priest, he responded with laughter. But he did fear the rigors of the Inquisition: "On the 10th day of November of 1595, the cleric Manuel Dias came before the Board to confess that in the chapel of the Espírito Santo . . . before other clerics, without respect for the place, he had broken wind."[138] Repentant, he asked to be forgiven for his irreverence.

The Virgin's human, female traits were highlighted. The New Christian Bento Teixeira (author of *Prosopopéia?*) swore by the Virgin's pubic hair.[139] How could Mary's status as a woman be reconciled with her role as mother of God? Her virginity was constantly questioned. Around 1616 the New Christian Manuel (or Francisco) de Oliveira stated near the São Francisco River that Our Lady had given birth twice. God had seen to this man's punishment *a priori:* he was "crippled in his feet and hands."[140] The sailor Manuel João, a native of Terceira Island and an inhabitant of Bahia, was condemned by the Holy Office "for being a Lutheran heretic and for pronouncing words against the purity of Our Lady Virgin Mary." On July 10, 1644, he appeared in an auto-da-fé in the center of Lisbon; he was scourged, gagged, and sentenced to three years in the galleys.[141] The shoemaker Frutuoso Antunes, a 55-year-old New Christian, went even further, declaring that "Our Lady the Virgin Mary had not been a Virgin before birth, nor at birth, nor after birth."[142] Here again, it is not the offender's Jewish roots that account for this irreverence toward Mary. Cathar peasants from Montaillou called the Virgin a "vat of flesh" in which Jesus Christ had come wrapped, yet they nevertheless worshipped her with chthonic force.[143] They did not believe in her virginity; Christ had been made "through fucking and shitting, rocking back and forth and fucking, in other words through the coition of a man and a woman, just like all the rest of us."[144] More than blasphemy, what appears here is the desire to make Christ and the Virgin into human beings like any others. Ruled by a sense of the practical, the miller Menocchio also failed to believe it possible for Mary to have given birth and still remain a Virgin.[145]

Unequivocally expressing their skepticism about the purity of the mother of God, Manuel de Gallegos and Francisco Mendes, both New Christians, had a one-eyed gray mare that they called Mary or dark-gray Mary. In jest, they would ask the scandalized sugar master Baltazar Pedro: "Have you seen our dark-gray Mary?"[146] Such irreverence was not always ironic, however. At Fernão Cabral's *fazenda,* a black woman from Guinea named Petronila, a baptized Christian, struck a blow against a gradine where Our Lady was represented, "declaring that that lady was worthless, that she was of wood, that better was her stone one, from the heathens, that moved when you approached it."[147] Around 1747, in Conceição do Mato Dentro, captaincy of Minas Gerais, Maria da Costa told a woman with whom she was arguing that she would strike her, for "she was a woman capable of striking Nossa Senhor do Pilar."[148] Some years later, also in Minas, this time in the town of Sabará, the Mina native Rosa Gomes, "finding herself in despair one day in her home between four walls, alone and wretched, implored to the saints and they did not respond, and finding neither a stick nor a rope with which to hang herself, so desperate and out of her wits, with a large knife she slashed the images of Our Lady, St. Anthony, and even the Christ Child, cutting off their heads and tearing off their arms." In the latter half of the eighteenth century, the Inquisition sometimes proved more complaisant than during the two previous centuries. Rosa was harshly reprimanded but was released, and her confiscated goods were restored to her.[149]

Gilberto Freyre captured the affective side of colonial religiosity quite well: sterile women rubbing up against images of St. Gonzalo of Amarante, seeking his aid in this intimate fashion:

Get me a spouse, get me a spouse,
Dear St. Gonzalo,
For to thee shall I pray
My dear little saint.

Or in another version:

> St. Gonzalo of Amarante,
> Matchmaker of old women,
> Why dost not marry the lasses?
> What harm have they done thee?[150]

Freyre also underscored the familiarity with St. Anthony. Asked to find husbands and locate lost objects, the saint might be hung upside down inside a cistern or well, or even placed inside an old privy, so that he might fulfill a promise more swiftly.[151] Freyre noted the popularity of St. John the Baptist, "feasted on St. John's Day as if he were a handsome young lad and lover let loose among the marriageable maidens, who address to him such nonsense as this: 'Whence comest thou, St. John, that thou comest so moist?'"[152] Freyre likewise pointed out St. George's and St. Sebastian's roles as holy captains or military leaders, "like any powerful plantation owner."[153] He mentioned St. Peter's ability to marry off widows.[154] Generally speaking, Freyre saw the saints as catalyzing a great procreative tension among the Portuguese, who sensualized saints and religion. This stimulation of love and fertility crept into colonial cuisine and manifested itself in suggestive names: *suspiros-de-freiras* [nuns' sighs], *toucinho-do-céu* [heavenly back fat], *papo de anjo* [angel's belly], *levanta-velho* [raise-the-old-man], *língua-de-moça* [maiden's tongue], *mimos-de-amor* [love's caresses].[155]

In his brilliant interpretation, Gilberto Freyre focused on the cultural expressions of the social elite and of sugar planters (especially in the northeast) while leaving aside the practices and beliefs of Brazilian society's middle and lower ranks. The adoration of saints had expanded remarkably, starting in the fifteenth century and continuing throughout the sixteenth—"polytheism was about to be reborn," as Delumeau put it, in exaggerated terms.[156] These saints were relied on as great go-betweens.[157] But in their ambiguity, they could be good or evil, generous or vengeful.[158] They could therefore awaken anger and violence in people—and the harsher the concrete conditions of existence, the more legitimate such reactions. This ambiguity could be seen in the colony as well, where sources document attitudes of affection as well as of wrath and disrespect.

During the 1618 Visitation, the New Christian merchant Domingos Álvares Serpa was accused of saying that St. John the Baptist "had been a sinner, like any other man."[159] Called before the board, he confessed his guilt. Speaking with friends, "they came to discuss who would be the greatest saint in heaven." Pero Vilela, a barber, had said the ranking fell to St. John the Baptist—the plantation maidens' handsome saint. The merchant "replied that St. John the Baptist had sinned."[160] Around the same time, the priest Hieronimo de Lemos declared before witnesses that "when St. Peter had slashed Malcolm, he had had two drops, implying that St. Peter had had his fill of wine."[161] At

Nossa Senhora da Ajuda Church, during Holy Week, the New Christian Duarte Álvares pulled at the beard on an image of St. Peter—the solicitous widows' matchmaker—and told "how this wicked villain would raise the wine bag back when he was a fisherman."[162] Of the blessed St. Francis, Gaspar Roiz said that "the saint had gone some leagues to see a handsome woman."[163] Lázaro Aranha invoked the aid of St. Anthony while playing cards and thanked the saint, calling him "that little scalawag" when he drew the desired card.[164] Antonio da Costa, a 40-year-old *mameluco,* vowed to celebrate a mass to St. Anthony should he get a runaway slave back; as soon as he had his hands on the black man, he "said that little scalawag St. Anthony was a lecher for he knew full well that [the saint] did not want him to come upon the Negro till after he had promised the mass."[165] Finding himself in a similar spot, Lázaro Aranha, mentioned earlier—who must have been a devotee of this saint—promised St. Anthony a coin as alms should he find a vanished black man. But once he had found the slave, he tricked the saint, saying ironically: "That rascal St. Anthony thought I would give him a cruzado!"[166]

In this affective relationship with religion, an effort was made to draw it into daily life. Associations were even made between saints and living, known people. Diogo Lopes Franco, a 26-year-old New Christian merchant, admitted to having compared the figures of the apostles arranged in the countryside chapel of Nossa Senhora da Ajuda during Lent "with some men of this land, and of one of these it had been said that he resembled the Meirinho do Mar [bailiff of the sea]."[167] In a way reflecting the blurring of the sacred and the profane that was so typical of the Middle Ages and that lasted into the Early Modern age, this identification with the saints at times went even further. Domingas Fernandes, from the Portuguese town of Aveiro, wandered begging about the fields of the Recôncavo, in the company of the famous Maria Gonçalves, known by the sobriquet Butt-That-Burns. Maria would tell people that her traveling companion was a saint "and that touching her or being touched by her was a virtue."[168] Arguing with a man about some of the figures in his account books, the Old Christian merchant Manuel Barroso said that "just as the evangelists had spoken the truth in the Gospels, so did he . . . speak the truth in the additions in his books."[169]

José de Jesus Maria, or José de Moura, took this association with the saints even further. A hermit from Montemor and inhabitant of Lisbon, he was banished to Brazil after being imprisoned, tortured, and tried by the Inquisition; he appeared in an auto-da-fé held on October 22, 1656. He himself had come before the Tribunal of the Holy Office to report the extraordinary things that had happened to him. While he was praying before images, particularly those of the Virgin and of Jesus Christ, when "something presented itself to him in his heart, he would inquire of the Holy Images whether it would be good to do so, or refrain from doing so, and they would indicate that yes he ought to, or no he ought not to do that which presented itself in his heart, and he would comply with this, and he had never been wrong." The images expressed their sentiments by nodding or shaking their heads and also through eye movements. The hermit had been inspired to seek their counsel for a wide variety of motives: if he should make a certain white and blue habit, "with a belt to gird himself"; if he should or should not go into a certain church, follow a certain procession, change his name, practice self-mortification. It is not known whether José de Jesus Maria continued his eccentric practices in the colony.[170]

As seen earlier, relationships with the saints were predominantly affective and characterized by a desire for closeness and greater intimacy. But as like-wise underscored above, there were moments of anger and strife, within the framework of a religious economics where an act of barter may not have been reciprocated. Francisco Lopes, the curious New Christian *mameluco* from Pernambuco who despised priests, was enraged by some oxen that had entered his pasture and damaged it. He directed his wrath toward the saints, renouncing all of them indiscriminately.[171] Cristóvão Dias Delgado, a 27-year-old bachelor who worked as an overseer for his brother, a farmer, discharged his family tensions onto the saints. On the morning of Our Lady's day, before mass, the butcher Jorge André went to his house to collect eleven mil-réis "that he had lent him for some business of his said brother. And since his brother then questioned payment of this debt, he, the Confessor, became vexed and in anger said that he renounced his father and his mother and his grandparents and all the Saints that be in paradise." Saints became mixed up with family in this repudiation of the established powers that op-pressed him. The brother-boss rushed to defend order, intent upon reestab-lishing it: "The said brother hastened to reprehend him . . . and advised him to come forward and accuse himself, and he, the Confessor, then silenced himself, and . . . he asks forgiveness for this offense."[172]

Besides hatred and rebellion, there was always the carnivalizing approach, perhaps still more irreverent. It was common practice to attribute this kind of attitude to the New Christian, perpetual dissident and critic of established values.[173] Around 1613 a typical meeting of goodly men took place in the city of Bahia. The host was chaplain at the Santa Casa da Misericórdia, and among those in attendance were a town councilman (the accuser himself); a New Christian, son of a wholesale merchant from Lisbon; and the captain of Fort Santo Antonio, Afonso de Azevedo, who was a member of the Order of Christ and an official at Santa Casa, the almshouse. The conversation was precisely about the needs at Santa Casa. The captain was explaining how critical the situation was, to the point where it would be necessary to sell a church ornament. Manuel da Silva, the New Christian, replied that "he would purchase the said ornament as a feed bag for his horse." All were scandal-ized. Holy ornaments were not to be sold for animal feed bags, the captain retorted, perhaps not realizing the New Christian's good-humored riddling when he offered to save the Santa Casa and, moreover, inverted the signifi-cance usually attached to religious ornaments.[174]

There was also an archaizing element that blurred the nuances between the representation and what was being represented. Why revere a mere ornament? Why believe in the power of some simple round beads? The New Christian Frutuoso Antunes, skeptical about Mary's virginity, one night called "his wife to bed." But since she was praying, she did not want to go. Disappointed, the husband exploded: "[T]he prayer beads were made of wood . . . , one did not pray the words of God with them."[175] Perhaps implicit in his outburst was an idea similar to that of someone else accused by the Visitation Boards: that a Christian served God as well with his wife in his house and in his bed as did a cleric in divine service. Analogies with medieval religiosity, replete with the vitality of life, are again inevitable, especially in such heretical manifestations as those of the Cathars, advocates of free love.

A certain sensualization of religious matter at times bloomed more intensely. Three young men who worked at Dom Jerônimo de Almeida's house were discussing the dogma of the Most Holy Trinity, inspired by a picture one of them had nailed on the wall, "with Our Lady and the Holy Spirit above and some angels in a circle around." Suddenly their attention was diverted to the sensuality of the little angels' plump legs, "those angels that were painted there with fat little legs."[176] They then returned to the topic at hand: what was the order of the persons in the Most Holy Trinity? If, when crossing yourself, you said, "Father, Son, and Holy Ghost," the last must be the third person, said one of the fellows. Another thought the Holy Spirit would be the second person, for that is how he was portrayed in the picture.[177] How can one abstract what is being represented from its meaning?

Dogmas contained in the body of doctrine, such as the Last Judgment, Everlasting Life, and the existence of purgatory, were also the object of daily discussions among the colonists, who simplified them and stripped them of the abstractions common to theological ponderings, rendering them more concrete by bringing them into their daily lives.

The gypsy Tareja Roiz denied the existence of Judgment Day, and for this she was again accused before the Board of the First Visitation to Bahia.[178] Antonio Dias de Morais, a New Christian, did not believe there would be a Judgment "once the body died."[179] The subject came up in a conversation with an Old Christian, Francisco Pinheiro, who had said they should not work so hard, for "some ten years from now, Judgment Day shall come." The New Christian replied that "it would be when God so willed, and that once dead we become a bit of rotten flesh of the basest content there is, and that there is no Judgment."[180] This episode is interesting because it shows a certain convergence in the two men's conceptions, suggesting that what mattered more than Jewish roots was the interpretation of different beliefs that, in the final analysis, wove the fabric of colonial religiosity. The old Christian declares that it is useless to work so hard—after all, everyone will die anyway, with Judgment Day coming in ten years (Sebastianist millennialism?), and what matters is the here and now. The New Christian retorts that it is

God who decides everything and that we are worthless once we die—which is another way of saying that nothing but life matters! "Popular religion does not concern itself with eternal salvation but endeavors to attend to the multiple—even if modest—exigencies of daily life."[181]

Once the body is dead, the soul dies, Menocchio said in northern Italy in the late sixteenth century. He was arrested twice and executed on the second occasion. In the first year of the seventeenth century, a deponent informed the inquisitor from Friuli—Menocchio's home—that at the time of the miller's execution he had come across an innkeeper in Pordenone who told him that in that place lived a certain Marcato, or Marco, who held that once the body had died the soul did as well. "About Menocchio we know many things. About this Marcato, or Marco—and so many others like him who lived and died without leaving a trace—we know nothing," states Ginzburg.[182]

Neither is anything known about those who, like Antonio Dias de Morais, believed the body was nothing more than rotten flesh. Yet there is no doubt these people existed. This radical attachment to the material world and to the pleasures of this life gives a glimpse into their conceptions of eternal life. "In this world may you see how well I live, for in the next you won't see me suffering," said Estêvão Cordeiro, who lived on a plantation in the parish of Santo Amaro.[183] Paulo de Abreu, resident of Igaraçu, believed "there was no other world beyond this one."[184] And if one did exist, it must be an extension of earth. The *mameluco* Manuel Gonçalves, sugar master on a plantation in Várzea do Capibaribe, went about with black women and when reprimanded used to say that "they should let him fornicate well in this life, for he would be well fornicated in the next as well"—and this he had heard from others.[185]

In the captaincy of Paraíba, around the same time, similar exchanges took place. Gonçalo Francisco, a *mameluco* sailor, was so young that he barely had a beard, but he was nevertheless very fond of female charms. One day, on his "way to Varadouro, the said Gonçalo Francisco took a *brasila* [indigenous woman] and he, the Denouncer, told him to leave the black woman alone." "Be still," the young man replied, "for whoever does not sleep with women in this world, the devils will sleep with him in the other." Like the Pernambucan Manuel Gonçalves, he responded to his friend's reprimand with these words: "he had heard that before from other men."[186] In evening conversations among men, three friends were talking about a young married woman, "quite handsome" but "very wanton" because, since her husband lived away, "she used her body wickedly," giving it "to whoever asked her." Then one of the men, Sebastião Pereira, who made his living by bringing slaves from Angola, pronounced the following words: "Leave her be, leave her be, she does very well, for if she does not get her fill here, she will not make out well for herself in Paradise."[187]

Within popular consciousness—"not very open to the eschatological concepts of the times," as the historian Aaron Gurevich has pointed out—the content of the story of salvation penetrated the present, that is, each individual's life. In confronting the present moment with eternity, people moved easily from the world of the living to the kingdom of the dead, as was the case in medieval journeys to the Beyond.[188] For this reason it was possible to fornicate in the other world. If the people of the colony recalled the Middle Ages when they brought the eschatological concept of time into their daily life, however, they stood apart from that era when they rejected the holy story, through sacrilege and irreverence toward dogma. In this aspect colonial people were eminently early modern.

Although the idea of purgatory had enjoyed great popularity in the Christian West since the twelfth century, in the colonists' consciousness it was a matter of some confusion. The notion was a relatively recent acquisition and, moreover, had been the target of harsh criticism from Protestants; Luther spoke of it in ironic terms, calling it the "third place."[189] In the last years of the sixteenth century, the inhabitants of the captaincy of Pernambuco still were unclear about the place where sins were purged. It would be better to pay for sins in this life than in the next, said one Pero Correia, from Olinda, about the torment meted out by the Inquisition. Disagreeing, the soldier Domingos Ferreira said that the sins not paid for in this life would necessarily be paid for in the next. But he was a bit uncertain: he thought that those who died after confession and communion would not need to pay for their sins in the next life, "nor would they go to purgatory." Pero Correia detected heretical propositions in his companion's speech and warned that such words could take him to the gallows. But Domingos Ferreira stood firm in his viewpoint. He told the story "of a thief who confessed to a hermit and that the thief had been saved and the hermit lost." Before the Visitation Board, he confessed he had always held that "purgatory was not for those who died after confession and communion, but rather for those Christians who died without confession." He had not heard these ideas from anyone but held them solely out of "his ignorance" and did not even know that they ran counter to the church's teachings.[190]

In 1594 Manuel Pinto, formerly a carpenter but now a farmer, denounced the Flemish man Antonio Vilhete for not believing in purgatory. "Blessed was he who went to Purgatory, for he had hopes of going on to glory," Manuel Pinto said. Vilhete laughed and scoffed at him, saying: "Purgatory [is] there next to that tree and along that path, and wherever God so wants Purgatory."[191] Probably he was a Calvinist. But what his words underscore is the notion embraced by so many Catholics living at the same time and even much later, like the Jesuit André João Antonil: that the colony was a purgatory. According to the testimony of another witness, Salvador Jorge, the Flemish fellow had said that "there was no separate purgatory because purgatory was next to a tree, or a sugar plantation, or a trail."[192]

At various times, God's commandments were relativized in the colony as well. Killing one's adulterous wife was not a sin, declared Estêvão Barbosa, basing his statement on the Law of Moses.[193] Baltazar da Fonseca, a stonemason born in Coimbra and now living in Itamaracá, said in anger that it was not a sin to murder a thief; he was "reproaching a man who always stole chickens, suckling pigs, tools, and other things from him."[194] During the 1763–69 Visitation, the *mameluco* carpenter Pedro Rodrigues and the native Brazilian Marçal Agostinho were charged with spreading the belief that it was not a sin "to kill children inside the womb," especially among "the women Indians who were great with child." They said that after the babies were dead their souls would come to speak with them—this according to what the Virgin herself had told them.[195]

"Tolerating thoughts was not a mortal sin," Bartolomeu Barbosa commented in a conversation in Rio Vermelho with the New Christian Bento Sanches in 1615.[196] In the distant colony, the feeling sometimes was that offenses would go unpunished, and these breaches were not necessarily even seen as such. "Fornicate, fornicate to your fill, for the land is of the King, for never did anyone go to hell for fornicating," Pero Gonçalves happily told two friends after a dinner where he had "eaten and drunk over half a pint of wine."[197] Sex ranked high among colonists' concerns, perhaps because of the scarcity of women in the earliest days. Around 1580, at the Santo Amaro plantation in the captaincy of Pernambuco, the manioc farmer Gonçalo Ferreira had come to speak with Domingos Pires about the sin of the flesh. Domingos stated that "sleeping carnally with a Negro woman or a single woman was not a sin and that it was only a sin to sleep with a married woman."[198]

About ten years later, something similar happened on the *fazenda* of the New Christian Diogo Nunes, in Paraíba, where Antonio de Góis was working as a mason. In 1594 Góis went before the Visitation Board to accuse his ex-boss. One day after lunch, boss and employee had been enjoying a casual conversation about the sin of the flesh, when Diogo Nunes declared that "he could very well sleep carnally with any Negro woman from the town and that in this he would not be sinning if he gave her a shirt or anything." The employee disagreed, saying that it would be a mortal sin, but the boss insisted, firm in his notions of mercantilized love: "sleeping carnally with a single woman was not a mortal sin, paying her for her work."[199] Jerónimo de Albuquerque's *mameluco* son, Salvador de Albuquerque, mentioned earlier, would dupe women with whom he wanted to have relations by saying that "asking them to sleep with him was not a sin." This was what he did with Pelônia (Apolônia?) Ramalho, "single woman of the world," as well as with a number of black women and with his brother João de Albuquerque's indigenous slaves, Antonia and Felipa. He deliberately fooled them, knowing the carnal act was sinful.[200] Gaspar Maciel and Bento Cabral, on the other hand, were uncertain about the matter, which no doubt was quite pertinent to the former, married in Bahia but living in Pernambuco. Bento Cabral believed that simple fornication, namely, "a single man sleeping with a single woman, was only a venial sin, saying that, on the other hand . . . , the sin of copulating with a virgin woman or with a married woman was a mortal sin and was more serious than that of simple fornication." Gaspar Maciel contradicted him, saying that simple fornication was likewise a mortal sin. "Then he, the Confessor [Bento Cabral], replying to him no further, silenced himself and held in his breast as truth that which the said Gaspar Maciel had told him."[201]

We looked earlier at colonists' uncertainties regarding the state of matrimony versus that of the unmarried clergy. Doubts and hesitations about the other sacraments abounded as well. For example, concerning the baptism of heathens: it must be a sin "to baptize Negroes in Angola, as long as . . . they had the same customs as when they were heathen," argued the stonemason Antonio Pires in 1595 in Olinda.[202] Whoever "received the water of baptism could not go to a wicked place nor lose himself," believed Diogo Carneiro, sugarcane farmer in Itamaracá.[203] A baptized child would carry with him throughout life a kind of immunity to error. "If later, as a man and sinner, he should come to die with sins, he would not be lost," he further stated, after being interrogated by the Visitor.[204] It was as if the sacraments held a magical power—something the people of the Middle Ages had ascribed to them.[205] The New Christian Fernão Pires, known by the epithet Mija-Manso ["Gentle Pisser"], baptized dogs and christened them.[206] Here again, it cannot be argued that this practice derived from his ancestors' having kept the Laws of Moses. In Pontifical Rome itself, in the enlightened eighteenth century, "all quadruped folk" in the city gathered before the church of Santa Maria Maggione on January 18 to receive a blessing in the name of St. Anthony: "oxen, cows, mules, and asses appeared in great number, decorated with flowers and fruit. Domesticated dogs and cats were not excluded. A priest wearing a surplice and stole gave holy water to all of them."[207]

The sacramental oils were often renounced: in gambling, as in the case of the farmer Miguel Pires, from Olinda;[208] in fights with slaves, as in the case of Isabel Fernandes and Jerônima Baracha;[209] in fights with a young son who had gotten into some mischief that shortly thereafter was completely forgotten, as in the case of Bárbara Fernandes, from Itamaracá.[210] Not much importance was paid to the obligation of partaking of communion on an empty stomach. Francisco Henriques, a New Christian, had imbibed a dipper of water after midnight and taken communion the next morning, with no scruples whatsoever—worse yet, boasting about his deed, he said that "it was not a sin to take communion after having drunk."[211] Not satisfied with having eaten some bananas at home, Jerônimo Nunes, a 20-year-old New Christian, went to Passé Church eating sugarcane along the way. Indignant, two friends who accompanied him denounced him publicly before all those attending mass. The priest also reprimanded him.[212] During this same Visitation (the Second), João Garcez accused the ex–field captain Domingos Gomes Pimentel of eating lunch before taking communion.[213] The sacraments were thus demoralized, but not as Eduardo Hoornaert has contended; rather, they were disrespected by the colonists themselves, rebellious, skeptical, or stubborn when it came to meanings that seemed absurd to them in the context of their daily lives. Would God be happier if one walked kilometers on an empty stomach or if one heroically passed the night suffering the torment of thirst caused by Bahia's climate?[214]

As Philippe Ariès said, pure Christianity was always an imaginary model. In the fifteenth and sixteenth centuries, the European masses had felt a real need for religious life, and the Christianity manifested in their religiosity was authentic even though it was basically lived rather than conceptualized.[215] In the distant colony, always terrified by the possibility of inquisitorial visits but still distanced from the horrifying tribunal by an ocean, these features remained more intact and lingered longer. As I have endeavored to show, religion and its symbols and dogmas occupied a considerable space in the daily concerns of colonial man. And for him, everything that related to consecration and communion—perhaps more than any other religious dogma—was imbued with magic and shrouded in mists that lent these sacraments a high degree of incomprehensibility.[216]

During the First Visitation, in the city of Bahia, two women confessed to similar practices involving the words stated at the moment of consecration. On August 20, 1591, Paula Sequeira, forty, who had Flemish blood on her father's side and was married to the bookkeeper of the Royal Treasury, confessed not only to practicing homosexual acts but also to using the words of consecration during the sex act. She had learned this twenty-three years earlier from a cleric who was a distant relative, when she was a newlywed and still living in Lisbon. She was supposed to say "the words of the consecration of the mass wherewith the host was consecrated into the mouth of the said husband when he slept, and he would be tamed and would give her all of his affection, and for this end the said cleric had given her, written on a paper, the said words, and she, the Confessor, said the words sometimes into the mouth of the said sleeping husband." A good while later, in Salvador, Isabel Roiz (or Boca Torta ["Twisted Mouth"], who was accused of sorcery on several occasions, as seen in the next chapter) had told her to say the same words—*hoc est enim*—under the same circumstances and for the same purposes.[217] Married to a shoemaker, "daughter of a bailiff of the sea, serving the voyages of ships to India," Guiomar de Oliveira, thirty-seven, confessed to the same offense on the day following Paula Sequeira's confession. She had learned the spell from another notorious sorceress, Antonia Fernandes, Nóbrega by nickname. But her version was two words longer: *hoc est enim corpus meum* was the infallible formula that "a person during a dishonest carnal act" should say into the other's mouth, "for they would make him mad with love and desire."[218]

Also in Salvador, the sugar planter Bernardo Pimentel, a married man, went before the board to denounce Violante Carneira. She was the widow of Antonio Roiz Vila Real, a New Christian that the Inquisition had burned in

Coimbra. She had "conversation" with Bernardo Pimentel and on two occasions said the holy words into his mouth; "and he, feeling this be evil, found it strange, and she celebrated greatly with laughter, showing that she had already captured him, by having said the words to him, so that he would want her."[219] The next year, two more men who had an "illicit friendship" with Violante Carneira went to denounce her to the Visitor: the widower Cosme Garção, a captain from Itaparica, and the *mulato* Simão de Melo, master sword-fighter. The woman was arrested around this same time, and from her confession it is known that she was nine months pregnant by the church canon Bartolomeu de Vascogoncelos [*sic*]. In the trial records—very confusing, out of order, with obviously garbled dates—Heitor Furtado de Mendonça wrote in his own hand that the sentence would be served only after Violante had given birth. She should appear in an auto-da-fé holding a burning candle in her hand, remain standing throughout celebration of the mass, and then hear her verdict read. This auto-da-fé—one of the few held in the colonial territory—took place on January 24, 1593. The offender was sentenced to four years of exile in Itaparica. Eight months later, she asked that her punishment be reduced, alleging that she was very poor, had many children (one of them still nursing—the words of consecration had brought forth fruit!), was always sickly and received no medical care, and was going hungry. She was repentant and asked for forgiveness and "mercy upon the five wounds of Christ Our Lord."[220] It is not stated whether her request was granted.

These blasphemies and acts of sacrilege can often be separated into groups: against God, the saints, the Virgin, the commandments, the sacraments, and dogma like Everlasting Life, the Last Judgment, purgatory, and Mary's virginity. But there are times when these offenses are all committed together, out of the mouths of great blasphemers who seem intent upon demolishing the entire structure of faith and religion in one fell swoop, as if they were a sort of "Luso-Brazilian Menocchios."[221]

In 1763, in Grão-Pará, the young *cafuza* [person of indigenous and black blood] Joana Mendes, nicknamed Azeitona ["Olive"], was thrown in jail together with some women friends. One night, perhaps in despair over her misfortune, "she had taken the rosary that hung round her neck and had broken the string, spilling the beads upon the floor" and stomping on them. She renounced the Most Holy Trinity and the Virgin Mary; unmoved by her cellmates' protests, she insistently repeated these offenses. She lamented not having with her an image of the crucified Christ that she used to keep at home; for if she had it there, she would throw "it out into the street so that all could see that sacrilege."[222] She wanted her fury to become public.

Two years later, in Belém do Pará, another wrathful prisoner lambasted the dogmas of faith. In front of others in jail, Francisco José, formerly a soldier and tailor, declared that God did not exist, "and that the God that does exist, he trod him under his feet." He refused to kneel down when the

Holy Sacrament passed by outside, turning his back instead, stomping his foot on the ground, and calling it a filthy dog. He denied that he was a child of God; "rather would he be of the devil than of God, for God had no power whatsoever, but only the devil did." He did not attend mass, "and on purpose and with considered intent . . . for when the priest celebrated mass at the altar outside the jail, and the other prisoners were listening to it, he would turn his back to said altar, at times laughing loudly, and at other times committing the abominable sin of sensuality." He was an inveterate masturbator, and when they told him this was a most serious offense, condemned by St. Paul, he replied that "St. Paul was a drunkard and an ass who knew not what he said." He turned his back to the other prisoners when they pulled out a rosary, and no one had ever seen him say any prayer or pronounce any word that might give the slightest hint that he was a Christian. The other prisoners, who were in the habit of kissing the feet of the crucified Lord, asked him to do so as well. Francisco José replied that they should get the image out of his sight "and stick it in the most filthy part of the human body." He suggested that the same be done with the images of Our Lord of the Navigators and his crown, with the image of Our Lady of the Rosary, and with the palm of St. Rita. He prided himself on having one day gone to confession at the church of the Nossa Senhora do Carmo Convent; "and when they had given him communion, he had taken the wafer out of his mouth, and in truth, he had placed it inside the barrel of a shotgun, so that the devils would take the host."[223] His dissatisfaction with the Catholic religion is crystal-clear. He did not want that God, preferring the devil instead; he did not accept the priests' prohibitions; he did not worship their saints; he did not believe in the Eucharist; and he hated the symbols of faith. They deemed him a heretic. At no time did the ex-soldier and tailor propose an alternative religion, however, or suggest the merest outline of one. He said he believed in the devil, but more by negation than out of any deep conviction. He expressed a wild, indeterminate rebelliousness and most likely found the passive, well-behaved piety of his cellmates irritating.

In contrast, the old woman Ângela Micaela, who lived on her daughter's *fazenda* on the island of Marajó, seemed to profess the rudiments of her own unique faith. She did not worship images but rather left them tossed behind a trunk, covered with dirt, "and this same dirt moistened, and with much indecency." She insisted that her children not worship God Our Lord, "on the grounds of his being solely God of the dead, and not of the living, for he had died on a cross." They should instead adore the Sun, the Moon, and the Weather, "for only they ought to be worshipped as lords of the living." If her children worshipped them, "they would go with her to the next Kingdom, where they would be princes, and she queen, becoming immortal as she already was." She had friends who came to speak to her at night in the form of figures that climbed to the treetops. She did not pray, saying she had already served God well throughout her entire life, "not needing to serve him longer, for if she died, she would soon be saved."[224] Unlike Francisco José, Ângela Micaela believed in positive values, in another life, in a vital and primitive God, perhaps influenced by the region's indigenous beliefs. (Were the beings that appeared in the treetops spirits?) In her idealization of another kingdom, where she would be queen and immortal, there perhaps lay some distant echo of Sebastianist millennialism, syncretically blended into a body of popular religiosity.

A final example is the extremely religious stonemason Baltazar da Fonseca, thirty-five, an Old Christian who lived in Itamaracá and who was mentioned earlier because of his hatred of thieves. On December 15, 1594, he went to confess before Heitor Furtado de Mendonça's Visitation Board. For twenty years he had refused to believe in Our Lady, St. Peter, St. Paul, or any other saint and did not believe in the cross or worship it. "He only believed in and worshipped one almighty God." On a number of occasions he had said that "a man could very well eat meat on any prohibited day, even if it be Maundy Thursday, and that, eating salted fish on Easter, one would do for the other." He had no doubts that Christ had died on the cross, nor that Our Lady was a virgin. He knew the saints were saints and that they dwelled in paradise and were greatly close to God. But he thought that "God Our Lord is the center and the purpose wherefrom all emanates, and he worshipped and believed only in Him." He saw that other Catholics worshipped the cross, the Virgin, and the saints, but "for himself he believed that those who did so did not understand as well as he." He saw they knelt down, asked forgiveness for their sins, and beat on their breasts; however, he thought that "neither the cross, nor Our Lady, nor the saints have the power to forgive sins, but rather only God Our Lord." Therefore he "for himself believed that one need not worship anyone other than only God Our Lord." He had often been reprimanded by the vicar of the main cathedral in Itamaracá but had never paid any attention to these reprimands. His faith seems to have been personal, autonomous, and deeply rooted. Because he did not believe "in the wee donkey and in the pack-saddle on which Our Lady had gone to Egypt, and in the chains with which St. Bartholomew had captured the demon," the vicar publicly took him to task. Baltazar da Fonseca wanted to bet him two chickens that he would not be judged guilty by the *ouvidor* Diogo do Couto if a record with his peculiar beliefs were drawn up; the vicar turned down the bet.[225]

Before the board, they asked him from whom he had learned his beliefs. He "answered that he had heard in his youth, from whom he did not recall, that so it was said in some preaching from pulpits, and that henceforth this had remained with him till now." He had been born in Coimbra and denied having had any contact with Lutherans, Lutheran writings, or heretics. He had realized something was wrong with his beliefs when, "from the gallows that were built that past October in Olinda in Pernambuco," he had heard the sentence of an individual who had renounced the cross and the saints;

"and that he at once became perplexed," having gone to confess before the board and promising to "cast aside his error." For many years, the possibility of his own religion, internal and personal, had been open to him, directed at the worship of one sole almighty God, like so many heretics in medieval Europe who absorbed ancient popular traditions. But Baltazar da Fonseca did not want a direct confrontation with the official church; nor did he want anyone to think he was a heretic or apostate. "His intent had never been nor is it to believe, nor to have, nor to go against the truth of the Holy Mother Church, and . . . never before now had he known he was going against it, but it seeming to him that he was correct, he had done and said what he had, and if he be wrong, he asks mercy for his offense."[226] The unassuming mason recognized his errors only in part, subordinating them to a conditional clause: "if he be wrong." Even in an intimidating situation, with the Visitor before him, he left open the possibility that he was not all that wrong. He had not blasphemed and had not disrespected the saints, the Virgin, or the cross. He simply thought that, compared with God, they were not so important, and he wanted his church to allow him room for this conviction.

The Demonization of Social Relations and the Divinization of the Economic Universe

The Inquisition routed out devils in the colonial world, often seeing them where there were none. But the men of the early colonial centuries shared their daily lives intensely with devils, demons, and fiends. Even when they knew it was illicit to do so, they could not help but invoke them time and again.[227] As fear of the Visitations spread—with the Inquisition seemingly ready to pounce upon the colony's towns at any moment, particularly during the Philippine period—the demons became confined to hidden and many times unconfessed practices.[228] But during the sixteenth century and into the seventeenth, they inhabited everyone's day-to-day life, as if they were private, almost inoffensive divinities. At the very least, the colonists' understanding of these entities differed substantially from those that demonologists outlined in their treatises and that ultimately became the touchstones of inquisitorial procedures.

Within the realm of elite thought, the early Middle Ages had witnessed the steady demonization of daily existence, a process of externalization of Satan in relation to God.[229] In the twelfth century, works like the *Elucidarium* sought to systematize and vulgarize demonological elements disseminated in Christian writings since the church's earliest days.[230] The Protestant Reformation and the religious upheavals of the sixteenth century further strengthened Satan's presence on earth.[231] During the same era when "Paris saw itself dominated by a forest of belfries whose pious sound never ceased," Jean Wier registered the existence of 72 princes and 7,405,926 devils, divided into 111 legions, with 6,666 members each.[232] They were igneous, aerial,

terrestrial, aquatic, subterranean, and lucifugous.[233] They dwelled on gla-
ciers, possessed the bodies of rodents, controlled storms.[234] Boniface VIII
and Guichard kept their private demons inside flasks.[235] Antonia Fernandes,
nicknamed Nóbrega, the sorceress mentioned earlier in this chapter, had promised to give Guiomar de Oliveira a private demon inside a bottle; he spoke,
answered questions, and supplied information. But he also had to be handled
properly: "On certain days of the week, one had to take the care to place
onion and vinegar nigh to the said glass, for that which was inside of it was
fond of such food."[236]

In a nonrationalized world, everything could be explained by the action
of supernatural forces: either God or the devil. Neither force seemed abnor-
mal, and the popular mentality saw the two as approximating each other.[237]
As Christianity advanced in its triumph over pagan survivals and folklorized
religion, the devils of Christian theology lost their role as "operative forces
of magic," becoming primarily tempters and enemies of God, "those who
seek to seduce souls in order to tear them away from God and drag them
into hell."[238] At the close of the fifteenth century, preachers and clerics satu-
rated their sermons with a diabolic vocabulary.[239] In the catechism of the
Jesuit Peter Canisius, the name of Satan is cited sixty-seven times while that
of Jesus appears only sixty-three.[240] This shows us how in elite thinking the
notion of an inevitable struggle between God and the devil endured for quite
some time.

The insistent presence of the Prince of Darkness in Jesuit letters shows
that even before Canisius, the Ignatians were concerned about Satan's unrestricted freedom on earth.[241] When Manuel da Nóbrega offered to venture
into the *sertão* to build a house and chapel for the indigenous population, he
saw his plans blocked by the ill-will of the governor, who initially seemed to
approve of the idea. This change in Tomé de Souza's enthusiasm is blamed
on Satan, who features in Nóbrega's text just like any other character: "This
could not be hidden from Satan," says the priest, "for, the governor having
said to me that it appeared well to him that we enter, once he knew that we
were taking a chapel and singers, and that we would be building a house, he
hindered us by all means."[242] The devil also interfered when Nóbrega sent a
brother into the *sertão* who knew how to speak the indigenous language.
"We have ascertained that the demon desires to kill him along the way,"
wrote Father Pero Correia from São Vicente. This was why he had caused
"two sticks thirty to forty palms long and thick as a leg" to fall on the brother's
head and had also afflicted upon him "a most great pain in the eyes."[243] In
São Paulo de Piratininga, Pero Correia also said the priests had "many com-
bats with the devil, and still have now." This struggle manifested itself through
the death of many members of indigenous groups. But God got the better in
the end: "We held nine processions to the nine choruses of angels against all
of hell, and the deaths soon ceased."[244] When they headed toward Laguna,
among the Carijó people, the Jesuits again found themselves contending with

infernal ambushes. They embarked in a small canoe, taking with them a trunk of ornaments, a cask of wine, and a gradin with relics, which belonged to Father Jerônimo Rodrigues. "As the devil so greatly felt our coming into the land, *which for so many years he had possessed,* he ordered, *God Our Lord so permitting,* that the volume be so greatly increased . . . and thus, the canoe overturning, all sank to the bottom . . . from whence with great labor everything was removed, wet and damaged."[245]

On the opposite side, Luther said in his *Large Catechism* of 1529: "[The devil] constantly seeks our life, and wreaks his anger whenever he can afflict our bodies with misfortune and harm. Hence it comes that he often breaks men's necks or drives them to insanity, drowns some, and incites many to commit suicide, and to many other terrible calamities."[246] In the Early Modern age, the ecclesiastical discourse of both Catholics and Protestants was heavily imbued with the notion that the devil was a most nefarious force working for disorder. In a kind of foreshadowing of the "scandalous affairs" of seventeenth-century France, it was predicted that the struggle between God and the devil would reach into the convents. The decree handed down by the twenty-fifth session of the Council of Trent determined, among other things, that "nuns will go to confession and communion at least once a month, so that armed with this salutary safeguard they may boldly overcome all attacks by the devil."[247] It was thus in the early days of the Early Modern age and not during the Middles Ages that hell and its inhabitants invaded the Western imagination. Demonological science reached its apogee around 1600. At that time, the demonologist Martín del Río affirmed that the human struggle against the devil would be perennial: "perpetual war, right from the birth of the world."[248]

In the colony, the Jesuits found autochthonous populations that also viewed the devil as an active, powerful force, in the form of multitudes of spirits wandering around about the dark forests and in sinister places. Ultimately the priests further demonized these indigenous notions and eventually—as paradoxical as it may seem—became demonizing agents of everyday life in the colonial world.[249] The indigenous peoples were so terrified by the idea of the devil that some actually died in pure fright of hell.[250] Or, like the indigenous people mentioned in a letter by boys at the Jesuit school in Bahia in 1552, they became terrified and alarmed at the possibility that the bad would die and go "to hell to burn with the devils."[251] Frightened of evil spirits, they nevertheless integrated them into a corpus of beliefs where they held a specific meaning, making it possible to circumvent their negative aspects and coexist with them. The Jesuits and their greatly demonized European notions rendered the idea of evil unbearable. For these Europeans, the Otherness of indigenous culture was diabolical, as mentioned in the last chapter, and the colony was the land where hosts of Satan's servants evolved. Consequently, the Europeans always considered indigenous and African religions to be "satanic aberrations."[252]

Within the universe of popular culture and syncretic religiosity, two possibilities existed: either God came out on top or the devil did. Hence the popular Brazilian saying about lighting one candle for God and another for the devil.[253] On the occasion of Heitor Furtado de Mendonça's Visitation to Bahia, the topic of discussion was which of the two forces was more powerful. Leonor Velha complained about her husband, saying he was bad; her friend Catarina da Fonte comforted her by saying that "God is mightier than the devil, and that she should not be vexed; and [Leonor] responded that God was not mightier than the devil, that never would her said husband be good, nor would he mend his ways." Catarina da Fonte reprimanded her: "God was mightier than the devil, she should not talk like that." Recalcitrant, Leonor Velha retorted that "yes, she would talk like that, giving as examples other men of sinful living that never mended their ways."[254] The devil had the power to trouble married life, inciting discord and misunderstanding. His strength lent him credibility and, once again, placed him in opposition to God, his chief adversary. Pero de Albuquerque, *fazendeiro* in Pernambuco and member of one of the captaincy's chief families, did not believe in God and the Virgin, "adding further that he ere believed in all the devils." "I do not believe in God, nor in the Virgin Mary, if such be the truth I ere believe in all the devils," he had the habit of saying when coming across something amazing.[255] Tired of waiting at the door of Nossa Senhora de Ilhéus Church, where a large crowd had gathered one day for mass, André Gavião said that "if one would have to wait so long at the door of Paradise, he ere wished to go to hell."[256] At every moment in daily life, the possibility of choice presented itself. There were those who made such choices: suffering from a discharge all over his foot, Lázaro Aranha, mentioned earlier, said that "God is the devil."[257] Eager to play cards, the New Christian Pero Fernandes had asked them to let him into the game "for the love of God"; later, after he had played three or four hands, he said to the onlookers: "Let me play, for the love of the devil."[258]

People's attitudes toward the devil might be passive. For example, adherence by process of elimination, which was the case of the sugar master Gaspar Roiz, who suffered from constant pain: "Considering that God did not have the power to remove his pain from him, let the devils come and take him."[259] Adherence might also be involuntary. Residing on São Francisco Street, in Salvador, Henrique Barbas once found his wife, Antonia de Barros, "behind a door or a crate quite suffocated by the devils that were suffocating her."[260] Irrespective of what Salvador da Maia might really have believed, the collective imagination seemed to associate this accused New Christian with Satan. He was denounced for his Judaizing practices, which included the eating of lamb during Holy Week. His accusers did not forget to describe his physical defects: as in medieval representations of the Prince of Darkness, Salvador da Maia was "lame in one foot."[261] Pero Fernandes, the New Christian who asked that he be allowed to play cards, was likewise stigmatized: he too was "crippled in his feet."[262] Convicted of adulterating crated sugar with sand, the merchant André Fernandes, beardless, his face marked with slash scars, wanted to lead the good life in this world: "in the next, may all the devils take me," he acquiesced resignedly.[263]

But adherence could also come about intentionally. In Itaparica, it was rumored that Gaspar Pacheco had given himself to the devils.[264] In Ceregipe o Novo, Captain Tomé da Rocha had arrested the Portuguese vagabond soldier Pedro de Mendonça by order of the Holy Inquisition; word among the soldiers was that the jailing was "because he had delivered himself to the devils." His action must have worked, because ten days later Pedro de Mendonça had already been released.[265] Whenever some annoyance occurred, Simão Pires Tavares—whose anticlericalism was highlighted earlier in these pages—had the habit of "offering himself to the devils, saying that he offers himself to the devils so that they will take him, and this with wrath."[266] Five years before the First Visitation, the seaman Manuel Faleiro despaired of his poverty: "Being at home, in anger and wrath, not having food to give his children, who asked him for something to eat, he said that he gave himself to the devils."[267] He perhaps hoped his fortune would improve under the new order. Remembered at moments of misfortune, the devil was also evoked at moments of leisure. A scribe in the city of Bahia, Antonio Guedes sparked envy with his sleights of hand. Asked by someone to teach him "how to perform the sleights that he did, he replied that it would be necessary to give a buttock to the devil."[268]

Rare indeed, perhaps even a singular instance, was the attitude of superiority over the devil adopted by Lázaro Aranha, mentioned earlier. When he played, he often called on the devils to deal him a particular card. When the carpenter João Brás asked him why he did so, "he replied that he called upon them because they were his dogs."[269] Until the fifteenth century, the devil had *served* humans, with varying degrees of subjugation. In this sense, Lázaro Aranha's prepotency in treating the devils like dogs is still medieval. Beginning in the fifteenth century, the situation changed radically, with the devil going from servant to master.[270] Although the opposite may at first seem to be the case, attitudes of subjugation to the devil are therefore early modern. Active postures differ somewhat from passive ones, with adhesion to the pact being more transparent in the latter cases. Yet both contain the implicit idea that it is the devil who subjugates and who deals the cards. Lázaro Aranha's arrogance toward his dogs may be more markedly popular, reminiscent of a folkloric time when demons were personal, domestic. "In the popular fantasy," Oronzo Giordano reminds us, "there were also good, happy, meddling devils, like the hobgoblins and gnomes of Germanic mythology, always eager to jest and joke."[271] In the instance of passive attitudes toward the devil, which is most often the case in the examples studied here, we hear the echo of demonological formulations, theorizations on pacts with demons, and the devil's inordinate power over the earth.

It is too early to affirm that the discourse of high culture had made strong inroads into the popular universe, dictating norms; the intertwined weave of these discourses will be discussed later. For now, what should be noted is that despite their distance and isolation—and perhaps thanks to Jesuit influence—the colonial populations were not indifferent to the demon-craze that swept over Europe in the early days of the Early Modern age.

In a colony that often took on the features of hell, as seen in the last chapter, a variety of forces worked to demonize everyday life. As the process of colonization advanced, slavery perhaps became the most evident of these. Its vices were elements that dissolved the social formation and threw the people of the colony into the arms of Lucifer. In the early eighteenth century, Benci censured them vehemently. Veritable "Lucifers on earth" were the masters who closed their eyes to the errors of their slaves and, worse yet, incited them to error by forcing them to carry "illicit messages and embassies" that served their sinful needs.[272] Many masters, "so as to maintain their slaves," ignored or overlooked the sins they committed. Nuno Marques Pereira's Pilgrim likewise reproved this attitude.[273] As stated earlier, closing one's eyes was very often a way of manipulating syncretism for ideological purposes. For the clerical culture, and for certain segments of the elites, syncretism was diabolical and as such should be combated.

Slavery thus swept masters and slaves into hell. By countenancing African heathens, indulging in lechery with black female slaves, and prostituting a good number of others, the masters turned themselves into Satan's cohorts. The slaves, by maintaining their religious practices—so-called satanic aberrations—also collaborated with the enemy. The Christianizing efforts initiated by the Crown and by the missionaries sometimes seemed ready to crumble under the pressure of the contradictions inherent in colonization. The tendency was for syncretism to spread. "I do not know if [syncretism] passed from the slaves to freedmen, and to white men as well, for want of punishment," the Pilgrim stated in horror.[274] By dissimulating their slaves' vices, the masters were in fact multiplying them. "Therefore, how may it now be permitted that they use such rites, and such indecent abuses, and with such thunderous noises, that it would seem to us that the demon desires to proclaim his triumph to the sound of these infernal instruments, with the end of demonstrating to us how he has achieved victory over the lands, wherein the true God has raised his Cross at the price of as many Laborers as have introduced to this new world the true Faith of the Holy Gospel?"[275]

Daily life in the colony at times seemed irreversibly demonized. A clear vision of hell was sketched within the popular mentality. The *Compêndio narrativo do peregrino da América,* which compiled countless popular traditions in vogue during the first quarter of the eighteenth century, established the image of one of these possible hells—one similar to the hell that was envisioned by Europeans in their own imagination and that high culture incorporated into demonology beginning in the early Middle Ages. What

Nuno Marques Pereira describes is a "terrible place," where "one continually sees and hears flashes of lightning and rumblings and crashes of thunder, and many other torments as well, which here are found congregated together, this being the saddest and most frightening place one can imagine." Hell was the basest, most infamous place that could exist, located in the middle of the earth, uniting in one spot all the filth produced by putrefaction: "serpents, scorpions, snakes, lizards, toads, and all sort of poisonous creatures"—the same ones, in fact, that the detractors of America had described when they spoke of the New World.[276] As if this were not enough, there was also the "most horrible and alarming sight" of countless demons and the damned, squeezed and crowded together in such a way that the "authors, and most competent mathematicians," used their imaginations to pack so many beings into a space that was no greater than two or three leagues "in width and circuit."[277] In addition to painting this panorama, the Pilgrim of the book's title is also author of the first literary description of a *calundu,* that is, a colonial session of Afro-Brazilian Candomblé, which he likewise portrays with diabolical features. It is as if there were the European hell, the African hell, and the hell of syncretism.

Daily life in the colony was thus permeated by demons. In contrast, the economic universe was often associated with divine elements, as if the colony were really a place of passage, a proper place for purging sins committed here or in the metropolis. Portugal was the final destination, the place of desired return after penance had been paid, as well as the destination of colonial production.

This divinization of the economic universe may at first seem a dubious notion. If, however, the analysis is taken further, it is not surprising to find that the colony's output—with sugar at the top—at times gained superhuman features, both because of the value gained on the foreign market and also because of the tremendous efforts expended in its production. On the long road from deforestation to tilling of the soil to planting and harvesting to the milling, purging, and packing of the cane, human lives were lost. In a land of slave labor, which had consumed considerable capital investments, the prime goal was to produce much and maximize profits. For the colonists, planters, merchants, and constellation of individuals who made their living off colonial trade, both in Brazil and in the metropolis, the product of slave labor was more important than the producers' human attributes—or even their very lives. Even clerics like Benci and Antonil theorized about how best to punish a slave without hampering the productive process.[278]

Pero de Carvalhais believed there were no friars in heaven but rather *lavradores.* The clerics lived like pigs while the farmers lived like angels.[279] "He was thoroughly examined by the Board, who sought to find in the Defendant doubts about the value and validity of members of the clergy."[280] The tribunal had obviously stumbled down the wrong path. Pero de Carvalhais was doing no more than depicting reality as he saw it in original fashion. In the colony, not only were farmers worth much more than clerics, but if they were rich, they would live a much better life.

The New Christian Pero Nunes, a renter on an *engenho real* [water-powered sugar mill], revealed an extremely curious aspect of the slave-master mentality when, "seeing the sugar that had been separated to tithe to God lying on the ground, brown and raw, he said, for this is your God, in this way you treat him, calling sugar God."[281] His words are of double significance. First, they suggest that the Christians did a bad job of worshipping their God: they tithed but in point of fact lacked a more refined spirituality; their spirituality was instead rough and crude like brown sugar, dark and full of impurities. Second, these rough men's true God was the sugar they produced: in addition to serving as currency in the religious economics of the barter system—for sugar pays tithes—it was so important in their lives that it could be compared only to God.

Lázaro Aranha, introduced earlier, scandalized those present when he said that "in this world there existed an immortal thing, which was the coal lying beneath the earth"[282]—the same coal that fed the furnaces and purified the sugar. Along with reflecting his disbelief in, and even ridicule of, the Catholic dogma of everlasting life, the blasphemer's words highlighted the importance of a product of the land that, in the context of European peasant culture, could display a magical significance inherited from secular pagan traditions. Human lives would pass, and coal would continue underground, always ready to be dug up in order to generate wealth. It was immortal like a god.

Sugar master and New Christian Fernão Roiz was known for saying that "he would stick Our Lady in a sugar mold."[283] Father Brás Lourenço attributed nearly identical words to a sugar master from São Vicente: "[As] a sugar master [was] placing the sugar in molds, he said that if Our Lady were there he would likewise place her into that mold."[284] It is hard to know whether this was the same person and same episode or if the repetition of the story testifies to an idea common in the colony at the close of the sixteenth century. The historian Gonçalves Salvador stressed blasphemer Fernão Roiz's Jewish roots,[285] reading into the episode nothing more than disrespect for the mother of Jesus. As in previous cases, however, there is a second significance, one that divinizes the economic universe: the place where the precious product was molded was sacred; it could even shelter Our Lady.

The most extraordinary document attesting to this divinization of the economic universe is chapter 12 of the second book of *Cultura e opulência do Brasil,* entitled "Do que padece o açúcar desde o seu nascimento na cana até sair do Brasil" [Concerning what sugar suffers from its birth in the form of cane till leaving Brazil]. In this section, Antonil describes a saga that can be understood as a grand metaphor for the suffering of slaves in colonial lands. In comparing the path taken by sugar (from planting to marketing) to the Passion and Death of Jesus, Antonil realizes the divinization of the economic universe through images. The narrative seeks to capture not just the Calvary of the blacks but also the tendency of the colonial social formation to dehumanize that which is human and to dignify, through sacralization, that which lies within the realm of the productive world's economic values.

The life led by sugar is "filled with such and so many martyrdoms that those that the tyrants invented have no advantage over them."[286] Following untold suffering and offenses that are described in minute detail—and are always endured—sugar leaves "purgatory and imprisonment, as white as it is innocent."[287] A new cycle of suffering then begins, from crating through marketing. As in a Holy War, there is also the danger of falling into the hands of infidels and the risk of "being taken to Algeria among Moors" (pirates or Protestant competitors who might intercept the ships carrying sugar to Portugal?).[288] Everything is endured with courage and resignation, the sugar "always sweet and vanquisher of bitter hardships." At last come the "great profits for the plantation owners and sugar farmers that pursued it and for the merchants that purchased it and carried it to ports, banished away, and profits even much greater for the Royal Treasury at the custom-houses."[289] Christian-like, through its Calvary, sugar ultimately brought good to its tormentors; like Jesus, it died on the cross to save those who had tortured it.[290]

The Cuban historian Manuel Moreno Fraginals, advisor on historical matters for the movie *La Santa Cena,* put the following words into the mouth of a sugar master: "In this world, everything that is white had to have been black one day." This is a superb allusion to slavery, to *engenhos,* and to the Catholic religion that provided the ideological framework for the early modern colonial system. The formulations of Luso-Brazilian colonists, together with the superb metaphor created by Antonil, seem to reiterate this felicitous statement, insinuating that in the colonial hell it is through production—is not sugar itself purged?—that one can achieve divine grace.

In this divinization of the economic universe, references to sugar predominate. But there is also a curious passage where the praises of manioc are sung. A tailor and domestic servant, Gaspar Coelho, went to mass and saw that there were not enough wafers for the crowd of faithful. He then suggested that tapioca cakes be distributed among them, as if they were hosts. This way of solving the problem fit such uniquely colonial molds that the Visitor needed clarification to understand it: "and asked by the visitor what thing be tapioca cakes, he replied that they are some cakes that in this land are made from bread flour, that it is a manioc root from which the flour is made, from which said tapioca cakes are made, which are like wafers, which is the common provision in this land of breads."[291]

Even if this was a mockery, the episode reveals two complementary tendencies: it assigns a holy character to a staple of the land—thereby divinizing the economic universe—and at the same time humanizes and secularizes the sacrament, imprinting a nearly lay character on religion. In making a communion wafer, why would "a little flour from Portugal"[292] be any better than tapioca, a local product, cheaper and better suited to the population's habits and needs? In the end, how could that markedly elitist and formalist metropolitan religion penetrate deep into the colonists' unpredictable, chaotic daily life, impregnated with syncretic rites?

A yawning gap separated the religious stiffness of the watchful Portuguese Inquisition and the Catholicism lived by the colonists every day, and mutual misunderstandings were a constant in their discourses. Nevertheless, when it came to talking about purgatory, *tacheiros* [workers who tended large sugar pots], sugar masters, sailors, slaves, merchants, carpenters, soldiers, and plantation owners were doing nothing more than discussing a question that had similarly gnawed at Luther decades earlier. This mutual incomprehension thus could not be blamed on incommunicability between different cultural levels.

In the colony's everyday life, heaven and hell, sacred and profane, primitive and European magical practices approached each other at one moment only to pull violently apart at another. In the fluid, transitory reality of colonial life, however, the blurring of distinctions was more characteristic than dichotomy. When dichotomies did appear, they were almost always encouraged by missionary ideology and by the action of the nascent machinery of power, striving to separate the different parts with a view to seizing upon heresies. What almost always rose to the top was religious syncretism.

As we saw in the excerpt from *Peregrino*, syncretism was one of the faces of hell. African and indigenous beliefs were constantly demonized by elite thought, incapable of comprehending colonial religiosity in its ever more multifaceted expressions. As the colonizing process advanced, definitions would become clearer cut. The complexity of a social formation based on both slavery and Christianity pulled the colony toward infernalized images, where Satan had the role of confirming God. Hell was the social tensions; the poisoning of masters; *atabaque* drums beating in the slave quarters and dark alleyways of colonial towns; *quilombos* of runaway slaves haunting the forests, trails, and wild lands; the *catimbós* of northeast Brazil that called forth ancestral spirits; magical healing and divinations. On the other hand, the colony's identification with the metropolis likewise pulled it toward the paradisiacal pole: one could reach heaven by reciting the creed of Portugal and invading European markets with sugar, tobacco, gold, diamonds.

Between one pole and the other, the colony affirmed its purging role. It was a purgatory where the penalties and evils inherent in social tensions were cleansed and where salvation was sought by divinizing the productive universe.

This divinization of the productive universe may seem less significant here than the demonization of social relations. As the former topic has never been explored, these few pages suffer the consequences of this silence. I nevertheless hope that they will serve as a point of departure for further studies and that more light will soon be shed on the fascinating being-and-not-being of the colonial world, "a land rich in diamonds and impieties."[293]

PART II

Sorcery, Magical Practices, and Daily Life

The sorceress who lights her embers in a clay pot will never tell us what she knows and what we know not.

—Rimbaud

When he described eighteenth-century Brazil as a "land rich in diamonds and impieties," the novelist José Saramago was displaying an acute understanding of history. Representing the main portion of Portugal's colonial empire in the 1700s, Brazil fed Dom João V's megalomaniac delirium and the inquisitorial bonfires at one and the same time. In reality, gold bars and sacks full of diamonds were more numerous than impious colonists. But the colony's stigmatized image as a producer and perpetuator of impieties still retained enough strength to emerge in the words of the Portuguese writer two centuries later—impieties that when purged yielded brilliant diamonds. As so often stated in this book, the colony-purgatory purified itself into white gems, the currency used to purchase metropolitan imports and serve as an ephemeral palliative for Portugal's economic and social ills.

Diamonds and impieties went together. Both were plentiful in colonial lands, nesting together like two opposite yet complementary puzzle pieces. New Christians, sodomites, Calvinist heretics, sorcerers, wise men, and diviners can only be understood within their own context—that is, within the colonial universe in all its enormous complexity and as part of the colonists' daily lives and varied aspirations, at times noble and legitimate, at times petty and mediocre.

The Portuguese reached Brazil at a time when Satan's presence among men was especially notable. Monsters, animals, and diabolical beings, the colonists were also sorcerers, about whom the European imagination fashioned and developed a series of notions. Indigenous peoples from America, blacks from Africa, and whites from Europe blended together to produce extremely complex and original magical practices and sorcery.

Any study of this topic—sorcery and magic—will need to cope with multiple contexts and cultural heritages, at times circumventing these issues by returning to the always comfortable Indo-European source, as Julio Caro Baroja has done.[1] This author differentiates between two types of *maleficia:* on the one hand, *encantos* (charms) and *sortilegios* (sortilege), which entail individual practices; and, on the other, *brujería* (witchcraft) proper, whose collective, associative characteristics are part of a true cult.[2] The English historian Norman Cohn adopts the same position: witchcraft is collective; magic, individual. But he also distinguishes sorcery (a *technique* that *induces* evil) from witchcraft (where the *person* is the *source* of the evil).[3] Gustav Henningsen draws a fine distinction between witchcraze and witchcraft. The first is collective; boasts a broad, systematic mythological superstructure; is defined by a pact; and does not figure in regulating or maintaining society and therefore cannot be studied by anthropology. The second is individual; has a deficient, asystematic mythological superstructure; is not defined by a pact; and plays a regulatory, preserving role in society, meaning it can be the object of anthropological approaches.[4]

Constituting a milestone in the tendency to adopt an anthropological approach, Edward Evans-Pritchard's study of the Azande also served as a point of departure in distinguishing between witchcraft and sorcery, which he sees as the difference between an imputed act that is impossible and an imputed act that is possible.[5] Robert Rowland believes that only British witchcraft, quite distinctive within the European context, displays similarities with African witchcraft. Throughout Europe a uniformity of beliefs could be identified in various societies; in Africa, on the other hand, types of sorcery varied from one society to the next.[6] French has only one term for the two practices, and Robert Mandrou defines it quite simply: *sorcellerie* exists when there is a contract or pact with the devil.[7] Keith Thomas, for his part, sees no great utility in the anthropological distinction between witchcraft and sorcery. According to him, it may be said that the sorcerer relies on material objects while the witch does not. However, Thomas believes that in the English case there was an interpenetration and exchange between the two, making them part of the same type of offense.[8]

In this book, I am not concerned with drawing a fine distinction between witchcraft (*bruxaria*) and sorcery (*feitiçaria*): as far as I have ascertained both terms refer to identical practices, and here I draw support from Thomas. However, like Mandrou, I do differentiate between sorcery and magic, based on the existence of a pact or not. Consequently, I use the expressions *sorcery* and *magical practices* in distinct ways.

I must also point out that what interests me more than tracing the possible kinships of magical practices in the colony is ascertaining how and as a result of what context they came to intermix. Colonial sorcery, which was almost always individual and of little significance when compared to the madness of European witch-hunts, can shed light on life in the colony over the course of its three centuries. Sorcery was one of the ways that colonists found to adjust to their surroundings; sometimes it afforded protection from conflicts, while at others it responded to the unbearable tensions troubling their day-to-day lives. It helped the colonist bind a lover, kill off a rival, get rid of the envious, fight oppressors, build a cultural identity. Very often it solved problems related to the next world; at other times, it cast the colonist into a terrible abyss. But it was almost always a bridge to the supernatural.

During their earliest moments, still in the sixteenth century, the cultural kinship between sorcery and magical practices was nearly transparent. One can easily trace their European and indigenous features and more rarely their African ones (for the slave trade was just beginning). As time went by, these features began blurring and interpenetrating, and one sole body of syncretic beliefs began to emerge. It was then that uniquely colonial forms, unlike all others, were born.

CHAPTER 3

Material Survival

And then let pleasure and distress
Disappointment and success
Succeed each other as they will;
Man cannot act if he is standing still.
                    —Goethe, *Faust*

Divination

Broadly disseminated throughout the Christian West, the practice of divination was often associated with the devil. As in so many other areas, St. Thomas Aquinas played an important role in this demonization. For him, attempting to foretell the future and going "beyond what can be foreseen by human reason or what has been revealed by God" was a grave sin, indicative of a diabolic compact: "The sinful nature of this act is deduced from the fact that it is only possible through the intervention of a demon."[1] From this point on, even civil law would view divination as an offense incited by Satan. In Portugal, statute 3 of the Philippine Ordinances, which addresses the subject of sorcerers, also deals with the question of soothsaying: hydromancy, crystallomancy, looking into mirrors or metal images, scapulimancy using sheep, and divination using heads of animals or bodies of the dead. The punishment for these acts was severe: the condemned might be flogged with a hemp rope and paraded by a crier through the streets of the town where the offense occurred; ordered to pay three mil-réis to the accuser; and, curiously, be banished to Brazil.[2]

Local diviners were joined by those from the metropolis, individuals who, like the farmer Álvaro Martins—arrested by the Inquisition in 1557 at the age of eighty—responded to their communities' very real needs through divination. The diviner Álvaro Martins used the stars to look for lost objects, money, animals, and slaves.[3]

Soothsayers employed countless forms of sortilege during colonial times. One of the most common involved a sieve and shears or lady's slipper or—an apparent variation of the first—a basket. Its use is recorded as early as the sixteenth century, in Pernambuco, attributed to the *mulata* Felícia Tourinho, daughter of a cleric. Felícia was arrested for hitting an honorable woman in church. When Domingas Jorge lodged an accusation against the *mulata* before the Visitation Board, she was implicitly stigmatized: after all, she was a bastard daughter, an offender punished by law, and dishonest, unlike the woman she assaulted. As will be seen many times in this chapter, the stigmatization of women—and more rarely of men—played a major role in the collective construction of a stereotype of sorcery.

While under arrest, the *mulata* Felícia had once taken a pair of scissors and stuck them into a shoe. Then, "with both forefingers set beneath the rings of the shears, she raised the slipper into the air," saying: "[D]isheveled-haired devil, big-eared devil, shaggy devil, thou shalt tell me if a certain man go down such path . . . ; if this be true, thou shalt make this thing move, if this be not true, thou shalt not make this thing move." The scissors and slipper then turned round, tilting to one side. It was later learned that the man had indeed gone to the place in question.[4]

Antonia Maria, born in Beja, had left Portugal in 1713 after being convicted by the Holy Office. Accused of sorcery, she was banished to Angola for three years. For reasons known only to God, she ended up in Brazil, where she lived on Laranjeiras Street in Recife, Pernambuco. Francisco Xavier de Viveiros was her neighbor, their residences sharing a common wall. Noticing one day that Francisco seemed sad, the sorceress asked him what the matter was. We know the details from the denunciation Francisco Xavier lodged against his neighbor on July 21, 1718. Francisco replied that he was downhearted because he wanted the bishop to admit him to the clergy, but the man was taking his time processing the request. "Do not be troubled, for you shall be a cleric by this bishop," his neighbor Antonia Maria said to ease his mind. The future priest was intrigued. Some days later, "the said Antonia Maria came to the house of him, the Witness, and said: 'Come now, and see whether you shall be a cleric: give me four vinténs, a glazed earthen basin, some water, a paper from a notebook, a sieve, and a shears.' " Antonia poured the water into the basin then dropped in the coin (which sank) and the sheet of paper, which did not sink and remained dry on top. She took the sieve, stuck the two points of the open shears into its rim, took hold of one side, and gave the other to Francisco Xavier to hold. She then told him to repeat everything she said, negating her words. And she recited: "By St. Peter, and by St. Paul, by the door of St. Iago, Francisco Xavier shall be a cleric." The sieve circled round, while the scissors did not move. When Francisco Xavier negated her words, the whole contraption stood still. He was ordained a priest shortly thereafter, firmly convinced the basket ritual had depended upon the existence of a pact.[5]

In Maranhão, around 1750, Margarida Borges used the basket ritual to solve crimes of thievery, as in the case of a shirt stolen by the black woman Mariquita. No reference is made to shears, but otherwise the procedure is the same: one person utters the prayer while the other negates it. The difference is that a series of names is pronounced. When the name of the pilferer is stated, the basket inexplicably turns of its own accord. The prayer is also a variation in Margarida's case: "By St. Peter, by St. Paul, and by the hole of St. Iago and by the invested Priest and by the consecrated host, A, B, or C hath stolen the thing lost."[6]

A number of cases involving divination by basket and shears were recorded in the state of Grão-Pará. The black slave Maria Francisca, who lived with her master on Formosa Street in Belém, made recourse to the basket and shears method to divine the theft of some coins. She murmured: "Come St. Pete [*São Pita*], come St. Paul, to the door of St. Iago," and then she named the suspects.[7] Manuel Pacheco Madureira used the same sortilege and same prayer to find out who had stolen one of his shirts; he had learned the technique from an indigenous woman.[8] It was likewise from a native Brazilian—this one by the name of Quitéria—that the slave Marçal learned how to use the shears and basket ritual, accompanied by a prayer to St. Peter, St. Paul, and the doors of St. Iago, in order to discover who had committed a theft.[9]

The popularity that this practice achieved among indigenous peoples and the mestizo population in northern Brazil offers a fine illustration of the syncretization of magical practices in the colony, a process that advanced along with colonization and intensified during the eighteenth century. An unknowing reader familiar only with the cases in Pará might even think this divination with a basket, shears, and sieve had indigenous roots, but the method was also employed in eighteenth-century Lisbon. Domingas Maria used the sieve ritual, but with a slightly different prayer: "By St. Peter and by St. Paul, by the crucified Jesus, by Barabbas, Satan, and Caiaphas, and by as many as they are, by Dona Maria Padilha and all her company, tell me, sieve, if the said two people have been captured or not, collected the money, or done the business they were about, that I shall give thee one vintém of bread and another of cheese and greatly shall I esteem thee in my heart."[10] Even more curious is the fact that the sieve and shears ritual was known in sixteenth-century England, where it was often employed to solve robberies and recover stolen goods.[11]

The case of the lady's slipper—sortilege performed by Felícia Tourinho—and the case in Portugal have something in common: they are the only situations where divination is used in combination with a medieval-flavored conjuration of demons, accentuating its traces of ritual magic. The other episodes, such as those in England cited by Thomas, have kinship with the popular European tradition that sees magic strength in Christian prayer; they are therefore more influenced by folklorized religion than by ritual magic. In any case, the deeper meanings of the sortilege and the words pronounced have been lost in the night of time.

A divination similar to the sieve or basket and scissors was performed using a key and an Our Lady Psalter.[12] During the Second Visitation, it was ascertained that at least three women resorted to this method in the city of Bahia: Ana Coelha, a carpenter's wife; Madalena de França, a seaman's wife;

and Maria da Penhosa, who confessed having learned the practice from the other two. As with the shears and sieve, this divination was a means of locating stolen objects. An Our Lady Psalter was opened and a padlock key placed inside, with the larger part sticking out. After closing the book, the key was grasped with one finger and the other end given to a young boy to hold. While the book hung suspended in mid-air, the suspects would be named one by one until the book turned, thereby indicating the thief. As in the case mentioned above, words were also pronounced: "I conjure thee on the part of God and the Virgin Mary by the virtue of this book to tell me who has taken the stolen object."[13] At the root of this practice perhaps lay the *sortes sanctorum* of the late Middle Ages, where one's fortune was read or the future foretold by reading the Gospel. People thought this was a method of consulting God directly, since the clergy taught them that the Gospel held His words and His will. At first leery about such activities, St. Augustine ultimately tolerated them, for they were preferable to worse divinatory magical practices. He did not reprove the exercise itself; "what displeased him was that the words of the Holy Scriptures were used to orient matters and trivialities of daily life."[14] Indeed, these exercises were meant to resolve everyday troubles. This divination by book and key was well known throughout the Middles Ages, persisted into the Early Modern age, and, according to Keith Thomas, was still current in many rural areas even in the nineteenth century.[15] The sixteenth-century English version differed slightly from Brazilian colonial practice. The Bible was usually used, and "the names of possible suspects [were] written on pieces of paper and inserted one after another in the hollow end of the key. When the paper bearing the name of the thief was put in, the book would 'wag' and fall out of the fingers of those who held it."[16]

There were simpler divinations, which relied solely on prayers. The prayer of St. Peter, St. Paul, and St. Iago might be used alone to discover the author of a theft, as transpired with Captain-Major Gonçalo de Castro and his slave Luís in the *sertão* region of Caracu [*sic*], in Pernambuco's hinterlands.[17] Before her exile to Brazil, Antonia Maria, mentioned earlier, would pay devotion to Our Lady at the foot of the cross "to bring to knowledge and divine future contingencies." She would kneel down before the image with her hands raised and with

> the rosary in them, she would light three white waxen candles, all three being alike, the middle one in honor of Our Lady, the one to the right in honor of Our Lord, and the one to the left in honor of the Evangelist, and, they being lighted, she would beseech Mary thus: "God save thee, Virgin of Piety, thou art sanctuary of the Most Holy Trinity, as this be true, Lady, attend to my need, Thou, Virgin, know it well, right it for Thou canst. I beseech thee, Virgin, to show me: if such shall be so, stay in thy candle, and if it shall not be so, remain in that of the Evangelist." And she, the

Defendant [Antonia], believed that if the two wee candles then went out by themselves, and that of Our Lady remained lighted, she would secure that which she desired.[18]

As with the shears and basket, the prayers used to attain concrete objectives had more to do with folklorized religion than with ritual magic or sorcery. They bore a certain flavor of the belief in the specialization of saints, ridiculed by Luther and commented on in the previous chapter. People in the Christian West resorted to such methods quite naturally and only learned to fear them when the machinery of power identified them as offenses against the faith. Within the colonial context, the Inquisition played this role.

Many of the divinations used water as a ritual recourse. Such was the case with one anonymous diviner in Recife around 1728. He was approached by Faustino de Abreu, a *pardo* [person of black and white blood] who lived in the parish of Vargem and who believed that a woman by the name of Marciana had been bewitched. When consulted, the diviner revealed the authors of the sorcery in a basin full of water, where they appeared so clearly that Faustino had no problems recognizing them.[19] Cota Marouta was also a diviner in Recife, where she lived on Trincheiras Street. A fellow from the *sertão* by the name of Manuel Machado went to her for advice because he had been robbed and hoped to recover his money. Manuel suspected a man called Cosme de Souza. Cota Marouta carried out the divination right in the suspect's home. She called "three young maidens to bring to knowledge the evildoers inside a glass of water, and in the said glass this woman placed some straw rushes, all of them split." She prayed and blessed the glass, but, according to her accuser, nothing happened.[20] The divination by egg and water on St. John's Eve, still current in Brazil, was already known to colonists in the northern part of the country in the mid-eighteenth century. Isabel Maria da Silva learned it from another woman, of unknown name, and used it a number of times. She would fill a glass "with water from the night of the said saint" and toss the yolk and white of an egg in it, forming a cross and praying a Paternoster and an Ave to St. John. She asked the saint to show her what was going to happen to the person she named. This was how Isabel Maria foretold that a student she knew was going to be ordained a cleric.[21]

Looking for treasures or possessing the talent of divining where they were hidden was considered a serious offense. In 1403, in a law against sorcery, Dom João I banned the search for gold, silver, or any other valuables by means of rods, mirrors, or other devices. It was believed that such activities were privy only to sorcerers, aided by the devil's agents.[22] Portuguese tailors invoked devils to unearth buried treasure. One of them even stored eighteen sacks of coins given to him by Satan in his house.[23] Treasure-hunting was a very common paradiabolical practice in Europe. There was no banking system at that time, and "the possibility of coming across hidden treasure was by no means a chimera," as Keith Thomas has pointed out.[24] People turned to the aid of a "specialist" in the matter. Engaged in such hunts because they claimed to possess special talents for finding valuables, these diviners argued that the treasures, which had generally been buried during times of disturbance and unrest, were guarded by demons that had to be neutralized through conjuration.[25]

In the colony, conjuring demons to find buried treasure does not seem to have been a common practice. Under the colonial system, wealth leaves the colony and is accumulated in the metropolis. In the popular imagination this is where treasures may thus be found. But one interesting episode did take place in Brazil. The Mina slave Domingos Álvares had lived for many years in Rio de Janeiro, where he became a famous *curandeiro* [healer]. He apparently was the head of a kind of *terreiro* [religious sanctum], of what would now be known as Candomblé. Arrested by the Inquisition, Domingos appeared in an auto-da-fé on June 24, 1744, where he was sentenced to exile in Castro Marim, a *couto* located in Algarve. There he resumed his illicit life. But thanks to an impressive ability to accommodate, he added another activity to his practice as a *curandeiro:* he began hunting for treasures that belonged to or were guarded by Moors, which appears to have been a deep-rooted tradition in Algarve.[26] Domingos accounted for his divinatory talents by saying he "knew what was inside the earth and within a creature's body." He would order excavations and declare what would be found: sludge, stones, sandy earth, and so on. As the digging progressed, he would throw some powders into the hole. The process was enveloped in a whole ritual: he wrapped himself up in a sheet, lit a candle, and murmured some unintelligible words; "sometimes he would lie down like a dead man, at other times he would stand still without moving so that he seemed of marble." His assistants would see blue lights and hear the throwing of stones and pounding of hooves as if of small beasts. The black man said that one of the female Moors keeping guard over the hidden treasure wanted her spell removed so she could return to her native land. Another Moorish guard was half-man, half-serpent, and needed a kiss to remove his bewitchment. But Domingos was reluctant to kiss him because he found the monster revolting and was afraid of the Moor's embrace, "for he might squeeze most hard."[27]

Since Domingos Álvares could see inside bodies and the earth, the Holy Office again imposed penance on him, and he appeared at another auto-da-fé, this time on October 20, 1749. The image of the bewitched Moor who longed to return to her homeland was perhaps a projection of Domingos's own story of exile and captivity, and his magical cures were a kind of recovery of Africa. The Moor-serpent reveals Domingos's capacity to merge and further develop traditions. It also makes it evident how monstrosity and allegedly illicit sexual desires are always found together—hence his great fear of the Moor's tight embrace and the salvational kiss.

Certain practices of African origin remained quite unchanged throughout the colonial period. In Bahia during the First Visitation, André Boçal, a slave from Guinea, was accused of divination using a moving pot or bowl. He would place the object on the ground, step away from it, and "move his fingers about, and with his mouth say some words in his tongue in a soft voice." Soon "the said pot or bowl would gain a fury to move from there." Anyone who touched it could feel that it contained a force "as if someone were throwing it." André would ask it things—for example, the whereabouts of a slave who had escaped from Gaspar Pereira. The pot moved toward the island of Maré, and the runaway slave was found.[28] Years later, in 1618, an old black man belonging to São Francisco Monastery priests performed divinations using bowls of water or wine, once more finding runaway slaves. His masters—the priests—seemed to have no complaints about his practices.[29] Around the same time, people in the city of Bahia would call upon a young black boy by the name of Bartolomeu. He was only twelve but had already earned fame for his ability to divine by speaking "in his chest a kind of whistling."[30] In the eighteenth century, the black man José synthesized all of these techniques, in Conceição do Mato Dentro, in Minas. He performed divinations by placing a plate of water on the ground and burying a sharp knife in the earth next to it. He would ask questions, "which a small voice, like the squeaking of a bat, answered from next to the plate," providing clarification about the maladies and chronic ailments "that each had."[31]

Healing

Africans, native Brazilians, and mestizos were the great *curandeiros* of colonial Brazil. Their knowledge of herbs and ritual procedures unique to their cultural universe coupled with the legacy of European folk medicine. There were some European *curandeiros,* but a much smaller number. Yet, as in Europe, the number of male *curandeiros* was much greater—an exception, in fact, to most magical practices, performed chiefly by women.[32]

Magical healing was of great importance in indigenous cultures. The successful treatment of disease stood as proof of the talents of Tupinambá sorcerers.[33] Brazil's earliest chroniclers made allusion—often in an admonishing tone—to African skill in healing through herbal infusion. Recognizing the slaves' special gifts in this field, Brandônio narrates an episode involving one of his female slaves. Poisoned by a black man, she survived thanks only to a serum administered by the very fellow himself—a bushy herb that the herbalist kept a careful secret.[34]

In traditional European society, sickness was also seen as something supernatural that could be combated only by resorting to similar means. There were no satisfactory explanations for sudden deaths (nowadays attributed to heart trouble) or infectious diseases (since there was as yet no germ theory). "Lacking any natural explanation, men turned to supernatural ones."[35] This is how people still thought in seventeenth-century France, where it was believed the gift of healing was hereditary. Although official medicine deemed them charlatans, empirics figured importantly as well; and even during the century of Enlightenment, practical books abounded.[36] In England, a man like Francis Bacon "thought that 'empirics and old women' were 'more felicitous many times in their cures than learned physicians.'"[37] Life expectancy in England was extremely low in the third quarter of the seventeenth century: 29.6 years. Medicine "began at home," and "every housewife had her repertoire of private remedies."[38]

Using supernatural means to heal thus brought these popular therapeutics closer to the realm of sorcery.[39] Illnesses, sunstroke, and discomforts like toothaches were cured, but so too were spells. As evident in the episode cited by Brandônio, *curandeiros* had a paradoxical role to play: identified with the sorcerer, they were often requested to undo spells, and their actions could consequently appear ambivalent. In Minas, in the second half of the eighteenth century, there was a black male sorcerer who was capable of healing but also of praying some words that would leave a person disabled and unfit for work.[40] In sixteenth-century Bahia, there was talk of a woman known as Mineira and a man named Velho Quatro-Olhos ["Old Four Eyes"], who used herbs to heal through the devil's art. The positive aspect of their work— the cure—outweighed the negative aspect—recourse to the diabolic.[41] Also in Minas during the gold century, the Episcopal Visit reprimanded Captain Manuel de Oliveira da Silva for procuring the services of a *curandeiro* to heal one of his slaves: "he ought not again expect to obtain the health of his ill slaves through such remedies."[42]

In colonial Brazil, *curandeiros* could restore lost harmony and bring the sick back to health, but they could also unleash maleficent magic. Rarely was there a functional division like that existing in Gaul at the close of the sixteenth century, where female witches unleashed evil and sorceresses did away with it.[43]

A few cases are suggestive of an incipient specialization. The black widower Jorge Ferreira could divine when poison had been administered and made herbal physics to discover the nature of the illness caused by the poisoning.[44] Antonio Mendes, a freed black, also employed physics to cure the bewitched.[45] Perhaps there were differences between *curandeiros* who healed maladies, *curandeiros* who cured those under spells, and spell-casters themselves (actual sorceresses), while the era's repressive machinery led to a homogenization of these activities, accounting for the form in which they have reached us. The question remains unanswered.

Blowing out air and suction played a major role in curative magic as well as in provoking maladies and *maleficia*. Claude d'Abbeville points to the Tupinambá belief in the powers of both. *Pajés* "cause the people to believe that it suffices to blow on the ill part so as to heal it." Sick Indians sought remedy from *pajés,* who would "immediately . . . begin to blow on the ill part, sucking and spitting out the evil and introducing the cure."[46] Like the Tupinambá, sorcerers of the Apopocuva and Chipaia groups also had the habit of blowing hard on their patients with the intent of breathing magic force into them.[47] Perhaps among the indigenous peoples this technique could also have the same negative potential attributed to it in Europe; in France, people believed that human breath could be deadly and could bewitch.[48] But all available records on the colony refer only to the positive effects of this technique. Suction was also a common technique among Africans and was employed in Portugal as well—here again revealing magical practices common both to tribal societies and to preindustrial European societies, which rules out the possibility of drawing a clear distinction between them. Leonor Francisca, dubbed Sarabanda, healed the sick in Lisbon by sucking on their toes and head; she cured children by "sucking on their fontanel, navel, and the soles of their feet."[49] She did just the opposite of many witches who sucked on children to kill them, as will be seen later. Yet she was still labeled a sorceress and appeared in an auto-da-fé, where she abjured *de levi* (appropriate in the case of lesser offenses). Two centuries before Sarabanda, a heathen sorcerer in the Bahian *sertão* cured cold feet by sucking on them.[50]

In the mid-eighteenth century, in Sabará, the *calunduzeira* Luzia Pinta ordered the sick to kneel down before her and would then breathe on them and sniff them to discover what ailed them.[51] She was black and from Angola. Thirty years earlier, likewise in Minas, in the parish of Nossa Senhora de Nazaré do Inficcionado, a black male slave belonging to Bernardo Pereira Brasil paid a high price for his work with magical cures. He removed bones and *drogas* from his patients' bodies by sucking them out. The Episcopal Visit believed that in so doing "he, the aforementioned, worked by virtue of the devil." The church officials ruled that his master should give him sixty lashings in the main street of the *arraial* [settlement].[52] In northern Brazil, in the state of Grão-Pará, the slave José, born on the Mina coast, had cured the *fazendeiro* André Fernandes of the agues from which he suffered. He took hold of one of André's hands "and, sucking hard and vehemently with his mouth on said hand," he gave the patient some relief on the spot; André enjoyed full recovery shortly thereafter. José had also cured the attorney José Januário da Silva of his headaches by devising a kind of herbal smokehouse and directing the smoke toward the patient's head. He also blew on him, uttered some strange words, and sucked his neck, spewing out a white matter resembling phlegm.[53]

Breath and suction could remove a spell from a victim's body, causing it to be expelled orally, rectally, or vaginally. When called in to heal someone who had been bewitched, the *curandeiro* also undertook a kind of prospecting expedition on the grounds around the bewitched's residence, where he or she would find various *maleficia* that were blamed for the patient's ailments and maladies. Sucking, blowing, vomiting, defecating, and unearthing things were thus procedures guided by a common principle: they were meant to expel or neutralize a type of negative, destructive energy responsible for maladies and misfortune.

Around 1718 the stonemason Domingos de Almeida Lobato was a victim of Antonia Maria, the sorceress from Beja who had been banished to Pernambuco, where she had resumed her diabolic activities. Finding himself in the grips of a nonstop attack of the hiccups, the mason blamed it on the ill intent of Antonia, hired by a woman who wanted to marry Domingos despite his lack of interest. He first went to Antonia herself to have her undo the spell. She went to his house, picked some sprigs of herbs in the yard, gathered up traces of his footprint, mixed it all in a pot, and added some sugarcane rum. Antonia put the sprigs in one by one while she said: "Satan—Barabbas—Caiaphas—Lame Devil—your wife." She lit five pieces of green twine, smoked out the little pot, and invoked the devils again, calling them her soldiers of valor and ordering them to find a remedy for the ailment in the ocean waves. Domingos was supposed to fumigate himself with the pot on the coming Tuesday and Friday and then toss its contents in front of the door of the woman whose love was unrequited. He did everything Antonia told him to, as well as using a ritual that involved a napkin and some coins. The hiccups worsened. Giving up on Antonia, he decided to try a black healer by the name of Domingos João. The latter first put some powder in the palm of the bewitched man's hand and told him to snuff it through his mouth and nose. The healer also told him to bury at his threshold a special root given to him for this purpose. He next had the afflicted man imbibe "a drink that appeared to be the juice of chopped herbs, and right at the same moment he spewed from his mouth in vomit a creature in the form of a horse, . . . dry from the middle part down." When the creature finished drying, the mason would die. Most extraordinary of all, just after the animal had been spit out, "a chicken suddenly flew over his [the healer's] wife . . . , who was next to the door, and descending to the basin wherein the creature was, it carried it off in its beak, the said chicken no longer being seen, nor found, and the healer said that it had come to fetch it so that its body would not turn around backward." The mason's throat was very sore for some days afterward, but the hiccups went away, and "from then on he was well."[54]

This remarkable account shows how ingrained syncretic magical practices were in early-eighteenth-century colonial life. Recourse was made to *curandeiros* and sorceresses to resolve matters of love and to cure ailments. The solutions encountered ranged from invocatory magic of a more notably European tone—where demons were still the medieval-flavored soldiers of valor—to the *curandeirismo* common among African peoples, also including extremely old folk traditions like the practice of lifting the footprint of the one who would benefit from the magic forces. If his health had not been restored after expelling the creature, it could be expected that the mason Domingos would have turned to church exorcisms, as so many other colonists did in such cases.

In 1615 the black man Mateus, Pedraluz Aranha's slave, was very sick.

Antonio da Costa then called upon a black man owned by Inês de Barros, said to be a sorcerer. "The Negro came, and healed the other sick Negro and on the same day made him well, with a cupping glass taking a clump of hairs from the place where it pained him, which he said was the spell that had caused the said Negro to be sick."[55] Like blood, sperm, and urine, hair had curative properties.[56] But because these things constituted vital energy (hair and nails especially, since they continue to grow after a person's death), they could be used for either positive or negative purposes.[57] A substantial number of spells meant to cause *maleficia* and misfortune involved the use of hair. So nothing would be more natural than for the bewitched to expel hair when the spell was properly broken.

At the time he lived in Brazil, Domingos Álvares—the one who hunted for enchanted treasures in Algarve—was in great demand because of his skill in herbal cures. He became an herbalist thanks to his knowledge of the art brought from his homeland, the Mina coast. He spent much time in the woods in search of the right herbs and preferred those still moist with dew. He used them to make potions, ointments, and brews. When brought panic-stricken before the Inquisition Tribunal, he said his healing was a result of herbal properties and not of any contribution from the devil. He had once given a patient a mixture of sugarcane rum and a powder made from ground roots and herbs, and he had blessed the brew. That night the sick person coughed and "spewed in vomit from his mouth some hair, and from his *via prepóstera* [rectum] some small bones that appeared to be of chickens, and hawk's talons." Domingos Álvares, digger of treasures, also dug up gourds to help his clients; they would prove to contain hairs, bones, and sorceries. Once when the gourds were uncovered they had caused the healer to fall on the ground as if dead—as if he were a kind of lightning rod for the malefi-cent forces emanating from the gourd. In Algarve, Domingos continued to detect *maleficia*. In the doorway to Antonio Viegas's house, he found a doll stuck with thirty-nine pins, human and dog hair, sulfur, bones from the dead, snakeskin, shards of glass, and kernels of corn. He handed out small cloth bags he himself sewed; when a female client of his opened one, she discov-ered it was filled with hair.

Causing *maleficia* by burying spells was a common procedure in colonial Brazil. Some cases recorded in northern Brazil perhaps best illustrate the specialization mentioned earlier, whereby the sorcerer who cast a spell was distinguished from the sorcerer who counteracted it. This chapter will make frequent reference to an indigenous woman named Sabina, who was a kind of counter-sorceress often called upon to detect maleficent magic. It was said, for example, that she had unearthed from Jacinto de Carvalho's thresh-old "the claw of a tapir covered with black wax, having inside it a wee piece of white stone." The witness who narrates the episode expresses a belief similar to that held by Domingos Álvares regarding the extreme virulence of maleficent forces concentrated in buried spells; she did not even want to look at them, "for she had been told that when one Indian had touched such spells, his arm had fallen asleep and he had suffered from great headaches the entire day."[58] One of the authors of spells neutralized by Sabina was Hilário, of indigenous blood. She accused him of having buried a bundle of shellfish teeth and some fish bones beneath the hammock where Gregório Gervásio da Silva Mata usually slept, at his home in Porto Salvo (Calvo?). Sabina also blamed him for a *maleficium* involving a bone of unknown origin, inside of which there was "a root called *tajá* [a type of caladium], with which it is said that such sorcerers are accustomed to performing diabolical operations." If these spells had not been detected in time but had remained "in the places where they were till taking effect," Sabina said "it would inevitably happen that everyone in the place would die." She ordered the spells thrown into the sea. With the community growing ever more suspicious of him, Hilário began moving from place to place, living with a series of small farmers. One of the witnesses who testified against him, an *alferes de auxiliares* [militia ensign], advised Gregório Gervásio, then sheltering Hilário at his farm, "that he not permit him in his home, nor even in his neighborhood, and that it would be better to send him to town, to the Most Illustrious and Most Excellent general, before he would perhaps bewitch everyone."[59]

At the time when Geraldo José de Abranches installed the Board of the Visitation to Grão-Pará, there were myriad cases of bewitched individuals who—like veritable wicked sisters of fairy tales—spewed countless beasts and filth from their mouths and other orifices. The black man José mentioned above, who specialized in healing through breath and suction, was once called in to see a black female slave who had taken ill. Even before he began treating her, she had been "spewing forth from her *via da madre* [vagina] diverse creatures and live vermin the color of bronze." As soon as he stepped into the slave-master's house, "seeing a creature that the said Negro woman had spewed out, he said that she still had more within her." He began uttering unintelligible words, administered to the sick woman an herbal infusion he had prepared himself, and went into the yard to bury an ear of corn. In the end, the patient "hurled out a thing like a pouch or sack in the form of a bladder skin, wherein, after being rent, three live creatures could be seen: one resembling a small frog, another resembling a tiny alligator, and another resembling a small hairy lizard, and each of the three said creatures was of a different color."[60]

Denunciations against the Indian Sabina are filled with descriptions of strange creatures being regurgitated and of buried spells. In the 1750s the small farmer Manuel de Souza Novais sought the advice of this indigenous woman famed for discovering spells. His family was suffering from generalized *maleficia*; and he believed these were spells, because bundles of bizarre things would appear about the cacao trees. He sent for Sabina at the Acará River where she lived. She had scarcely arrived at Manuel's *fazenda* when she ordered them to dig on the stair landing, where they discovered "the head of a pit viper all withered, and solely of bones."[61] Her client paid with a cut of cloth.

Some time later, another small farmer, Domingos Rodrigues, asked Sabina to treat his sick wife. The *curandeira* said the malady had been brought on by the spells of a Tapuia who lived in the house, and Sabina called the woman to undo the harm. She ordered the accused to dig beneath the bed and in other places around the house, and from each of the holes she removed bundles containing bones, feathers, fish bones, and pierced lizards. The suspect eventually confessed that she had done it all with the help of the devil. Sabina also had the stricken woman use an herbal fumigator, which caused "diverse live creatures like small lizards and other vermin" to leave her body. Still not content, Sabina wet her hand in holy water and removed a lizard from the sick woman's mouth. Finally, she advised the woman to seek the help of the church's exorcists.[62]

When the governor of Grão-Pará, João de Abreu Castelo Branco, once took ill, off went Sabina to the palace. She asked for a pointed knife and used it to jab holes in the mud wall plastered with lime, where she found a bundle containing small bones—spells against the previous governor, José da Serra, by then deceased. Sabina made a fumigator for Governor João de Abreu, rubbed his leg, and extracted from it three very soft live creatures the size of chickpeas.[63]

To treat Raimundo José de Bitencourt, *ajudante do terço dos auxiliares* [adjutant to a militia regiment], Sabina smoked a pipe and then puffed into the sick man's eyes. She next stuck her tongue into his eyes, rolled it around, and vomited out creatures: one of them had a belly full of dead offspring and looked rather like a fish. Saying it was for hygienic purposes, Sabina repeated the operation with her tongue, and each time she would spit filth from Raimundo's eyes: ashes, sand, dead wasps.[64] In treating other patients, Sabina vomited angleworms, snails, rattlesnakes, and shrimp eyes.[65]

Narrating a contemporary *catimbó* session, Francisco das Chagas Batista, folk poet from Paraíba, gives evidence that magical practices are a continuous, age-old part of Brazilian folk traditions:

> He put it in his pipe, lit up
> And began to puff,
> He fumigated the ill
> With the smoke he sucked . . .
>
> During the fumigation
> The sorcerer said:
> "Come, Urubatan, take
> This frog from his head
> And take this mewing beast
> From his belly."[66]

In the early seventeenth century, Abbeville witnessed members of the Tupinambá group in Maranhão sucking on diseased parts of the human body. "They at times hide pieces of sticks, iron, or bones, and after sucking on the diseased part, they show these objects to the victim, pretending to have removed them. Ofttimes they are cured, but thanks to their imagination or to superstition, thanks to diabolic arts," the Capuchin said.[67]

Around the same time, the auto-da-fé in Logroño was delineating various aspects of the Spanish stereotype of witchcraft. According to what was said at that time, sorceresses would concoct diabolic ointments on the *akelarre,* or sabbat, under the demon's supervision. The ingredients? Vermin, toads, snakes, geckos, lizards, slugs, snails, bones, and the brains of the dead.[68] So in mixing their potions, the witches used the same creatures that the bewitched colonists—white, black, indigenous, or mestizo—expelled from their mouths, rectums, vaginas, or even skin. Is this an archetypal coincidence or the superposition of various cultural traditions? It is hard to tell. What appears undeniable is that in the earliest years of the seventeenth century members of Europe's cultured elite—like Abbeville and the Inquisitors at Logroño—shared similar views of the devil, while this understanding differed greatly from indigenous beliefs regarding evil spirits. It was then thought that indigenous *curandeiros* could remove evil spirits from the bodies of the possessed by sucking, but they did not yet extract the geckos, lizards, and vermin of 150 years later. It would be wise to remember that Catholic Europeans were the great demonizers of indigenous magical practices. Even if Geraldo José de Abranches, Heitor Furtado de Mendonça, Marcos de Noronha, or any other Holy Office dignitaries had not come to Brazil, the indigenous Sabina's devil and the spells of the black men João, José, and so many others would remind us of practices in Logroño, in Loudun, in Lancashire, and in Val de Cavalinhos: they were part of life in the colonies.

Cures also entailed hard-to-define magical procedures, often semiritual in nature. In Maranhão, the slave João blended *curandeirismo,* divining, and ritual proscriptions. He was summoned to heal Catarina Machada, wife of a boatman, who had taken seriously ill. The black man prepared some shallow earthen basins with water, herbs, and a stone like those found on some fish heads, saying the devil would appear in them. He dripped a bit of this mixture into the eyes of those watching so they could better see the apparition. João mixed another basin, filling it with water and covering it with a large plate; he said "it was for the sick woman to drink of and heal the sores in her throat." He twisted some rope out of white and black strands and used them to tie up the foot and head of the cot where Catarina Machado was lying; whoever touched this rope would drop dead. João swayed around the room with a gourd in his hand, murmured incomprehensible words in his native tongue, and shouted in Portuguese: "Come, devil, come, devil." The sick woman's relatives and friends were gathered around to share her final moments of life, accustomed as they were to what Philippe Ariès has called "domesticated death."[69] Children ran in and out, taking little note. One of them bumped against the ropes and immediately began shouting: "Here I have touched the ropes, and even so I did not drop over, nor did I die!"[70] Catarina died shortly thereafter.

Domingos Álvares, the disenchanter of Moors, cured a variety of diseases that not even surgeons could remedy: paralysis, coughs, cankers on the face. In the latter case, he administered powders, cleansings prepared of cooked herbs, and nettles with honey. He cured the stone malady, using the stone from the head of a fish called a *xaréu*. It was in Brazil that he had learned this practice, which reminds us of the fish stone João mixed into the basin water. In Algarve Álvares continued to make successful recourse to it.[71] For aches and pains, he prescribed unsalted sheep tallow; in cases of various other maladies, he rubbed his patients with a baby chick and a ten réis coin! He had learned how to cure sunstroke from whites in Brazil: he had the patient stay in the sun from eleven in the morning till noon, with a folded napkin on his or her head; a glass of water was placed upon it turned upside down, which soaked the napkin until absorbed. The procedure was to be repeated several days in a row until a marked recovery was noticed.

José Januário da Silva, a 40-year-old white man who worked as an attorney, came voluntarily before the Visitation Board to confess to a number of offenses, including his remedies "to remove the sun, a malady that produces headaches." He would first take an open napkin and make the sign of the cross over it diagonally while he recited a Credo. He would then fold the napkin, place it over the mouth of a cupping glass filled with water, and put "it all on the sick person's head, with the napkin next to the head and the bottom of the cupping glass up in the air, with the water inside."[72] José Januário would make two crosses over the bottom of the cupping glass, saying: "Sun and Moon, begone with the sign of the cross." This was followed by Paternosters and Ave Marias in the name of the passion and death of Our Lord Jesus Christ and by crossing himself in the names of the members of the Blessed Trinity.[73] This model, more sophisticated, accompanied by prayers, must have been the basis for Domingos Álvares's simplified version. What is most remarkable is that exactly the same remedy for sunstroke remains in use today, practiced by blacks and mestizos in Paraíba, where it is known as *sol-na-cabeça* ["sun on the head"].[74] If Domingos Álvares was correct when he stated that this technique was common among white settlers, here again we have a process of transmitting and syncretizing a practice down through the centuries: in today's Paraíba, these *rezadores* [healers through prayer] are always practitioners of *catimbó*.

In Europe, toothaches commonly were cured by using a nail and invoking the name of God, something the church deemed a mortal sin.[75] But records of this practice in colonial times have more to do with a variation that combines the sacred and the occult. Flemish by birth but a resident of Bahia, João Poré had learned the procedure from some Italians in Madrid around 1610. The method consisted of "taking a new nail and touching the aching tooth with it, and also writing on the wall with it the name of Maccabeus, and if the said tooth is in the right part, by nailing the said nail to the first A of the said name, and if the said aching tooth is in the left part, by nailing it to the last A."[76]

Common all around Europe, these magical cures through words reflected a longtime belief in the curative power of the medieval church. The procedure that Margaret Hunt confessed to before the Commissary of London in 1528 bears great resemblance to many of the methods we have seen so far: she would first pronounce the names of the afflicted persons; then she would kneel down and pray to the Most Holy Trinity and ask for protection from their enemies. The ill were to say five Paternosters, five Aves, and a Credo for nine consecutive nights, all in the name of the Holy Spirit.[77]

In Brazil, this kind of remedy was used especially for *quebranto*, a weakness or illness caused by the evil eye; for evil eye per se; and for erysipelas. Cures for *quebranto* were in use all over the colony in the eighteenth century. In Minas, in the *arraial* of Tejuco, a *parda* by the name of Aldonça was famed for "curing *quebrantos* by means of words."[78] In the north, José Januário, mentioned earlier, and the Indian Domingas Gomes da Ressurreição healed *quebranto*. José Januário defined the ailment as encompassing headaches, fever, and bodily weakness.[79] To combat it, he blessed the patient's whole body with his index finger and thumb or with the cross on his rosary. While he made the sign of the cross, he would say: "So and so, with two it hath been given to thee, with three it shall be taken from thee. In the name of God and of the Virgin Mary." He then said one Paternoster, one Ave, and a Gloria Patri in the name of the sacred passion and death of Jesus.[80] Domingas Gomes had learned the cure from her mistress, who could no longer practice it since she had received the sash of St. Francis (which did not keep her from teaching it to the slave!). Domingas would say: "Two evil eyes have given it to thee, with three thou shalt be cured." The three eyes were an allusion to the members of the Most Holy Trinity. The prayers were the same, except for the Credo; honor was paid to souls in purgatory as well.[81]

José Januário and Domingas also remedied evil eye, but by recourse to different prayers. The native woman made signs of the cross over the sick person's face, saying: "Jesus Christ hath marked thee, Jesus Christ hath created thee. Jesus Christ sayeth to thee, behold who hath looked at thee in evil."[82] Januário, who made signs of the cross as well, prayed: "St. Anne begot Mary. Mary begot Jesus Christ. St. Isabel begot St. John the Baptist. As certain as these words are, so shalt ye, so and so, be free of this evil or of this eye, by St. Peter, and by St. Paul, and by the crucified Jesus."[83] Domingas also had a prayer against erysipelas: she would take a knife and touch it against the affected place, making the sign of the cross and saying: "White rose, I cut thee. Black rose, I cut thee. Scarlet rose, I cut thee." At each utterance, she would touch the person twice with the knife. And she would end: "I command thee for the sake of God and of the Virgin Mary, if thou be wildfire or erysipelas, do not afflict God's creature."[84]

In the Brazilian northeast, magic formulas for combating *quebranto* and evil eye still survive, many of them in verse form. As in colonial days, when the praying is done, oblation is made to the holy passion and death of Our Lord Jesus Christ, concluding:

Just as he was made free
Safe and sound from his afflictions
Thus ye believe, so and so,
Ye shalt be made free of evil eye
And of all hidden evils.[85]

An amazing mixture of religiosity, occultism, magical cures, and, in a way, Satanism is found in the charges brought in the 1740s against Friar Luís de Nazaré, a Carmelite from Bahia. The friar was an exorcist in great demand for his ability to cure the sick, and he would often administer a physic. Once he ordered a pig bought in order to make this household remedy. He said the animal should be slaughtered and the quarters and the side pork sent to him so he could prepare a salve to rub into the invalid's belly. The animal's entrails should be cooked and placed at a crossroads late at night. The patient in question, who was a female slave, died. The priest told her masters to give away or sell the dead woman's clothes and that no one should wear them. He probably believed they were impregnated with evil forces.[86]

In the cities and countryside of Europe, priests had practically no choice but to double as doctors. One of their most sacred duties was to offer spiritual comfort to the sick, "helping them to profit of the illness and, in some cases, to have a good death."[87] In fulfilling the role of curative priest and exorcist, Friar Luís found himself struggling with repressed desires—with a sexuality that exploded violently and destructively because it was illegitimate and guilt-ridden. Yet he was no poor soul brutalized by the rigid, hypocritical morals of his time; when it came to women—particularly those of lower social status—he took full advantage of his prerogatives as an exorcising priest, as a man of the cloth, someone relatively well educated in a colony of illiterates.

Hundreds of denunciations document his favorite habit. When summoned to see someone who had taken ill, Friar Luís would state that the only road back to good health was through the administration of certain cleansings and fumigations. One of these episodes was witnessed by Feliciana Pereira da Cruz, a black *crioula* who would later denounce the priest before the Holy Office's commissary. Tomásia, a female slave who worked in the same house, fell sick around 1736. Her malady was "extraordinary and unknown" and failed to respond to medical treatment. Her masters then sent for Friar Luís de Nazaré and asked him to exorcise their slave. Arriving at their house, the priest took his stole, "read some books that contained the exorcisms," and caused Tomásia to experience "some tremors and convulsive writhings twice." He then ordered that the sickly woman be moved to another room, taking with him as assistants the subsequent denouncer, Felícia, and a *parda* named Tereza. He ordered them to "remove all of the ailing woman's clothing, and rub her belly, having placed a charcoal in the mouth of each." He then told them "each to cut the hair of their privy parts, and that they cut the hair on the invalid's head." Together they should make some fumigators for the stricken woman. Friar Luís returned the following day, repeated the exorcisms with his stole, and "placed himself over the same ill woman, telling the assistants to turn their faces the other way, and he engaged in an act of carnal copulation with the woman, and then another with the denouncer, and another with the aforesaid Tereza; both reviled him but were vanquished, and he aided by saying that the book with which he performed exorcisms so ordered, wheretofore they submitted to the said Priest, who told them they need have no scruples, for it was to cure the sick woman."

If the slaves who were asked to lend their assistance rebelled against the priest's efforts to force them into sexual relations, he would send them away and ask the mistress of the house to find him new assistants. Intimidated by the exorcist's prestige, the slaves kept a pact of silence for a long time. The exorcist told all of them to "clean the seminal matter from said copulations with a piece of cloth and spread it on the sick woman's belly, and that they ought, on every occasion, to wash their privy parts with water, and keep [the water] in a pot so they could continue to wash the said sick woman with it." All this paraphernalia notwithstanding, the patient died.

In some cases Friar Luís actually forced the women to have sex with him. He confessed to having done this with a slave owned by one João Francisco, who lived in the *sertão*. The priest would make certain demands: in order to cure Father Francisco Quaresma, resident of the Recôncavo region, he required "a clean, tidy woman" who could help him do some cooking with *ervas de São Caetano* [a local herb]. His intentions were in fact otherwise.

Friar Luís perhaps believed in the curative power of sperm, like so many Europeans of his time.[88] His skullduggery is undeniable, but it reveals a mysterious, syncretic world where magic and popular religiosity intersect, regardless of his status as a man of the cloth. In this sense he reminds us of the superstitious, "ignorant" priests mentioned in the previous chapter. Many years before charges were brought against him, Friar Luís was asked to exorcise a sick woman by the name of Dona Antonia de Lacerda, who had supposedly been hexed. One day when he was arriving at the patient's home, the priest was approached by her unmarried sister, Dona Rosa, who said she suffered from great stomach pains during each monthly cycle. The priest called her to an inner room, told her to lie down, and, "ordering her to raise up her shirt, placed the scapular of his habit over her stomach, and prayed the Magnificat, whilst at the same time he had his hand holding the said scapular over her belly, and he was standing; once finished praying, putting aside the scapular, he ran his hand downward till touching her privy parts with the intent of having carnal copulation with her, which she resisted, and he then left her, but some time later he was unchaste with her several times through consummate voluptuousness, approaching his privy parts to those of the said Dona Rosa de Lacerda, although he never consummated carnal copulation with her, for she was reputed to be a maiden."

Not all of the infirm took unkindly to the exorcist's curative procedures. Married and seriously ill, Tereza, a slave of Colonel Custódio da Silva and resident in Bahia, copulated with Friar Luís. According to what he later confessed, it seemed she felt "the same way she could if she were well."

On occasion, Friar Luís lent a bit more sophistication to his cleansings, adding to the water such local herbs as *erva espinheira* and *erva de São Caetano;* a mordant known as *bolo-armênio;* or charcoal. He was arrested by the Inquisition and sent to Lisbon in 1740. Terrified before the inquisitors, he made a total confession, lamenting and regretting his acts. He admitted to having greatly offended God, blinded by his lust, "in which he admitted having been more than excessive." Like an ungrateful son, he blamed his sins on his condition as a resident of the colony: "in those parts of Brazil where he found himself," lust enjoyed "great strength and dominion." He disdained and humiliated the women with whom he had copulated: they had been credulous "because they were ignorant and simple women, and . . . in those lands of Brazil, they are easily misled by anything told to them, *especially when these are people whom they hold in some regard.*"[89] The Inquisition read the verdict before the board, banished him to the most remote monastery of his province for five years, prohibited him from returning to the city of Bahia, and banned him forever from practicing exorcism—but allowed him to remain a priest.

Superstitious Blessings

Blessing animals had been a common practice in European societies since the late Middle Ages. Gregorius of Tours left a remarkable account of this custom: bulls, sheep, and pigs would be taken for ritual blessings, turning the basilica into something like a modern Texas ranch.[90] This widely employed practice was an effort to save animals essential to a subsistence economy.[91] For a long time, these blessings were better tolerated by the church than were other types of ritual used for the same purpose. In 650 the Synod of Rouen banned charms that used breads and herbs hidden at crossroads for the purpose of protecting herds and flocks from epidemics.[92] At the end of the Middle Ages and dawn of the Early Modern age, a greater intolerance began to appear. In 1499 Dom Manuel ordered that blessers, along with sorcerers, have the letter "F" (for *feiticeiro*) branded on both cheeks.[93] The defamatory punishment of the iron was later suspended, as the Philippine Ordinances dealt less harshly with the offense of superstitious blessing. "We uphold that no one shall bless dogs, or beasts, nor other dumb animals, nor shall do it, but that he shall first obtain our permission, or that of the prelates, to so be allowed."[94] Offenders were to receive the customary punishment: a flogging, a fine of one mil-réis paid to the accuser (or two mil-réis if the accuser was a squire or of higher rank), and banishment to Africa for men and to Castro Marim for women.

Colonial documents have little to say about these blessers. It is hard to tell whether there were indeed so few of them or whether the Inquisition, episcopal Inquiries, and other powers were so unconcerned about them. Since superstitious blessings are still practiced in Brazil today, the second hypothesis seems the more likely.[95]

The First Visitation to Bahia investigated charges against João Roiz Palha, a 62-year-old farmer. In his confession, the man says that fifty-two years earlier, while still in Portugal, he had charmed cattle to make bugs fall off them. "He picked nine stones from the ground and uttered the following: I charm by the greater devil and by the smaller, and by all the others." He repeated these words nine times, "and each time he finished saying them, he threw one of the said stones toward the place where the cattle were walking." Three days later, all the bugs fell off. Asked his reasons for engaging in this practice, João Roiz Palha replied that "he did it because in those days he saw almost all shepherds of that land generally doing it."[96] A long-standing tradition thus justified his action and lessened his guilt.

In the eighteenth century, in Nossa Senhora da Conceição dos Carijós, Minas, the overseer Francisco Martins spoke blessings on animals afflicted with maggots, and they became "rid of them and healthy."[97] He therefore played a very useful role in the community, but the long arm of inquisitorial power did not have the habit of delving into the merits of social harmony. When the visitor Friar Domingos Luís da Silva traveled to the gold-mining region at the order of the bishop of Rio de Janeiro, Dom Friar Antonio de Guadalupe, he lodged a denunciation against Francisco Martins for his activities as a blesser.

The Overseas Universe

Divinations, magical cures, and superstitious blessings were an attempt to respond to the needs and events of daily life, making things a little easier at a time of frequent hardships. They were often used in combination, as part of an effort to ameliorate the impacts of one of the most important components of daily life, directly tied to the colonists' subsistence-level living conditions: the overseas venture.

One-fifth and at times even one-fourth of Portugal's population was engaged in the overseas effort. This meant an average of one or two people per family.[98] At a time when little was known of technology, the sea easily incited fear. It was "the privileged dominion of Satan and of infernal forces."[99] So despite their long tradition as a seafaring people, the Portuguese feared for their relatives far away, who were battling waves, whirlpools, typhoons, and giant Adamastors.

In Brittany, where sailors were also numerous, their wives resorted to sortilege to get them back: they cleaned the chapels near their towns and threw the dust into the air, hoping favorable winds would bring their husbands home as a result.[100]

Many have argued that the Basque maritime endeavor accounts for the great upsurge in Basque sorcery in the early seventeenth century. Pierre De Lancre, the terrifying judge of Labourd, was perhaps one of the first to draw this link; for him, the beautiful Basque women who were left home alone by their fishermen husbands summer after summer insinuated "dangers of love and sortilege" with their eyes.[101] But it was Dr. Martínez de Isasti who went further. In *Relación que hizo el Doctor don lope de ysasti presbytero y beneficiado de leço . . . ,* Isasti constructs a brilliant explanation: "Women witches, because of the pact they have made with the Devil, can give news of what is happening at sea or at the ends of the earth; sometimes they are right and sometimes wrong in what they say, but there have been people who have known about events that occurred a hundred or five hundred leagues away the day after they happened, and who have been right. . . . And this is their chief motive for becoming witches, to get news of their husbands and sons who are on their way to the Indies, Newfoundland, or Norway."[102] If so many sixteenth- and seventeenth-century people in fact believed the sea to be the dominion of Satan, nothing could be more natural than sorceresses' knowing its secrets better than anyone else.[103] They learned these from the devils, which often dwelled on ships or in the ocean depths. The devil that helped the *cafuza* Maria Joana with spells and conjurations sometimes failed to appear because he was not on land but "on a ship that he could not leave."[104] Maria Barbosa, *parda,* would summon an ocean demon in her prayers: "Great demon maritime, unto thee I deliver this pine."[105]

Trobriand Islanders believed that shipwrecked men fall helplessly into the hands of flying witches who go about at night with the intention of drowning sailors at sea.[106] In the Middle Ages, certain demons were specialized in sinking ships.[107] Colonial witches did not sink ships, but they could interfere with and change their courses. The infamous Butt-That-Burns [Arde-lhe-o-rabo], "for two cruzados that were given her, caused a ship going from Bahia to Portugal to make port, by the power of the Devil."[108] Also in the sixteenth century, it was rumored in Bahia that the *mulata* Beatriz Correia, on her way to the Kingdom, "carried three snakes inside a jug on board ship and caused it to make port."[109] Antonia Fernandes, known as Nóbrega, was the only woman accused of sorcery by the First Visitation to Bahia who actually came before the board to confess. She had been banished from Portugal for acting as procuress for her own daughter and was the widow of one João da Nóbrega, "a man who traveled as a provisions clerk on Lisbon armadas." Because she was a single, middle-aged woman (she was fifty) suspected of being a procuress, the community began to view her much as a stereotyped witch. Among the numerous charges of sorcery lodged against her, one was that she had caused "a ship from India to make port."[110] Like the women De Lancre and Isasti spoke about and like those in Brittany who threw dust to control the direction of the winds, Nóbrega was married to a man who earned his livelihood in the struggle with the sea. In the eighteenth century, the overseas horizon still occupied the colonists' imagination. At the *calundu* sessions held by Domingos Álvares when he resided in Rio de Janeiro, one of the possessed "responded by furnishing news about what had happened at sea with vessels, and in other lands most far away," after which she fell dead on the ground.[111]

Curiously enough, there is at least one case of two men who also altered ships' courses. Around 1668 the Holy Office charged the young barber Manuel João with sorcery, and the episode appears to have caused quite a stir in Belém. One of the witnesses who testified against Manuel João was the merchant Salvador de Oliveira. He told the board that he had inquired as to whether the sorcerer had news about the caravel due in from Lisbon and that the accused "had replied that he had ascertained that the caravel was not lost and that within three days it would arrive in Maranhão."[112] The slave Manuel da Piedade had been born in Bahia but later moved to Portugal, where he resided in a number of cities. While still living in the colony, a fisherman passed to him the prayer of the Just Judge, said to work well for escaping blows and dangers at sea. He was accused before the board of having performed a ceremony to keep a ship from making port, unleashing unfavorable winds by blowing and spitting.[113]

Daily life in the colony depended greatly on the fleets that arrived from Portugal bearing news, goods, loved ones, and on occasion unpleasant orders from the Holy Office and even mandates for arrest. It was important to know when a ship would arrive, when an awaited voyage to Lisbon would finally be made, whether the husband who sent no news had died in the struggles in India or had been swept away in the Atlantic waves.

The colonists missed Portugal, longed to go back, and sometimes had a vague feeling of inferiority because they lived in the colony, an inferior region of the planet. Projecting deep-seated desires, Dona Lianor claimed she could go from Bahia to the Kingdom in one night, which placed her under suspicion of sorcery.[114] Put in jail and stigmatized as a diabolical sorceress, Boca Torta ["Twisted Mouth"] "said that she saw what was said and done in Lisbon."[115] More magnanimous, Isabel Maria de Oliveira boasted she could take people from Belém to Lisbon by means of some glass rings she had bought in the Terreiro do Paço, in Lisbon. On other occasions—perhaps to provoke the envy of acquaintances—Isabel Maria claimed she went to the Kingdom just to buy ribbons.[116] She could supposedly transport people wherever they wished to go as well; all they had to do was embark in a canoe in the company of a black rooster, not utter the names of Jesus or Mary, and not carry any gold or silver coins. In her confession, she admitted to claiming she could make these secret trips as a joke.

The licentiate André Magro d'Oliveira was held at the Recife jail because people accused him of betraying the Spanish king and of serving Dom Antonio, prior of Crato. One day the *mulata* vendor Brígida Lopes—"considered and called a sorceress"—had gone up to the jail bars and muttered in his ear that he would be embarking for Portugal "and that at sea he would do battle with a thieves' ship, and that he would not be captured but would reach the Kingdom, and there he would be released and would return to this Brazil, released and free." The vendor knew this because she had performed "some spells and rituals with water and lead." Everything turned out just as she predicted: the licentiate embarked, did battle at sea with an English ship, reached Lisbon, was released, and returned to Brazil. As a result, he had a "bad conceit of her" and denounced her to the Visitor in 1593.[117]

Maria Barbosa, a *mulata* with a dubious past, lived in Bahia in the early seventeenth century. It seems she had previously been banished to Angola for sorcery. Once in Brazil she became a repeat offender. Among the many denunciations against her, an old episode was brought to light. In a basin of water she had shown Manuel de Silveira, governor of Angola, the image of his wife, who lived in Portugal. She had also predicted how long his administration would last in Angola, "and so as she spoke, so did it happen."[118]

The baker Maria de Escobar lived in Recife and was married to a ship's pilot who was off in the area of India. She thought her husband had died and wanted to confirm this fact so she could remarry. She sought out Domingas Brandoa, known as a sorceress, "and requested that she do something to discover whether she was to marry the said man." The witch asked her to maintain total secrecy. She took "a twig broom and dressed it in a shift and placed a towel on it like a woman, and with it thus decorated stood it against the wall, and in a loud voice, standing in the middle of the house, she began to speak, summoning Barabbas and naming other names and things." Once the ceremony was over, she told the woman to go home, "for it was certain that she was to marry the man that she intended to marry."[119]

Isabel Maria da Silva's spells also served romantic purposes. She performed the St. John divination mentioned earlier, breaking the white and yolk of an egg in the shape of a cross inside a glass of water. Appearing before the board of the Visitor to Grão-Pará, she recounted the sortilege. A young maiden had sought her help to discover whether she "was to marry a *mazombo* [person born in Brazil of Portuguese parents] or a man who would come from the Kingdom." When the sorceress employed her technique, "there appeared before her a ship that she clearly saw." The girl married the man from Portugal. Another woman who asked for the same divination had different luck: no ship was spied in the glass, and she married a man from Brazil.[120]

In Lisbon, a terrified woman sought out the sorceress Domingas Maria. She was crying and said her husband had arrived in the fleet just in, and rumor had it he intended to kill her. She wanted to know if this was true. Moved by the woman's tears, Domingas Maria performed the egg ritual using a urinal and also taught the woman countless prayers to be said at certain times and in certain places.[121] The Portuguese sorceress Sister Maria do Rosário, who had gone by the secular name Maria Tereza Inácia, also intervened in favor of a suffering woman whose husband was far away. The woman complained about her spouse's lengthy absence. After hearing out her complaints, the sorceress decided to help her. Together with some women friends and the demon, they went to India in the form of ravens, where they found the man lying sick in a bed. They placed him in a vessel and carried him home through the air, depositing him at the door of his house.[122]

In one of her prayers, the aforementioned witch Dona Paula spoke of "faithful saints of the God of distant seas, of near seas."[123] Tried by the Portuguese Inquisition in 1582, Ana Gómez confessed she had been initiated into the secrets of sorcery during the twelve years she spent living with a famous sorceress in a town in Portugal. She had later married, and her husband had gone to fight in Africa. Because she wanted news of her spouse, she invoked the devil using words in a book. Satan said her husband and his friends as well had perished in the African venture.[124]

If God was worshipped in the near seas and overseas, Satan was too, reigning over ocean swells and whirlpools. At a time when the colonial system encompassed a large part of the globe, it is natural that dreams, longings, desires, and imaginary projections would reflect its importance, evincing the system's impact on everyone's daily life, personal relationships, and very survival. Furthermore, sorcerers circulated within the heart of the colonial system. Lists of autos-da-fé include a substantial number of sorceresses whose close relatives (husbands, fathers, or brothers) were sailors. When convicted of sorcery, a good share of these women were banished to Brazil, especially in the seventeenth century. Those accused of false beliefs were likewise exiled to the colony: *beatas* and visionaries. So documentation again demonstrates the curious role the colony played in the early modern European imagination: the place where sins were purged and where paradisiacal visions alternated with infernal ones.

The three lists below serve to illustrate the relationship between sorcery and the overseas world. The first enumerates sorceresses related to men engaged in the overseas endeavor; the second is a list of Portuguese sorcerers banished to Brazil; and the third is a roster of Portuguese *beatas* banished to Brazil.

Witchcraft and the Overseas Universe[125]

1. Maria da Conceição, widow of Manuel Fernandes, seaman: Auto-da-fé (AF) May 16, 1594.
2. Maria Vicente, married to Pedro Mendes, or Martins, sailor: AF October 11, 1637.
3. Maria Gorjoa, married to Pedro Roiz, seaman: AF December 15, 1647.
4. Joana da Silveira, daughter of Manuel Rodrigues, seaman: AF August 18, 1661.
5. Maria Jacome, married to Domingos Romeiro, seaman: AF September 17, 1662.
6. Monica Gomes, married to Antonio Delgado, pilot: AF September 17, 1662.
7. Francísca de Sá, widow of Manuel Galego de Oliveira: AF August 17, 1664.
8. Maria da Silva, married to João Esteves, sailor: AF August 17, 1664.
9. Luisa Pereira da Silva, married to Gaspar da Costa, pilot: AF March 31, 1669.
10. Luiza da Silva, widow of Marcos Lucas, sailor: AF August 8, 1683.
11. Maria da Conceição, widow of Manuel Fernandes, seaman: AF May 16, 1694.
12. Josefa Hilária, a.k.a. Hilária Correia, married to Manuel da Costa Palma, seaman: AF October 14, 1714.
13. Tereza Maria, known as Valente, married to Matias dos Santos, seaman: AF November 8, 1750.
14. Maria Tereza, known as Rata, married to Crispim dos Santos, sailor: AF September 24, 1752.

Portuguese Sorcerers Banished to Brazil[126]

1. Catarina Barretta: AF December 10, 1573.
2. Suzana Jorge: AF April 5, 1620.
3. Jerônimo de Souza: AF January 10, 1621.
4. Ana Antonia: AF May 5, 1624.
5. Simão Ribeiro: AF May 5, 1624.
6. Maria Ortega: AF October 11, 1634.
7. Marta Nogueira: AF February 25, 1645.
8. Francisca Cota: AF December 15, 1647.
9. José de Jesus Maria: AF October 29, 1656.
10. Tomé João: AF December 15, 1658.
11. Amaro Fernandes: AF October 17, 1660.

12. Manuela de Jesus: AF September 17, 1662.
13. Francisca de Sá: AF August 17, 1664.
14. Luzia Maria: AF August 17, 1664.
15. Maria da Silva: AF August 17, 1664.
16. Caterina Crasbech: AF June 24, 1671.
17. Domingas da Silva: AF June 24, 1671.
18. Maria de Seixas: AF December 10, 1673.
19. Paula de Moura: AF December 10, 1673.
20. Úrsula Maria: AF December 10, 1673.
21. Maria Pinheira: AF May 10, 1682.
22. Maria de Souza: AF August 8, 1683.
23. Maria Simões: AF August 21, 1689.
24. Paulo Lourenço: AF September 21, 1689.
25. Domingas Fernandes: AF July 1, 1691.
26. Simão Luís, known as Castelhano: AF July 1, 1691.
27. Maria Manoel Beleza: AF June 14, 1699.
28. Manuel Pereira: AF September 12, 1706.
29. Manoel Rodrigues: AF November 18, 1708.
30. Isabel da Silva: AF June 21, 1711.
31. Antonio Nunes da Costa: AF May 17, 1716.

Portuguese Beatas Banished to Brazil[127]

1. Luiza de Jesus: AF December 15, 1647.
2. Maria Antunes: AF December 15, 1658.
3. Joana da Cruz: AF October 17, 1660.
4. Maria da Cruz: AF October 17, 1660.
5. Luíza or Luzia do Santo Antonio: AF October 19, 1704.
6. Felipa Lopes: AF June 30, 1709.

CHAPTER 4

The Onset of Conflict

For the insolence of the Defendants was so extreme that among the most injurious derisions that they cast in the face of the Plaintiff was the scandalous and most injurious name of sorceress, by which she fears the Defendants have defamed her before all her acquaintanceship; hence the Plaintiff worries that in this manner she shall come to be reputed as such.

—Libel Suit, Rio de Janeiro, 1772

Before the European witch-hunt released its full fury, magic had been associated with a logical order and a social order, as is still the case today in many communities studied by anthropologists. This integration, found among Germanic and Slavic peoples, for example, was thrown somewhat off balance during times of tension by the predominance of maleficent magic.[1]

In a slave society like colonial Brazil, this tension was ongoing, a constituent part of the social formation itself, reflected in many of the magical practices and sorcery used by the colonists. Through these, the colonial inhabitants at times sought to safeguard their physical well-being and at others to do evil to possible enemies. Therefore such practices fulfilled a dual role: they were offensive, that is, meant to attack, and they were defensive, meant to protect and preserve.

These practices were found in all social ranks, where participants could be both subject and object. Not all such practices were directly related to the tension existing between masters and slaves, though a good share did indeed reflect it. They were very often an expression of personal rivalries or conflicts between neighbors, so common in European villages, where such tensions likewise gave birth to spells and *maleficia*. Many of the practices recreated centuries-old fantasies from the European imagination within a new context. Finally, some were unique to the world of slavery and colonial life.

Spells intended to do harm or even to kill must have been a very common part of daily colonial life. That they were so commonplace may explain why the era's documents contain so many merely vague allusions to their practice, as if there were little point in dwelling on something so routine. For example, in Recife around 1728, the slave Luís was denounced as a reputed sorcerer and for "having a compact with the devil, for taking lives, and doing other things."[2] In Conceição do Mato Dentro, when gold production was already declining, the black woman Luzia Lopes was said to be a sorceress; she was publicly flogged in the local chapel by a missionary on his way through the town. She used powders, ointments, bones, skulls, roots, and leaves, and the devil had tempted her into killing a female slave of mixed blood with the aid of such ingredients.[3] In São João del Rei, in the third quarter of the eighteenth century, Custódia was professed to be a sorceress, though no concrete accusations were lodged against her. The only thing known was that a certain woman had fallen sick after premature childbirth, and when they had gone about "burying the blood of the birth, . . . the said Custódia found herself attending to this burial and had most eagerly asked to do so herself, and that later a bundle of silk or taffeta had been found, which resembled the clothing of the said Custódia, and that in the said bundle a small amount of blood from the same birth had been found, together with fingernail parings, hair, bones, and a spine of a [illegible] coendou [hedgehog]." Everyone suspected the bundle belonged to Custódia.[4] To judge by the arsenal it contained, the young woman most certainly must have been a sorceress: after all, bones, menstrual blood, fingernails, and hair were always tied to spells.[5]

There were more specific spells and *maleficia*, intended to achieve a given end and hurt a certain individual. The same Beatriz Correia who forced the ships in which she traveled to make port sent Fernão Cabral de Taíde "the belly of a fish stuffed with things of sorcery," just to upset him.[6] In the early seventeenth century, the bishop of Brazil, Dom Constantino Barradas, was at constant odds with Governor Diogo de Menezes. The former accused the latter of covering up the offenses and indecency of Maria Barbosa, a woman eventually tried for sorcery in Lisbon. Maria Barbosa paid the bishop back for his hatred in kind: she sought out the old black woman Domingas Velosa, pestering her to arrange "some sorcery or some outright malevolence to kill the bishop." Maria said, "[F]ind me something through which the bishop will get me out of here or make him go to the devil." She also specified what kind of poison she wanted: a certain variety of beans and a small manioc bug, both of which were venomous.[7]

Married to a small farmer, Rita Maria supposedly caused serious disturbances in the district of the Santo Antonio chapel, in Pitangui. She was accused of bewitching the wife of Francisco Fernandes, Quitéria, who had fallen hopelessly ill. When Rita went to visit her, the sick woman's condition worsened dramatically. In despair, Quitéria's husband wanted to murder the alleged sorceress. But they held him back, arguing that "if he killed her, his wife would also die." A black man by the name of Ventura tried some countercharms, but he himself died a few days later, "lamenting that the said sorceress was killing him because he had aided the infirm." The community was terrified by the reach of Rita Maria's powers. Francisco Fernandes, the sick woman's husband, rounded up three men and went to Rita's house on horseback. "Placing her under arrest and leading her out of her house, they said they would kill her if his wife did not heal, for she was having fits and close to death." Rita Maria calmed the husband down, assuring him that Quitéria would not die, which she did not. But Rita left other victims in the community: the daughter of Domingos Ferreira Pacheco and the entire family of Escolástico Vieira Antunes.[8]

Tensions between Neighbors

Denunciations of sorcery often reflected tension between neighbors, acquaintances, enemies. Accused of sorcery by her master's entire family, as will be seen later, Luzia da Silva Soares was also incriminated by a black man named Francisco, who wanted to have "illicit dealings" with her but was unsuccessful in his efforts.[9] As in Europe, petty concerns and village gossip laid the ground for denunciations and the creation of testimonies.[10] Through the collective construction of the witch stereotype, a way was found to settle conflicts within community life, by "identifying and excluding those responsible for misfortunes."[11] One case followed another—like that of Jasmin's witch, to cite just one, rediscovered by Le Roy Ladurie.[12] At the same time, many sorceresses bragged to their neighbors about their powers in order to gain notoriety, attract clients, and eke out an existence. Both situations—when neighbors or acquaintances believed a woman wielded evil powers or when the sorceress made this claim herself—provided a justification for inquisitorial persecutions and created material for Inquiries and Visitations to the colony.[13]

The story of Antonia Maria, mentioned earlier, provides a fine illustration of the link between sorcery and conflicts between neighbors. From the time she had lived in Portugal, this witch upon request had offered up prayers meant to neutralize conflicts. She taught a lovely prayer intended to obtain someone's forgiveness. Holding a bowl of water in her hand, she would say: "The heavens I see, the stars I find, Lady St. Anne, oh what can I do, for I have not yet seen so and so [male] today, nor so and so [female] . . . nor Noah, nor anyone who would give me news of them. Lady St. Anne, as the sea floweth, the heavens shine with stars, and the wind bloweth, and the fishes cannot enter the sea without water, nor the body without soul, so is it that so and so [male] and so and so [female] cannot stay without forgiveness granted." Antonia would then put her mouth to the bowl; strike the ground with three switches from a quince tree; and invoke Barabbas, Satan, Caiaphas, Maria Padilha and all her company, as well as a "seahorse that shall in all haste bring them along their way." She would next toss a bit of altar stone, wolf lip, lavender, *sangue de leão* [lion's blood, a Brazilian plant] and *barbasco* [a plant used to render fish poison] into a boiling pot.[14]

Another example from the realm of conjuration incorporating Catholicism was the following supplication for pardon, also part of Antonia's repertoire: "*Donia* is *Donia,* sweet is God; *Requiem eternam* for the souls and saints, faithful servants of God—God save thee, faithful saints of God; God save thee, save thee God. Those who walk in church plazas and holy places, be they baptized or yet to be, may it please all to gather, and incorporate, and enter unto the hearts of so and so [male], and of so and so [female], and grant her pardon; may eating and drinking and sleeping be gone, and may they call for so and so [male], that he desire to grant forgiveness." When the purpose was to free a prisoner, Antonia's ritual magic would be addressed to the presiding judge. She would first put to boil an animal's heart pierced by three needles and three pins and then place it in a new pot with a bit of vinegar. Next she would recite: "So and so [naming the judge], here I boil thy heart, with all the nerves that are in thy body. With Barabbas, Satan, with Lucifer and his wife, may it please them all to gather and unto thy heart enter so that thou cannot be nor have rest save thou rule in favor of so and so, and all that he shall ask of thee, may it please thee to grant."

Antonia was a veritable repository of prayers. Not only did they reinforce confidence in the medieval church's curative power, but many of these supplications contained mutilated bits of semireligious verses that described episodes in the life of Christ or the saints. "They reflected the ancient belief that mythical events could be a timeless source of supernatural power," as Keith Thomas has pointed out.[15] A model example here is Antonia's formula for seeing an offense pardoned. Standing before a boiling copper pot containing an infusion of vinegar, altar stone, and *barbasco,* she would recite these words:

> When this *barbasco* flowereth, then shall so and so cease to love and want his kin. . . . When this altar stone be consecrated, then shall so and so fail to grant this pardon [and she would throw a chicken's head into the boiler]. . . . When this cock croweth, then shall so and so fail to grant this pardon [and she would stir the mixture with a spoon]. . . . As St. Erasmus's insides were stuck and wound on a sheave, thus shall so and so run and walk to this house [and she would strike three switches from a quince tree on the ground]. . . . Blessed St. Erasmus, I pray thee, may it please thee to grant this to me, and may thou enter unto the heart of so and so, and such tremors may thou bring him and his wife that they will not stop, till this pardon be granted.

In the Maria Padilha prayer above, and in another one likewise seeking pardon for offenses, a new element appears: the emphasis on certain herbs and plants, generally medicinal, employed here in ritual fashion.[16] In the supplications above, lavender and *barbasco* are mentioned; the next prayer makes reference to three green switches that should be gathered in the valley of Lucifer, sharpened on the stone of Barabbas, and stabbed into the heart of the person whose pardon is sought: "With one, thou piercest his life, as such people have their pain and weariness; with another, thou piercest his heart, as such people have their pain and passion; and with the other, thou piercest his soul, as such people have their pain and sorrow." Finally, the souls were urged to gather and incorporate: "Go and fare in these nine days, that I pray thou grant me."

As seen earlier, Antonia Maria was arrested, tried by the Inquisition in Lisbon, and ended up in Pernambuco around 1715, together with another sorceress, Joana de Andrade. She found herself a house on Trincheiras Street, with a yard adjoining that of the 43-year-old mason João Pimentel. This neighbor was married to Bárbara de Mello, but the sorceress's proximity, the adjacency of their houses, and, ultimately, "human weakness" compelled him to have illicit dealings with her, "spending on the said woman his meager earnings." When Bárbara de Mello saw that her husband had lost his head over their neighbor, she began harassing Antonia. Meanwhile, the mason curbed his amorous whims, fearful of his wife's wrath. But Antonia was persistent and started going over to her ex-lover's house on the pretext of visiting Bárbara, who had fallen ill. After Bárbara recovered, she learned from Joana de Andrade that the sorceress Antonia had cast spells at her door to harm not only herself but her husband and household slaves as well. Antonia was particularly interested in doing evil to a young black slave, because her ex-lover had refused to give her the woman as a present. Indeed, the black woman and all the others soon took seriously ill. João Pimentel sought the aid of a Carmelite cleric to exorcise all members of the household. The place was sprinkled with holy water and fumigated with incense. João began "casting forth . . . from his body, out of his *via do curso* [rectum], much of the herb known as sedge, wood shavings, whole human teeth, bones, charcoal, little trees with branches, fish bones, pieces of stone, human hair, and much beach sand; and while the exorcisms were being performed, many stones were thrown, which fell off the roof into the house, and at night it sounded as if goats were running over the roof." His wife and slaves also cast out the same "filth," and they finally rid themselves of the spells only by resorting to purgatives of herbs and roots prepared by a black male *curandeiro*.

In addition to reflecting a conflict between two neighboring women over the love of a man, Antonia's story is indicative of tensions between two sorceresses prompted by mutual jealousy over professional prestige. Antonia and Joana had been friends ever since their days in Portugal. During the course of her trial, perhaps to attenuate her crimes, Antonia stated she had learned everything she knew from Joana de Andrade, in Beja. They had arrived together in Brazil and had resumed their sorcery and divination together as well. But, according to Joana, her friend had gone even further, refining her technique in the colony through the teachings of a skilled sorceress named Páscoa Maria (the colonial world accentuated demoniacal vocations). Joana was resentful of her then-friend's success. Taking deathly ill, she accused Antonia of trying to murder her, because she was fearful of the competition. When Antonia came to visit, Joana said: "Antonia had already seen what she wanted, which was to see her dead because she was robbing her of her livelihood." Indeed, before getting sick and ultimately dying, Joana had worked as a counter-sorceress against Antonia's spells. Joana had informed on her to Bárbara de Mello and had attempted to undo the maleficent magic she claimed her friend had performed against the mason's family. Antonia never forgave this meddling in her affairs: she paid Joana back by killing her.[17]

Infanticide

Tensions also manifested themselves in the form of infanticide, actual or imagined. In Europe, one of the most generalized witch-beliefs was that these women murdered children. In the south of France, it was believed they suffocated babies in the cradle and that an infant's body would bleed when a witch passed by.[18] Infanticide was the crime with which the witches of Logroño were most frequently charged.[19] Those sent to the stake in Lisbon in 1559 had gone about murdering children at the devil's orders.[20] In the seventeenth century, in the duchy of Luxembourg, a great many children died due to their own parents' neglect, since both had to work to support the family. References to consequent accidents were often cold and hard: "a one florin fine for a child destroyed by a pig."[21] During a time of crisis, blaming this kind of death on witches was perhaps a way of alleviating stress and assuaging guilt.[22]

The terror of infanticide lingered on in the popular mentality. Sick, rachitic children were thought to have been sucked by witches.[23] The soles of old shoes were burned to drive these witches away, and unsheathed swords were hung at the heads of cribs.[24]

In the late sixteenth century, the gypsy Joana Ribeira was accused by the Visitation to Bahia of bewitching a child through a magical procedure based on what certain authors have called the *law of similarity*.[25] Joana had gone to visit a gypsy friend in her child-bed. The infant had been born with its head wrapped in the afterbirth, and Joana had taken it home and salted it. The newborn started to get sick "and to turn black, and some thirty days suffered thus, without suckling nor opening its mouth, and wasting away, unable even to cry." The mother then remembered the afterbirth and Joana Ribeira. She went to Joana's house, opened a chest, and "found the said afterbirth made into a ball salted with church salt left over from the baptism." The infant died.[26]

It was common to link nursing problems and the infanticide practiced by witches. Among the evil talents attributed to witches in Gaul was the ability to dry up a mother's milk.[27] In Pernambuco at the close of the sixteenth century, Isabel Antunes had been bedridden for six days after giving birth to a baby girl, when through her door walked a woman she knew only by sight and who was said to be a sorceress. It was Ana Jácome, a cross-eyed, husbandless woman. The newborn was lying near Isabel Antunes, and in the bed next to her was a 3-year-old slave. The stranger approached and said: "If thou dost not want the witches to come into thy house, take a table and turn it with its legs pointed upward, and a trivet with its feet turned upward as well, and with your broom atop, all behind the door." She went up to the little *mulata* girl and murmured: "Thou, godchild, hast lived, whilst my daughter hath died." She then spat three times all over the bed and went out the door, saying: "Now stay ye." The new mother and the slave girl were immediately stricken with fever and the chills; the baby, which had not yet been baptized and "had always been of good health and suckled well, began to cry loudly, and succoring the child, they found it to be hexed, with its mouth sucked in both corners, with a black spot with bite marks in each corner of the mouth, and on its groin too another suck mark and black spot on both sides." The baby never again nursed, "nor could it take anything into its mouth." Baptized at home, the child cried incessantly till it could no longer open its mouth, and then it died.[28]

Ana Jácome's story meshes with similar reports from Europe and seems to belong to one of the groups of stereotyped witch-beliefs. In the early seventeenth century, in the south of France, the sorceress Marie de Sansarric breathed into the mouth of a small child, hexing it; never again was it able to speak or shed tears, and it died some time afterward.[29] Using their sight, touch, or breath, the Portuguese witches burned at the stake in 1559 would leave a child "so dazed and poisoned that it no longer suckled and died in a few days."[30] The demons of Logroño sucked small children "by their nature" (genitals), leaving them feeble; they would squeeze them "fiercely with their hands and suck them hard."[31] Sucking blood was also said to be a practice of Yoruba sorceresses in twentieth-century Nigeria.[32]

In eighteenth-century Minas, in the region of Ouro Preto, Florência do Bonsucesso seduced "some men into using her in an evil way." For this purpose she kept "a shriveled child at home, wherefrom she removed dry meat and reduced it to powder to use in her sorceries."[33] Luzia da Silva Soares, a sorceress who lived in the *arraial* of Antonio Pereira, had learned a number of magical practices from the black man Mateus, who carried round with him "a shriveled child whom he had hexed, kept in a shepherd's leather bag" for use in spell-making.[34] In the collective imagination, these mummified children were the very embodiment of society's fears of infanticide by witches.

Tensions between Master and Slave

Among many other crimes, Luzia was accused of killing two of her mistress's children. She had used the brains of one to prepare a porridge or potion to make her boss sick.[35] But Luzia da Silva Soares's practice of infanticide illuminates yet another facet of the matter: the tensions between master and slave. This was not the death of just any child but of children belonging to the master's family.

As seen in earlier chapters, demoniacal traits had been attributed to Brazil ever since its discovery. Indigenous peoples, blacks, and, later on, the settlers were viewed as a race of demons. Settlers who were also slave-owners—and who, beginning in the eighteenth century, would be seen as potential demons with a penchant for rebellion—often had a demonized view of their captives. Concomitantly, slavery itself pushed slaves toward demonization. Bastide has shown how, through slavery, "African culture ceased to be the communal culture of a global society and became the exclusive culture of a social class, of one distinct group in Brazilian society—a class that was economically exploited and socially subordinated."[36] In this context, maleficent magic or sorcery became a *necessity* for a society based on slavery. It not only furnished weapons with which the slaves could wage a silent battle against their masters (quite often the only battle possible); it also legitimized repression of and violence against these captives. Keith Thomas documents how the inhabitants of sixteenth-century English villages committed acts of extreme violence against sorceresses, believing they could in this way undo the spell.[37] In Brazil, this belief in the redemptive, purifying power of physical violence found a powerful ally in slavery's need for exemplary punishment. Slaves could be punished for legitimate reasons since they were also sorcerers. Seeing them as sorcerers was in turn an expression of the paranoia of the masters.

The association between sorcery and punishment appears in the very early days of colonization. Brandônio tells us that he had a *mulata* slave of whom he was very fond. She once informed him about a theft by a male slave said to be a sorcerer. The girl then fell gravely ill: she gasped for air, rolled her eyes, ground her teeth, and foamed at the mouth. Her master soon concluded that the sorcerer was the author of the *maleficia* vexing the slave girl. He summoned the alleged sorcerer, "stating to him that he would have no longer life than that which the girl enjoyed" and stating further that if he did not lift the spell, "he would be passed through the mill shafts." Terrified, the slave "agreed to cure the sick girl," asking only for permission to go into the woods to pick some special herbs. Zealously wishing to control everything that happened within the realm of his plantation, Brandônio told a trusted slave to follow the herbalist and discover which herb would be used as an antidote. "But the other was so sly that, with the intent thereby to protect against this, he gathered many and diverse herbs, amongst which he included that of which he had need." So the spy was unable to ascertain the proper herb for such cases. Once administered to the sick girl, the herb did its job; she soon reacted, opening her mouth and eyes, "purging greatly below and above."[38]

Masters were thus taking precautions against their slaves' magical powers from early on. Their fears lasted as long as slavery. In the early eighteenth century, in Pernambuco's parish of Santo Amaro do Jaboatão, Captain José Carneiro wanted to keep his distance from his slave Marcos; he did not like to see the boy in his house and had in fact relocated him to a different farm, because rumor had it he was a sorcerer.[39] José Francisco's master "did not wish his Negroes to use any prayers, for he was afraid that they were mandinga." He must have punished them harshly for this practice, because a frightened José Francisco threw out all the pouches he carried with him.[40]

Expressing a still incipient tension concerning their masters, the slaves attempted to deliver themselves from castigation by using spells. Although mutual accusations of sorcery at times reflected friction among the slaves themselves, they also served as an escape route to avoid possible punishment. Luís da Silva was a slave in a house where Luzia da Silva Soares lived.

His foot swelled up after he stepped on a thorn while stealing corn in the field. Afraid to confess this deed to his masters, he accused Luzia of putting a hex on him.[41] Many slaves in Minas believed that "the wheat root that grew in the swamps" had the power to save them from punishment.[42] Others, like the black man Manuel da Piedade, would scrape the soles of their masters' shoes to avert beatings.[43] Marcelina Maria, who had been born in Rio but went to live in Lisbon while still young, kept the scrapings from her mistress's shoe soles wrapped in two small bits of paper. When the moon came out, Marcelina would make three crosses in the moonlight, place the papers between her legs, and go to sleep like that; afterward she would store them "in the tuck of her skirt." She changed masters quite often and always abhorred bondage and punishment. In despair, she at times "desired to be sold to the Brazils," land of her birth. Her mistresses were jealous of Marcelina and their husbands, who in turn were jealous of the boyfriends Marcelina would arrange to meet on occasion. One of her masters, João Eufrásio,

> due to receiving news . . . that she was the mistress of a Negro house slave, ordered her to strip naked, tied her hands, one Negro taking hold of her, and another flogging her, and the most shameful for her was that she saw herself unclothed before six or seven men, one of whom was the said master of hers, and his eldest son, seeking to know from her, by means of this harsh punishment, how many times she had copulated with the said Negro man, who was present as well and was also flogged at the same time and on the same occasion.[44]

Sortilege involving shavings from soles or ground trod upon by the intended victim was also common among European populations. In the early seventeenth century, the Portuguese sorceress Maria Cebreira was accused of bewitching people by taking earth from beneath their feet.[45] Under France's ancien régime, people were advised to spit in their right shoe before putting it on in order to ward off *maleficia*.[46] It is hard to tell whether this was likewise a current practice among African populations or if slaves like Manuel and Marcelina had picked it up while living in a European city. In any case, it is interesting to note that when employed by captives it took on a new connotation: it was meant to ward off the punishments inherent in the slave system. Once again, the colony recast magical practices and endowed them with a singularly colonial meaning.

At a second level of tension, sorcery and magical practices were a way for slaves to get out of the system without destroying it. This option could be paternalistic in nature. For example, when called upon by Catarina Pereira da Matta, Friar Luís de Nazaré (whose name appeared earlier) cooked pig's blood, cut the pork into pieces, and went to throw it all at the door of Catarina's husband with a view to obtaining the freedom of a slave named Inácio.[47] The slave José Francisco, who also resided in Lisbon, performed spells at the behest of other slaves to obtain their freedom. Sought out by

Antonio, who wanted his foreign-born master to sell him, José Francisco asked Antonio to "bring him, from the house wherein he gave assistance to the said master, a small amount of rubbish . . . , and to scrape the sole of his shoes, and to bring some phlegm of his." He mixed it all together with a bit of sulfur, mashed it, and put it in a small cloth bag, "which, cooked, he gave to the said Negro, telling him to bury it next to the door through which his master entered." Three days later, he should dig up the bag and keep it, and soon after he would be sold. José Francisco was also called upon by four black men who wanted a prayer that would enable them to open a certain door; inside the house they would find a great deal of money, with which they intended to buy their freedom and "some things needed for their use." A letter was supposed to be drawn up in the terms of a diabolic contract that would hand their souls over to the devil, but it was never written. In his state of delirium under torture (which will be analyzed later), José Francisco told how he had counted on the devil's aid to free himself from captivity.[48]

At a third level, slaves could turn against their masters' property, initiating a more direct kind of protest against the slave system. Gratuitously—or rather because "the demon had tempted her"—the Mina slave Joana killed a slave belonging to her mistress, Dona Maria de Sá Cavalcante, in Conceição do Mato Dentro.[49] Another Joana, slave at the Nossa Senhora de Guadalupe sugar plantation in the state of Pará, raised a knife against her mistress. Such attitudes led the second Joana's masters to keep a careful eye on her. During interrogations meant to ascertain the slave's guilt, her masters said that "she does not have a very good nature and is fond of doing and saying evil." Their distrust had prompted them to warn the indigenous slave Filipa Josefa to be wary of Joana. But when Joana offered Filipa a gourd full of the delicacy *tacacá*, "which is the juice of manioc roots," plus three stewed fish, the Indian could not resist. That very same night, "she began, with a series of vomitings, to spew from her mouth a most great abundance of blood." Her masters first punished Joana on their own. They must have tortured her (though no specific mention is made of this in the records), and they put her in the stocks. When they decided to take her to the town jail, in effect shifting the matter into public hands, the unfortunate woman had to be carried on her husband's back, "for she was unable to walk on her own feet, due to being hobbled by the long time she had spent in the stocks." Once in the clutches of the Inquisition, she confessed that because of her masters' constant punishments, she had decided to arm herself as best she could. She had learned sortilege using roots of the *cipó picão* vine, with which she rubbed her wrists in the form of a cross, saying: "Master *paitinga* [literally, white father], as thou hast wrath against me, so shalt thou warm thy heart." Whenever she went to speak to her master, she would place a piece of this vine under her tongue to protect herself. She had grown to hate Filipa because this other slave was "very attentive to her master," and so she accused Filipa of doing evil and provoking punishments against her. She put *tajá* roots in Filipa's food to poison her.[50]

Joana attacked one of her master's slaves, thus repaying her punishments by causing monetary damages. But she also wanted to kill her mistress. Luzia da Silva Soares, the sorceress from Antonio Pereira, performed generalized witchcraft against her master's whole family. Among the many accusations hurled at Luzia were that she had hexed gold-mining operations so they would produce no more and that she wanted to see the master's entire family dead so she could take over the plantation herself.[51] Crimes against the master's property mingled with crimes against the physical safety of the master and his family, perhaps constituting the most direct contestation of slavery through recourse to sorcery. A cause of much worry for masters, suicide itself was a crime against their property. Antonil astutely perceived the close relationship between murder and suicide and always made references to them together: if "punishment be frequent and excessive," the Jesuit said, "either the slaves shall leave, fleeing into the woods, or shall kill themselves, as they are accustomed to doing, smothering themselves or hanging themselves, or they shall try to take the lives of those who treat them so ill, resorting (if need be) to the *diabolical arts.*" Captured in *mocambos* in the woods where they fled, "it may be that they shall kill themselves, before their master flogs them *or before some relative of theirs takes vengeance into his hands, either through sorcery or through poison.*"[52]

In situations of extreme despair, masters were murdered, shaking the slave structure through violence that was often spontaneous and not always conscious. The black woman Josefa would wash her nether parts and put the water in her masters' food to do them harm.[53] She lived in Minas, like the Coura slave by the name of Quitéria, who in the mid-eighteenth century had performed spells on her mistress and left her on her deathbed. Under punishment, Quitéria "had confessed that a Negro man, José Mina, slave to Gabriel Gonçalves, had given them to her to place in her mistress's food, and in her bed as well."[54] Another Minas resident, the same Joana mentioned earlier (who succumbed to the devil's temptation to kill female co-workers), ended up making her mistress Maria de Sá Cavalcante a widow.[55]

Although it really only came into existence in the early eighteenth century, Minas Gerais had always led other regions of Brazil when it came to clashes between masters and slaves involving magical practices and sorcery. It outranked Bahia, where the slave population was even greater in number, undoubtedly because the slave system in Minas was more complex and existed within a more extensively urbanized environment.[56] Conflicts erupted there constantly, upsetting the gold-rich *arraiais*. The greatest concentration of *quilombos* could probably be found in Minas Gerais during the colonial period.[57] The African cultural complex was also best preserved there, as will be seen shortly.

Mandinga Pouches

In terms of magical practices and sorcery, colonial tensions found their most consistent expression in *bolsas de mandinga,* also known as *patuás.* It can even be said that these mandinga pouches were the most typically colonial form of sorcery in Brazil: first, because of their popularity and the broad extent of their use. From northern to southern Brazil, people of the most varied social ranks (admittedly, almost always men) would carry them. Therein lies the second argument: use of these bags was not unique to one segment of society, though they were widely employed by slaves. Third, they were perhaps the most syncretic of all magical practices and forms of sorcery utilized by Brazilians, a unique fusion of European, African, and indigenous cultural habits that combined the European tradition of amulets with Amerindian fetishism and the customs of African populations. Finally, they were typical of the eighteenth century, with no mention of their use during the First and Second Visitations; the first reference to them dates to the late seventeenth century, while all others come only in the eighteenth century. This information is of marked significance since amulets were an age-old custom and in the previous two centuries the Brazilian colonists would have been familiar with them. Why then did the habit of carrying these little pouches become widespread only in the eighteenth century? Perhaps the answer is that it takes time to construct a syncretic practice with a highly symbolic meaning. The time that it took for the use of mandinga pouches to become widespread was, curiously enough, the same time taken to construct a colonial mentality, that is, the perception of what Luís dos Santos Vilhena was to call "living in colonies."[58]

Mandinga pouches seem to have been most popular in northern Brazil, that is, in the regions corresponding to the states of Grão-Pará and Maranhão. Yet it is hard to know whether they were really more common in this region or whether this was merely apparently the case, since the only eighteenth-century Visitation of which there is any knowledge took place in the north. The seventeenth-century mention of the bags noted earlier involved a barber from this region. Manuel João, originally from Maranhão, moved to his grandfather's house in Grão-Pará at the age of sixteen. Accused of being superstitious, a sorcerer, and a devil conjurer, Manuel was found wearing one of these pouches round his neck when he was arrested on May 9, 1668. The *ouvidor* had the pouch removed and inside it discovered a paper with the Our Lady of Montserrat prayer (found in the sepulcher in Jerusalem), intended to ward off danger, with "four marked rules" on it; a piece of torn paper; a crumpled paper containing many pieces of Agnus Dei; some garlic; two stalks of rue; and a bone the size of a fingertip, wrapped in a paper "and appearing to belong to some dead man, for the paper wherein it was wrapped had a spot, whereby it appeared that the bone had been wrapped in it still fresh."[59]

From the late Middle Ages, fashioning amulets had been considered one of a sorcerer's main activities. In *Decretorum libri,* Burchard of Worms censured the use of herbs, magical words, and pieces of wood or stones and condemned both those who made amulets and those who asked others to do so for them, with the intention of wearing them sewn into their clothing or attached to their bodies.[60] Cesarius of Arles likewise condemned use of so-called characters: pieces of wood, stone, metal, fabric, or parchment covered with signs. In 813 the Third Council of Tours banned carrying about on one's person the bones of dead animals and charmed herbs.[61] Shortly before that, St. Boniface had listed the works of the devil: magical filters, charms and sortilege, the belief in witches and werewolves, the practice of abortion, disobedience to masters, and carrying amulets on one's person.[62] Known as *ligaduras,* amulets attached to the body—on the arm, leg, or neck—were believed to safeguard against illness and accidents.[63] Manuel João had thus committed an offense defined centuries before. But he found himself in the company of some illustrious individuals: in 1597 Elizabeth I gave the earl of Essex a coin from the time of Edward III to protect him during his expedition to the Azores.[64] Manuals popular under the ancien régime explained how to make talismans.[65] Europeans resisted the ban on them: "Why is it that using a key of St. Peter, namely, the key from a church dedicated to St. Peter, which must be placed on the back to protect against wrath, is condemned as superstitious, while carrying round an Agnus Dei, clothes of the Virgin, or scapulars is encouraged as protection against all disease?" asks François Lebrun.[66] Why was the use of scapulars accepted, while the use of mandinga pouches was rejected in colonial Brazil?

Both talismans and mandinga pouches can be considered part of what Étienne Delcambre classifies as the "law of contact."[67] In terms of magic, it was believed that beneficial fluids emanated from the objects inside the bag or from the talisman itself. The Mandinga or Malinkê were the people that inhabited one of the Muslim kingdoms in the Niger valley in the eighth century, the kingdom of Mali. In Brazil, this name became transformed into Malê. In Rio as well as Bahia, Malê were considered masters of black magic.[68] It was their habit to wear amulets around their necks, containing Solomon's seals or bits of paper with verses from the Koran.[69] It is hard to tell whether it was really the Malê who introduced mandinga pouches to the colony. But it is interesting to note that in the eighteenth century, for a series of reasons, the expression *bolsa de mandinga*—which was linked to the colonial system and to the Africans who were forced to serve as colonial slaves—came to refer to a specific kind of talisman that blended European, African, and, in a certain way, indigenous practices as well.

In the eighteenth century, the earliest references to these pouches come from Pernambuco. While not describing the object as a mandinga pouch, Antonia Maria's trial narrates how this sorceress gave out bags of wolf lip and altar stone so that whoever carried them would be successful in buying and selling. A prayer went along with the bag: "Altar stone, Altar stone, that was found in the sea, and consecrated on land, as the bishops and archbishops, friars and clerics, cannot say mass without thee, so be it that all creatures that shall touch me cannot be without me, and shall give me all that they have, and shall tell me all that they know, and shall desire to buy all my fabric, and where I am shall no one else be able to sell, nor to buy."[70] About ten years after Antonia was tried, another Recife resident, who lived on Água Verde Street, used a pouch to "seal his body" [*fechar o corpo*]. His informer was the licentiate Caetano da Silveira, in whose home the following episode occurred. João de Siqueira Varejão Castelo Branco, the accused, "had said that nothing of iron could enter him, and he showed him a large pouch that he hung round his neck." When the licentiate expressed skepticism, João de Siqueira called a house slave—"a person of small wit"—and "cast the pouch about his neck, and wanted to plunge a sword through him, to which the Denouncer did not consent, but said that in such things he did not believe, and at the Denouncer's many pleas he removed the pouch." But still João de Siqueira did not give up trying to prove his talisman's powers. He hung the bag around his own neck, laid the sword on the licentiate's bookshelf, and, "placing the point at his left breast, with fury and wrath he pushed himself onto the sword, which curved but did not in any wise harm him, and he soon became angry, and wrathful." Inside the bag there were some "communion cloths and purificators, and other little things."[71]

By the first quarter of the eighteenth century, the union of the mandinga pouch with sacred elements had been defined. The altar stone was a piece of marble with an opening where relics of holy martyrs were placed and over which priests consecrated the communion host and wine. It possessed great magical meaning, for it was indispensable to the mystery of the Eucharist. The *Constituições primeiras do Arcebispado da Bahia* referred to it as a "portable altar" because whenever a cleric said mass other than at the church altar, he was supposed to bring the altar stone with him and place it upon a table, where mass would be celebrated.[72] In the European popular mentality, the altar stone's significance must have intermingled not only with that of the stones of virtue from the tradition of marvels—which only the best knight could approach—but also with a whole gamut of holy stones: Roman ones, used to delimit the boundaries of provinces and private properties, and barbarian ones, revered by Germanic peoples.[73] As to people who carried bits of altar stones to bring them luck—such as the Portuguese witch Dona Paula Tereza de Miranda Souto Maior, mentioned earlier—it was recommended that they not wear them during mass.[74] Despite this appreciation of the stone's religious significance, the tendency was to turn it inside out—that is, its magical meaning was simultaneously a product of its religious meaning and of its negation. For Mandrou, the tendency to invert church rites constituted an indication of the devil's intervention in human life, manifesting itself not only in the sabbat—an inverted mass—but also in the sorcery derived from these rites, at times resorted to even by priests.[75]

A *sanguinho,* or purificator, was a thin piece of napkin-shaped cloth that priests used to wipe off the chalice after consecrating the wine into Christ's blood. It was usually kept in the sacristy after mass, and stealing it was like having the blood of Jesus.[76]

Something that would later become a mandatory feature of these mandinga pouches was already appearing in Pernambuco: pieces of paper or letters where prayers and cabalistic signs were mixed together. Antonio José Barreto carried one of these in his pocket, with an inverted creed, an Ave Maria, a "sign of Solomon," and words supposed to defend him from armed fights and to ensure him numerous friendships.[77] Often engraved on the doorways of Portuguese houses to ward off the evil eye, the sign of Solomon or *saimão* traced its roots to ancient traditions.[78] This six-pointed star had been widely used in ritual magic and conjuration during the Middle Ages.[79] From the early days of Christianity, using the name and writings of Solomon in certain magical practices and amulets was a common practice, as attested by Origenes. Over time these were replaced by verses from the Gospel and by the relics of saints, as St. Jerome observed women doing in the Christian communities of Palestine.[80] In the popular mentality and within the realm of magical practices, however, the Solomonic tradition maintained its allure over the centuries, reaching colonial lands.

One very curious fact about the mandinga pouches is that much of our information on them comes from trials involving slaves residing in Lisbon. In the first quarter of the eighteenth century, Lisbon's population included a substantial black contingent. Many of the Portuguese government employees brought their captives back with them when they returned to the metropolis. Large numbers of black Africans consequently roamed the streets of Lisbon, having first lived on the Atlantic islands or in various captaincies of Brazil; others had only stopped at these places along their way, as the slave ships carried them to the Kingdom. Some saw their stay in Portugal as temporary and longed to return to Africa or Brazil. The fact that they circulated in the midst of the colonial system, disseminating African cultural values and (among other magical practices) the use of these bags, again underscores the uniquely colonial character of these practices.

Although there was a close link between the colonial universe and these pouches, their use was not limited to slaves and settlers. Many whites born and raised in the metropolis soon took up the custom. In 1700 Manuel Lopes, cabin boy and son of a tavern-keeper from Batalha, was condemned on presumptive evidence of a pact and for carrying a pouch. In 1711 it was the turn of Francisco Xavier, *ajudante de auxiliares* [militia adjutant] from Galvêas. But greatest usage was observed among slaves and settlers. In 1704 Jacques Viegas, a black man born on the Mina coast and a resident of Lisbon, was accused of carrying one of these pouches; his trial ended in an auto-da-fé. In 1714 the same thing occurred with Francisco Lourenço de Vasconcelos, a white man born in Angola. Two years later, the freedman Diogo Lopes Pereira, originally from Cape Verde, met with a similar fate.[81]

In the early eighteenth century, use of these pouches gradually defined itself through these interactions involving Portugal, Brazil, and Africa. Although the practice was adopted on both sides of the Atlantic, it would gradually come to be associated with Brazil, where it was to achieve final form under the name *bolsa de mandinga* or mandinga pouch.

In August 1731 Miguel Vieira, apprentice to a tinsmith, went of his own accord before the Board of the Holy Office to denounce a black slave named Mateus. The story seems to omit some facts. The denouncer, son of a deceased commissary in Brazil, had run into Mateus one night at the door of his house. Mateus gave him a pouch and asked him to keep it for him. Miguel did not open the bag and had no idea what it contained; he nevertheless put it away in a box until one day, following the advice of his neighbor, a priest, and of a young man named João, he decided to take the pouch to the Board of the Inquisition and lodge a denunciation. He finished his narrative by stating that Mateus had earlier asked him to transcribe a prayer of Our Lady of Montserrat, which he did without ever knowing what purpose it would serve. He stressed that he had acted innocently in regard to both the bag and the prayer.[82] The denunciation makes no reference to the bag's contents.

To my knowledge, three of the most complete trials involving mandinga pouches occurred in the years 1730 and 1731. Two of these were related, as the defendants were friends and had acted together. As to the third man, although it seems quite likely he had contact with the first two, there is not enough information to confirm this. The third man was Manuel da Piedade, a slave to Captain Gaspar de Valadares who had been born in the city of Bahia and later become a resident of eastern Lisbon. He was arrested in March 1730, one year after a number of slaves in Coimbra had denounced him as a *mandingueiro*. His accusers included Luís de Lima, Antonio Criança, José Luís, Sebastião Rocha, and Ventura Ramos, most of who were from western Africa's Mina coast. Shortly after his trial began, Manuel da Piedade confessed that he carried a prayer of the Just Judge in his pocket, which afforded protection against the dangers of the sea and of beatings. In common use in Brazil, it had been given to him by a young man when he lived in Bahia. He had later resided in Pernambuco, Porto, Vila de Viana, Esposende, Braga, and finally Lisbon, where he ended up after fleeing from his master. The strongest accusation against him was that he sold the ingredients needed for mandinga pouches, which he prepared with the devil's assistance in the countryside near the cities where he lived. One of these ingredients was a certain prayer whose efficacy depended upon its being placed under an altar stone, where three masses should be celebrated.[83]

The other two black men were José Francisco Pereira and José Francisco Pedroso, slaves to two brothers, João Francisco Pedroso and Domingos Francisco Pedroso, respectively. In this case the intellectual mentor for the sorcery was José Francisco Pereira, while the other slave simply carried out his orders. Both of them had the habit of placing prayers beneath altar stones, like Manuel da Piedade, and of making mandinga pouches for sale. The slave Pedroso named a number of his customers, who always had some kind of tie to Brazil: José, "who lives in Remolares, slave to a man who came from Rio de Janeiro on the last fleet"; "Francisco, slave to Matias da Guerra, who lived in Jesus, and was already deceased, which Negro embarked with a fleet from Bahia to Maranhão"; "the Negro Antonio, slave to a cleric, who lives in the woods of Alcântara, and also has houses in Confeitaria, and was sold to Pernambuco"; "a Negro named Miguel, slave to the bishop's assistant in São Paulo, and who was sold to Bahia"; "Ventura, last name unknown, slave to Paulo Rodrigues, understood to be a businessman, resident across the street from the Casa da Moeda, and [who] went to Rio de Janeiro." All of these and other black men from Alfama, whom Pedroso was unable to name, "had purchased mandingas from the said Negro José at the time of the fleet."[84]

Pedroso had lived for some time in Rio, where he had been baptized and confirmed and had first heard of mandingas, "and that they served well to protect from knife slashes." As soon as he arrived from the colony, Pereira was badgered by black men asking him for mandingas: "Since he . . . had a short time before come from Brazil, many Negroes beleaguered him . . . so that he would give them mandingas, for he must have brought some from there."[85] For slaves who lived in the metropolis, and for the inquisitors as well, Brazil was a demoniacal land where sorcery flourished. One of the mandinga ingredients prepared by the two friends was a root that the demon gave them "so that, when they tarried in the house, their masters would not beat them." They did not know what plant it was, only that it "smelled much, and comes from Brazil."[86]

The pouches were made of cloth, almost always white, and were basically intended to protect their bearers from knife or gunshot wounds. They contained flint stones, onyx, sulfur, gunpowder, a lead bullet, a silver vintém, a dead man's bone, and the famous writings that were supposed to have spent time under an altar stone. The papers were covered with letters and figures written with the blood of a white or sometimes black chicken or else with the blood of José Francisco's own left arm. The prayer of St. Mark was also included: "O glorious St. Mark, St. Mark mark thee, Jesus Christ soothe thee, St. Manso [literally, St. Gentle] calm thee, the Holy Spirit humble thee, my St. Mark, glorious saint, I ask thee that my blood not be spilled nor my strength be taken nor my enemies encountered, by the power of God the Father, God the Son, and God the Holy Ghost, that if my enemies have eyes, that they not see me, and if they have mouths, that they not speak to me, by the power of Lucifer, at all times be with me, where I encounter my enemies." An acquaintance of José Francisco Pereira would copy out the prayers since the slave was illiterate. Once ready, the bag was fumigated with incense. Sometimes the contents were buried at midnight and then dug up before being placed in the bag. On St. John's Night, the sorcerer would place the bags under the bonfire to render them more efficacious.[87]

In 1743 numerous people came before the Board of the Inquisition in Lisbon to denounce the slave Antonio Mascarenhas as a *mandingueiro*. The accused eventually presented himself and confessed to engaging in magical practices. He had been born in Angola but had left there when still a child and had gone to Funchal, in Madeira. He had also spent time in Rio de Janeiro, the island of São Miguel, Lisbon, and Mazagão. Some nine years earlier, in Rio de Janeiro, he had learned of mandinga pouches from a ship captain's slave, who had given him "a letter that he said was from a mandinga, with diverse figures painted in red ink, whereupon there was an image of Christ Our Lord crucified, and an ugly figure that resembled the face of a person, and many other things in the way of trivets and gridirons, and more figures." The letter would safeguard its bearer from fights and rows and prevent injuries. With it in hand, Antonio returned to Madeira, where he gave it to the student Antonio da Silva for transcription. The student copied the writing and also taught him that "for the mandinga to be most strong, he must place it between the altar stone and altar cloth so that mass would be said upon it."[88] Notions about mandinga pouches and the letters placed inside them were therefore circulating around the Portuguese colonial system in the eighteenth century. But their paternity was always assigned to the Brazilian colony.

In the mid-eighteenth century, use of mandinga pouches had become prevalent in Bahia. In Vila de Cachoeira, in 1749, Miguel Moniz, *pardo,* was arrested at the order of the district's *ouvidor geral* [superior magistrate]. In his house, inside a basket, he had found a "small bundle, with two covers, one of flaxen cloth, the other of fine cotton sewn around, wherein was held a little bundle of black hairs that appeared to be of an animal, tied with a string of white thread, half a sheet of wrapped paper written in block and, inside of this, some powders with beads of quicksilver and other hairs." They also found a half-sheet of paper "written along a border, and a fourth sheet also written on one part, which contained prayers with strange words in honor of saints." Although his name was inscribed on these papers, Miguel denied having anything to do with them. He claimed that he had no idea what they were all about and that they had arrived inside the basket, unbeknownst to him. He was removed to the Salvador jail and eventually released, in April 1750, receiving pardon along with other prisoners on Good Friday.[89] At no time did the secular or ecclesiastical authorities refer to a mandinga, although this was the object described. Was it possible they were unfamiliar with the term?

Around 1750 three friends, all of them slaves, were arrested in Jacobina for using mandinga pouches. Their stories are intertwined: they had all traveled together to Portugal, shared time in prison, and probably appeared in the same auto-da-fé, although the Inquisition found them guilty at different levels. Their names were Luís Pereira de Almeida, twenty, slave to Dona Antonia Pereira de Almeida, residing at her small farm in Riachão; Mateus Pereira Machado, fifteen, slave to Veríssimo Pereira Machado, residing in the countryside of Vila de Cachoeira and assistant at Vila de Jacobina; and José Martins, twenty-six, a black freedman, son of freed black parents, married, born and residing in Riachão, at the small farm called "Joana de Andrade." José Martins's father had given him a mandinga pouch meant to instill bravery; it contained prayers in the Holy Name of Jesus and of St. Cyprian, along with a purificator and altar stone. Some time later, José sold it to Mateus, who gave him a dog in exchange.[90] All indications are that Mateus had another pouch, holding not only an altar stone and purificator but bits of a paschal candle, a consecrated host, an inverted creed, and the following words:

> So say I . . . that the sea shall give me its fleets, Jesus Christ, His power: O, my altar stone, that in the sea hath been created, and on land found, in Rome confirmed, I ask thee and pray thee by the seven virgin maids, by the seven godmothers, by the seven married women, by the seven devout women, by the seven bishops, and by the seven archbishops, and as the Supreme Pontiffs cannot celebrate mass without thee, I ask thee and pray thee by the seven hanged men, by the seven [illegible] men, by the seven men shot down by a strong man that is Barabbas, and Satan, and Caiaphas, and Lucifer that is my king, my duke, prince of my battles, victor of the army, that all these shall be in my favor and aid in my intent, and [illegible] me [illegible] . . . winds like a soldier in the field.[91]

Luís, however, was not really an advocate of mandinga pouches, although he was arrested and tried in Lisbon. His offense was keeping one of Mateus's bags for a while.[92] It is the words of Luís—as reported by José Martins—that reveal the scope of this custom among Bahian blacks. The two friends had been talking about the seizure of one of the bags when Luís revealed to José that it held small consecrated hosts. "We are lost," said a distressed José. His friend calmed him by saying that, after all, numerous blacks carried such hosts around in bags.[93]

José Fernandes, a free *pardo*, widower, and shoemaker, also ended up in an inquisitorial prison because he used a mandinga pouch. He stole a small host from mass and carried it around, along with superstitious prayers, "for the indecent purpose of warding off dangers and not being harmed by any weapon." A week later, repentant, he swallowed the communion wafer and prayed an act of contrition. In a palm tree in the woods he hid the cloth in which the wafer had been wrapped, but he kept the bag round his neck. His reason for resorting to the pouch was a little different from that of so many fellow Bahians. The widower had fallen in love with a married woman and was having an affair with her. His beloved had begun to ask him to kill her husband, who in turn was going around saying he would kill the rival courting his wife. José Fernandes turned to the amulet's powers in hopes of acquiring strength to resist the temptation of adultery, while at the same time it made him feel safer, with his body "sealed."[94]

During the course of the eighteenth century, the use of mandinga pouches became better defined and more complex. Paschal candles and communion wafers were also utilized in Europe. Around the sixth century, Eucharist bread was stolen for use in apotropaic rites and magical practices in general.[95] Six centuries later, Hugh of St. Victor accused sorcerers of using baptismal water and holy chrism oils in the making of amulets.[96] In fourteenth-century Ireland, Lady Alice Kyteler kept in her closet a "wafer of sacramental bread which was said to be stamped with the Devil's name."[97] One century later, the *Constituições do Arcebispado de Lisboa* condemned use of the consecrated host and holy chrism oils in the preparation of spells.[98] In early modern Spain, Rodrigo de Reynosa's "Coplas de las comadres" leaves a record of the use of wax from paschal candles to "make spells and things for romantic purposes."[99] Communion wafers were stolen to make ointments under France's ancien régime.[100] In 1651, in a village in the duchy of Luxembourg, a poor woman stole the host lying on the altar and ate it, thereafter bleeding greatly from the mouth and nose. She was eventually burned at the stake. Her sacrilege was punished, but word spread of the miracle, which was nevertheless exalted—"as superstitions indeed are repressed, while the worship of saints and the veneration of relics are exalted," in the words of Marie-Sylvie Dupont-Bouchat.[101]

There had thus been a long-standing tradition of employing the communion wafer as a magical element that lent strength and supernatural powers, sealing the body against acts of aggression. But it was only around the mid-eighteenth century that the tradition took firm root in the colony, merging with practices already in place, such as the use of papers covered with signs from ritual magic and the utilization of altar stones, purificators, and other ornaments from mass. Perhaps one day it can be clarified why certain practices preceded others. For now, my concern is to show how they gradually became interwoven and overlapped, ultimately constituting a magical procedure singularly colonial in character.

The path that led to this unique magic syncretism was neither linear nor cumulative. Around roughly the same time that blacks and mestizos in Bahia popularized the use of communion hosts in mandinga pouches, two artisans from Minas were seized by the Inquisition for engaging in similar practices. Salvador Carvalho Serra was a carpenter and lived in the *arraial* of Tapanhuacanga, on the boundary of Vila do Príncipe; his brother Antonio, a shoemaker, lived in the *arraial* of Conceição do Serro do Frio.[102] Together they trod a veritable path to Calvary because they stole some consecrated hosts, wrapped them inside a bit of paper, and carried them in their pockets for a time. The two brothers' goal is not wholly clear, unlike the Bahians'; the siblings never did confess what they expected to gain from the hosts, but upon every interrogation simply repeated that they viewed them as relics.

Their attitude was more archaic and not directly part of the magical practices through which others sought protection within a society suffering great tensions and conflict. Rather, the two brothers' behavior stemmed from a pervasive sacrality dating back to medieval times, when the faithful saw communion primarily as a form of magical contact with the divine, a way of "taking out a security on the mysterious and terrible divinity in whose name the saints performed great miracles."[103] So during the same period, similar behaviors bore different significances.

Mandinga pouches were also in use among indigenous peoples and mestizos of Grão-Pará in the eighteenth century. During the Visitation of Geraldo José de Abranches, some of these individuals were arrested, leaving us a record of their practices. A number of those accused knew each other, suggesting that some people made the bags while others distributed them among friends and customers, much as in mid-eighteenth-century Lisbon.

Although the episodes narrated in the inquisitorial records occurred in two different towns—Benfica and Beja—their similarities are surprising. Both involve the theft of communion wafers around the same time of the year: April 1764. It can be inferred from one of the trials that it was Easter week. For uneducated colonists professing a uniquely and sharply syncretic religiosity, this was perhaps the time of year when the body of God was most heavily imbued with magical potential, since it was when He had risen from the dead.

In the town of Benfica, on Palm Sunday, the vicar noticed that some communion cloths were missing. The following Friday—that is, Good Friday—he discovered that the altar stone from the head altar had been moved and its cover was unraveling along one side. When he went to look closer, he saw that it was ripped down the middle and that a piece of the stone was missing. More communion cloths disappeared on Easter Sunday. After some investigating, suspicion fell primarily on Anselmo, a 15-year-old indigenous lad who worked as a sacristan for the vicar. When questioned by his friends, Anselmo explained his intentions: he wanted a communion wafer so that he would "be strong, and neither knives, nor swords, nor sticks could harm him." He also said that it "was for a protective medicine, and to have a mandinga." Warned that he might be excommunicated, Anselmo replied that "excommunication would do him no harm." Likewise accused were Joaquim, mentor for the theft; Francisco, who became frightened and returned some of the communion cloths to the sacristy; and Patrício—all three men of indigenous origin. Joaquim believed that a mandinga pouch containing wafers, an altar stone, a purificator, Baby Jesus ribbons, and candle wax would be most helpful in coping with daily dangers and conflicts. It would deliver him from the evil that his enemies could do him, as well as from wildcats and snakes. "It served to assure that arrows, knives, or gunshots would not enter the body of whoever carried it with him." In payment for the stolen altar stone, Joaquim had promised Anselmo a shirt of fine cotton. Evidently he later vacillated about paying the debt, offering Anselmo part of the altar stone instead. In the end, he hid it inside a box belonging to Anselmo, wrapped in a piece of red taffeta.

At a time when communication was basically oral, news of this theft spread quickly throughout the population. Anselmo learned of his coming arrest from João, an indigenous canoe man, who advised the boy that he was suspected of having stolen communion cloths from the sacristy. When Anselmo was taken to Belém after his arrest, he heard the true story of the Indian Francisco's participation in the episode from the mouth of the canoe man who transported him, an indigenous man by the name of Simão.[104]

The episode in Beja took place some fifteen days before Holy Week, but also in 1764. The key protagonist was Joaquim Pedro, nineteen, indigenous and a sacristan like Anselmo. And like Anselmo he too was asked by friends to steal a piece of altar stone and some wafers so they could make pouches. They put a brick in the spot where the stone was broken off and sewed the cover over it. As in the previous case, pieces of communion host and altar stone later mysteriously appeared at the bottom of a chest, wrapped in the pages of a breviary and in crimson taffeta. The discovery incriminated Lázaro Vieira, another native Brazilian, and triggered persecutions of a large number of indigenous youth, all enticed by the powers of the altar stone and host. Manuel de Jesus, the only black person involved in the episode, was thirteen years old and wanted a pouch with an altar stone and host so he would enjoy success with women. Judging Manuel to be still a child, Joaquim was reluctant to give him the relics. But he had given them to Francisco, only ten years old, and to the 15-year-old son of the native Brazilian João Lourenço. Even the settlement's sergeant-major, Domingos Gaspar, a rather well-respected married man of indigenous blood, had gone to Joaquim to ask for a pouch and had promised him nine tostões in payment. Matias, twenty-two, wanted a pouch to make sure he did not die without confession and so that he would be "delivered from drowning to death, and from being bitten by snakes, and preserved from wildcats, and from everything that could hamper him." Luís Antonio, twelve, wore a pouch round his neck so he would not die a sudden death; he made other pouches at home, perhaps to sell. When he was arrested, Joaquim was carrying a pouch; the wafer inside had already crumbled to bits from his perspiration. He believed that whoever carried one would be delivered from a "knife or a sword entering his body, for all broke against the body." He was preparing another one at home to sell to Matias. Lázaro Vieira, mentioned earlier, and Angélico de Barros, both indigenous, were also on the list of altar stone and host customers who pressured Joaquim Pedro into obtaining them.[105]

In northern Brazil more than in any other region, the magical significance of the altar stone found fertile soil in which to flourish. It perhaps acquired such importance partly because indigenous people also revered it highly.[106] It was their way of seeking protection from the routine, everyday hardships they encountered: ferocious animals, flooded rivers, and the arrows of fierce Indians. Through the stone, wafers, and pouches, they created a parallel universe where the obstacles of daily life dwindled in strength. The balancing role of this universe was to deny the limits of the human condition and nourish the hope that fate could be conquered.[107] This often required overcoming specific tensions. Perhaps the mandinga pouch's greatest virtue was the way in which it metamorphosed and molded itself to respond to these tensions—hence its importance within the colony's magical universe.

CHAPTER 5

Maintaining Bonds of Affection

Outside the town, there near the tanneries, on the bank of the river,
this good woman hath an isolated house, rather dilapidated, not in
good repair, much less well-provided for. She had six trades, to wit,
seamstress, perfumer, skilled maker of cosmetics and re-maker of
virgos, procuress, and a bit of a witch.

—Fernando de Rojas, *La Celestina*

Homer's Circe, Euripides' Medea, and Horace's Canidia were witches of classical times who resorted to magical practices for amatory purposes when dealing with unbridled human passions.[1] During the Renaissance, a new archetype of the sorceress entered the Latin world, common to the urban environments of both Spain and Italy: Celestina, heavily laden with symbolic meaning and created by Fernando de Rojas. It was Caro Baroja who classified her as an archetype: "Celestina, and all her disciples and children—legitimate and illegitimate offspring—is a woman of ill repute, who has passed her youth giving love for money, and becomes a procuress or go-between in her old age. She acts as advisor to a series of prostitutes and panderers; is a skillful maker of perfume, cosmetics, and other beauty products. But she also indulges in witchcraft, erotic witchcraft in particular."[2]

Devising philters, potions, and salves and relying on various types of sortilege to help amorous relationships along is therefore quite an ancient procedure. Maybe this is why the judges and inquisitors handling crimes of sorcery tended to sexualize them and often viewed witches as prostitutes or semiprostitutes. The repression of sorcery and the repression of adultery, incest, or sexually deviant behavior frequently went hand in hand.[3] Sometimes illegitimacy and sexual promiscuity played a part as well, as was the case in England, where "the more blatantly sexual aspects of witchcraft were a very uncommon feature of the trials," except perhaps during the period of the barbarous Matthew Hopkins.[4]

In one of his most brilliant and fanciful passages, Gilberto Freyre revealed his perception of the magical syncretism visible in sorcery of a sexual nature. He pointed out that while the phenomenon was often attributed to African influence, it could also be traced to European Satanism. To explain his thesis, Freyre cited cases of sexual magic from the First Visitation. He stated: "Witchcraft in Portugal revolved around the driving force of love. Indeed, it is not hard to understand the vogue of sorcerers, witches, *benzedeiras*, and specialists in aphrodisiac sortilege in a land that was so drained of people but that through an extraordinary effort of virility was still able to colonize Brazil. Witchcraft was one of the stimuli that somehow contributed to the sexual super-excitation that was, whether legitimately or illegitimately, to fill the enormous gaps left in the scant Portuguese population by war and by pestilence. The Portuguese settlers arrived in Brazil already imbued with a belief in sorcery."[5]

So it was following in the steps of fine Latin tradition that Portugal practiced erotic sorcery. As can be gathered from reading the Lisbon auto-da-fé of 1559 (when a number of witches went to the stake), the Celestina stereotype and the association of sorcery with prostitution were likewise not unknown to Brazil's metropolis. When practitioners failed to heed the Demon's instructions, he would react: "and if they do not do their trade well, he punishes them, giving them many lashings and beating them, *as a panderer may do to his concubine*."[6]

Cartas de Tocar

In her tent, the sorceress and procuress Celestina kept magnets that would attract the senses, grains gathered on St. John's Eve, and the nooses and bones of hanged men. She also had beans that assisted women and men in their romantic endeavors, so long as the name of the favored man or woman was carved in them. To seal a conquest, it was enough to touch the beloved with the bean.[7]

In Castela, it was commonplace to use beans in amatory conjuration. It is not possible to tell how or in what way these beans might have resembled the *cartas de tocar* ["touch-letters"] of the Brazilian colony. In any case, Celestina's witchery is, as far as I know, the only reference to a procedure that bears any resemblance to the amatory sorcery of *cartas de tocar* from Brazil's colonial times. Quite likely they were known in Portugal, from whence they passed to the colony. Nevertheless, even in the metropolis, the only mention of which I am aware involves a similar technique, yet one that is not precisely the same. Dona Paula Tereza, the early-eighteenth-century Portuguese witch mentioned earlier, would touch the image of the beloved with a bit of altar stone as it formed in a shallow earthen pan of water, thus ensuring his affection.[8]

At the time of the First Visitation, Isabel Roiz sold *cartas de tocar* in the city of Bahia. Francisco Roiz had used one "to touch a woman whom he much desired to wed."[9] Isabel Roiz, also known as Boca Torta ["Twisted Mouth"]—a sobriquet that recalls the stereotype of the ugly, deformed witch[10]—claimed the letter "was of such great worth that as many things as it touched, so would they follow it."[11]

In the eighteenth century, touch-letters were still in use in different parts of the colony. In Taquaral, Minas, amatory sorcery and sexual promiscuity appeared together. Agueda Maria "had a paper with some words and crosses that she said was for touching men so that they would have illicit dealings with her."[12] In Recife, Antonio José Barreto, mentioned earlier, had a paper with a sign of Solomon and an inverted creed that offered the double advantage of "sealing the body" and procuring women: "any woman that touched it would subject herself to his will."[13] José Francisco, the Lisbon slave, also possessed some *cartas de tocar* "for lascivious purposes," which he sometimes carried along with the mandinga pouches that protected his body.[14] In Grão-Pará, Adrião Pereira de Faria suffered through an agonizing trial because he had written *cartas de tocar* that conjured the Demon. Adrião promised his submission to the devil; in exchange he wanted to be "strong and courted"; to be protected against arrest and injury; and always to obtain the woman he desired.[15] His accomplice, Crescêncio Escobar, author of the letters, fled from Belém when his friend was incriminated. Some ten years later, terrified when the Visitation of Geraldo José de Abranches initiated investigations, Crescêncio voluntarily came before the board. He was a 33-year-old *mameluco* blacksmith whom Adrião had asked to transcribe a touch-letter of "unfailing power" for the price of three mil-réis. He had acquiesced "out of ambition." He repented before the Visitor, who nevertheless judged him suspected of minor heresy and read his verdict before the board.[16]

Prayers

The use of amatory prayers, a practice known worldwide, was very common in the colony. In this branch of ritual magic, the power of certain divine words was considered irresistible—above all the name of God. But practitioners might also resort to conjuring demons, who were commanded but not worshipped. As stated in the last chapter, prayers entailing submission to the devil represent the influence of the Satanism typical of the final days of the Middle Ages and are therefore of a more early modern nature than invocations where Satan himself is subdued.[17] In the Early Modern age, it was considered a deadly sin to utilize verses from the Psalms "to fool women and maidens, or secure their love and wed them."[18] The church therefore punished the early modern demonization of medieval conjuration prayers. There were also prayers of another type, which employed neither divine words nor demoniacal formulas.

During the First Visitation, Antonia Fernandes, known by the nickname of Nóbrega, was accused of deploying a number of spells. One involved praying alongside the beloved: "João, I bewitch thee and bewitch thee again with the wood of the *vera cruz,* and with the angel philosophers, which are six and thirty, and with the bewitching Moor, that thou shalt not be parted from me, and shalt tell me all that thou knowest, and shalt give me all that thou hast, and shalt love me more than all other women."[19] Nearly two centuries later, indigenous peoples from Grão-Pará were still invoking the cross in prayers used for amorous purposes: "So and so, I swear to thee upon this cross that thy blood shall be imbibed, that thou shalt not be able to eat, nor drink, nor rest, save thou come speak to me." At the same time the prayer was recited, crosses were scratched on the ground with the left foot.[20]

Maria Joana, likewise from Pará, was not of indigenous blood, but she knew countless magical practices of a broad variety of origins. Making signs of the cross with her fingers and head, she would pray: "So and so, with two I see thee, with five I command thee, with ten I bind thee, thy blood I drink, thy heart I take. So and so, I swear to thee by this cross of God that thou shalt follow me as the soul followeth light, that thou shalt go and come below, and be at home, and wherever thou be, thou shalt not eat, nor drink, nor sleep, nor rest, save thou come and speak with me." The generous Maria Joana created variations on the same theme, with her arms outstretched, standing like a cross at the doorway: "So and so, thou seest me in the form of a cross, and in me seest the Sun, and the Moon; no other thing shalt thou see; for me thou shalt be meek, and humble, and still, as God hath humbled Himself when they imprisoned Him. So and so, God can, God willeth, God endeth all for thee, and thou for me, all that I want for me."[21]

Antonia Maria, the Portuguese sorceress who had been banished to Recife, had her own priceless repertoire of prayers, employed primarily in her travels about the Kingdom. She would call upon souls to guarantee nuptials: "Souls, souls, of the sea, of the land, three hanged, three dragged, three shot to death for love, all nine shall gather and into the heart of so and so shall enter, and such tremor shall cause her for the love of so and so, that she shall not rest, nor be still, save she say yes to his wish to wed." Antonia advised the man to repeat this devotion nine days in a row. To divine marriages, she would pray barefoot before Our Lady of Grace: "Forgive me, Our Lady, if thus I offend thee, but my need forceth me. God save thee, Virgin of Bethlehem, honor and glory of Jerusalem, pleasure of Israel, by thy pure, clean, and clear conception, I beseech thee, grant my eyes what my heart desireth; I beseech thee, Virgin of Grace, show me if this be so, by turning toward the right, and if it not be so, toward the left."[22] In the case of romantic conquests, Maria Joana demonstrated less reverence before the Virgin than her Portuguese counterpart, going so far as to imply something of a religious anthropophagy: "So and so, the blood of Christ I give thee to eat, the milk of the Most Holy Virgin I give thee to drink; so and so, sighs, cries, and the pangs that the Most Holy Virgin felt when she saw her beloved son dead, the same cries and same pangs and same sighs shalt thou feel for me whenever thou comest not to speak with me." An ardent practitioner, Maria Joana would make signs of the cross with her head.[23]

During the second half of the eighteenth century, St. Cyprian's prayer was used for romantic ends. No mention of it has been found outside of Grão-Pará. Maria Joana would recite it, having learned it from an Indian: "My glorious St. Cyprian, thou were bishop and archbishop, preacher and confessor of my Lord Jesus Christ; for Thy Holiness, and for Thy Virginity, I beseech thee, St. Cyprian, that thou bring me so and so on his hands and feet, and crying, *Sato Saroto Doutor* [meaning obscure; perhaps inserted for the sake of rhyme], that he shall desire to take me in." So as not to lose the habit, she made her usual signs of the cross.[24] Manuel de Pacheco Madureira used a very simplified version of this prayer to warm hearts.[25] The *mameluco* soldier Antonio Mogo knew one practically identical to Maria Joana's; thanks to his aid and this prayer, the *cafuza* Lívia, a woman of questionable honor (she had been banished to Macapá for this very reason), won back the heart of the soldier João Ventura and had "illicit dealings" with him.[26]

In Grão-Pará, the most popular prayer for assuring success in romance was St. Mark's. During the Visitation, at least four individuals were accused of resorting to it: the same Maria Joana, Manuel Nunes da Silva, Manuel José da Maia, and Manuel Pacheco Madureira. Ten years earlier, Isabel Maria de Oliveira and Adrião Pereira de Faria had been tried for sorcery, and among the accusations against them was their knowledge and use of the prayer of St. Mark. Manuel Nunes da Silva pronounced the most complete version, containing elements common to the others, like Maria Joana's (quite complete as well); Manuel José da Maia's (quite muddled); and Manuel Pacheco Madureira's. Da Silva's went: "So and so [addressing a female], St. Mark of Venice mark thee, and the consecrated host and Holy Spirit confirm thee in thy will, wherewith all shall seem like earth to thee, and only I, so and so, shall seem like pearls and diamonds to thee. O glorious St. Mark, who hath risen to the mountaintops, hath stood against fierce bulls, with thy holy words hath warmed, so do I beseech thee, warm the heart of so and so that she may not eat nor drink nor rest, save she come to me, so gentle and humble as Christ hath gone to the tree of Vera Cruz."[27] In a much more simplified version, Isabel Maria introduced a new element: "Mark, Saint of Venice, mark thee, *for the host hath flesh.*"[28]

Maria Joana, veritable champion of prayers, knew other forms as well. These included typically European elements, as noted earlier, and narrated stories from Jesus's life or drew comparisons with plants.[29] For example: "So and so, may St. Mark mark thee, Christ warm thee, Christ was nothing, may he put thy beard in the earth, as the meek lamb of the tree of *Vera Cruz:* the herb [illegible] that [illegible] went to seek, whose branch is in the sea and its roots in heaven, as this herb be difficult to find, so thou, so and so, cannot be gone from me." Another starts out in similar fashion but differs from the middle part on: "May he put thy beard in the earth, where the son of God was nothing, may he warm thy heart; the heart wherewith thou makest me suffer, mouth wherewith thou speakest to me, eyes wherewith thou seest me, come to me in great peace and accord, as my Lord Jesus Christ when he hath gone the path of Jerusalem, met with his disciples, and said softly, my friends, so shalt thou, so and so, obey me."[30]

In the popular mentality, St. Mark's job was to mark, as in France it was St. Bouleverse's role to *bouleverser* [disturb]. A complex set of symbols surround St. Mark, who was celebrated in Europe on the first day of summer and last of winter, based on the old division of the year into two phases. In Spain, it was an occasion for commemorating a number of rites. The nature of these festivals was highly agricultural and pastoral and at times coincided with cattle fairs. The bull was the pagan representation of the saint, captured and crystallized in folkloric tradition.[31] Caro Baroja suggests that since many peoples have considered the bull a sacred beast, it evokes the Horned-God of the Greeks and Romans, thereby implying a parallelism between the rite of St. Mark's bull and the Dionysian ritual described by Pausanias.[32] So it does not seem mere happenstance that the Dionysian St. Mark was invoked by sorcerers (or was the patron behind their prayers) with the intent of sponsoring and facilitating illicit romances.

Not satisfied with the prayer's Dionysian potential, Adrião Pereira de Faria demonized it in a one-of-a-kind version. The beginning is fundamentally no different from the verses cited above, but toward the end Adrião verbalizes his fondness for the devil: "The demon shall cause it that thou cannot be, nor eat, nor drink, nor sleep, save thou come and speak with me."[33]

With a difference of one century, Maria Barbosa and Antonia Maria also made recourse to demonized prayers that replaced the customary pleas to saints, the Virgin, and Jesus with a kind of diabolic conjuration. As seen in chapter 3, Maria Barbosa had a special liking for the sea demon, whose help she sought in winning the affections of Diogo Castanho. "Great devil maritime, to thee I deliver this pine, and this pine I deliver to Diogo Castanho," she recited from prison, placing in the window a candle made of tallow that the devil "would swallow with a great shout and earthquakes."[34] Antonia Maria, the sorceress from Recife, had some demonized versions within her sizable arsenal of prayers. To bind a lover, she would cut a bit of goat cheese in three pieces and put it in the window between nine and ten o'clock at night. Then she would recite these words: "We wish to cut the first slice of cheese for Barabbas, the second for Satan, the third for Caiaphas, that all three shall gather in haste, and quickly, and this that we ask shall they grant, that so and so shall come fetch us and shall enter through the door, and without us cannot be, and all that so and so would ask of him, he shall want to do and grant." Should the request be granted, doors would open and close, guitars would start to sound, and stars to shoot; if not, asses would bray and dogs would bark. Antonia also knew how to attract desire, particularly men's. She was evidently a charming woman, "small in stature, with a pale face, and a broad one, dark eyes, and handsome ones." Seated at the doorstep of her house, she would say: "I come to sit in this door stead, and I see not so and so, nor be there anyone to fetch him; go Barabbas, go Satan, go Lucifer, go his wife, go Maria Padilha and all her company, and may all gather together and enter unto so and so's house, and not let him eat, sleep, nor rest, save he enter my door, and all that I shall ask him, shall he wish to do and grant, and if this be done for me, I promise to give thee a table." And once more Antonia Maria would begin throwing pieces of cheese to the three devils.[35]

Besides prayers that invoked saints and holy figures, there were those that turned to the stars, plants, and animals. The prayer of the three stars, of

European inspiration, was used by at least two of those accused in northern Brazil at the time of the Visitation, namely, Manuel de Pacheco Madureira and Maria Joana, who, like Antonia, boasted a vast inventory. Manuel's was simple: "Three stars I see, Jesus Christ and the three kings warm the heart of so and so."[36] Joana, a living archive of Portuguese and indigenous traditions, offered a more complicated version, which in all likelihood mixed elements of various prayers:

> Three stars I see, which are three kings, oh Jesus I open the heart of so and so with this [illegible]: so and so, I command thee, by Elis, Elucas, Eloquis, which are three strong horsemen that are shut inside a house, which shall not eat, nor drink, nor clothe themselves, nor see the light of day, *antum sum* shall eat and go unto the house of so and so, three jolts shall they give him so he be not able to eat, nor drink, save he come and speak with me. So and so, I command thee by seven virtuous friars, and by seven virgin maids, and the altar stone that was found in the sea, and consecrated on land, as the clerics cannot say mass without thee, thus thou, so and so, cannot be without me.[37]

This habit of invoking the stars while concomitantly summoning forth the three magi who paid homage to Jesus in Bethlehem is most certainly Portuguese. But conjuring by means of stars was common to early modern Europe, and Caro Baroja contends that similarities between Spanish and French conjuration are a product of the press's role in publicizing small books of medieval or Renaissance tradition; the magic of medieval conjuring as analyzed by Cohn is thus adjoined to the more demonized magic of the Early Modern age. Joana's prayer points precisely to the intersection of these two currents, one older than the other. Elis, Eloquis, and Elucas are the demons summoned forth by Joana, who subdues them in her conjuration. Beelzebub, Barabbas, Satan, and Lucifer are called upon in the Spanish version, while the French variant names not only Beelzebub but also private demons: Alpha, Rello, Jalderichel, and the Hunchback of Mount Gibel.[38]

In a most curious example of syncretism in progress, Maria Joana would learn prayers from indigenous people and then translate and shape them to fit the European mold of conjuration. From the *cafuza* Rosa she had learned the properties of a certain herb known as *supora-mirim*. She would use the plant in ablutions and then go to a crossroads at midnight, where she would say: "*Supora-mirim*, as thou sleepest not at night, may it be that so and so cannot rest without me." To attract men, she had learned a song from the *mulata* Luzia Sebastiana in an indigenous language and had then translated it into Portuguese. The English version is: "*Bemtevi* [a Brazilian bird], *bemtevi*, as thou art a *bemtevi*, and thou knowest not how to take leave of thy nest and offspring that be born from thee, and even as thou goest far, thou returnest there at once, so be it, so and so, O bemtevi, even if far he be, soon shall he return to me." Spitting and blowing, she would add: "Fly away, bemtevi. As thou art poor, even poor may so and so come fetch me." Luzia Sebastiana had taught her yet another song, already translated into Portuguese. In English it goes: "*Jabuti, jabuti* [a type of turtle], as thou art always in thy corner, thy eyes tearing and crying, thus shall so and so always cry with tears in his eyes for love of me, nor can he be wherever he be, nor can he eat, nor drink, save he come speak to me."

Maria Joana learned many other songs "that she herself [did] not understand for they [were] words known only to the Indians that dwell in the forests." Some of the translated ones bear signs of the region's geography: "Seagull, seagull, as thou, every day and every night, goest about seeking thy food with the blowing of the wind and swaying of the sea, crossing the bay of Marajó, thus shall so and so come to me through my door and behind my house every day and every night." Others referred to people's struggles against creatures that wrought havoc on their plantations: "Deer, as a field be planted and thou tirest not, save they kill thee, thus shall so and so not rest, save he come to me."[39]

Sortilege

Maria Joana used her prayers in conjunction with sortilege. She would fumigate her pudenda with smoke from the resin of an animal that resembled a small frog, called a *cunanaru*. Then she would say: "*Cunanaru*, as thou startest thy resin inside a piece of wood, and there dost thou eat and drink and never take leave of it, save thou finish it, so shall thou, so and so, never take leave of me." In the second quarter of the eighteenth century, the mestizo population of northern Brazil was therefore syncretizing prayers and sortilege known to the colony since the time of the First Visitation. It was from a *cafuza* of her acquaintanceship that Maria Joana had learned that "there was much worth for a woman to wash herself with water on her pudenda, on the soles of her feet, and in the pits of her arms, and then to scrape the soles of her feet with a knife and throw this water in a mortar, and the next day give it unbeknown in some drink" to her beloved so that he would desire her and be unable to part from her.

Maria Joana was set to marry a certain man, who lived with her in the same house. But he was so scurrilous that he brought into this house "a certain other woman whom he used without heed" to Maria Joana. So she had him drink this brew from the mortar, and her boyfriend "soon left said woman and acceded to the will of her, the Confessor." Indigenous females "from days of yore" also believed that herbal ablutions possessed sexual powers. They used the bark of a tree called *caure juira*; according to folk tradition, they would go up to the tree, knock on it "as if it be a door"; if a response came from inside said tree: "What dost thou desire?" then they would state the names of the one knocking and of the man they wanted to captivate. In reply, the tree would tell them to take a bit of its bark—a kind of syncretic, colonial version of the holy oak of classical tradition.

Maria Joana also knew that when mixed with pipe tobacco and given to a lover to smoke, the leaves of two other trees, the *caãxixo* (or tree that cries) and the *urubu giriá* (or raven that turns), had the merit of attracting men. For his part, João Mendos believed in the powers of herbal ablutions. He once coveted an unmarried indigenous woman who shunned him and said he was not about to have her. A male friend of indigenous blood then taught João an ablution using leaves and shavings from the root of the *tabarataseú* tree. He should thrice sprinkle his entire body and all his hair, invoking the demon. In the wee hours of the day on which this ceremony took place, the Indian woman he so greatly desired knocked on his door. He "drew her inside, and both soon offended God."[40]

In 1591, in Bahia, the sorceress Nóbrega (Antonia Fernandes) was already resorting to this kind of magic where the genital organs played a central role. In one case, the woman should take three hazelnuts or pinenuts, stick them with pins, remove their meat, and stuff them with hair from all parts of her body, as well as with fingernail and toenail parings and scrapings from the soles of her feet. She should then swallow the hazelnuts or pinenuts "and after [they were] spewed out below" should administer them to her beloved, who would be irresistibly captured.[41] Nóbrega advised her female acquaintances to make recourse to potions made from their lover's sperm: that "the seed of the man, given to drink, would make him desire greatly, it being the seed of the very man from whom affection was desired, after having carnal coupling and flowing from the woman's *vaso* [vagina], and that this seed, given to drink to the same man who spilled it, would make him feel great affection."[42]

A contemporary of Maria Joana's, the black slave Joana (who was harshly punished by her masters and had poisoned a fellow slave out of jealousy, as mentioned earlier) had learned from an indigenous woman how to bind a man using the water left after ablution of the pudenda. The first water should be cast aside, but the second kept and administered in food and drink.[43] Not long before this, in Lisbon, the young slave Marcelina Maria cooked an egg, slept with it between her legs, and then gave it to the man whose heart she wanted to win. She had been taught that "when she copulated with a man, she ought to moisten her finger in her *vaso natural* [vagina] and make two crosses over the eyes so that said person would always stay beside her and never take leave of her."[44]

Powders and roots likewise wielded magical power over sweethearts. Arde-lhe-o-rabo ["Butt-That-Burns," i.e., Maria Gonçalves Cajada] would hand out powders when her assistance was sought. They came wrapped in small pieces of paper and were supposed to be thrown at whomever her client wanted to secure.[45] Catarina Fróis asked her for some special spells to make her son-in-law satisfy all her daughter's whims. For this purpose, Catarina gave the sorceress a button and a scrap from her son-in-law's cloak, and in exchange Maria Gonçalves "gave her some powders, saying to her that they were from a . . . toad and that it had required much labor for her to make them, and that she had gone into the woods to speak with the devils and that she had come back wearied by them." Since Maria Gonçalves had come "out of the woods all disheveled," her person confirmed her words. She instructed Catarina Fróis to throw the powders beneath her son-in-law's feet, and he would be subdued.[46]

Maria Barbosa rubbed Diogo Castanho's dishware with wood dust, in the hopes of ensuring that her beloved would not leave her.[47] Isabel Maria de Oliveira placed scented roots inside the clothing of the men she wanted to win over; Isabel Maria starched and ironed for others, so she earned her living by working. Many people accused this unmarried woman of being a sorceress. They also said that when she was with her lovers—whether actual or potential—she would chew licorice root to make them fall madly in love. Interrogated by the Holy Office, Isabel Maria claimed that she used these roots so the clothes she ironed would smell fragrant and pleasing to her customers. As to the licorice, she chewed it to sweeten her breath.[48] Manuel da Piedade carried about some crumblike powders squeezed in his hands; as long as he held them so, "a certain woman . . . would not be able to take leave of him, and would only go once he had released said powders."[49]

There were various kinds of sortilege. Early in the second quarter of the eighteenth century, in Recife, Ana Ferreira counseled her betrothed daughter to go out at night in her petticoats, with her hair falling loose down her back, and to knock three times on a church door—and this would guarantee her marriage.[50] In the early seventeenth century, Maria Barbosa, mentioned earlier, gave her husband a broth to drink that put him to sleep for three days and three nights. The episode became public knowledge in Pernambuco, where her husband served as a soldier, in the town of Recife. The unfortunate man had left his barracks on Saturday and returned only on Tuesday. When questioned about why he had been away so long, he asked in astonishment if it was not Sunday morning; he had completely lost his sense of time. While her husband was sleeping, so went the gossip, Maria expended her charms on other men.[51] In the region of Ouro Preto, in 1731, Florência do Bomsucesso "took coals to the crossroads and invoked the demon, tossing the coals along the path and by such a feat the man she desired early the next morning would knock at her door and . . . dishonor himself with her."[52] In Minas Gerais, many people were accused of knowing secrets and spells that would "procure women for men for the purpose of having copulation together," like Timótea Nogueira, who lived by Brumado creek.[53] References were made to unspecific sortilege in Grão-Pará as well. Isabel Maria de Oliveira used superstitious sayings to subdue her paramours. She had lived some time with a soldier, but she said she was single "so she could, with greater liberality, live like a bawd."[54]

Unmarried women or those who worked for a living were almost always thought of as prostitutes. In the classic conception of the Renaissance procuress and perfumer, witches in turn were harlots, women of ill-repute. In colonial Brazil, of all those who worked with magic, perhaps women who sold love philters, taught prayers to bind men, and prescribed potions and herbal ablutions were stigmatized the most by a social perception that they were prostitutes. Sexual magic and prostitution always seemed to go together. The Minas *mulato* Antonio Julião, one of the only men accused of practicing amatory sortilege, lived in the midst of "*mulata*-ladies," as if he were a kind of panderer and thus involved in the world of prostitution as well.[55]

The crossed eyes, the twisted mouth, the "burning butt" that recalled prostitution, the disheveled hair, the nightly sojourns on the beach or in the woods, the sexual interest on the part of many men, the lovely dark eyes, the life of a rover, moving from city to city and house to house, knowledge of strange words and medicinal herbs—all this contributed to the collective construction of the stereotype of a sorceress. Witches "are enemies of society and, as such, embody whatever in that society is considered to be antisocial." Witches are indeed antisocial individuals, and ones that dwell in the midst of society.[56] Some social groups differentiated between "night-witches" (or flying witches) and "everyday witches." The latter shared backyards with the people that showed them animosity, while divining lost objects, healing aches and illnesses, and furthering romantic adventures; often they were "the image of what one would not wish one's neighbors to be, and many unpopular people have the qualities ascribed to witches."[57] Night-witches, on the other hand, were about flights, metamorphoses, crossroads, and demons that took their blood or, in the case of private demons, took up residence in their bodies, in their homes, in their bottles and household utensils. Perhaps this label serves first and foremost to designate sorceresses in their relationship to the mysterious supernatural worlds.

CHAPTER 6

Communicating with the Supernatural

Come, come, sir, this excited flood
Of rhetoric's quite out of place.
The merest scrap of paper meets the case.
And—for your signature, a drop of blood.
                                                    —Goethe, *Faust*

***

Dreams

In their dreams, the colonists would see heaven and sometimes purgatory. One morning when she was just twelve and still living in Angola, Luzia Pinta collapsed in the middle of her master's yard as if dead, "remaining wholly immobile and out of her senses." Knowing not how, she saw herself transported to the bank of a wide river, where an old woman asked where she intended to go. Luzia had no idea; she was just wandering aimlessly. She decided to take the old lady's advice, namely, that she should "go very far away, because she would soon return." Continuing along her path, Luzia met a rather young man who asked her the same questions as the old woman and received the same answers. Farther along she ran into another old woman, who once again repeated the question. Luzia expressed her desire to travel to the other side of the river. The old lady instructed her to take hold of one end of a very fine thread she was holding in her hand. As if by enchantment, the river dried up, and Luzia "was able to cross over, her feet dry and without any trouble." She then found herself at a crossroads where there were two other old women. Two pathways opened before her, one filthy and the other very clean. Luzia's first impulse was to choose the clean one, but the old women ordered her to take the other. Acquiescing, the slave girl arrived at a big house, "wherein she found an ancient old man with a long beard seated on a chair, and around him a number of young boys holding lighted candles." Luzia instinctively went up to the old man and asked for his blessing; he ordered her to return. When she reached the stairs of this great house, she woke up, "by virtue of medicines and fumigations that her said master had ordered made." Luzia went to speak to a cleric and narrated the events to him; he told her that the old man was God Our Lord, "which she thus came to understand."[1]

Luzia's dream contains a number of archetypal elements found in count-less fairy tales and mythical narratives: the river that must be crossed, the old women who give advice, the crossroads—where the most alluring path is not the one to be taken—and the long-bearded old man. First the river and then the soiled pathway (perhaps symbolizing how hard grace is and how attractive sin is) draw a clear separation between the world of the living and the world beyond.[2] For the slave girl, the big house where she found Our Lord evoked the world of white men who owned both slaves and land. Luzia asked God for His blessing as she asked it of her omnipotent master, who wielded decision-making power over her life and her fate.[3]

Maria Joana, who knew so many prayers for procuring women for men and who held conjuration ceremonies at crossroads, felt remorse for engag-ing in these practices. One day, lying in a hammock, she fell asleep and dreamt about the open heavens, "the size of a great room." Inside it, countless people dressed in colorful clothing were all joining "in a great party, to the sound of many and well-tuned instruments." In the space where heaven was, all was blue and filled with lights. From the door, someone garbed in purple stared wordlessly at Maria Joana. When she awoke, the young woman decided to change her way of life. She traveled with her children into the countryside, where her daughter died. In despair, she wanted to see in dreams where her daughter had gone. "At one moment she would be convinced [her daughter] was in purgatory; at another, that she was wandering the earth, purging her sins." Then one night Maria Joana dreamt she saw "the open heavens, very far off, and a great procession of persons dressed in white." An intense bright-ness enveloped everything; at the doorway stood "someone dressed in theat-rical style, who appeared to be an angel, with a burning torch in hand." The angel ascended back up into the heavens, followed by the entire procession. The heavens closed, and Maria Joana woke up, convinced her daughter was among those in white. Four times in her dreams she saw an angel "with a burning torch in her hand walking about heaven, and among clouds, till hiding in a most thick one."

Maria Joana always asked to see Christ or the Virgin in her dreams. Once "she had seen something like a staircase with steps, which began in the middle of the air and ascended up into heaven." Near it stood a huge multitude of people dressed in white. A cleric appeared from inside heaven. Covered with many lights, he descended the steps, "and with such resplendence, that it almost prevented her from . . . being able to see him as she would like." He always had his back to her; and when he reached the end of the stairs, every-thing disappeared. Maria Joana "believed that the cleric was Christ Our Lord."[4]

Maria Joana was white and of Portuguese ancestry. Despite her penchant for syncretic prayers, she saw heaven through the eyes of Catholic Europe's iconography. The stairs leading to heaven suggested an ascendant perspec-tive; the theatrical clothing, overwhelming clarity, and thick clouds recall baroque representations of saints and miracles, vulgarized by painters typical of the Counter-Reformation, led by the Carraccis.[5]

But such celestial visions of a bearded God the Father, of dramatic torch-bearing seraphim, of intense blues and blinding lights notwithstanding, the colonists were also inclined to infernalized visions. The Inquisition censured both but left greater records of diabolical delusions and obsessions with witches.

Everyday life and the imagination often intermingled, their boundaries growing hazy. But even when there is a clear-cut distinction between the two, understanding these so-called delusions and fantasies is indispensable to understanding the Luso-Brazilian colony's social formation.

Metamorphoses

In colonial days it was believed—as is true in many parts of rural Brazil even today—that certain people had the power to transform themselves into animals. This belief traced its roots both to European folk tradition, lost in time—when animals talked, when Beauties married Beasts—and to indigenous and African legends as well, when turtles, tortoises, monkeys, and oxen behaved like people.[6] Two stock characters were constructed in antiquity: the striga and the ass-man. Apuleius wrote of ass-men, while strigae can be found in Ovid, sucking babies' blood and shrieking harshly, a sort of combination of the owl and the vampire.[7] St. Augustine said that men *dreamt* that the devil transformed them into animals.[8] In the Early Modern age, European demonology borrowed elements of metamorphosis from centuries-old folklore tradition. As early as 1428, sorcery trials in Sion, in the canton of Valais, and in Todi, Italy, made mention of metamorphosis, associating it with witches' night-flights.[9] Witches were thus able to transform themselves into animals: those who were burned at the stake during the 1559 Lisbon auto-da-fé attended sabbats transformed into dogs or cats by diabolic art.[10] As further evidence that man and animals are archetypally linked in the realm of the divine, the Tupinambá of Brazil also believed that sorcerers could undergo metamorphoses and take on zoomorphic features.[11]

At the time of the First Visitation to Bahia, two respectable ladies from Salvador had been found "in the form of ducks," in Caminho de São Sebastião or Água dos Meninos. One of the women was Dona Mécia, wife of Francisco de Araújo. The episode became public knowledge. Isabel de Sandales was at her window talking with the priest of Vila Velha one day when Dona Mécia passed by on the street. "There goes Goody Duckling," said the cleric.[12]

Around the same time it was rumored that André Gavião's wife was a witch. Father Baltasar de Miranda, a member of the Society of Jesus, spied her trying to cross the threshold of a door whose latch was raised—but she failed, as often happened with witches. That same night a large cat came through the door, leaping over the candlestick and putting out the flame.

Suddenly those in the house realized that a 6-day-old baby, brother to the Jesuit, had been "hexed, with his chin sucked." The child died shortly thereafter. Transformed into a cat, the woman had been the perpetrator of the evil deed.[13]

Around 1550 Dona Lúcia de Mello had sheltered in her home in Bahia a poor woman married to a city jailer by the name of Godinho. Knowing her hostess was easily frightened, the woman said she would someday give her a real scare. One Saturday night, Dona Lúcia and her sister were busy sewing by candlelight when "a very big butterfly with very big eyes came along and flew round the candle so much that it went out, and the butterfly appeared no more." Dona Lúcia was afraid and told Godinho's wife of the incident, "[w]hereupon she answered that she herself had been the butterfly." Dona Lúcia thought the woman was teasing her but shortly thereafter learned that the woman had been banished from the Kingdom for practicing sorcery. She took to hiding her children so the odd woman would not hex them.[14]

In the mid-eighteenth century, Luzia da Silva Soares was accused of metamorphosing into a butterfly and passing through a hole in a window to suck a child's blood. She achieved this feat "as the witch that she was."[15]

Like the bat in the Azande world, the butterfly seems to have served as a vehicle for the witch's soul in the Brazilian colony.[16] This particular insect was seen as a psychopomp in Europe as well. In writing of the horrible agonies that plague mystical life, St. Teresa said that "Satan tries to unhinge the person who, like a moth round a lamp, . . . approaches too close to the divine sun."[17] In the *Auto de Guerreiros*, still current in mid-twentieth-century Alagoas, the butterfly symbolized a sorceress, in the broadest sense of the word:

> I am a butterfly
> I'm lovely, a sorceress
> I move about the room
> Seeking whoever wants me.[18]

Even more than witches, the devil himself enjoyed metamorphosing. He did not always take an animal form. Sailing to Lisbon to face incarceration under the Inquisition, José Martins saw the devil in the guise of a large-headed, hairy mestizo with a big mouth, fat from the waist up, thin from the waist down, poking fun and laughing at him.[19] The devil appeared to Manuel João, the young barber from Grão-Pará, in the form of a large talking beetle, which complained that the fellow had set fire to some haunted houses.[20] Antonia Maria spied the devil walking about her house in the form of a small black pig; in a menacing voice, it asked her for some kind of a sign. Antonia gave it a bit of blood, and the beast disappeared.[21] For Luzia da Silva Soares, it appeared as a foul-smelling he-goat.[22] In the fields of Massarelos, in Portugal, Manuel da Piedade saw the devil in the forms of a cat or dark-gray she-goat, a kid goat, and also a mulatto-like figure.[23] But the most diverse diabolic metamorphoses appear in the trial records of José Francisco Pereira. The demon appeared to him either as a white man or as a black man with the feet of a duck or hare; as a woman with her feet pointing backward; "in no wise seeming a person, in the figure of a black he-goat, a donkey, a lizard, a toad, a tortoise, a spotted cat," and a hen with chicks.[24] It was in the devil's slippery nature to fool people and surprise them with the unexpected. When coming upon an animal, no one could be certain it was not the demon.

At times an animal, at times human, the devil almost always exhibited some feature that betrayed his infernal nature. The butterfly had big eyes uncommon to its kind; the woman's feet were on backward; the man's feet resembled a duck's or a hare's; Manuel da Piedade's demon was mulatto-like, stigmatized by mestizo skin in a society of whites.[25] And what José Martins ran into at sea was an expression of discord in its strong upper limbs and scrawny lower ones. What appears in all these cases is a "fantastical accumulation of monstrous metamorphoses" that always produce a partial totality, a "sum of fragments that cannot be resolved into a whole." In the most diverse cultures, the diabolic form has always been distinguished by deformity, plurality, and chaos. Satan—God's monkey—fashioned monsters from the shreds of mutilated creatures.[26]

"If no devils, no God," it was stated in an English witchcraft trial in the last year of the sixteenth century.[27] The existence of the devil was the ultimate proof of the existence of God, as many seventeenth-century English thinkers rightfully asserted.[28] Historically, the devil has been linked to monotheism. The early Hebrews felt no need to personify the principle of evil, attributing it instead to the influence of rival deities. With the triumph of monotheism, however, it became "necessary to explain why there should be evil in the world if God was good. . . . The Devil thus helped to sustain the notion of an all-perfect divinity."[29]

The demon's physical imperfection not only mirrored his inner, spiritual imperfection but also stood as a counterpoint to divine perfection. Out of collective dreams, his image was crystallized in the discourse of high culture. De Lancre envisioned him as large as a tree, sitting limbless in a huge chair, a kind of goat with many horns, one of which shone to light the sabbat.[30] Reginald Scot—author of the first book on sorcery written in England and also the inspiration for *Macbeth*'s witches—described the Fiend as "an ugly devil having horns on his head, fire in his mouth, and a tail in his breech, eyes like a basin, fangs like a dog, claws like a bear, *a skin like a Niger* and a voice roaring like a lion."[31]

Animal Familiars

The devil's repugnant, sometimes terrifying appearance did not keep people from frequently invoking and conjuring him up. Recourse to diabolical forces seems to have been quite common during the colonial period. Numerous women bragged that they talked with demons, invoked them, went about with them despite grave danger, and tamed tumultuous passions with their help: Arde-lhe-o-rabo ["Butt-That-Burns"] and Boca Torta ["Twisted Mouth"] in sixteenth-century Bahia; Domingas Brandoa and Felícia Tourinho in Pernambuco; and Apolinária Dias in Minas Gerais.[32] Some commanded the devil, following the medieval tradition of conjuration. Timótea Nogueira "would make the demon come unto her presence whenever she desired."[33] Isabel Maria, from Grão-Pará, has already been mentioned earlier; she summoned the devil by knocking thrice on a tree.[34] Rosa, a *crioula* from Congonhas do Campo, was more playful and had the habit of going to "dance with the devil at the foot of a cross at midnight."[35]

Satan could send demon familiars to assist sorceresses. Many took the form of an animal and sucked the sorceresses' blood at certain spots, leaving indelible marks on their bodies.[36] They suckled at the witch's breast, which she offered them in delight. In Logroño, Beltrana Fargue nursed her toad familiar, who sometimes "would stretch up and jump off the ground" to satisfy its voracious appetite.[37] In the portal of the Moissac cathedral, under Satan's serene eye, a flaccid-breasted woman suckles two serpents, possibly familiars. Such representations persisted throughout the Middle Ages and can be found in Hieronymus Bosch as well.[38] Animal familiars were very common in England. In the days of Matthew Hopkins, a great many took the form of insects. "It thus became a common procedure in witch-detection to isolate the suspect and wait for some animal or insect to appear as proof of her guilt," according to Thomas.[39] In colonial Brazil, in the cases listed above, many of the peculiar animals generally thought to be sorceresses in metamorphosed form may perhaps have been animal familiars. The cat that snuffed out the candlestick and hexed the baby, the butterfly that frightened Dona Lúcia with its big eyes, and the one that sucked the blood of the master's little boy may have been familiars in the service of André Gavião's wife, Godinho's wife, or Luzia da Silva Soares.

At the time of the First Visitation, Nóbrega boasted she had a familiar called Antonim, while her daughter had another one in Portugal, named Baul.[40] Baul lived in a ring, and Antonim "was her private servant, and did all that she commanded him, and . . . Lucifer had given her for her protection."[41] It is not clear whether Antonim lived in a bottle, where Nóbrega kept "a thing that spoke and answered all that they desired to know, and on certain days of the week, care had to be taken to place onion and vinegar near the said glass, for that which was inside it was fond of such fare."[42] Perhaps the one who enjoyed well-seasoned food was a second familiar, heir to a long tradition. Guichard, the influential bishop of Troyes under Philip the Fair, had a familiar he held in great esteem; he kept him inside a flask and relied on him for valuable advice.[43] In 1326 or 1327 Pope John XXII issued the bull *Super illius specula,* directed against this practice, so common to ritual magic of the Middle Ages.[44] In 1612, some twenty years after Antonia had boasted of the advantages she and her daughter enjoyed thanks to the services of familiars, Evzen Gueguen's *Confessional* reiterated the position taken by the pope three centuries earlier: "keeping the enemy in bottles or rings is a mortal sin."[45] Baul, who belonged to Nóbrega's daughter, appears to be a corruption of Baal, the Canaanites' sun-god, who in the Old Testament is portrayed as the most fearsome of all heathen gods. In ritual magic, he ruled over all other demons, who, like the angels, often had names derived from the Bible.[46]

One curious case involved Leonor Martins, a single woman banished from the Kingdom for practicing sorcery. She lived on João Eanes Street, in Recife. One day Leonor summoned Madalena de Calvos, who resided in the home of Leonor's sister, Isabel Martins; she told Madalena that out of friendship she wanted to share a secret. "She raised up her skirts and on her left flank and next to the bottom of her back she showed her, in her own flesh, a concavity pushing inward, a rounded hollow as large as a coin, and inside the hollow, on her very flesh, there was fixed in the middle, and sticking out, a figure with a face like a human, and this was her very flesh, and when she showed this, she said to her that she was carrying a familiar there."[47] Like English sorceresses, Leonor bore on her body the unnatural mark that announced her ties to Satan, though it was more like a protuberance or cavity than the classic spot insensitive to pain.[48] Inside it dwelled the familiar, in symbiosis with the sorceress. Interestingly, the Azande believed witchcraft was an organic substance, and autopsies of witches showed it to be located in the intestines, precisely near the ilium.[49]

In her home in Pernambuco, Antonia Maria had a doll that talked to her, possibly a familiar.[50] Isabel Maria and Dona Isabel, both living in Grão-Pará, projected the inner demons of slavery on their familiars. Isabel Maria had some little black boys who did everything she ordered. Dona Isabel would summon her little black devils with song; she called them *xerimbabos* [wild animals raised as pets], and they would eagerly come running from a corner of her house, speaking an incomprehensible language.[51] The indigenous peoples wanted spirits that would serve them and help with daily chores as well. In Maranhão, a sorcerer claimed he had at his service "a most fine spirit, friend of God, not a bit cruel, which, to the contrary, seeks to do good: he eats with me, sleeps and walks ahead of me, very often flying in front of me; and when the time comes to take care of the planting, I do no more than mark the boundaries of my field with a stick, and the next day find everything done."[52]

Pacts

Familiars were a part of medieval magical tradition, of the days when—as seen in chapter 2—men ruled over demons, availing themselves of the services they could provide. Although pacts with the devil were a kind of semifeudal contract, they reflected a new, more early modern reality: under the aegis of Satanism and the emergence of an elite current in demonology, men who had previously subdued demons now became their servants. In the sixteenth and seventeenth centuries, there are growing numbers of references to such pacts, both written and verbal, often accompanied by sexual subjugation. As noted earlier, Mandrou contends that it is almost always a diabolic compact that defines a sorcerer as such. For Cohn as well, the conjurer of demons who wields power over them is not the Early Modern age sorcerer but rather the medieval magician.[53]

Compacts with the devil served to secure advantages, achieve success, guarantee political prestige—Oliver Cromwell is said to have made one on the eve of the battle of Worcester. Paradoxically, some English sorceresses justified these covenants based on their fear of hell.[54] In a context of tension and extreme inequality, like that of the colonial slave society, resorting to a pact with the devil was a way of resolving—at least in one's imagination—the hardships inherent in daily life. Giving oneself carnally to the devil was in turn a way of realizing sexual fantasies and often of compensating for loneliness and the absence of concrete emotional relationships.

At the time of the First Visitation, a woman known as Borges was arranging diabolic contracts for clients, taking their blood for the devil. In 1593 she took a carpenter to the bridge in Vila de Olinda, tied up his hands and feet, and poked him in the legs with a needle "to take his blood to give to the devils, and she called for them."[55] Nóbrega used blood from her finger to write a statement to the devils "in which she delivered herself unto them." In exchange, they taught her "many things of sorcery."[56] She tried to lure her acquaintances and bring new followers into the demonic sect. She said the devil always talked to her, in the guise of a man accompanied by many horsemen; he chose to appear as a human being precisely so he would not frighten his servants.[57] The famous Maria Gonçalves Cajada habitually spoke with devils and had dealings and slept with them as well. They helped her perform different types of spells, and in exchange she gave them her blood to drink. For this purpose she always had an open sore on her foot. "On certain days of the week, the devils would take a piece of flesh from that wound."[58]

In the first quarter of the eighteenth century, in Pernambuco, Antonia Maria accused her fellow witch Joana de Andrade of having persuaded her to make a compact with the devil, putting her blood on a scrap of paper. Antonia claimed she had succumbed to her friend's pressure, because she argued that they were both poor and had nothing to their names.[59] Around the same time, a black man by the name of Luís paid the devil back for his covenant by murdering at the evil one's orders.[60]

In lieu of payment for the blood due upon signing a diabolic pact, offspring could be given to the devil. In 1734, in the *arraial* of Tejuco, word had it that the prostitute Arcângela Pereira had given the devil a writing "so that he would help in her wantonness." They called her "the devil's wife," and it was said "she had made a pact with the demon, to give him the children such as she bore, in this way to come by good fortune." She had suffered certain health problems, and her own doctor, Henrique de Lemos, thought something supernatural might be happening to her. Time proved it was some sort of uterine trouble [*folhetos uterinos*]. A poor woman with nothing of her own, she still could never rid herself of the nickname, a constant reminder of her alleged supernatural consortium.[61]

Minas was also the setting of one of the most interesting cases of diabolic compact in colonial times. The key protagonist, Paulo Gil, was a *pardo* freedman who lived in the vicinity of Vila do Príncipe. Reputed to be a sorcerer, he was blamed for a number of deaths and suspected of having made a covenant with the devil. He had once taken a liking to a certain slave. When the young woman's displeased mistress reproached him for it, he responded with threats. Both the slave and the mistress then fell seriously ill and only recovered thanks to church exorcisms. João Batista, a 20-year-old *pardo* freedman, has left us a detailed account of Paulo Gil's witchcraft. The sorcerer asked João "if he wanted to have a mandinga pouch so that no one could bring him harm," and then he offered him some ground-up altar stone in a brew. João Batista turned him down, but Paulo Gil kept insisting for another eight days. João finally gave in and accompanied the sorcerer on a nighttime excursion to a crossroads, where he stayed by himself while Paulo Gil disappeared for a bit. Paulo returned a few moments later, together with seven or eight black figures, all human in form. The sorcerer said: "Here are our friends." Terrified, João Batista told Paulo he was going to leave for a moment but would be right back. He disappeared, seeking refuge at his house. The next time they ran into each other, Paulo Gil reprimanded him harshly and said it had been a big mistake for him to disappear. Paulo Gil again insisted on the mandinga pouch, but João Batista would not make up his mind. Some days later, João awoke feeling a great pain in his hips. Paulo Gil had wounded him in order to take his blood and give it to his "friends," who in exchange would guarantee him immeasurable strength. João Batista disavowed these friends, saying he wanted nothing to do with them. Immediately a terrible whirlwind came up, and the terrified young man began calling out for St. Anne. From that day on, he never again spoke to Paulo Gil.[62]

A classic sorcerer, Paulo Gil brought on disease and held diabolic meetings at crossroads—a sinister, dark place where good and evil meet that in ancient times had been held sacred by Hecate.[63] Having a compact with Satan, Paulo also served as middleman, insistently seeking new covenants and even stealing human blood in the still of the night. Here again, the blood was taken from the hip region, which became sore and irritated, as was always the case wherever blood was drawn to offer to the devil. In response to João Batista's desertion, the devil had shown his fury by unleashing a whirlwind.[64] The episode combines a number of elements common to European and African sorcery: the belief that disease is the work of witches; the role of the flank as a receptacle for witchcraft-substance; and the popularity of devil worship among slaves in Brazil.[65] Also present are certain features typical of popular colonial religiosity. St. Anne—who had begun to be venerated more intensely in Europe in the Renaissance—was a symbol of the master's house in Brazil, identified with the slave-owners' paternalism, within whose shade João Batista had sought shelter in his moment of panic.[66] Highly syncretic, the tale of Paulo Gil thus has a universal flavor precisely because it combines singular solutions with elements so general that they are archetypal. In the final analysis, the case of this *pardo* from Minas fits into a long tradition dating back to the Eastern legend of Theophilus and other diabolic pacts, a tradition that has had important repercussions even in literature—Gonzalo de Berceo's poem on Theophilus and Goethe's *Faust,* to cite only two.[67]

Born in Rio de Janeiro and a resident of Lisbon, Marcelina Maria, mentioned earlier, was driven to make a pact with the demon because her boss had mistreated her so badly. He demanded that all household chores be done on a tight schedule, and the slave felt incapable of getting things finished on time. So "it came to her thoughts to make recourse to the demon to help her with that work." Angry and "with the intent of becoming a sorceress," she began summoning up the devil while kneading two *alqueires* [roughly 80 pounds] of wheat bread. She was unable to do her job properly, for she was "greatly enfeebled and shortly before [had been] bled." And so it was that suddenly she saw the bread kneading and rising by itself, and in an instant she was able to roll it out and place it in the oven to bake. Dubious, she "did not wish to partake of it, and she well knew that only by the work of the devil could bread be kneaded and rise in so little time." Marcelina did not see the person who kneaded the bread, "but she saw very well that . . . it was making a great din, as it was being well kneaded." When she started asking how she would get all her work done by the hour appointed by her master, she heard a voice say: "If thou so desirest, seek in Campo Grande, for there they shall teach thee what thou must do so that thy labor shall all be done swiftly." Scared out of her wits, her hair on end, her body shaking, Marcelina kept staring fixedly at holy images, not knowing what else to do. Finally, at midnight, she decided to go meet the devil. She found the door of the house open, despite the lateness of the hour and the fact that all were asleep.

And she understood that the demon had left the door open and ready for her, so that she might seek him, and for this purpose she removed the beads from round her neck and went out in only her shift and flannel cloak, and heading for Campo Grande by way of São José Street, she encountered no person nor carriage nor animal; and, before reaching the Church of São José, near some fine houses that stand on the right side, she spied a very tall shadow, and it seemed that it was taller than she, in the figure of a he-goat, she knows not of what color, for upon the sight of it, her body trembled, and the light was gone from her eyes, and she heard the said shadow utter these words: "Whither goest thou?" and then there arose a gust of wind so great that she thought it would knock her to the ground.

In terror, Marcelina Maria replied that she "was going to fetch some good things," and she decided to run back to her master's house. In her rush to get home, she felt someone following her but saw no one. She found the door open, just as she had left it. She had barely come in the door when it slammed shut behind her. The slave spent many sleepless nights, until she eventually decided to take an image of Christ on the cross to bed with her and hug it tightly. From then on she slept peacefully.

Besides the elements that were standard fare in diabolic pacts and activities, this case illustrates an interesting replacement of diabolic possession by divine possession. When the slave, exhausted by insomnia, carries a crucifix to bed with her, Jesus replaces Satan as her lover. Marcelina's experience brings to mind the antagonistic yet complementary conceptions of mystical nuptials and diabolic weddings that took form around the sixteenth century. While female witches submitted to painful diabolic coitus on the sabbat, mystics as illustrious as St. Teresa of Ávila fell into ecstasy pierced by flaming arrows. Both were cases of sexual possession.[68] The beauty of the slave's testimony lies precisely in the ellipses, in what went unsaid but can be read between the lines. Farther along in the trial records, in the excerpt referring to the Examination [Exame]—when the inquisitor starts closing in on the defendant—Marcelina makes it apparent how she has sexualized the whole experience: "Knowing that the vile demon copulates with some women, and that he takes on the figure of known men, upon all occasions when she consummated the sin of carnal knowledge, with whomever it might be, she always blessed herself first, so that it should not happen that this copulation be with the demon."[69] In exposing her sex life, Marcelina became entangled in the Inquisition's net; for in the minds of demonologists, a sorceress would never be a virgin.[70]

Sabbats

As seen so far, despite metamorphoses, familiars, oral or written diabolic compacts, and allusions to sexual relations with the devil—couched in such terms as "dealings with the devils," "giving oneself to the devils," "receiving many blows from the devil"—Brazilian colonial sorcery makes no mention of the famous sabbats, so common in Europe. In Lisbon, however, three slaves—one a Brazilian and the other two having spent time in the colony—stated they had attended a meeting that could in a way be considered a sabbat. If so many practices of European origin found their way to Brazil, as seen throughout this chapter, why not the sabbat?

It is perhaps still a bit early to formulate an answer. Contrary to what certain historians have contended, however, it appears that the sabbat never truly existed as the powers-that-be construed it.[71] Here in the colony, far removed from the ongoing interference of these powers and of the interrogations that disseminated the inquisitorial creed and rekindled demonological fantasies in the popular imagination, the sabbat did not hold up. Elite sectors and popular sectors professed distinct ideas about the devil, and the colony seems to have nourished popular thought while dismissing elite thought.

Under brutal torture, Manuel da Piedade confessed that he had gone with some friends of his, all black, to speak with the devil in the fields surrounding the city of Porto. Appearing in animal form, the devil would ask for blood, guide the preparation of mandinga pouches, demand to be worshipped, and take pieces of shirts and pants from those in attendance. Ultimately, he would ask for their souls.[72] José Francisco Pedroso and José Francisco Pereira, the slave friends who served two brothers, constructed interwoven narratives in which they are both protagonists of the same episodes, along with other black men, all of whom met to worship the devil and run through the fields near Lisbon with him. The meetings took place primarily in Cotovia and Val de Cavalinhos—precisely where the Portuguese witches that went to the stake in 1559 used to meet.[73] Perhaps in an evocation of bacchanals and Dionysius, the demon would offer the participants wine and grapes. His assistants, almost all of whom were black, would square off against each other, run brawling through the fields, and sing black songs, some in the Mina coast tongue. Recalling the sabbats of England, France, and other non-Iberian countries of Europe, they would skin a goat and eat its meat, later carrying its hide beneath their hats to protect them from knife slashes.

At last came the part that the inquisitor so anxiously awaited: sexual relations with the devil. José Francisco Pedroso limited himself to saying only that the devil appeared before him thrice "in the figure of a woman, well dressed and well adorned. She gave him embraces and kisses" and "had vile dealings with him diverse times, repeating lascivious acts."[74] José Francisco Pereira, in contrast, generously shared the details of his matings with the devil and also narrated particulars of the other black men's relations, hence painting a portrait of the orgiastic features of the Val de Cavalinhos and Cotovia "conventicles."

It is symptomatic that the only account of sexual excesses under the command of Satan came from the mouth of an African slave and involved other slaves as well, native Africans like himself or born in colonial lands or in the metropolis. In the realm of the imagination, sexual pleasure appeared as both liberating and integrating, reestablishing the identity between nature and culture that was more intense in African lands, an identity that, like so many other cultural traits, had been destroyed by slavery. Scholars of witchcraft today often contend that "orgiastic practices evince a religious nostalgia, a powerful desire to return to a culture's archaic stage—the oneiric time of fabulous 'beginnings.'"[75]

In other words, for those who prefer a more anthropological approach, the Early Modern age sabbat violated what were then newly devised rules, that is, sexual and social conventions underpinning the construction of the idea of home, family, and social organization. Hence the attention focused on heterodox sexual practices like sodomy, incest, promiscuity, and homosexuality.[76] Finally, as a projection of the imagination, the sabbat exposed hidden recesses of the collective subconscious, where unrestrained sexual activity constituted both the culture's great taboo and the ultimate, unattainable desire. It is well known how much Christian tradition demonized sexuality, deeming satanic any practice that in other cultural contexts might have an important ritual meaning.[77] It is exactly this meaning that perhaps felt more familiar to a newly arrived slave from Africa; painfully, it would be resuscitated by inquisitorial pressure. Under the influence of the demonological perspective, present in each of the inquisitor's questions, sexual practices that were constituent elements of the African cultural universe and were crystallized in its imagination would attain a degree of demonization unthinkable in the original African context. Through a complex mechanism that worked much like a set of trick mirrors, the African slave would hand back to the inquisitor a discursive formulation wherein the latter would recognize the sabbat. Rather than integrating the slave into his or her new universe, this process shattered it even further.

José Francisco Pereira said:

> . . . the truth is, in the olive grove that lies in the valley, near the Convent of Jesus, he and his said companions Antonio Borges, Tomás, José Francisco, Pedro de Azevedo, Mateus, all of them together had vile dealings with the demon, and it was at night, it would be six o'clock, and at the time of the winter last past, he does not remember the month, and this happened on many occasions, he does not remember how many times it was, and in the same place and spot, all of them had copulation with the demon in the figure of a woman, in the figure of a man, for at each instant it would change from one to another figure, and when it took that of a man, it was by way of the *vaso traseiro* [rectum] that he had coition with him and with each of his companions.

All then worshipped the devil: they knelt down before him with their hands raised, "the demon in the figure of a man, and at each instant he would change colors, both in face as well as in dress, and before and after indulging themselves in venery, all did worship him and recognize him as their God."[78] In the devil's series of transformations, the slaves projected their longing for the fullest possible sexual satisfaction, which transcended the differentiation of the sexes and pointed toward the realization of desires often repressed within the limits dictated by anatomy, male or female.

The sabbat was thus present in the inquisitor's mental universe rather than in the colonists'. The confessions of the three slaves cited above are the sole references to participation in sabbats during the colonial period. In their relationship to the supernatural and in their invocations of the devil, the mestizo colonists expressed themselves primarily through ritual possession of indigenous or African influence. Because these activities were collective in nature and included the presence of the devil or of spirits that were often wicked—or at least ambiguous and ambivalent—the inquisitors were led to see sabbats in them. But they actually were something quite different, found at the root of today's Umbanda and Candomblé: *calundus* and *catimbós*. If a differentiation between sorcery and witchcraft based on the individualistic character of the first and collective character of the second were in fact valid, it could be said that colonial witchcraft resided primarily in the *calundus* and *catimbós*.

Possession

Just as there were no sabbats, there is nothing to suggest that the colony witnessed cases of collective possession like those that brought renown to the French convents of Loudun, Louviers, and Aix in the seventeenth century. The only episode in which several people were stricken by demonic visions is narrated in the trial of Manuel João, the young barber from Grão-Pará arrested by the Holy Office in the late seventeenth century. Largely at Manuel's insistence, his female cousins, aunts, and some slaves in the house of Manuel Soródio (his grandfather) began having visions of angels and strange figures. They witnessed extraordinary happenings, heard voices, and lost their senses for up to forty-eight hours. Those who had been bewitched were eventually taken to Belém, where they could receive the aid of the church, including exorcism by Mercedarian friars.[79]

The custom of exorcism dates back to the early days of Christendom. In the third century, Tertullian and Cyprian viewed the Christian ability to exorcise demons as the surest proof of Christian truth, representing Christ's victory over pagan deities.[80] Exorcism was given a high profile by the Catholic Church of the Counter-Reformation, which published a number of practical manuals on procedures for casting out devils.[81] Friar Luís de Nazaré, who copulated with young girls and then used the washings from their pudenda to make physics, employed the books *Mestre da vida* and *Opus de maleficiis,* written by Friar Candido Brognolo. At the time of Friar Luís's trial, the inquisitors alleged that these works had been banned—something the cleric did not know, or so he said. He had achieved prominence in Salvador as an exorcist, and when evidence of his improper behavior began piling up against him—a "wooing" priest who deflowered maidens—the ecclesiastical authorities were incredulous.

It is well worth registering here one particular case of possession where Friar Luís was called in. The vicar of Cotegipe had sent Leonor da Silva, bewitched, to see the friar. After exorcising her, Friar Luís was approached by a young boatman, named José Romeu, who had escorted the girl to the priest. José asked the priest to give him confession, and among other sins he stated that "all that said maiden was suffering was pure deceit, for in truth she was neither possessed nor did she suffer from anything, and that she pretended in that fashion solely for the end of wedding him, which her mother and relatives forbade her, and she, to convince them and persuade them, showed herself to suffer from such complaints." The friar volunteered to remedy the situation. He called the young woman's parents and relatives and advised them to take her to a country house where she often went. He arranged things so that he was alone with the girl "and had carnal copulation with her, availing himself for this purpose of that which he had heard in the said *mulato*'s confession." Finally, he took some alms and joined the couple in wedlock, and the story ended there.[82] Such was the conduct of Friar Luís de Nazaré, who in the words of José Roiz de Oliveira, Commissary of the Holy Office, was "known and held" in Salvador "to be a serious cleric, and reputed to be virtuous." He was a Commissary of the members of the Order of Carmo and was charged by "his office publicly to exorcise the possessed and others that turn to him in their illnesses."

Calundus

Whenever he saw that his exorcisms were doing no good, Friar Luís recommended consultations with black *calundureiros*. Tomásia, slave to the businessman José da Costa, was exorcised by Friar Luís several times. He eventually ascertained that she "had spells such as those called *calundus* among the *negros,* and they consist of saying that the souls of deceased relatives come to speak through the mouth of the bewitched, which is very common in [Brazil]." The priest told the patient's master and husband that they should "send her to the healers called *calundureiros,* inasmuch as . . . *exorcism does not remove that kind of spells, for they are a diabolical thing.*" This sentence sounds contradictory, since the goal of exorcism is to expel demons from the bodies of the possessed or rid them of spells cast by devils and their henchmen. But Friar Luís was actually displaying an astute sensitivity: the *calundu* demons were not the same ones the church dealt with, and so it was necessary to call upon specialists who would know how to handle them. Furthermore, Friar Luís demonstrated that he was attuned to his patients' spiritual needs. For the slave Tomásia, *calundureiros* were closer to her than Christian clerics and could therefore be more efficacious in helping with her troubles. So whenever he deemed it necessary, the priest would direct the possessed or the bewitched to black *calundureiros.* Such was the case with the *parda* Apolônia Góis and the *pardo* Inácio Tinoco. Friar Luís was quite familiar with *calundus* and most likely had attended some, although he did not openly admit this; he claimed he had become versed in the subject merely out of curiosity, by asking questions of the black people who participated in these events. He knew such festivals were very common in the city of Bahia and its surroundings. The blacks in attendance would leap about, oddly contorting their bodies and screaming till they fell down upon the ground as if dead. "There they remained for some time, and when they would later rise up, they would say the souls of their deceased relatives had come to talk to them" during the time they had been passed out.[83]

These observations by Friar Luís are dated 1740. In Bahia, ritual African practices were already known as *calundus*. Around the same time, in Rio de Janeiro, Domingos Álvares—the one who unearthed buried treasure—practiced what was apparently *calundu* as well. He led a ceremony in which a basin of water was placed on the ground with a sharp knife stabbed into it, with a number of people standing around. In the middle of the circle, next to the basin, was "a woman possessed by a demon called Capitão, who danced and jumped about." Domingos threw some black powder at her, "whilst placing his finger on the fontanel of her head." He asked the possessed woman about the *maleficia* and cures to be done and also inquired: "Capitão, are we friends?" The woman replied affirmatively. "Am I in hell?" The woman said no, adding: "For thou art more able than I, and whither thou goest, we cannot go." Domingos fumigated the possessed woman, "wherewith she became furious and grew more incensed," saying she was blind.[84] About thirty years later, in 1772, Rita Sebastiana referred to her enemy Ana Maria da Conceição as a *rabicha* [big butt] and *calundureira*. In the trial records, *calundu* is defined as the act of "jumping diverse dances" and performing deeds offensive to God and His creatures.[85]

But it was in Minas that the *calundu* seems to have gained wide-ranging ground earliest, confirming Bastide's thesis that it was Brazil's cities that best preserved archaic African traditions.[86] Minas was the colony's most heavily urbanized captaincy and likewise the captaincy with the most robust slave system in the eighteenth century. The region's sizable contingent of slaves made more intense social fellowship possible, including the organization of *quilombos* and *confrarias,* the former outside and the latter inside the system. If whites enjoyed all the rights, the black was left to find refuge in mystical values, "the only ones they could not take away from him."[87] So resistance to the white man was expressed on both the social and religious planes.[88]

Some references to the *calundu* in Minas are vague and imprecise, just as the rite itself must often have been vague and imprecise. In Curral del Rei, around 1756, one of Inácio Xavier's slaves revered the god of his native land by hanging a pot from the ceiling of his home and worshipping it. He would put stews and old household utensils on the table, ask its permission to eat, "and round the same pot, hold his festivals and *calundures.* . . . It is said that this man is a sorcerer."[89] A few years later, in Congonhas do Campo, a black man wrought cures through sorceries, holding gatherings of black men who danced and engaged in *batuques* [ritual dances of African origin, using *atabaque* drums] in his house. He had even been arrested for these offenses, which was reflected in his name: everyone called him Domingos Calandureiro.[90] The black woman Antonia Luzia, together with two other companions, summoned "Negro women and *pardas* to worship dances" and used dead persons "to tame the masters' wills."[91]

In none of these cases is the ritual clearly defined. Violante Coutinho, who lived in the *arraial* of São Gonçalo, in Paraúna do Andrequicê, "danced and did *calundures*," and in her house black men would beat *atabaques*.[92] In Sabará, a black woman of Angolan origin was suspected of summoning up demons through recourse to the "abominable merriment" of the *calundu* dance.[93] Some masters allowed their slaves to practice these rites, in an astute attitude that was—as far as we know—inaugurated in Brazil by Fernão Cabral de Taíde (see chapter 2). Gaspar Pimentel Velho was one of these. He knew his slaves held "superstitious *calundu* dances," and for this the Pastoral Visitation obliged him to pay a heavy fine. He was also instructed to prohibit such dances, "not only because they were heathen, but because it can be presumed that demons participate in said dances."[94] Yet again, an African practice was demonized by the ecclesiastical authorities. In 1753 the slave Maria Canga earned a bit of gold for performing ritual divination. "She would invent a *batuque* dance, in the middle of which something began to leave her head, which was called wind, and she began to divine that which she desired."[95]

In 1728 Nuno Marques Pereira left us one of the first literary descriptions of a *calundu*. While staying at a planter's home, he could not sleep at night because of the infernal "din of the *atabaques*, tambourines, *canzás* [recorecos], *botijas* [musical jugs], and castanets" played by the black slaves, which made "such a terrible clamor" that the Pilgrim thought it the mayhem of hell.[96] His host seemed quite tolerant of the slaves' noise, and explained to the Pilgrim: "These are festivals or divinations that the Negroes say they were accustomed to perform in their own lands. When they get together, they perform them here too in order to bring to knowledge all manner of things, such as what is causing illnesses, or to find lost objects, also to have success in hunting or in their fields, and for many other purposes."[97] Always virtuous, the Pilgrim had a word with his host, demonizing the *calundu* and declaring it a most horrible offense against God. For Bastide, the Brazilian slave endeavored not to let "vital values inherited from his ancestors perish but to reestablish them, either in the secrecy of the *calundus* or in the armed isolation of the *quilombos*." The white colonists even referred to these *calundus* as *mocambos* or *quilombos*,[98] revealing both the terror the African slaves' cultural expressions instilled in them and their own awareness that such expressions represented a danger to the established order. Another recognition of this danger was evinced in the employment of so-called *capitães-do-mato* [slave hunters], hired to repress these manifestations of African religiosity.[99]

The slave-owner's tolerant, understanding paternalism and the Pilgrim's dogmatic, orthodox intransigence are thus two sides of the master stratum's ideology. The first—much like Antonil, and perhaps even more advanced—

viewed African practices (already somewhat syncretic) as a necessary evil if slave labor was to be sustained. The second, whose viewpoint was perhaps more heavily bound to the metropolis, associated the Africans' unique cultural identity with a serious crime against the faith and against the king: "It is the rite these heathens are accustomed to practicing and bringing *from their lands.*" Once in the colony, they had to be converted since it was catechization that justified slavery.[100] What lay beneath the Pilgrim's arguments was the bothersome certainty that preserving the blacks' cultural identity would lead to class consciousness and thereby jeopardize the colonial system.

The letter that accompanied Luzia Pinta to the Inquisition at Lisbon said she was publicly reputed to be a sorceress, "making diabolical apparitions by means of dances, which are commonly called *calundus.*" In order to divine the whereabouts of lost objects or money, she would don "certain clothing not used in that land" and commence dancing to the sound of drums or cymbals played by black people encircling her. She would sniff some *bentinhos* [scapulars] that she kept in a box; in apparent anguish, she would tremble violently, as if out of her senses. She would even divine secrets: Domingos Pinto had sought her assistance because he had been robbed of some oitavas-de-ouro, and she told him the author of the theft was his Coura slave, with whom he had slept without giving her anything in return. The letter states that "it was correct that Domingos Pinto had slept with one of his Negro women, and had not given her anything, and had the said Negro women in his house."

One of the descriptions of Luzia's ritual bears great resemblance to what we know of Candomblé today. She would perform *calundures*

> on a little altar with a canopy, a scimitar in her hand, a wide ribbon tied round her head, with the ends of the ribbon toward the back, garbed in the manner of an angel, and two Negro women, Angolans as well, would sing while a Negro man would play an *atabaque,* which is a small drum, and they say that the Negro women and Negro man are slaves of the aforesaid, and they play and sing for a length of one to two hours, [and] she would appear to be out of her mind, saying things that no one understood, and the people she cured would lie down on the ground; she would move over them diverse times, and it was on these occasions that she said she received winds of divination.[101]

The myths symbolized in rituals like *calundu* may have been lost or altered substantially over time; as seen in chapter 2, the selection process that occurred in the heart of African religions in Brazil ultimately placed greater esteem on bellicose warrior gods. But the rite itself as established during the colonial period has remained remarkably the same until today. As Bastide wrote: "Those who perform the rite are not always completely cognizant of the underlying myth." Indeed, the rite cannot vary much, as it "is encaged in the matrix of muscular capacity. . . . The scope of myth, on the other hand, is the almost infinite one of the creative imagination."[102] Practically stowed away in hiding places or "niches," the African cultural traits that were successfully preserved would help in the effort to reconstruct African society, in a movement that, for Bastide, "was accomplished in a downward process"— from the superstructure to the infrastructure.[103]

Traits unique to each group ultimately formed one culture, as ethnicity and culture became dissociated. Distinct legacies and additions to them very often merged in a single cultural expression, like *calundu*.[104] As described by Luiz Mott, an interesting dance called the *tunda* or *acotundá* took place in Paracatu around 1747; it illustrates this Afro-Brazilian religious syncretism and points to nuances within African rites themselves. When this dance took place, the Mina woman Caetana

> said that she was God, that she had made heaven and earth, the waters and rocks. To join in this dance, they first set in place a doll they had made with the figure of a head and nose imitating the Devil, pierced upon an iron tip and with a cape of white cloth that covered its head, and the end of his snout and his blood-shot eyes appeared. And they placed him in the middle of the house, on a small carpet on top of some crosses with nine crossbars on each point and some pots in a circle, and inside them a few cooked herbs and in others some raw herbs, and in another a piece of foul-smelling dirt. And after placing this platform for the doll, they all went in to dance and say their words, that this was the Saint of their land and thus they showed favor to the doll.[105]

According to the testimonies, the blacks sang in the Coura tongue, and some of them proclaimed words of the Holy Catholic Faith. Near the altar were a number of gourds, water-filled clay pans, a pot painted with blood, fish bones, and seashells. They said their black man came from the land of Coura, "and that he came baptized by Our Lady of the Rosary and St. Anthony, and that he came to work miracles in this land of Paracatu."[106]

Divinations were performed during the ceremony. Devotees of the *acotundá* dance were arrested in 1747 by *capitães-do-mato,* confirming once more Bastide's thesis that *quilombos* and *calundus* resembled each other as forms of protest against slavery. Known as *courá, courano, curá, curano,* and by some other terms, primarily in eighteenth-century Minas, the Coura people were Sudanese, neighbors to the Minas, and from all indications belonged to the Yoruba language group.[107]

There is a kind of uniformity in all these practices: ritual possession (the winds of divination); the evocation of spirits (usually of the deceased) and offerings to them; clothing of African inspiration; divination and at times *curandeirismo;* music sung to the rhythm of percussion instruments; and their collective nature. But there was heterogeneity as well, with the variations eventually converging in the *calundu*. They flourished in Minas more than anywhere else in the colony during the eighteenth century; at least available references to Minas *calundus* are more numerous—even more so than references to *calundus* in Bahia, now the land of Candomblé. Here again it must be remembered that Afro-Brazilian religious syncretism, religious persecution, and slavery were traveling companions in colonial territories, so Minas stands out; after all, in 1733 Simão Ferreira Machado called Vila Rica, "for the circumstances of its nature, the head of all America; for the abundance of its wealth, the precious pearl of Brazil."[108]

Catimbós

Displaying characteristics quite similar to those of *calundus*, indigenous rituals of possession also drew the Inquisition's rage. These rites occurred almost solely in northern Brazil, and all references I have located refer to Grão-Pará. The descriptions that have reached us must already display a certain degree of syncretism, not always easy to detect.

In 1767, on the Tajurá River, a number of people—the majority indigenous—engaged in "activities of sorcery invoking the demon, pretending they called down spirits, foreseeing the future, and discovering hidden things, with the intent of thus healing and curing the ill."[109] All the cases involve a very similar practice. Ludovina Ferreira, a white woman, had learned curative magic from indigenous peoples. Around 1735 she performed cures together with the native Brazilian Antonio. She had once gone to a sick friend's home, where she and the Indian sat down on the woman's bed. With the room in darkness, her maraca in hand, Ludovina chanted incomprehensible songs and smoked a *taquari* or cigarette made of tree bark. Outside the bedroom, members of the sick woman's family heard thunderous noises on the rooftop—the sound of people jumping about, whistling, hoarse and sharp voices that asked questions and then answered. Ludovina suddenly appeared with the head of a snake bearing a pepper in its mouth. She told those in attendance that these things were spells buried at the front door and that the *pajés* had come to get them.[110] Back in the bedroom, she balanced the maraca over a water-filled gourd and placed them both under the sick woman's bed. After the session was over and Ludovina had left, the indigenous man remained prostrate on the ground, as if dead. The residents of the house went looking for Ludovina the next day since they had no idea what to do with him. Ludovina returned and blew smoke over her friend, whereupon he got up as if nothing had happened.[111]

Three years earlier, Dona Antonia Jerônima had been involved in rituals similar to those employed by Ludovina. She had been suffering from fevers, headaches, and strange movements affecting her whole body. Some indigenous people told her that the Indian Antonio could heal her. Summoned by the afflicted woman, Antonio gave her scrapings of tree bark and roots to drink. He also said that the lights would have to be put out in the house so he could better consult with his *pajés* and discover what was wrong with her. Antonio began chanting in his native language. When he finished his songs, "a most violent gust of wind was heard on the housetops" and the roof shook. "Soon there was a loud din as if someone were jumping up and down." After wishing her good evening, a voice asked Dona Antonia Jerônima how she was, to which she replied that she felt most ill. The voice said that God would reestablish her good health by means of physics made by the native Brazilian; furthermore, her sickness was the product of *maleficia*. When Dona Antonia asked who was responsible for the *maleficia*, "the said voice responded that it had not come to lay blame on others."[112]

Another practitioner of such divination ceremonies was Maria, a black slave; a commotion would likewise be heard on the rooftop, along with unfamiliar voices and a loud rumbling like an earthquake.[113] Other practitioners included the native Brazilian Domingos de Souza, his wife Bernardina (also indigenous), the *mulata* Lourença, and the *cafuza* Teresa. They covered themselves with bird feathers, played maracas, and sang unknown words next to the sick person who had bid them come. When the lights went out, the uproar would be heard on the roof: the stomping, the unfamiliar voice replying to questions asked of it. At the end of the ceremony came a new clamor: the figure (which no one ever managed to see) was leaving, after having cured the illness.[114]

The Indian Marçal Agostinho's confession, which commenced on May 9, 1765, offers an interesting demystification of these healing and divination rituals involving the invocation of spirits, which appear to be a kind of *catimbó*. About forty years old, Marçal was a small farmer in the town of Bulim, in Grão-Pará. He often attended the gatherings of Indian men and women sponsored at night by an indigenous carpenter named Pedro Açu. At these events, Pedro would speak with souls, foretell events, and heal diseases. There would also be singing, dancing to the sound of maracas, whistling, and "unfamiliar voices, some more melodious, others sharper, in accordance with the age of the one who was singing, and people who had passed away." Ceremony participants put questions to the deceased, many about the final destination of their loved ones. Marçal Agostinho admired Pedro Açu's talent, even though he was a little suspicious that his practices involved diabolic art and familiarity with the devil. He envied the Indian's prestige among his followers and decided to ask Pedro Açu to instruct him in these techniques. Agreeing to Marçal's proposal, Pedro first taught him a song that should be chanted at the gatherings.[115] Later, after he had gotten to know his disciple better and felt certain he would be able to keep a secret, Pedro Açu told Marçal that "all that he had seen him do was trickery, with which he fooled the observers so that they would respect him, because no souls came from the other world to be at the gatherings; nor did he go up on the rooftops to call them: and all the voices that were heard were his, which he caused to be higher or deeper as circumstances required, and that it was he himself who supplied the answers that were heard to all that was asked; however, he, the Confessor, should not reveal this secret to any person, if he wished to be respected by the Indians."

Marçal Agostinho then began the second stage of his specialized training. Though he now knew it was all fakery, he continued to engage in these practices to earn the respect of the other Indians. He called a meeting at his farm and followed Pedro Açu's instructions to the letter. He led the dancing and singing to the sound of maracas. It was in the darkness of night, and he could pretend that he went up on the rooftop, that it made much noise, that the souls descended one by one, at his command:

> and after pretending that the souls with which those of the assembly desired to speak had come, he himself, the Confessor, began to greet the onlookers with voices of diverse qualities, one by one, feigning to some that he was his father's soul, or mother's soul, to others that he was their son's or daughter's soul, to others that he was the soul of a relative or certain friend, all remaining in silence while this feigning went on, and he, the Confessor, responded only to that person who asked about the place to which a soul had gone, saying to some that the soul was in heaven and to others, that it was in hell.

When he came down from the roof, Marçal Agostinho made a show of being very tired and said he had come from a secret place about which nothing could be revealed. He became famous and was highly sought after for his sessions. Considered a disciple of Pedro Açu, he was called *pajé* and prophet, "in addition to enjoying the advantage of drinking as much as he desired at such assemblies, till he became drunk, as very often was the case." He pretended that the souls drank so he would have a reason for drinking more himself. When brought before the Visitation Board presided over by Geraldo José de Abranches, the indigenous man said he deeply regretted his behavior and asked that his sins be forgiven.

Charges were brought, and the trial opened with a series of depositions, all incriminating Marçal Agostinho. He was accused of cheating his fellow man, supporting abortions, and taking advantage of women who trusted him. On August 28, 1766, Father Inácio José Pestana, presbyter of the Order of St. Peter, certified that "on the first octave of Easter . . . the Indian Marçal Agostinho had been found dead in the morn, in one of his houses located on the banks of the Piri in this town, and he had been buried in the plaza of the Church of São João." Nothing in the written document indicates the cause of death. Perhaps he was murdered for having divulged the secret of the ritual so dear to the indigenous peoples. In disobeying Pedro Açu's instructions, he did not maintain silence and therefore probably was not respected by them.[116]

These varied ways of foretelling the future, discovering the whereabouts of lost objects, healing disease and undoing spells, recovering animals essential to a subsistence economy, and achieving some kind of control in the maritime endeavor meant that magical practices and sorcery figured very importantly in the daily life of the colony, alleviating the hardships and threats posed by the material world. While guaranteeing daily sustenance, they also addressed situations of conflict, sometimes exacerbating them, sometimes ameliorating them. They kept watch over the colonists' affective lives, sealing and breaking unions, stemming the flow of blood from romantic wounds, and opening up new perspectives. In short, they were the primary means by which the colony communicated with the supernatural, from whence peered the figure of Pero Botelho, the sometimes friendly image of the devil from popular lore. The devil, magical practices, and sorcery were very often regarded quite naturally, as part of everyday life. They had traveled to the colony together with the Portuguese, and their roots had been lost in the darkness of time, in European folk tradition. Grafted together with other cultures here in the colony, they took on new shades. A synthesis of African, Amerindian, and European beliefs, the mandinga pouches or *patuás* worn round the neck and the equally amalgamated *calundus* were the two great creations of colonial magic and sorcery. Both date to the eighteenth century, as if the process of magical syncretism required time to mature and, moreover, moved parallel with development of the colonial consciousness.

Brazil's most harshly repressed attempts at political emancipation were the Inconfidência Mineira in 1792 and the Revolta dos Alfaiates [Tailors' Rebellion] in 1798. There is no record of any sizable colonial rebellions in the sixteenth century. In 1591, however, the Inquisition was already treading on American soil, on the trail of heresies, sexual deviance, magical practices, and sorcery. Brazil had just become a colony, and the legal trials of its residents were already being sent to Portugal. So from the very outset the colonists and the Inquisition disagreed about religion, magical practices, and their role in daily life.

PART III

Culture, Imagination, and Everyday Life

'Tis wonderful from how many idle beginnings and frivolous causes such famous impressions commonly proceed. . . . To this very hour, all these miracles and strange events have concealed themselves from me: I have never seen greater monster or miracle in the world than myself: one grows familiar with all strange things by time and custom, but the more I frequent and the better I know myself, the more does my own deformity astonish me, the less I understand myself.

—Montaigne, *Essais* (book 3, chap. 11, "Of Cripples")

CHAPTER 7

Intertwined Discourses

Whilst we live in the fear of Hell we have it.

—Richard Coppin

The most defenseless tenderness and the bloodiest of powers have a similar need of confession. Western man has become a confessing animal.

—Michel Foucault, *The History of Sexuality, Volume 1: An Introduction*

The onset of the witch-hunt, the creation of the centralized state, and the inauguration of the Early Modern Inquisition were tightly linked contemporary phenomena. Sorcery and inquisitorial persecution played out their momentous roles on stage against a gruesome backdrop of fear—the age of fear that Delumeau has addressed in so many of his works, particularly his most recent,[1] and that accounted for the occurrence of the West's two religious reformations: the Catholic and the Protestant. Born in the surge of the fourteenth-century crisis, the early modern state was both an integral part of and possible solution to the era's dilemmas. Along with its birth came expansion of commercial capitalism and colonization of the New World—in the final analysis, creation of the mercantilist colonial system or of early modern world economics, as some authors would have it.[2]

Looking at the Inquisition, sorcery, and the absolutist state as *early modern* phenomena, it can be noted that it was the witch-hunt's "immense fiery cross" that enveloped Europe most evenly, from "Scandinavia to the Mediterranean, from the British Isles to Poland," its flames singeing the Americas as well, though not uniformly. In Brazil its presence was felt more intensely in the north, more tenuously in the south.[3] In Europe witches were persecuted even in regions where there was no centralization of monarchical power, such as the severely punished Swiss cantons and especially German principalities. Sorceresses were also burned or hanged in parts of Europe where the Inquisition did not venture, confined in the Early Modern age to the Iberian peninsula, the Mediterranean islands under Spanish rule (Sardinia and Sicily), plus certain areas of Italy, primarily in the north. Curiously enough, given the scope of the regions involved, early modern sorcery resembled another phenomenon that similarly connected diverse and geographically distant areas: the construction and operation of the old colonial system. Of course there is no necessary relationship between one phenomenon and the other, notwithstanding a few interesting isolated observations, as mentioned in earlier chapters—those of De Lancre and Isasti. Yet in the case of the present study, sorcery and the colonial system are interwoven insofar as the former derives singularity from the latter. Numerous authors have aspired to comprehend European sorcery through the prism of the absolutist state and the wars of religion. Among others, Hugh Trevor-Roper and Franco Cardini contended that persecutory fury was greater in Protestant regions, while Delumeau tried to demonstrate the inimitable ferocity unleashed against sorcery in Catholic countries, where a process of political centralization was under way.[4]

None of these authors turned their attention to the colonial system, because they were focused on the European witch-hunt. But this book cannot explore sorcery as a phenomenon without establishing just such a relationship. My object of study is sorcery in colonial Brazil, and I endeavor to portray it by exploring the tangle of its interwoven threads, which lent it a historically constructed form, at once universal, archetypal, and unique.

Witch-Hunt and Inquisition: Early Modern Nightmares

The Inquisition was established in the thirteenth century as a religious tribunal charged with judging and punishing crimes of heresy, in the hopes of halting the Cathar advance.[5] Appointed by the pope and accountable directly to Rome, medieval inquisitors devised the procedures that would later be adopted by Early Modern age tribunals, namely, by the Spanish and Portuguese Inquisitions. Their guidelines were laid out in the manuals *Practica Inquisitionis haereticae pravitatis,* written in the first quarter of the fourteenth century by Bernard Gui, and *Directorum inquisitorum,* authored by the Catalan Nicolas Eymeric some fifty years later. While addressing the question of heresy, both the inquisitors and their manuals nevertheless contributed to the construction of a symbolic model of sorcery. In blaming heretics for offenses long ascribed to minorities or marginalized groups, they allowed such offenses, organized into a model, to become associated with sorcery.[6]

From the late Middle Ages on, all of folkloric culture had been rejected by ecclesiastical culture, as Jacques Le Goff has brilliantly shown.[7] Interpenetrations notwithstanding, the educated clerical stratum managed to equip its cultural system to preserve its cohesion and enable itself to perpetuate one given form of thought—that is, "rationalism" of Greco-Roman roots—to the detriment of another, much more ambiguous and equivocal, that is, the folkloric system. The Carolingian period saw a strong revival of folkloric traditions, expressed later in such "concessions" by the ecclesiastical elite as establishment of the Day of the Dead, which occurred in Cluny, or the upsurge in devotion to saints and in hagiography. At times it was thus necessary to respond to popular concerns, and again it is Le Goff who has demonstrated how this can help us understand the "creation" of purgatory, a true need felt by Europe's Christian masses in the twelfth century.[8]

The installation of the medieval Inquisition was a watershed marking a new trend that would be inexorable and dominant into the Early Modern age: the intolerance of the Western Church, a deadly tempest that would spawn two Reformations and fell thousands of victims on European soil. In Cardini's eloquent words, "the twelfth-century Church—the Church of the University and of the canonistic and theological *Summae,* master of all science and lord of all power, on its way to realizing the hierocratic dream owed largely to Innocent III—could no longer view with the same tolerance the survival, even on the fringes of Christianity, of ancient, nonintegrated traditions."[9] During the following century, not even sacred forms predating the advent of the church "and therefore not necessarily opposed to its message" would be countenanced any longer.[10] Menacing, alarming, the shadow of heresy began creeping over formerly tolerated magical practices and postpagan superstitions that were constituent elements of Europeans' daily lives. The ruling culture gradually demonized both heresy and sorcery, within an already early modern context where the devil would be forever horrendous and never again a buffoon.[11] In the Early Modern age, sorcery would ultimately become a form of heresy.[12]

Responsible in Europe for the burning of some 20,000 individuals over a period of 250 years, the witch-hunt reached its apex between 1560 and 1630.[13] Some of these mass murders left their imprint on an entire era: the 900 executions so proudly ordered by Nicholas Rémy in Lorena between 1576 and 1591; the executions in the Jura region of France that took nearly 1,500 people to their deaths between 1537 and 1685; the slaughter in Catalonia, which wiped out 300 lives between 1616 and 1619; and the sentencings in Finland that sent 152 unfortunate souls to their graves between 1665 and 1684.[14] There were other famous tribunals that caused much ado even though large numbers of sorceresses were not always sentenced to death. Such was the case of the 1610 trials in Logroño, Spain, against the witches of Zugarramurdi;[15] the Lancashire trial, the most famous in the history of English persecution;[16] the notorious, scandalous trials of seventeenth-century France—in Aix (1611), Loudun (1634), and Louviers (1647)—explored in Robert Mandrou's model study;[17] and the Salem witch trials in the United States, which in 1692 terrorized New England.[18] In all these trials, sorcery was punished as the gravest of human crimes and a horrendous sin against God, a crime of *lèse majesté* both divine and human: "Divine because it aggrieved God Himself, putting Satan before Him. Human because, like all offenses of whatever degree, it aggrieved the interests of the prince and of Justice."[19]

Church and state, justice and religion, thus bore down on sorcery in the Early Modern age. As Muchembled affirmed, the witch helped promote a new model of humankind, meeting the absolutist need to augment authority and control. By exorcising demons, Europeans could better impose a model of political and ideological domination. In the process of investigating, imprisoning, and torturing sorceresses, the new judicial structure—intended to keep a controlling eye on people and to unify penalties—served the interests of the recent organization of the state while strengthening its own hand.[20] In other words, emerging from new political structures—those of the absolutist state—criminal law created the conditions for persecution while solidifying and legitimizing itself in the process.

Just as Europe legislated against the marginalized masses whose numbers multiplied as the crisis of feudalism reached its crest, so did Europe write laws against witches. Repression of sorcery and repression of vagrancy, beggary, and pauperism thus emerged as correlated phenomena.[21] In 1484 the church's overt struggle against sorcery became irreversible with the papal bull *Summus desiderantis affectibus,* a veritable "war cry from hell."[22] But even before this, civil powers were already enacting laws against sorcery. To cite only the Portuguese case, the famed Carta Régia of 1385 was, in the words of Oliveira Marques, meant to "cast out idolatry to please God in the grave situation then prevailing."[23] This was when the *magistratura citadina* [urban magistracy] of the "justice of the wedded, paramours, and sorceresses" was created, with Gonçalo Lourenço as its first head. The aim was to expunge idolatry and standardize customs, that is, render them moral.[24] On March 19, 1403, in Santarém, Dom João I returned to the attack, publishing a law against sorcerers.[25] Across much of Europe, civil tribunals sent hapless victims to the stake and to the gallows—in France, in England, in Switzerland. At the dawn of the seventeenth century, when the Portuguese Inquisition was already more than fifty years old, the Philippine Ordinances still legislated on sorcerers, as seen in earlier chapters. At least in theory, crimes of sorcery were on the roster of offenses falling under more than one jurisdiction—a topic that greatly merits a study of the attributions of each power: civil, ecclesiastical, and inquisitorial.

Even when judgment fell specifically to one or another of these three powers, crimes of sorcery contained a complex intertwining of different discourses: learned, popular, lay, religious, metropolitan, colonial. Bernard Gui and Eymeric, who played such important roles in designing the procedure later adopted against witches, even by lay judges, were members of the clergy. Some of the most renowned demonologists—such as Heinrich Sprenger and James Kramer (authors of *Malleus maleficarum,* 1486) and Martín del Río (who in 1599 wrote *Disquisitiorum magicarum libro sex*)—were likewise members of the cloth. Combining the attributions of judge and theologian, these authors were read and adopted by secular courts all over Europe.

A subject matter as complex as sorcery could not have produced judges of a unified voice. Even before the aforementioned skepticism about sorcerers had become more generalized, criticisms of unbridled persecution were often insinuated or implied. Among judges, Salazar Frias is famed for his dissenting stance in Logroño. Among demonologists and theologians, at the height of what Mandrou has called the crisis of Satanism, the Jesuit Friederich von Spee cried out against torture in his *Cautio criminalis* (1631). Reginald Scot studied sorcery with a skeptical eye, earning the enmity of Scotland's James IV, who, once seated on the throne of England, ordered copies of

Scot's 1584 *Discovery of Witchcraft* burned.[26] In the fifteenth century—when the papal bull *Summus desiderantis* and *Malleus* were both introduced— men like Ulrich Molitor (*De Lamiis et Phitonicis Mulieribus,* 1489) and Johannes Tinctoris (*Tractatus de secta vaudensium,* circa 1460) espoused much more flexible positions than Cologne's two inquisitors.

This is not to say that any of them doubted the existence of witches. In the opinion of Trevor-Roper, witch-belief was an inseparable part of the era's philosophy (and here Jean Bodin, economist and jurist, must once more be remembered). Men like Scot and Spee believed in witches but questioned *early modern* methods of detecting them.[27] Contrasting Molitor with Sprenger and Kramer, Cardini calls our attention to the early modern singularity of the witch-hunt. He argues that Molitor's *Tractatus* is an anti-*Malleus,* written in dialog form and representing "an eloquent product of court literature"; Molitor dedicated the book to Austria's Archduke Sigismund.[28]

So, curiously enough, it was reactionary forces—those with the strongest ties to feudal and knightly values—that proved the most moderate, tolerant, and skeptical about the power of witches. The official culture's most progressive camp had blindly embraced the Thomist thesis of the reality of magical facts, "a cause that would triumph in the following century, the century of the modern Absolutist States." The reality of sorcerous powers made it necessary to repress them once more, "which is revealing," Cardini claims.[29] In a century of upheaval, the same author goes on to say, "reason and tolerance found themselves on the side of reactionary forces, while intolerance, dogmatism, and persecution were on the side of progressive forces"—a paradox comprehensible only within the context of the traumatic shift from feudal to early modern values, to the values of the absolutist state.[30] What triumphed at the close of the century was the position represented by Sprenger and Kramer, the position that would be defended again one hundred years later by Bodin, Rémy, del Río, Jean Boguet, De Lancre, and so many others: "the line of intolerance and of the stake."[31] Satan's prime realm was therefore the realm of early modern times and not of the Middle Ages.[32] Until the eighteenth century, European states would deal ever more brutally with sorcery, once more exposing the relation between absolutism and demonic obsession.[33] Jacques-Bénigne Bossuet, the great theoretician of absolutism by divine right, lamented that all the sorcerers in the world did not share a single body, so that they could be burned together in one bonfire.[34]

On the Iberian peninsula, the Inquisition was an essential element in the consolidation of the state apparatus. It was the "leviathan's best helper," a tool of the monarchy, and a device for managing relations between royal power and inquisitorial power.[35] In Portugal, where the social body displayed more archaic cultural features—perhaps too "gelatinous," to use a term outside the historical context of the Early Modern age—the society's more traditional sectors also waged a more intense battle against the historical process that would destroy them. The Inquisition was a prime arena for this conflict. Owing to the specific characteristics of the Portuguese case, the opposing forces at times turned the Holy Office more into a state *above* the state than a state inside the state or alongside it.[36] The "helper" consequently became more powerful than the main protagonist. Providing evidence of these clashes and conflicts between social strata, the long arm of the Inquisition overrode the interests of slave-owners in the colony, arresting captives and detaining them in prison for years on end.[37]

If the major onslaught against Judaizers in Spain occurred during the earliest days of the tribunal, with the hunt growing more diversified in the seventeenth century, the New Christians and *conversos* were the main targets of the Portuguese Holy Office.[38] Perhaps it is this quasi-specialization in persecutory activities that accounts for assertions that the Portuguese Inquisition used a gentler hand in dealing with magical practices.[39] I do not agree. Overall, it appears to me that the Portuguese Inquisition was more rigorous than the Spanish. A case in point: there is nothing to indicate that individuals in Portugal who had been accused of offenses eligible for judgment in a mixed forum either desired or petitioned to be judged by the Holy Office.[40] On the contrary, as I will try to show, Portugal's inquisitorial procedures sowed terror and panic on both sides of the Atlantic, fraying the social fabric even when directed at offenses that were less profitable and incited less greed, like sorcery and magical practices.[41]

Paradoxically, the Portuguese Inquisition had only one colonial tribunal, that of Goa (1560), while Spain had three: Lima (1570), Mexico (1571), and Cartagena (1610). Furthermore, all indications are that it was under the union of the two Crowns—or, better put, during the time of dual monarchy—that efforts to establish a tribunal in Brazil were most intense. Rumors to that effect circulated in the colony, and Pyrard de Laval witnessed the New Christian terror at the possibility that the Inquisition would be introduced in the early seventeenth century.[42] The New Christians supported the Bragança dynasty, while the Portuguese Inquisition supported Spain, tightening the noose on the New Christians.[43] Spain's colonial tribunals likewise dealt harshly with the Portuguese New Christians residing in lands under Spanish control.[44]

Throughout the colonial period, Brazil thus answered to the tribunal at Lisbon, which, from Portugal, was responsible for cases in the colony. The Holy Office's already sluggish proceedings became even more so given the distance separating metropolis and colony.[45] Outside the periods of Visitation—of which there were three for certain—the Holy Office's Commissaries and Familiars snooped among the colonial population to uncover offenses that could be brought before the Lisbon Tribunal.[46] Cases could also be raised by some of the colonial bishops. It is known, for example, that in 1579 the bishop of Bahia was vested with the duties of an apostolic inquisitor.[47] Ecclesiastical or civil inquiries (Devassas) were brought before the Council General of the Inquisition at Lisbon, which issued an official opinion concerning the listed offenses. Should these merit further attention, witnesses would be cross-examined pursuant to the terms of the Inquisition's Instructions [Regimento].[48] It was only then that the Holy Office would consider bringing a case to trial. If things got this far, the accused would be taken to Lisbon, held in custody, and submitted to questioning. Once his or her guilt had been established, the interrogations would continue in the Inquisition's so-called secret prisons, where the detainee would often be tortured. As far as I am aware, trials were always held in the metropolis, except during periods of Visitation.[49] On these occasions specific charges would be drawn up, separate from the Visitation Books, that is, from the records of interrogations presided over by the Visitor.

The colonists dreaded the arrival of the ships, which often carried inquisitorial paperwork ordering arrests or further interrogations. Antonia Maria, the "relapsed" witch who performed sorcery services in Pernambuco, asked that all witnesses who testified against her be cross-examined. She was already in Lisbon then, detained in the Inquisition's secret jails, where she remained for quite some time.[50] Isabel Maria's trial provides us with an example of a written record entrusting the defendant to a ship captain:

I, João de Freitas Monteiro, hereby state, as captain of the ship *Nossa Senhora da Madre de Deus, São José e Almas,* being at anchor in the port of Pará, bound for the city of Lisbon, that it be true that I received from Manuel Pedro Nunes and José Gonçalves Chaves, on board the said ship, Isabel Maria, arrested at the order of the Illustrious Apostolic Inquisitors, at the Imposition of the Court and the city of Lisbon, *from the hand of said Familiars.* I likewise received a paper bundle, which contains a filigree cross and a chain bracelet with a vernicle carved with the image of Our Lady of the Immaculate Conception and St. Benedict, and a gold ring with a counterfeit stone, which is said to weigh six *oitavas* [total of nearly 40 grams] less fifteen *grãos* [total of 0.75 grams], to be delivered on the account and at the risk of the said Isabel Maria to the Treasurer General of the Holy Office. As I have also received the *bundle of papers* drawn up to be delivered to said Holy Tribunal, having received all listed herein from the aforesaid Familiars, I wholly do oblige myself, God granting me the good safety of this ship, *to deliver said prisoner to the Keeper of the Jails of the Holy Office; and the gold to the Treasurer General of the same.*[51]

The letter is dated November 25, 1756. Two years later Isabel Maria appeared in an auto-da-fé suspected of minor heresy. Her trial, as well as that of Adrião Pereira de Faria—who was convicted in the same auto-da-fé and who, in addition to being flogged, abjured *in forma*—must have related to the Visitation that had reached Grão-Pará five years earlier, headed by Geraldo José de Abranches. Both of the accused were from this region and were prosecuted for sorcery.[52] Isabel Maria's *auto de entrega* [record of delivery] exemplifies what must have been usual procedure and reveals the network of Inquisition bailiffs active in the colony. But it also evinces the complexity of the colonists' living religion and the gulf between the elite notion of sorcery and popular experience: the defendant, a sorceress, was carrying images of saints on her. Finally, the document points up the inordinate greed of the Holy Tribunal, which did not overlook even the most humble contributions—everything was worthy of confiscation.

The three Visitations to Brazil focused on the colony's economically significant regions: Bahia, Pernambuco, and Grão-Pará (to which Pombal directed special attention, appointing his brother governor of the state).[53] The inquisitors apparently exercised heightened zeal in dealing with colonists from Brazil's most affluent areas throughout the colonial period: "The Holy Office of the Inquisition always sought and kept a vigilant eye on the most prosperous regions of Brazil," states Anita Novinsky.[54] A breakdown of offenses by region and period (see tables 1–3 in the appendix) shows us, for example, that Minas led in the eighteenth century—and this during a period when no Visitations took place, that is, the second quarter of the century. It is northern Brazil that stands out at the end of the century, when Geraldo José de Abranches established his Visitation there. The predominance of sorcery in the colony's richest regions indicates that syncretism and magical practices were intensifying and gaining in complexity in tandem both with the process of colonization and the production of wealth and with the increased number of African slaves. In the case of New Christians, it is of course logical that the wealthiest would be found residing in areas of greater prosperity.[55]

In overall terms, it seems clear that in these areas of Brazil both the Inquisition and the Crown strove to render the population more "well-ordered" and homogenized, since heresies, spells, dissidence, adultery, incest, and bigamy were a greater menace and therefore less tolerable at these nerve centers. The very existence of episcopal Devassas is evidence of this normatizing concern. Ordained by the *Constituições primeiras do Arcebispado da Bahia,* these Inquiries were part of the post-Tridentine effort to gather the faithful to the bosom of the church, stamp out idolatry, and divest popular religiosity of any folkloric traces.[56] In this case, inquiries should have occurred throughout the colony, from north to south. Yet to date they are known to have occurred in only three regions: Minas Gerais, where they were more periodic and broader in scope and in range, held from the early 1720s through the dawn of the following century; Mato Grosso, where an episcopal Inquiry took place in the last quarter of the eighteenth century, at a time when the region had already entered a sharp decline;[57] and Ilhéus, Bahia, which still played an important role in the colonial economy in the early nineteenth century, when the inquiries occurred.

As far as the inquiries in Minas and Bahia, the economic importance of these regions justified such efforts to "normatize" the colonists' lives. In Cuiabá, in Mato Grosso, in contrast, the initiative was inspired by this border zone's strategic role.

From all that has been stated so far, it seems clear that the powers of state in the colony were helped by the Inquisition, acting autonomously at given moments. In the colony, the power structures likewise flexed their muscles and endeavored to attain legitimacy by persecuting and punishing heterodox and deviant behavior. Like the monotheistic God who can only exist in opposition to the devil, the Inquisition and the state looked for the elements of their lifeblood in the midst of the colony's mestizo population, syncretically religious and indisputably different from European models.[58] Visitors were not exactly "moved by love" to come to the colony, contrary to what one historian has argued.[59]

While the Inquisition spread its network of Familiars, Commissaries, and Visitors throughout Brazil, availing itself as well of offenses detected by episcopal inquiries, civil authorities created legislation for a populace that fit ever more poorly into the metropolitan mold as the eighteenth century advanced. During those hundred years, Municipal Councils were ordered to verify whether sorcery was practiced in their communities and if there were any witches curing animals by blessing them, making recourse to diabolical relics, or entering into compacts with the devil.[60] In 1780 the count of Povolide informed Martinho de Mello e Castro that open-air ceremonies were being sponsored by blacks from the Mina coast, where a centerpiece of the rite was an altar bearing idols, live goats, cock's blood, and corn cake, offered to the participants—in short, precursors to sessions of Candomblé. In tune with the European trend of demonizing expressions of popular culture, Povolide saw this event as a sabbat and tried to place it within the same framework as sorcery in Portugal.[61]

As noted in these pages, it appears evident that the witch-hunt could only have come to pass during the Early Modern age. Employed since time immemorial by a broad gamut of peoples, sorcery and magical practices altered their semblances in response to the new ways of organizing institutions and power structures that began emerging in the late fourteenth century. Intolerance of witches, procuresses, and diviners grew in tandem with the irreversible changes under way: the feudal system came undone, power was organized into monarchical states, and the church recognized its limitations in defending and propagating Christianity as the hegemonic religion. Sorcery was therefore not the "daughter of misfortune" depicted by Jules Michelet in the nineteenth century. Rather, it was a by-product of the birth of a new era, one symptom of a painful delivery that was to produce the precapitalist legions of dispossessed people, the mentally ill, and so many other excluded categories.

Among these categories, sorcery stirred the most hatred because it epitomized the clash of two worlds: the world of popular culture and oral, unlettered tradition—shared by the bulk of Europe's population—and the world of high culture, educated, written, and limited to a restricted number of intellectuals, who were about to be struck by the advent of the printing press. A multifaceted, polyphonic phenomenon, this clash of two worlds was connected with a series of contemporaneous transformations. Hence the numer-

ous explanations for its emergence: the wars of religion;[62] the disenchantment of the world prompted by the dawning of Protestantism; the intensifi-
cation of tensions between neighbors within an impoverished society;[63] the
church's realization that it was becoming an isolated citadel;[64] the acculturation of the Flemish and French countryside;[65] and many others. Nearly all
recent studies raise the issue of this conflict between two distinct worlds but
offer different interpretations and inferences about what has otherwise become a near consensus.

French historians ascribe great import to the existence of these two levels—the popular and the learned. While recognizing the interrelation between them, they tend to place more weight on the side of the elites.[66] In
examining the devil's presence in daily life during the Early Modern age,
Mandrou assigns it dual ancestry: judicial and theological literature, on the
one hand, and oral tradition, on the other.[67] But when he delves deeper into
his analysis, he links the witch-hunt to the judges' persecutory attitude and
argues that the French magistrates' early acceptance of enlightened ideas
accounts for the disappearance of the hunts. Muchembled, so concerned with
the question of popular culture, ultimately finds himself not far from
Mandrou, affirming that when the demonological doctrine fashioned at the
top found its way down into the hands of civil servants zealous in its application, the persecution intensified.[68] Viewing sorcery from the point of view
of persecution, Delumeau and other French historians, including Muchembled, characterize it as "the ruling ethics' self-defense" against an "invading" popular culture. From this perspective, Bodin, James I, Rémy, Boguet,
De Lancre, and del Río constituted a "frightened elite" engaged in a veritable "enterprise of expropriation" directed against popular culture and tradition.[69] Although the demonological construct is seen here as a mixture of
elitist obsessions and fragments of social reality and popular culture, the
former and not the latter would constitute its main ingredients.[70] Emphasizing persecution thus has the effect of accentuating the elite's "terrorizing
theology" and fails to draw a sufficiently clear picture of the twisted route
by which the stereotype itself was constructed.[71]

Albeit at times caught up in a fascination with sorcery as a mental construct imposed from the top down, English historians have nevertheless made
greater inroads in deciphering the various forces at play in the formulation
of the early modern idea of sorcery. Keith Thomas has endeavored to show
how the elites reworked the age-old notion of *maleficium* (according to which
certain people are capable of causing injuries), eventually engendering the
notion of the witches' sabbat, which was originally of a different nature and
grounded in theological writings.[72] Thomas also detects a popular hatred of
witches, which demonological literature and the advent of the witch-trials
adroitly took advantage of.[73] Drawn to the idea of a stereotype constructed
by the elites, Cohn at the same time offers an interpretation analogous to
Thomas's, wherein he highlights the fact that inquisitorial procedures were
brought to bear on *maleficium* in the Early Middle Ages.[74] Rowland, whose

analysis is of a more anthropological bent, has shown that the relation between sabbat and *maleficium* depended on formulations with distinct formal structures. Rowland feels that the lives of saints, magical popular tales,
and confessions of sorcery offenses display a diachronic structure, based on
the sequence of events and essential in translating relations between the natural
and supernatural worlds. By contrast, scholasticism's demonological concept is abstract, atemporal, synchronic.[75] At the height of the witch-hunt,
these two concepts merged to produce a new myth.[76] In the words of Rowland,
witch-beliefs derived from the process of institutional mediation between
cultural levels within a complex society.[77]

Gustav Henningsen makes what appear to be some contradictory assertions. He states that the "demonic mythology of witchcraft was a product of
the cultured elite and not of the popular mind." Nonetheless, he regards
witchcraze as the "fruit of a mating" between popular culture and high culture and believes that "in areas where there were no popular witch-beliefs,
there was likewise no persecution of witches."[78] With Carlo Ginzburg's analyses in mind, I believe it is valuable to stress that witchcraft raises the issue of
the circularity of cultural levels, which often hampers our ability to tell when
the elite sectors predominate over the popular sectors and vice versa. The
cultural elites reworked expressions of popular culture from the perspective
of demonology, and demonology in turn could not have been constructed
without recourse to long-standing folk traditions. In other words, demonology as a field of knowledge belonged to the educated elites; but it was still
never devoid of the silent, steady presence of popular elements.

Ginzburg did a model job of demonstrating how Menocchio, the Friulian
miller, constructed a heretical cosmogony that intertwined popular and elite
themes, often taken from readings like *The Decameron* and *A Thousand and
One Nights*.[79] Based on Ginzburg, it should also be said that much as this
mating occurred, a rift could still be perceived between one level and the
other. The early modern church and state were amazed by the myriad religious concepts and social realities that had to be administered and, in their
eye, homogenized. Their awareness of the immense gulf lying between these
two clashing universes generated and legitimized repression. Yet this was
often a suicide mission, insofar as one world was intertwined with the other.

Finally, it should be stated that witch-beliefs were a generalized phenomenon in Portugal, as indicated by the laws cited earlier and by various types
of documents. Still, sorceresses were persecuted less in this country than in
other parts of Europe. The mere existence of a belief thus does not suffice to
account for a greater or lesser degree of repression.

The polemic surrounding sorcery will remain alive for a long time to come.
In this regard, lying at the intersection of distinct cultural levels, colonial
sorcery is an object of study with exceptional explanatory potential, as the
clash between the popular and elite worlds becomes exacerbated within the
colonial system and within a social formation so complex from myriad angles.
I believe colonial sorcery acts as a kind of magnifying glass in the study of

these intertwined discourses. In the crossfire between them, the inquisitor's metropolitan condition also intersects with the defendant's colonial condition, undeniably another source of intimidation.

The Inquisition's Task: Spreading Persecution and Awakening Memories

Witchcraft is by definition an impossible crime, says Gustav Henningsen. This author tells us that "what is characteristic of the witch's role is that it is a fictitious one, imputed and vacuous: a witch can neither fly nor destroy anything with her look (evil eye)."[80] From the perspective of reason, Henningsen is right. In a famous essay on sorcery, contemporaneous with the immense fiery cross upon which humans were roasted, Montaigne had long before manifested his perplexity that people charged with these impossible crimes would be burned.[81] And as Mandrou has demonstrated, it was necessary for the entire belief system supporting the intertwined discourses on sorcery to fall apart before the rationalist, enlightened position could triumph.[82] Montaigne's concerns found practically no echo, unlike Nicolas de Malebranche, who wrote in the late seventeenth century; only then did Montaigne's assertion prevail: that cooking men and women alive was too high a price for such conjectures.[83]

As it captured and promoted the intermingling of elite and popular formulations, the inquisitorial procedure was exemplary in creating and perpetuating the stereotype of sorcery, driving the accused to confess.[84] For the most part, it acted on two fronts: the individual, by awakening memories and scrutinizing lives, fears, and desires; and the collective, where it aggravated social conflicts and interpersonal tension and created a channel where accusations, hatred, and sinister procedures could multiply. In short, spreading inquisitorial activities would allow the tribunal a much broader reach than it could achieve alone as an institution.

Colonial Brazil did not have its own tribunals, unlike Spanish America. But like Spanish America it experienced the dread of inquisitorial investigations. So it was familiar with the "microphysics of power" that emanated from the Inquisition, even at a distance; as Gonçalves Salvador observed, its tentacles reached Brazil.[85] Every year on the first Sunday of Lent, an edict that established the offenses falling within inquisitorial jurisdiction was read out and posted in the churches of the Kingdom and the Empire's overseas dominions.[86] Thus was the door opened to denunciations and accusations. The fear of Visitations in Brazil even prompted denunciations of dead people.[87]

Through arbitrary mechanisms—but nonetheless perfectly in keeping with the early modern notion of justice—the defendants were entangled in a web from which they could not extricate themselves. The Portuguese Inquisition permitted *testemunhas de ouvida;* in other words, hearsay was deemed admissible evidence. Furthermore, witnesses were not required to prove their own character, and any testimony counted, even that of children.[88] Famous judges and demonologists like Boguet and De Lancre placed great store in depositions of this kind, even when they were extracted under torture.[89] By virtue of the very fact that guilt was assigned *a priori*, "everything was done to facilitate the lodging of denunciations, while everything was done to hamper their elimination or exclusion."[90] In Portugal the Inquisition even resorted to what Saraiva has called the "curious device of multiplication": if witnesses were few, the Instructions determined that a different question would be asked at each repeated act or ceremony. Denunciations were thus augmented to give the defendant the impression that they were greater in number than they really were.[91] Finally, an informant could hide behind a cloak of secrecy, which by the same token meant that the defendants could be kept in the dark regarding their true situation or regarding any means by which they might dodge the inquisitorial trap set up at each interrogation. In the complacent words of Caro Baroja, the Holy Office was an "enigmatic tribunal" grounded in secrecy.[92]

For Bartolomé Bennassar, by contrast, the secret procedures that the Iberian Inquisition developed "to perfection" are consonant with "that era's trend, which we can identify with the development of the Modern State and its desire for power and control over its subjects." In Spain, men like Ferdinand of Aragon, Cardinal Cisneros, and Charles V devoted immense energy to preserving these procedures, despite the initial scandal this raised.[93] In Portugal, the Instructions themselves were secret, although printed; access was reserved to judges of the Inquisition and perhaps the prosecutor, while it was closed to the public and to the defendant, attorneys, and most civil servants. This meant that those accused had no knowledge of trial documents, the organization of the trials, the norms governing them, the law that would judge their crimes, the judges' decisions, or the individuals accusing them.[94] In the case of documents whose contents were to be read to the accused— such as the Statement of Charges (Prova da Justiça) and the Verdict (Sentença), announced during the auto-da-fé—the language was vague and elliptical when people and places were mentioned, with the intent of protecting informants, all in accordance with the Instructions. For instance: "A witness of the Court, sworn in, ratified, . . . states that he knows, for the reason given, that the Defendant, José Francisco, was found in a certain place and in certain company, whom he asked to go to a Church to place some papers beneath an altar stone so that some masses might be said above them." A second example: "Another witness of the court . . . states knowing, for the reason given, that the Accused, José Francisco, was found in a certain place, where he read to a certain person for the purpose of transcription. . . ."[95]

This blurring of people and places in the Statement of Charges as well as the Verdict seems to have the intent of highlighting the accused's crimes, which were described in minute detail even when repeated by a number of witnesses. The verdicts in the two trials of the relapsed heretic Antonia Maria, for instance, form a veritable compendium of magical prayers and spells, reconstructed from depositions by people who remained anonymous to the public. Names are omitted even in the Inquisition's transcriptions of the defendant's confessions: "She said, and confessed, that on a certain occasion, because she found herself in prison, a person she knew consulted with another that she might teach her some remedy to free said person; and indeed, both prepared a brew." Then follows the description of the ritual, while farther on it is stated: "And another person had asked her to make some remedy, so that someone, with whom she had maintained an illicit friendship, should desire to continue the wicked dealings as hitherto, making her a certain promise, if the results were achieved. And moved by these interests, she, the Defendant, went to the home of said person, and after she asked for a piece of goat cheese, they both went to a window."[96] The fact that these data are omitted even when the defendant tells her story and names the supporting actors lends credence to the notion that the intent was not only to preserve an informant's identity but also to magnify the suspect's guilt by means of this formal expedient. In the realm of crime and punishment, he or she alone gains an identity; he or she is the only actor.

Making recourse to Familiars and to means of persuasion—like sermons, processions, autos da fé—the Inquisition crept into all corners of daily life and, according to the liberal historiography of the nineteenth century, transformed "humankind into a band of informants and Christian society into a horde of spies."[97] This persecutory furor took advantage of personal or social antagonisms and indeed reproduced and perpetuated them.[98]

As in Spain, most denunciations in colonial Brazil came from neighbors, relatives, and friends.[99] In the late sixteenth century, Madalena de Calvos was friend and confidante to Leonor Martins, who went by the nickname of Salteadeira ["Leaper"], a single woman found guilty of sorcery and banished from the Kingdom. Leonor had confided to Madalena about the sorceries she knew and had even shown Madalena the familiar branded in the flesh of her flank, mentioned in earlier chapters. When Heitor Furtado de Mendonça's Visitation reached Pernambuco, Leonor was panic-stricken. "She begged [Madalena] to keep secret all the said things she had disclosed to her and that she do her no harm and not denounce these things, nor state them before this Board [of the Visitation], and she, the Accuser, promised her that she would not disclose them."[100] But Madalena betrayed her friend and appeared before the board to recount what had happened, revealing the sorceress's frailty before the menaces of this world and the violence of the power structures. Mutual denunciations also spread widely among the Bahian group arrested in the mid-eighteenth century for carrying mandinga pouches. The circumstances, however, were different: the friends began pointing fingers at one another after they had been arrested, and the incriminatory testimonies fell mainly upon Mateus Pereira Machado, accused by both José Martins and Luís Pereira de Almeida.[101] The same thing occurred in two other trials, where the defendants were involved in the same offense: José Francisco Pereira and José Francisco Pedroso, charged in Lisbon with taking part in the sabbat in Val de Cavalinhos and in Campos da Cotovia.[102]

Yet there were shows of solidarity between prisoners as well, chiefly when they were not prior acquaintances or involved in the same offense (for in the latter instance they all fended for themselves as best they could). When the *pardo* carpenter José Fernandes was locked up in the dungeon in Bahia, his cellmates frightened him by saying that "if he would make the same confession before the Holy Office as he had made there, they would certainly order his life taken."[103] Confessing bit by bit, as the inquisitorial noose tightened— a standard procedure among prisoners of the Holy Office—the black woman Joana was called to task by the inquisitors. They wanted to know why she had not confessed at once to the episodes she eventually disclosed. "She said that her reason for not confessing to everything immediately was because the other prisoners had advised her to deny everything that she could deny, and not to admit to her offenses."[104]

Informants often found themselves caught in the Inquisition's net too, as illustrated by the trials of Violante Carneira and "Butt-That-Burns." On August 22, 1591, Violante had voluntarily testified against Maria Gonçalves Cajada (Arde-lhe-o-rabo i.e., Butt-That-Burns), accusing her of being a sorceress. She reported the episode examined earlier, namely, that the famous witch of the time of the First Visitation allegedly had the habit of nourishing the devil with flesh from a sore on her foot. What Violante Carneira could not know was that by then she herself had been denounced by a former lover; two days earlier, on August 20, 1591, Bernardo Pimentel had of his own volition come forward to accuse her of uttering words from the mass during carnal relations.[105] Impassively, without tipping their hand, the inquisitors took first one and then the other denunciation. Hanging over every witness's head was the risk of being transformed into a defendant, by the same process through which he or she had voluntarily accused someone else. In other words, the Inquisition turned every witness into a potential suspect. But instead of discouraging denunciations, this menace spurred even greater numbers to testify, all trying to save themselves from possible denunciations and earn the inquisitor's confidence by appearing before him as an informant. Hence so many voluntary appearances and denunciations—aided further by the fact that church confessors prodded their lambs to appear before the Visitation Board whenever the priest deemed that a sin fell within the Inquisition's scope.[106] Thus diffused, the power of the Holy Office created chains of accusations, impregnated by a pervasive, omnipresent dread.

This generalized persecution fed on various types of animosities. Antonio Carvalho Serra, who along with his brother Salvador was accused of stealing sacred hosts and using them in a mandinga pouch, spent fifteen months imprisoned in the colony; he was later sent to Lisbon, where he eventually died. At one point in the proceedings, the vicar of Conceição do Mato Dentro Church certified that the case all boiled down to the false witness of an enemy of the defendant, who wanted to sleep with his sister-in-law.[107]

Antonia Maria, trapped a second time in the Inquisition's net, alleged that the accusations against her had been lodged by "mortal enemies"; Bárbara de Mello supposedly despised Antonia because she suspected the woman of having an affair with her husband. Bárbara wanted Antonia as far away from Pernambuco as possible and had threatened her, saying that "she would see that she would be cast out of that land." Antonia Maria's landlord allegedly had been induced by the woman to kick her out, which he did. The jealous wife said that even if she had to sell the veil on her head, she "would seek out false witnesses so that she, the Defendant, would be arrested again for the same crime for which she had been banished to that town." The stonemason Domingos Gonçalves had gone to Antonia Maria seeking relief from the attack of hiccups tormenting him. Antonia's remedy did no good, and the man "went to the home of her, the Defendant, most wrathful and furious, saying that he would hit her, the Defendant, with a stick and that he would whip her and accuse her before the Holy Office, making many insulting remarks in all the places he would go, slandering her, the Defendant, with very offensive names."

Listed among Antonia's many alleged enemies was Joana de Andrade, with whom she had a professional conflict, as mentioned earlier. Antonia Maria ended her contestation by stating that she "was a foreign woman who went to said town without having any kin there who would believe and defend her from so many defamations as her enemies raised . . . , and as these enemies were native to said town where they had kin and friends, it was easy for them all to unite to do this harm to her, the Defendant, and cast her out of the town in revenge, for the hatred they harbored against her, and in this manner not only would the witnesses that she had contested swear falsely but also the others whom she does not remember now, who would be kin and friends of the said enemies of the Defendant."[108]

Permeating the fabric of social relations, the persecution instigated by the Holy Office intensified existing tensions and sparked new ones, winning adherents who became veritable heralds of the ideology it embodied. On many pages of the *Compêndio narrativo do peregrino da América* are traces of the procedures devised by the Inquisition. When Nuno Marques Pereira criticizes the African slaves' *quigila,* he does so following the line of the inquisitors' demonological thinking:

> It is an explicit pact, which these heathens enter into with the devil, upon which is based some bodily convenience desired by the party who made it: such as having good success in war, fortune in the hunt, in planting, etc. These pacts, and *quigilas,* derive from the fact that *the devil is greatly envious of the rational creature,* and wants by diverse means to lead him to sin, making him lay aside his rules, and commandments, to the end of casting him into Hell. This *quigila,* or pact, *is passed on by tradition to children, grandchildren, and other descendants;* however, as these were not the instigators of the pact, it is tacit in them: and *as they are ignorant of the cause, their offense does not have such gravity as that of their parents and ancestors,* who did it expressly.[109]

When Nuno Marques Pereira adopts the idea that sorcery is hereditarily transmissible, when he differentiates between a tacit and explicit pact, and when he opposes magic to rationalism (that of the scholastics), he signals his adherence to the entire arsenal of ideas shaping the ideological framework of the early modern witch-hunt. The object of his repudiation is one of the constituent elements of the Afro-Brazilian religion that was then gradually being constructed in the colony; his discourse consequently illustrates the intersecting levels of the popular universe and elite universe. Perhaps the Pilgrim was a Familiar of the Holy Office as well. Or perhaps his adherence to the tribunal's ideas is merely proof of its efficacy as an apparatus of power that intruded into daily life and molded mentalities.

The microphysics of inquisitorial power thus constituted a complex process whereby both the collective and the individual universe were simultaneously undermined by a powerful institutional network, which in turn was bolstered by its collaborators' efforts and the concoction of arbitrary trials. In Spain the Inquisition already had been in force for fifty years, and there its devastating effects had become irreversible, engraving the traces of terror on people's memories.[110] Even today, the population of Galicia identifies the Inquisition with all it deems repressive and arbitrary. Recapturing that distant era, the region's inhabitants say the men of the Holy Office would appear like a vision, silently, evoking surprise and fear. "The ironically entitled Holy Inquisition has consequently become a symbol of disorder, of insecurity, of the violation of a person's innermost sanctum," Carmelo Lisón-Tolosana concludes.[111]

To enhance its results at the individual level, the Holy Office relied on confessions. These had been the key to the ancien régime's penal system, and in the case of the tribunal were taken as a sign that a trial had proceeded efficaciously, the grand finale of a successful interrogation.[112] The inquisitor should be "fanatical about detail," faithful to the spirit of the Manual governing him: "Even when the denunciation lodged shows no glimmer of truth, nevertheless the inquisitor shall not discard the trial that has begun, which he shall always move ahead with, for that which is not discovered today may be achieved tomorrow."[113]

Michel Foucault is the author of one of the finest analyses of the significance of confession in Western societies. According to Foucault, from the time of the Middle Ages, confession has been an important ritual for arriving at the truth, while corresponding interrogation methods have been gradually devised. We have become a "singularly confessant" society, building knowledge upon these foundations: hence *scientia sexualis:*

The confession is a ritual of discourse in which the speaking subject is also the subject of the statement; it is also a ritual that unfolds within a power relationship, for one does not confess without the presence (or virtual presence) of a partner who is not simply the interlocutor but the authority who requires the confession, prescribes and appreciates it, and intervenes in order to judge, punish, forgive, console, and reconcile; a ritual in which the truth is corroborated by the obstacles and resistances it has had to surmount in order to be formulated.[114]

Friar Luís de Nazaré, the debauched priest, and Maria Joana, the walking compendium of syncretic prayers, were both overcome by a veritable frenzy of loquacity during their interrogations. Furnishing much detail, the priest narrated episodes that were extremely similar to each other, even recalling events from long before, as if entranced with recapturing them. He was humble and plaintive and exaggerated his regret, blaming the error of his ways on his "wretchedness" and "weakness."[115] Maria Joana likewise did service to detail with great ardor, listing an impressive number of magical-religious prayers and dredging up from memory the places, people, and circumstances involved, as if she too, through her confession, were pursuing an identity lost in the course of the trial.[116] It was as if the impact of the interrogations had unleashed an identity crisis within the accused, traumatically dissociating the elite and popular levels intertwined in their everyday practice. Acting against their own best interests, the defendants succumbed to an "eagerness to confess and to expiate" in their desire to forge an alliance with the inquisitor.[117] The epitome was adherence to all the inquisitor said and the belief that what had been confessed had in fact taken place.[118]

The realization of guilt often was triggered by the forces of repression. At the time Heitor Furtado de Mendonça was making his way around Pernambuco, for example, Beatriz Martins and Gaspar Francisco became aware of their violations when they heard that the Inquisition regarded them as such. Beatriz had heard the announcement "of the documents of the Holy Office," which condemned affirmations that the state of matrimony was better than that of religious vows. Pressured by her fears, Beatriz recalled the time when she had first started thinking that way: "It seemed to her that she, being a young girl, had heard [these ideas] from a woman, her mistress, who had taught her to cook and to wash in her homeland [Mérida]."[119]

Gaspar Francisco gave a most interesting testimony that exemplifies this introjection of the inquisitorial mechanisms of repression. While still living in Lisbon, he had declared that the state of matrimony was better than that of the clergy. Shortly thereafter, he discovered that he "had spoken badly," according to the general monitory and edict of faith announced in the See, in São Domingos and São Roque, and "he immediately cast aside the error." He went to confession and received absolution, along with a warning that he should go before one of the inquisitorial boards in Lisbon to report his offense—which Gaspar failed to do, "out of carelessness." After moving to Pernambuco, he heard the announcement of the edict of faith ordered by Heitor Furtado de Mendonça, which again indicated that Gaspar's earlier assertion, made in Lisbon, was a heresy. Once more he felt pangs of guilt and sought out a Jesuit to make confession. Curiously enough, the priest "told him that there was no danger here that witnesses would come forward to accuse him, that he could be exempted from going before the Board; and for such reason he had not come." But his fears once again got the better of him when, "during the public act held at the main cathedral, some were given penance for this very reason." He went to another confessor, "who wanted not to absolve him, and ordered him to come before this Board, for which reason he now comes and asks forgiveness."[120]

As soon as he discovered that he had acted against the precepts of the church, Gaspar grew uneasy and tortured by fear and guilt. Through one confession and then the other, he sought assurance that his sin would be forgiven. But not even his confessors managed to give him a straight answer. One of them said that in the colony—land of sin—no one would denounce him; the Inquisition was a whole ocean away. The other, within the context of the Visitation, encouraged him to report his offense—for the threat was now at hand.[121]

The foreman Baltazar da Fonseca—whose peculiar religious views were seen in chapter 2—was made aware of his error thanks to the auto-da-fé held in Olinda, where he heard a penance given to someone "who had renounced the cross and the saints, and hence he was perplexed and for this reason he has now come before this Board to denounce himself, and henceforth he shall believe and hold to that which this Board teaches and orders him, and he has come forward with this intention, so that if he be wrong, he may cast aside his error, being herewith declared and enlightened."[122] His testimony is a sincere example of how the colony's living religion differed subconsciously from that postulated by the Inquisition.

The news going round about the all-powerful Holy Office and the announcement of monitories, sermons, autos-da-fé, and banishment all induced people to denounce themselves and others. Meanwhile, the inquisitors stirred the frightened memories of the suspects and defendants caught in their net, unearthing corpses. When the memory of a possible violation had been lost somewhere in the passage of time, the interrogation endeavored to revive it—for example, in the instance of Brásia Monteiro, in Pernambuco: "Asked if she knows or suspects for what reason she has been summoned, she responded nay; . . . if she knows something that someone has done against our holy Catholic faith, she responded that she knows no more than that which she has already said before this Board. . . . Further asked specifically what person is it that she knows to have lashed a crucifix *she said that now she remembers that many years ago, she knows not how many, Branca Dias being alive. . . .*" And she began her denunciation.[123]

The net of denunciations entrapped people who might not have come forward spontaneously to testify before the Inquisitorial Board. The Holy Office's terrifying eye, ever-watchful and probing, discerned crimes where ordinary people would often not so much as glimpse them. João Antonio, a 27-year-old carpenter, took part in a conversation with Pero Gonçalves, likewise a carpenter, and with the stonemason Antonio Martins. At the time, João thought there was nothing unusual about their topic.[124] The Inquisition rekindled his memory during interrogation; it shifted his recollection out of the context in which it had been recorded and dressed it in new clothing, the tone being set by the offense: "Asked from whom he had heard it said that no one goes to hell for women or like matter, he responded that he does not remember having heard such a thing, and was thereupon admonished to tell the truth, if he had heard this from one Pero Gonçalves, carpenter, because this Board has information that he was present, *and that if he does not speak the truth, he shall be punished. He responded that now, after the specific case had been stated to him and the circumstances surrounding it, he recalls and remembers that it is true that. . . ."* And he went on to denounce his friend.[125]

Francisco Cortes asked forgiveness for the blasphemy he had uttered fifteen years earlier, in Barcelona.[126] Salvador Carvalho Serra, arrested and tried for stealing hosts, remembered an old incident of a pact during his interrogation.[127] At the time of the Visitation to Grão-Pará, Crescêncio Escobar came before the board of his own volition to confess to a compact dating nine years earlier; he had reasons to be terrified, since his cohort, Adrião Pereira de Faria, had been arrested and prosecuted by the Holy Office and had fled to the interior.[128] Ana Seixas's testimony before the board in Pernambuco is moving. In 1594 she had been married fourteen years, and she confessed to having had anal relations with her husband twice, although he had ejaculated in her *"vaso natural* [vagina]." She asked forgiveness and said that "she had agreed to said relations to do the will of her husband." She added that she was "happily married in love and friendship with the said husband." Divulging the smallest details of his intimate life and contributing to the construction of what Foucault called *scientia sexualis,* the husband went to unburden his conscience too. The first time anal relations had occurred, he had been drunk, and "the said sins he had done against the will of his wife, who, out of fear of him, had consented."[129]

Particularly when it came to sexual matters, confessing was not enough— the violation had to be dissected and the acts described and disclosed before the inquisitor's sick curiosity. João Batista, a lad of fifteen, worked as page for one Lopo Soares, a bigwig in Pernambuco's colonial administration. Before the board, he naively told that he had gone to fetch a pair of his master's slippers from the shoemaker, who had raped him. Pressed by the Holy Office, he was compelled to recount the event in minutiae: "He was warned that he should state if the said shoemaker had penetrated with his member in his breech, and that he should speak the truth about all that had happened, for if he should tell a lie or silence the truth before this Board, he shall for this reason be punished; and he responded that the said shoemaker had not entered nor penetrated his *vaso traseiro* [rectum], for the reason that he, the Accuser, had not consented nor given opportunity for this, and everything that he has said is true."[130]

The Inquisition thus engendered the perception of guilt, pried it from memory through its interrogations, and then, reversing direction, introjected this guilt into the defendants, prompting adherence to the inquisitorial discourse, as stated earlier. José Januário da Silva cured *quebranto* with magical words and prayers, as seen in chapter 3. When questioned by the inquisitor, he replied that he had faith in the words he pronounced. The inquisitor then warned that the devil was quite fond of mixing good words (those of prayer) with empty words (those of superstition), to which the poor prisoner responded that if the words he had said entailed diabolic concert, he had used them without realizing it, naively. The dreadful inquisitorial logic eventually defeated him:

> Asked if he, the Deponent, knows that the words "St. Anne begot Mary, Mary begot Jesus Christ, and St. Isabel [begot] St. John the Baptist" may contain a blasphemy and slander against the Most Holy Virgin and her Most Holy Son; for it being certain that Our Lady the Virgin begot, remaining always a virgin, and that Jesus Christ Our Lord was born without it being the deed of a man, none of these attributes are found either in St. Anne or in St. Isabel, or in St. John the Baptist; and that for this reason, there being no difference in the said words, and considering Our Lady the Virgin like St. Anne and St. Isabel, and Jesus Christ like John the Baptist, then they are denied those unique qualities that are due them: to Our Lady as ever virgin, and as mother of God, and to Jesus Christ as conceived by the Holy Spirit, without concert of any man.[131]

The cure for *quebranto* had been transformed into an attack on Mary's virginity. The defendant had not thought of this but ended up recognizing that he had blasphemed; he regretted it and asked forgiveness.

The Indian Domingas Gomes da Ressurreição, who likewise cured *quebranto,* saw her knowledge of folk medicine ridiculed by the inquisitor, who strove to confuse her and make her doubt her therapeutic powers. As explained in an earlier chapter, the formula Domingas used was a syncretic prayer that made mention of white, black, and scarlet roses. The inquisitor drew on the same argumentation applied to José Januário: that it was a sin to mix good words with vain ones. The indigenous woman revealed the doubt this stirred within her: "She said that only now, after she made her confession, did she become dubious of the words by which she performed cures, and for this reason she also suspected that there may be in them something of the superstitious." As soon as the Holy Office's visit was announced, Domingas had begun to have pangs of guilt and wished to confess. The inquisitor took advantage of her hesitations to introject more and more guilt feelings, resorting to wild argumentation: "If she, the Deponent, knows that the three colors, white, black, and scarlet, are opposite to each other, and could not be placed together on one ill part"—to which the accused acceded. Well, the inquisitor rejoined, if she knows that, she should also know that the words she used were vain and superstitious, grounded on a "clear and evident lie" and lacking any virtue save that communicated by the devil, "who is father of the lie, and always making use of them." When Domingas said she was curing the illness without curing it, she was clearly lying and in so doing "showed that she had dealings, friendship, commerce, and communication with the demon." The accused capitulated: "She has said that she now knows the error in which she has lived, using lying and vain words and actions, which may contain superstition; however, she has said and done all by material means because she was thus taught." Cautious, she denied any compact, stating that she wanted nothing to do with the devil, that "instead, she hates and loathes him, and flees from him as a common enemy that thinks only of taking souls to their damnation." Finally, she promised never again to practice such cures, which she finally realized were "questionable" and composed of vain words.[132]

The mechanisms that the Inquisition deployed against individuals, leaving them at its mercy and reshaping them according to its creed, also made any chance of escaping this subjugation seem very remote. Mateus Pereira Machado had been arrested in Bahia in 1750 for carrying mandinga pouches. He reached Lisbon in 1753 and was taken to the inquisitorial prisons. One year later, when the testimonies of other deponents arrived from Bahia, the defendant was transferred to the Inquisition's secret jails, which is where he was the day the 1755 earthquake struck. Interrogations were resumed on May 19, 1756, at which time the inquisitor asked him what he had been doing during his period of freedom, since the tragedy had destroyed the Inquisition palace.[133] Mateus then told how on the day of the earthquake, after Aves (i.e., late afternoon), he had managed to break down the door with the help of two companions, one of whom was his Bahian friend Luís Pereira de Almeida. They had left by the hallway, with the fire at their heels, consuming everything. They had then joined some other blacks. The next day they had gone to Rocio at the jailer's summons and had signed an agreement promising not to run away. "And so long as he had been in freedom, he had occupied himself with the work of clearing away rubble in the streets to earn a few vinténs for his sustenance, *appearing many times at the door of the pavilion where matters of the Inquisition were processed to see if anything was desired of him.*"[134] One week earlier, on May 12, 1756, he had been taken anew to the Inquisition's jails, by then rebuilt.

During the six months he had been free, he had not attempted to run away or escape trial or slip out of the clutches of the Holy Office but had instead passively accepted his fate. One month later he was convicted at an auto-da-fé and in August began his banishment in Castro Marim, a sentence he served out conscientiously until 1760. He had given ten years of his life to the Portuguese Inquisition, which he was unable to evade even when by chance he had gained his freedom.[135]

The Inquisition's Task: Hunting Down Pacts with the Devil, Degrading the Colonial Condition, Shattering Human Lives

As we have seen, confession was the key to the legal system organized during the Early Modern age. For the judges who dealt with sorcery offenses, what mattered most was extracting confessions of diabolic compacts from the defendants. Again borrowing a formulation by Franco Cardini, this covenant was the "fundamental theme around which the theological and juridical image of truly heretical sorcery could be constructed."[136] It was debated whether or not such pacts were actually a fabrication, and each author held his or her own opinion about their true nature, illusory or concrete.[137] In general terms, however, from the fifteenth century on, the idea that it was heretical to invoke the demon *with supplications* predominated; in other words, the viewpoint was no longer that applicable to ritual magic in the Middle Ages, which aspired to master or command demons.[138]

In capturing and reconstructing the imagination of Europe's elites at the close of the Middle Ages, it can be said that demonologists and theologians established one of the currents of thought that supported the construction of the sabbat—in its essence, a myth foreign to the popular mentality.[139] But this elite current was not the only one at work; it was an integral part of a cultural complex further composed of dispersed elements of popular culture that had been fused in the crucible of the Inquisition.[140] The sabbat was therefore one of the main mental constructs introduced thanks to the confluence and interpenetration of elite and popular concepts that occurred in the early days of the Early Modern age, often in traumatic fashion. Diabolic pacts and the sabbat went hand in hand, almost always impossible to disassociate. Once an inquisitor had extracted a confession of a compact, he started on the trail of the sabbat.

As Carmelo Lisón-Tolosana has observed, in inquisitorial mythology it is the defendant who is portrayed as powerful. He or she is the author of the pact, the person who must be exterminated or cleansed.[141] The inquisitor hunts about in search of this diabolic covenant, probing among practices buttressed by popular tradition. Some of the condemned bravely denied the accusation; others, intimidated even if not tortured, confessed whatever their opponent wanted to hear.

Antonia Maria, tried twice, confessed to reciting a number of magical prayers and to practicing romantic sorceries but firmly denied any covenant with the devil. At most, she pointed her finger at her enemy Joana, with the clear goal of freeing herself from inquisitorial insistence on this topic. But even in the absence of proof, it was acceptable to make allegations: "the Defendant being a baptized Christian, and as such obliged to hold and believe that which the Holy Mother Church of Rome holds, believes, and teaches; and with her life and habit to set examples, not using spells, superstitions, and brews, and other things, by means of these to achieve diverse ends, she has done the opposite, and from some time thenceforth, forgetting her obligation, has used the said things, desiring through them to achieve the purposes intended, *which could not be without the Defendant having a pact with the demon.*"[142]

It was the first quarter of the eighteenth century, but the Holy Office's stance still resembled that of late-sixteenth-century judges and demonologists, when "Butt-That-Burns" [Arde-lhe-o-rabo] had been accused simultaneously of sorcery and of being a "dishonorable woman," a double stigma that fit like a glove in the case of single, penniless women. Like Antonia Maria, the sorceress of the colony's early days negated the reality of the magical practices so skillfully insinuated by the inquisitor: "She, within her inner self and her soul, never had erred in our Holy Faith, and never had she spoken with the devils nor had dealings with them, nor possessed bones of the hanged, and never had gone to the abyss of the ocean, and never had buried jugs with sorceries . . . but all the things she *had said and feigned doing, all being false,* to fool the said people who asked her for spells, to take from them money and things to eat."[143] Antonia Maria's trial records show the intersection of two concepts under debate since the Middle Ages: the actuality of sorcery and its fictitiousness. The former concept was embraced by the elites, while the fictional interpretation was invoked by the sorceress to justify her social role as the community witch; since the community saw her as an intermediary between themselves and the supernatural, she responded to this popular need as a way of making her living.

Arrested in 1756 and sent to Lisbon, where she arrived early the next year, Isabel Maria was insistently questioned by the inquisitor about the pact she had supposedly entered into with Satan: ". . . if by *maleficium* and diabolic compact, she had done or intended to do harm to any person's *life, honor, or property,* and if for this purpose she had contracted or sought to contract in any way friendship with the devil." The defendant had boasted she could transport people, go shopping in Lisbon, and subdue wills, but she denied any pact. The inquisitor insisted: had she made recourse to words for lascivious purposes or relied on the demon's concourse?—for God did not act in such a manner. Isabel Maria dodged first one way and then another, claiming ignorance as justification for her actions.

But the Holy Office pressed on, steadfast in its effort to hunt down a pact and extract a confession consonant with demonological theory, asking "if she had found herself with the demon at some gatherings of people where she had seen and known other persons with whom he had friendship, and who worshipped him?" In response, the defendant's despair: "She said that, for the mercy of God, never had such a thing come to pass with her." She perceived she would pay dearly for her cavalier proclamation of inconsequential words, when her sole objective had been to earn the admiration and envy of those who knew her. Then came the merciless verdict, grounded in her claims about nocturnal flights: ". . . boasting that she was one of the demon's favored so that she be feared and could hold subjugated to her those with whom she had dealings, all of which leads to the presumption that she, the Defendant, straying from the common practice of Catholic believers, does believe in the demon and with him has dealings and friendship." In addition to being convicted of minor heresy in an auto-da-fé, she was forced to serve out three years of exile in Leiria, Portugal, a great distance from Belém, where she had gone voluntarily years before at the encouragement of El-Rei [the king], who wanted "people to populate that conquered land."[144]

Nothing has been found to indicate the use of physical torture during Visitations to Brazil. The Inquisition did, however, resort to means of persuasion that terrified the defendant and had a powerful psychological effect. Joana Preta was suspected of having poisoned a fellow slave over a matter of jealousy involving their masters, as seen in chapter 5. As soon as Geraldo José de Abranches began his interrogation, he threw in the question of a pact, purportedly made with the intention of realizing certain desires. He pushed the defendant to confess. When she denied the accusations, he stated that superstitions were invariably "inventions of the demon . . . for it is certain that God Our Lord does not involve Himself in vain, worthless, and superstitious things." In the light of such evidence, to deny the pact was *insolence*. Intimidated, Joana began to give in: "She said that even though she had used the said things for the reasons stated, and even though she had been warned that they were superstitious and invented by the devil, *she had never made an express pact with him*; however, that if in said things there be a hidden, tacit pact, in this case she must have made one, for using the said things." She was not aware that this sortilege involved the devil's concert and only learned of it when warned by her confessors: "And she knows it now with greater clarity by the questions that have been put to her." The avid inquisitor wanted to know about promises made to the devil, about his appearances before her, about the body parts Joana had given him "as a sign of subjugation and that she was his slave, disciple, and friend," about the reverence she paid him, worshipping him as a god. After four years in jail, her verdict was announced at the Visitation Board. She abjured *de levi* and was exempted from banishment.[145]

The inquisitor interpreted the magical-religious prayers described in great detail by Maria Joana before the Visitation Board as presumptive evidence of a pact. She agreed that she trusted in the devil and admitted there may have been a tacit pact, but she firmly denied having entered into a pact per se.[146] The prayer to St. Mark pronounced by Manuel Nunes da Silva was also likened to a pact during his inquisitorial interrogations. At first he successfully dodged accusations, but two months later he ended up charged with a tacit pact.[147] The inquisitorial logic shook the convictions of the accused, who eventually caved in to the charges. Manuel Pacheco Madureira used prayers to achieve success in romance and was in addition a practitioner of the basket divination. Always on the prowl, the inquisitor asked if Manuel knew that Jesus and his saints were not in the habit of granting favors for vile ends. The defendant concurred: "All thus did he know, but his wretchedness and weakness had led him to this great precipice." The groundwork was laid for introducing the question of a pact: "If, as he says, he did thus know and understand, it was certain that he, the Deponent, could not expect, nor indeed did he truly expect, to attract the desire of the said woman for his libidinous purposes, save solely through the concert and intervention of the devil, entering into a pact with him and contracting his friendship by means of the aforesaid words, which he calls prayers." Cowering, Manuel Pacheco said that "he did not know how to answer the question, and he only knew that he had never made a pact with the devil." Under this pressure, he eventually affirmed—with no conviction at all—that he had invoked the devil twice and had promised him obedience only between the hours of eleven and twelve o'clock on the same day, regretting it immediately and confessing the next day. Triumphant, the inquisitor rejoined that this meant that on these two occasions he had entered into an explicit compact with the devil and that he should make a full confession. Vacillating at each new round of questions, Manuel responded that if he had made a pact, he had done so unawares, without deliberate intent.[148]

The inquisitorial logic did not always prove intimidating enough. The next step was then torture. By all accounts, Manuel da Piedade had fallen into the Inquisition's clutches because other prisoners had accused him. There were indications that he attended sabbats, and the inquisitors pressured him to confess something to this effect. In response to his denials, they tortured him. This triggered a deposition that is remarkable for its fluctuations: he confessed that "he gave the demon his blood, and then said that this was a lie, and again said that it was true that he had given him his blood, and his arm hurt, and he was wounded by a knife belonging to a Negro named João, he does not know to whom he is a slave, and then he said that what he had now stated was a lie, and then he again affirmed that he gave him his blood, and at Campo de Santa Clara . . . , but there was no sign of a wound, but never did he give him his soul or adoration." Dissatisfied with the tenor of his confessions, the inquisitors ordered further torture, which lasted about an hour. The next day, as was standard practice, they summoned him and asked if he remembered what had happened and if he confirmed what had been said following torture. "He said that he remembered the session that had occurred on the said days of the present year in the house of torture, where he was taken, and the confession he had made there, and the people of whom he had spoken, *which he did falsely, and he had said such things under the pressure of the torment whereto he found himself subjected, and that he retracted it all, and the lies he had told in the same confession for the said reason.*" The records of his testimony were taken and then read back to him. The accused listened and agreed, though he was incapable of signing "due to the suffering he had experienced during said torment." Ten days later, they summoned him yet again and questioned him about his testimony: did he recall having said, on the torture table, that he had gone to Campo de Santa Clara to speak with the devil? The defendant did remember, "but . . .

had said so falsely." The inquisitor refreshed his memory: he had said he had seen the devil in the figure of a dark-gray she-goat and of a cat and had given him his blood. Manuel remembered the confession, "but . . . it too was false." Faced with the Inquisition's insistence, Manuel said that "nothing had happened between him and the devil, and that which he had said had happened with him was false; . . . that he had never gone with anyone to the field, nor had he even left his house."

Seeing the chances for confession of a pact evaporating, the inquisitor closed in: "How could it be that he had not gone to the field in Massarelos with the Negroes, if he had named some in whose company he had gone to make a mandinga, and had said of them that he had seen them talking with the devil?" Manuel replied that it had been a lie, that he had never set about to prepare a mandinga, "and that he had always wanted and endeavored to be a good Christian. . . . If he had heard of mandingas, he had paid no attention and what he had said had happened with the devil had been out of fear and under the pain of torture." Because he was cruelly tortured, "that is why he spoke against himself and against everyone, and all falsely."

Impervious and obsessed with his hunt for the pact, the inquisitor judged Manuel "blind and obstinate in his guilt" and accused him of endeavoring to "conceal the devil and his cruelties, . . . moving from precipice to precipice" and aggravating and augmenting his guilt, "retracting his statements and contradicting all that he had said in that place, attributing everything to falseness and to the pain of torture." It had been fifteen days since his first session, and Manuel da Piedade was sent to the house of torture for the third time. The fruit of this further violence was of course his confession to a pact and to attendance at sabbat gatherings held in Campo de Santa Clara. Finally, this inconsistent finale shows the poor defendant's desperation: he affirmed that the devil had asked him not to attend mass but then added that

> *what he had said about the mass was too much,* and also that the devil had told him to talk to him every day, and had asked him for his soul, and he had said that he could not give him his soul, and [the devil] had asked for the blood of his body, and he likewise had not wanted to give it; and he said that he had given him his soul and his blood; he had not said prayers to him even though the devil had asked for them, nor did he take him as God even though the devil told him to take him as such, and then he said that he was confessing to everything that was not true, and he said no more.

Deeming his confession unaltered, the inquisitors subjected Manuel to a fourth torture session.

Five days later, the unfortunate man confessed to everything the inquisitors wanted to hear: a pact had been made; he had given the devil his blood, his soul, his worship; he had taken part in sabbats and the crafting of mandingas; he had abandoned the Catholic faith. His penalties were harsh: abjuration *in forma;* perpetual prison and penitential habit; and floggings *citra sanguinis effusionem* [until he began to bleed] through the streets of Lisbon. The Holy Office had shattered his pride and fashioned him into an obdurate sorcerer, exactly according to the book of European demonology. Manuel da Piedade was black, a slave, born in the city of Bahia.[149]

The trial records of another slave, José Francisco Pereira (mentioned earlier), offer one of the finest examples of the Holy Office's mechanisms for making the defendant introject the elite's concept of sorcery. As stated in chapter 4, which addresses tensions within the colonial slave system, José Francisco had been arrested in Lisbon in 1730 and charged with making and bearing mandinga pouches. Born on the Mina coast, he had lived for some years in Brazil and there had picked up the custom. He was known as a *mandingueiro* among blacks in the capital of the Kingdom, and it would appear that he had a small business going in amulets. Other than that, nothing concrete could be ascribed to him, and his first testimonies were centered on these facts.

José Francisco was, however, quite talkative, and he named many slaves who had asked him for pouches. The Inquisition construed these group connections as sabbat gatherings. By the time his Bill of Indictment (Libelo Acusatório) was read, the court had clearly solidified its presumption of a pact and had arrived at a negative judgment of him, ". . . from which it can be gathered that the Defendant's confession is fraudulent and deceitful, made solely for the purpose of escaping the great punishment he deserves, and not of healing his soul; and as such it is not admissible, nor is the Defendant deserving that any mercy be granted to him but all the rigor of justice, . . . that he be punished with the greatest and gravest penalties of the Law, which for his offenses he deserves, all in complete fulfillment of Justice."

The Statement of Charges published by the courts explains that José Francisco was accused of using blood from his left arm or from a chicken to write the letters that went with the pouches. Furthermore, he dedicated prayers to "Luçafé" in order to seal his body and avoid injury in disputes. Intimidated by constant threats of torture, he began raving; he described metamorphoses by the devil, who would appear in different guises, asking for his soul and for blood, traveling with him in ships, invading his home, demanding parts of his body, and urging him to attend diabolic assemblies in Val de Cavalinhos. José Francisco's frightened discourse is rife with confused notions derived from heterodox popular traditions: the devil would say that "everything was nothing like what the Ministers of the Church taught and advised him, that those matters of the Church were false, and when he went into a Church he should soon exit it, and when he entered it, he should cast the holy water behind him, for only Jews sought the Church and had the habit of staying there for very long."

The intimidating interrogations, detention in secret prisons, and the steady threat of torture awoke in José Francisco the need to talk more and more about his friendship with the devil and his option of an antichurch and of demystification; finally—in a conclusion rich in significances—it aroused in him an obsession with painting in minute detail "the point of weakness where evil portents reach through to us; the fragment of darkness that we each carry within us"—in other words, sexuality.[150] The inquisitorial methods stimulated him to wild imaginings about the numerous possibilities of coitus, which coincidentally were part of demonological knowledge: anal relations—painful, ice-cold, devoid of pleasure, and rife with guilt feelings.[151]

"He stated further that he was so intimate and familiar with the devil that for a long time his dealings with him were vile and lascivious . . . , the demon serving him in the figure of a woman to satisfy his venery, having carnal copulation with him for many years, with the demon always being a *succubus,* and sometimes the demon had sodomy with him, the same demon acting in the figure of a man, and penetrating his *via prepóstera* [rectum]." In the guise of a woman, the demon varied from ugly to beautiful; however, she was "always white in color," which held a special meaning for the black man José Francisco. The coitions he had consummated with the real women he had known were "more enjoyable" than diabolic coition "because he found more heat in these women, while in his coition with the devil, when the latter served him as a woman, he found roughness and ice-coldness." Even when the acts were heterosexual, they held within them the potentiality of homosexuality: "During this same act of coition he always saw the devil with both tools that differentiate the two sexes and by which they are known." It was easier to penetrate regular women and have ejaculations with them than with the devil; since dark and sinister desires flowed together in the demon— all was arduous and slow, spawning guilt and punishment. "He stayed on him much longer, and when this copulation was finished, he felt greatly enfeebled, with pain in his hips, his arms, and throughout much of his body. . . . His member was always left aching, showing some sign that a thin layer of skin had come off, always left battered and weak."

"He stated further that also with the devil he had vile and lascivious dealings, both in the form of men, putting their members between one another's legs and spilling between them; and that which the demon spilled was something cold, and when the demon sought his *vaso traseiro* [rectum], he always felt . . . great pain and roughness, his belly began to ache and he felt some swelling in it, and from his *vaso traseiro* blood would flow." Del Río always warned judges to keep a constant, watchful eye on accused sorcerers because even in jail they would copulate with the devil.[152] So it was with José Francisco: "After he came forward before this Inquisition, he still copulated with the devil, serving him in the figure of a woman, and the devil had him by means of sodomy . . . ; and the devil always warned him not to confess before the Holy Office to anything that had happened with him, telling him that if he confessed, he would punish him most severely, but he did not say what punishments these would be."

There was no preference for one form of sexuality or another, which was regarded instead as something unified and integral. Engaging in homosexual sex did not erase a desire for women, and the devil himself was an accomplice in this regard, giving José Francisco touch-letters he could use to seduce women.

As far as can be deduced from trial records, José Francisco revealed the world of his imagination to the inquisitor more because he felt intimidated psychologically than because of torture. This once more challenges the idea that the Inquisition tortured less than lay tribunals and therefore was more benevolent and less cruel. This slave's amazing case opens up countless analytical possibilities. Caught in the terrifying position of being charged by the Holy Office, the defendant not only revealed the frightened, guilt-ridden psychological universe that was also shared by the era's educated men but also confessed what they expected him to confess. His belief in amulets was transformed into adherence to the demon of the theologians, while it simultaneously caused an unearthing of all the dark, frustrated desires that Christian tradition endeavored to camouflage and disguise.[153] The inquisitor, dazzled by the world of the imagination that unfolded before his questionings, always wanted to know more and demanded further details, for in the black man's raving discourse he recognized the source of demonological theory. The inquisitor asked: "Which of the vile couplings that he had with the devil was most odious to him, whether it was the sodomy he consummated with him, or the coition, the devil playing the role of woman?" In addition, he asked whether José Francisco usually told his male friends about his sexual adventures with the devil, if they had sex together, if Satan brought other devils along to these diabolic assemblies "in the figure of women, so that together all could engage in the depravities that he declared"; if he usually assigned names to these *succubi,* if he spoke out loud with them or in whispers, if their meetings took place during the day or at night. At various moments the Inquisition sought to frame the universe of the imagination inside a logical discourse, running anew into the clash between symbolic and rational. The inquisitor grew elated when he detected in the poor defendant's speech echoes of Guibert of Nogent, who believed the devil unleashed his debauchery upon women;[154] of Caesarius, the monk from Heisterbach who attributed the origin of the Huns to intercourse between ugly Hun women and demonic *incubi;*[155] of St. Thomas Aquinas, the theoretician of explicit and tacit pacts and of the differentiation between *succubi* and *incubi;*[156] of De Lancre, advocate of the idea that diabolic coitus was cold and painful;[157] and of so many others.

José Francisco's trial records raise another question: the sincerity of belief in the pact. The moment the accused chooses to adopt a discourse that is the inquisitor's but that shares points in common with the popular imagination, he or she believes that everything actually happened as stated.[158] In this sense, José Francisco's story reminds us of the "Benandanti" of northern Italy, followers of a centuries-old fertility cult that eventually became transformed into a diabolic cult after more than a century of inquisitorial pressure.[159] It further brings to mind testimonies such as that of the Spanish sorceress La Solina, who, intimidated and tortured, produced a crazed account that likewise speaks of sodomy with the devil.[160]

Finally, the Calvary of José Francisco provides us with elements for rethinking the question of sorcery as a mythology exclusive to the European elite or as a cultural system where popular and elite elements interpenetrated. It once more raises doubts about whether it is possible to reconstruct the popular universe based on institutionalized repression and interrogations led by inquisitors, almost always skillful in manipulating the answers to their questions.[161] It leads to one certainty, perhaps the only one among so many questions that remain unanswered: that sorcery trials were a unique place where distinct discourses intersected and overlapped, weaving, perpetuating, and affirming a stereotype.

By the same token, these trials allow us to perceive moments when the gap between the popular and elite worlds is wider. This rift becomes apparent primarily when the inquisitor brings up the defendant's inferior condition, not always quite explicitly. During Manuel da Piedade's interrogation, the Holy Office wanted to know how he went about invoking the devil: if he had "whistled *as is the habit among Negroes.*"[162] Upon recording the black woman Caetana's accusations against Friar Luís de Nazaré, the assistant priests read her testimony back and then asked if what was written was the truth. She "responded in *her coarse and awkward way of speaking Portuguese* that all that she had thus stated was the truth."[163] José Francisco Pedroso declared before the Inquisition's board that he used mandingas because he believed them to be "a thing of God." "How could he believe that the mandinga was a thing of God if he saw that *only Negroes used it?*" asked the inquisitor.[164]

The defendant's inferior condition served to justify his or her repression. In a letter to the Inquisition in Lisbon, a member of the clergy—probably a Jesuit and Commissary of the Holy Office—stated that imposters pretending to be witches abounded in colonial lands. "And as they are commonly Negroes and Indians, it is necessary to have power here, so that those who use such impostures can be ordered flogged; and if not, they shall continue their whole lives with this behavior, with no one to reprimand them promptly."[165]

Added to the contempt felt for poor populations in Europe was the repudiation of popular culture itself.[166] And when it came to the New World's inhabitants, the European elites supported their stance by a new prejudice, directed at the *colonial condition.* As stated repeatedly in this book, the colonists were members of a singular, menacing humanity that often took on demonic hues.[167] Twentieth-century authors have interpreted expressions of popular religiosity like the *calundu* of colonial days as "coordinators of passions," possessing the ability to alleviate social tensions. Yet what bothered authorities in the Luso-Brazilian colony most of all—and what bothered the inquisitors themselves—was the *colonial* nature of these expressions, a threat to metropolitan power.[168] Measures like Vasco Fernandes César de Menezes's provisions against the *calundus* of blacks are part of this picture, their zeal justified by the need to defend the "republic's" interests and to "protect the peoples and service of God."[169]

Scholars who have studied the Iberian Inquisition contend that its activities were particularly intense through the seventeenth century, after which they declined. As far as Brazil is concerned, however, no such turning point can be observed. On the contrary, trials were especially numerous in the eighteenth century and, as can be seen in tables 1 to 3 in the appendix, there was an increase in the number of trials involving the most prosperous regions. Aimed at popular culture and tradition, the elites' "enterprise of expropriation" intensified in Brazil during the eighteenth century.[170] But it did cleverly undertake to don new attire.

According to Amaral Lapa, the Visitation to Grão-Pará occurred at a time when the Holy Office was in decline and when the Marquês de Pombal was battling to see torture abolished.[171] Taking a close look at how inquisitors dealt with defendants, some variations can be observed and, as of 1768, a sharp change in course: the arrogance and intransigence of Geraldo José de Abranches gave way to a more "reasonable" and tolerant position. As had happened before with the Bahian group in the 1750s and with the Carvalho Serra brothers from Minas Gerais in the 1760s,[172] Anselmo da Costa and Joaquim Pedro were arrested for carrying mandinga pouches.

But while their cohorts were shipped off to Lisbon, where they were tried and then appeared in autos-da-fé, these two indigenous men from northern Brazil received completely different treatment. It is true that they had endured four long, bitter years of incarceration—from 1764 to 1768—but when the Visitor sent a list of their offenses to the Council General in Lisbon, the latter ruled that the charges did not warrant a trial. It was stated about Anselmo that

> rather, the Defendant can be seen to desire the same sacred things with the decency and respect befitting his capacities, bearing them round his neck and hoping by means of them to free himself from greater dangers that he might come to encounter in his life, which he naturally seeks to preserve, and for this purpose all means that assist in this end are valuable, and even if these be, and are, improper, all must be attributed to the lack of education found in the Defendant, and not in any intent that he may have had to insult the aforesaid things. Likewise, the condition of the Defendant does not call for greater punishment, for, to offend religion, it is necessary to be instructed in religion and have an intent to transgress, all of which is lacking in the Defendant.[173]

Incapable of discerning the error of his ways, the accused could not possess the malice needed to commit the offense, "and without [this intent], *maleficia* cannot exist." Of Joaquim Pedro it was said that he knew "only those things indispensably necessary to Salvation, and this only in material terms and lacking that knowledge that enlightens the spirit, to preserve holy and sacred things pure and free of superstition, which is transcendent throughout that country." Finally, the inquisitors from Lisbon advised that the defendants should be released but nevertheless harshly rebuked before the board and educated in the mysteries of the faith, their "lengthy imprisonment" in the city of Pará for more than four years "having been overly sufficient punishment." It was further stated that in the case of Anselmo "heed should likewise be taken of his being a minor at the time of the wrongdoing, being only fourteen years old." It was October of 1768, and the days when sorcery trials were built around the testimony of children seemed to be fading into the distance.[174]

A number of witnesses denounced the black slave Maria Francisca for divining with a basket. The recording of her offenses began in 1753, and five years later the Lisbon Inquisition's official opinion reached Belém: "heeding her coarseness and want of education," and also because "in this Kingdom knowledge of the things of religion is different than in that State," the defendant should be harshly admonished but not receive any greater punishment.[175] After two centuries of intransigence, the Inquisition finally seemed to begin perceiving the singularity of the colonial populations' living religion, which could not be reduced to the dogmatic faith guiding the Holy Office's actions. Making constant reference to the defendants' coarseness and lack of education, the Inquisition also allowed itself to recognize the pertinence of the colonists' medical knowledge in northern Brazil. The Bill of Indictment for José, a black slave *curandeiro*, was likewise only seen by the Lisbon authorities four years after it had been written up; and as in the previous cases, the Council General dealt leniently with the accused. It was declared that the tribunal only punished "those who committed deeds that, exceeding the force of nature, must, by the circumstances of the Subject, be ascribed to the power of the Demon; and as it is befitting in the order of Nature to heal the ill by virtue of herbs and fumigators, there is no reason for why the aforesaid cures should be construed as offenses."[176]

With a delay of almost one century, the "supernatural omnipresence" (of God or the devil) in daily life was replaced in Portugal by a more rational understanding of existence; Satan's retreat "gave back to man and to nature an autonomy rendered impossible by the previously permitted mixture of natural and supernatural."[177]

What is noted in a first reading of these documents is that the Inquisition became aware of the gap separating elite religion from popular religion and that it began to demonstrate greater complaisance—and even take paternalistic stances—toward the coarse and ignorant colonists. This makes sense if the Holy Office is thought of as an autonomous, sovereign tribunal. During Pombal's reign as prime minister, however, efforts were made to restrain this powerful institution, culminating in enactment of the Instructions of 1774.[178] At the same time, Portugal's educated elite was growing steadily more convinced of the pressing need to solidify an economic policy that would guarantee preservation of the colonial condition and, in the final analysis, of its overseas possessions.[179] All the above-mentioned opinions issued by the Council General date from October 1768. It is curious that this shift in the inquisitors' attitude toward the colonists occurred between enactment of the Lei do Diretório dos Índios in 1758 and imposition of the new Instructions in 1774. This further coincided with the apogee of Pombal's reformist concerns and with the realization that—at that juncture of external dangers (foreign threats against political and economic control of the colony) and internal dangers (the possibility that the colonists might become conscious of their colonial condition)—the Portuguese colonial empire was facing the threat of ruin.

If the Inquisition truly lost autonomy under the pressure of the state, another look must be taken at this benevolence toward the colonists and what it may have meant. When Portugal adhered to a more rational form of thinking, one that called into question the reality of magical facts and sorcery, it was following the European trend that Mandrou has investigated so well in the French case. Together with this rising complaisance and even a certain paternalism, however, there was always a disdain for the colonists themselves: an ignorant people—black, Indian, or mixed-blood descendants of Portuguese—incapable of understanding the complexity of faith, of displaying reason, or of reaching a more refined spiritual plane. In the trial of Joaquim Pedro, the Inquisition took as its own the words of one witness, in whose opinion the young men involved in stealing altar stones possessed "that intelligence befitting the condition of Indians."[180] So even long before the colonists had constructed the perception that they were all "poor children of America, forever hungry and with nothing of their own"[181]—be they black, indigenous, or mestizo—the Inquisition took advantage of the prejudice and mistrust that pitted them against one another.

To some extent, this adherence to one of the facets of enlightened rationalism also explains the disdain for the colonists expressed by the Inquisition's "benevolent" and "complaisant" judges in northern Brazil in 1768. Once again, it is Mandrou who sets us to thinking: the thesis of witches' non-responsibility brought the culmination of the crisis of Satanism in France. The realization finally hit: the best way to eliminate witches was to make them look ridiculous.[182]

At the dawn of the Early Modern age, a rift had opened between popular culture, where beliefs in magical acts and *maleficia* were wholly integrated, and elite knowledge, which persecuted these practices yet did not fully relinquish belief in them—both the ordinary people and Bodin believed in witches. A new rupture, distinct from the previous one, began to take shape at the close of the seventeenth century. This time the enlightened elite parted company with popular beliefs, and in this new context a position like Bodin's became untenable. When the first rupture had taken place, the possibility of belief had been preserved. But now the division was governed by skepticism; and whereas persecution ceased, prejudice did not.[183] I would like to suggest that from this viewpoint, the Inquisition and the Portuguese state were collaborators in sustaining the rift between popular and elite, readjusting it in accordance with their concerns about preserving the colonial world. The colonial condition was thus eviscerated with a view to ridiculing it and, yet again, conserving dominion of the overseas world. Behind the inquisitors' apparent "benevolence" lay the true, hidden intent: to bring home the impossibility and incapacity of the colonist to decide his or her own fate. In the eighteenth century, the Holy Office no longer banished those accused of sorcery to Brazil.[184] The entire colonial system was then being reshaped and rethought, and the metropolis dedicated special attention to homogenizing and conforming the people in the colony. So what sense would there be in adding new numbers to the already menacing army of mestizos, coarse and ignorant, fated to a universe of dissidence and rebellion?[185]

Throughout the colonial period, the Inquisition was an organism that wrought terrible destruction on the social fabric and was responsible for collective panic and personal tragedies. Even when it did not murder, it incarcerated for years on end, isolating defendants in prisons far from their families and from any form of human contact; it tortured them and, not infrequently, drove them to madness. After condemning them to traumatic and often deadly stays in the Inquisition's dungeons, the Holy Office subjected the accused to public scorn, to ridicule, to the humiliation of grandiose autos-da-fé organized for the purpose of intimidating, impressing, and terrifying the spectators. Before returning the offender (now transformed into human refuse) back to society, the Inquisition sentenced her or him to banishment or to the galleys. Some heroes, like Adrião Pereira de Faria, managed to make their way back to family and friends after this Calvary.[186] But his case was certainly atypical. The devastating effects of the Inquisition sundered the social fabric and the collective memory. In the indignant words of two nineteenth-century Portuguese historians, what was taking place within the Holy Office was a "composite evil, fashioned from unprecedented monstrosities crafted for the perdition of humanity."[187]

For Henry Kamen, the prisons of the Spanish Inquisition were not dens of terror.[188] Perhaps here they differed from the Portuguese prisons, which Father Antonio Vieira described in these horrifying terms:

In these jails there are usually four and five men and sometimes more, according to the number of prisoners that there are, and to each one is given his water jug for eight days (and if it runs out before that, one must simply bide his time) and another for urine, with a chamber pot for one's needs, which is also emptied every eight days, and there being so many who are kept in this filth, it is unbelievable what these wretched people must endure, and in the summer so many are the bugs that the jails are filled with them, and the stench so excessive that it is a blessing of God if a man leave there alive. And well can we see on the faces of all who appear in the autos the treatment they have received therein, for they come out in such a state that no one recognizes them.[189]

It must have been common for prisoners to go mad in the jails, since the Instructions of 1640 address this topic in book 2, chapter 17.[190] Isabel Mendes, arrested in the late 1620s and charged with Judaizing and sorcery, went insane in prison "following seven years of grievous suffering."[191] Mateus Pereira Machado was afraid he would go crazy during his imprisonment prior to the earthquake of 1755: "He, the Defendant, was constantly distressed by his imprisonment, but nevertheless he did not swear falsely; however, he believes that this incarceration disturbed his thinking, for he remembers that at that time he suffered some forgetfulness, of which he is now wholly free, and for so being he gives much thanks to God."[192] Had the disaster not destroyed the inquisitorial jails and thus set Mateus free, it is likely he would have gone mad.

The saddest story I know is that of the *pardo* shoemaker Antonio Carvalho Serra, Requibimba by nickname, born in Mariana, Minas Gerais. He was arrested for stealing hosts in early 1757 and reached Lisbon in August of the same year. He must have taken ill in prison, because when he was brought before the court for examination two years later, he said he had known how to read and write a bit but could not do so after the sickness that had befallen him. It is impossible to say exactly when he lost his mind, but after two years in jail he was clearly mad. Before he was sent to Todos os Santos Hospital, in 1761, a number of depositions about his behavior were recorded. The prosecutor José Mendes da Costa stated that, "whilst at the start of this accusation, the Defendant had no defects in his thinking, although one could always perceive in him frenzy, and a greater resoluteness than is common, today he shows himself frenzied and visibly crazed, both by his actions and by the words he pronounces." He then advised that the defendant not be judged until he had recovered and shown signs of being in a perfect state of mind and "able to defend himself in the prescribed form"—which, given the way inquisitorial trials went, sounds like a joke.

The Holy Office's jailer underscored Antonio's rough and fearful temperament, recalcitrant even when medicine was administered; he testified that the defendant displayed "total impairment of his thinking, which is steadily worsening, because he undresses before all and no longer will tolerate clothing, being naked in his cell; he wants to eat nothing made in the fire, eating everything raw, even codfish." He would ask for food that was not part of his ration, would not tolerate cellmates, had lost his initial slyness, and could no longer be punished. The guards confirmed that Antonio was mad. One of them said that when Antonio had first come to the prison, he spoke without problems; but shortly thereafter he suffered a stupor and became partially impaired. Another guard, apparently a faithful follower of the inquisitorial ideology, said he had noticed *a disorder of some kind* in the accused and had attributed it to the "desperation born of his temperament." He added that the madness was partial, for the hapless man could still eat and sleep. Other witnesses described his gauntness, his body being nothing but skin and bones; his loud cries; his nightly singing; the filthy clothes he wore, "wandering about the place even while bleeding, talking as if he was speaking with his wife or some young boys"; refusing food for fear they would poison him; and "feigning like a rich and honored man." In 1761 it was decided that Antonio should be transferred to the hospital. The following year, when he died, Dr. Manuel José Monteiro, who nursed the deranged, signed his death certificate: "ACS madman; state, country, fatherland, and occupation unknown."[193]

There was physical torture too, of which the rack and the pulley were the most common in Portugal. The procedures took place in the house of tortures, "a kind of underground cave, all vaulted," with benches for the inquisitors, physicians, and surgeons and tables for the notaries.[194]

Cruelly tortured, Manuel da Piedade underwent torment nonstop for an hour during one session, "in which he called out for Jesus and [said] he wanted to die by Faith in Christ."[195] His verdict omitted the torture, stating only that the defendant *had wanted* to confess. In the case of the rack [*potro*], the defendant was placed on a board, and his or her four limbs were bound at two points each: thighs and calves, arms and forearms. When he was tortured on May 31, 1756, Mateus Pereira Machado was tied "at six points only, for he had a wound on one arm." He cried out greatly, beseeching the wounds of Christ to succor him, "together with the crown of our lord King Dom José." Three times he begged for mercy, saying he was going to finish confessing. But when he added nothing new, his torture was resumed until those examining him on the board were satisfied and sent him back to prison.[196] After three torture sessions, the Bahian shoemaker José Fernandes— who had stolen consecrated wafers around 1760—was saved by the doctor, who stated that "the said Defendant was not fit for more torment, from which he was promptly removed, where he had spent twelve minutes and had called out repeatedly for Our Lord Jesus Christ, and Most Holy Mary, to succor him."[197]

All indications are that about ten autos-da-fé were held in Bahia and Pernambuco between 1592 and 1595.[198] They must have been modest and meager compared to those in the metropolis. Maria Gonçalves Cajada, or Arde-lhe-o-rabo, was one of the Brazilian sorceresses who appeared in an auto-da-fé in the colony, which took place in Pernambuco in 1593; it was recommended that Maria not be publicly flogged since she was ill.[199] Starting in 1595, all those convicted in Brazil appeared in autos held in the metropolis. Although some Portuguese witches were sent to the stake, there is no indication that any Brazilian sorcerers were "relaxed."[200] But the Brazilian offenders were scourged, some until blood gushed from their wounds, and in their disgrace and humiliation were paraded about the streets of Lisbon before the eyes of the king, the princes, the inquisitor general, the jailers who had interrogated them for months, and all the people. Their offenses and secrets were exposed and read in public. In the case of José Francisco Pereira, for instance, his verdict was read in its entirety, including the descriptions of diabolic intercourse and the sabbats in Val de Cavalinhos. He was *encarochado* [made to wear a conical witch's hat], abjured *in forma,* and was obliged to serve out a sentence of five years in the galleys.[201] Manuel da Piedade, José Fernandes, and José Martins were among others flogged *citra sanguinis effusionem,* and Manuel was condemned to wear a *sanbenito* or penitential habit for the rest of his life.[202] Next came banishment: five years in Angola for José Fernandes; five years in Castro Marim for Mateus Pereira; the same in Miranda for José Martins; five years in the galleys for Manuel da Piedade; and six years in Miranda as punishment for the relapsed heretic Antonia Maria.[203]

After this, they were free to return to "normal" life. Until their deaths, they would carry with them the stigma of having been accused by the Holy Office, many wearing *sanbenitos.* What may have been the destinies of the Brazilian colonists who, after years of captivity and terror, found themselves free in a strange land? Very little is known about the sorcerers. One illustrious defendant, Bento Teixeira, appeared in an auto-da-fé in 1599. He was sentenced to life but received permission to live in freedom. He lasted just one year, struck down by a lung disease that took him to his death, spitting blood.[204] Antonio Serrão de Castro, apothecary and poet, was absolved in 1682 following two years in the cells. Nearly blind, "he found it necessary to beg, although of an advanced age, so as to support himself, two children, who had been born demented, and a second sister, a widow."[205] His other elderly sister had died in prison as a result of punishments.

Considering the cold reality of numbers alone, many past and present scholars have asserted that when all is said and done the Inquisition killed very few and that the lay tribunals that judged sorcery were more cruel and destructive.[206] Fortunato de Almeida justified the Inquisition's actions with a formulation that stands as a true pearl of reactionary thinking: "The number of victims would have been much greater *if the Inquisition had not rid the country of the horror of holy wars,* which caused the spilling of tides of blood in the countries where the Protestant Reformation penetrated."[207] Sônia Siqueira adopted an analogous stance, underscoring what she deems a "meritorious achievement" on the part of the Holy Office: "The minute percentage of deaths, in relation to the number of reconciled, reaffirms the Holy Office's *good intentions* of cleansing the faith and *bringing back into the fold* believers who had strayed."[208]

Any believers who may have been brought back into the fold by the Inquisition—annihilator of lives and of wills—would have been frightened, broken people, hypocritically convinced of the truth proclaimed by the tribunal. Contemporaries of the horrors of the Inquisition protested against its operation and its existence.[209] In the early twentieth century, Antonio Sérgio assessed the destruction wrought within Portuguese society by the Inquisition and concluded that it hindered the flowering of critical thought within the realm of culture.[210] The Inquisition's deadly consequences cannot be measured or translated into figures.

Looking specifically at the repression of sorcery, it can be said that the Tribunal of the Holy Office reflected the clash between two different cultural universes, in which the one personified by the court held the upper hand and was momentarily embodied by the defendant. In the course of an inquisitorial trial, the figure of the witch depicted in the inquisitor's symbolic universe was momentarily absorbed by the accused or superimposed on her or his beliefs. Popular tradition in Portugal was unfamiliar with the sabbat, and yet people confessed to having attended diabolic assemblies.[211] Always ready and eager to transform individual practices into collective ones (i.e., sabbats), the Inquisition thus endeavored to justify its discourse and its repression. After undergoing the trauma of incarceration, torture, and an auto-da-fé, the accused might return to their previous beliefs sometime later; hence the backsliding of individuals like Antonia Maria and Domingos Álvares, who eventually resumed the practices that had originally incriminated them.[212]

This is not to say that the Inquisition "created" the stereotype of the witch—as asserted by so many of the historians analyzed in this chapter. The tribunal tampered with the inner workings of the popular cultural universe, altering and expunging the significance it assigned to magical practices. Cases where previous practices were resumed illustrate how the Inquisition's devastating impact could be overcome and the popular cultural universe reorganized.

Reverence for the supernatural and belief in magical acts were constituent elements of both universes, but with different meanings assigned to them by each. The witch-hunt in early modern Europe was an attempt to standardize these differing concepts. In Portugal, the intertwined discourses that echoed through the trials of the Holy Office provided a fertile arena where the stereotype of the witch could be constructed, affirmed, absorbed, and, in the end, demoralized.

On the theoretical level, it should be said that this was the confluence, struggle, adoption, renunciation, or dismantling of two distinct cultural universes. What is appalling is that during this clash, in the complex weave of these discourses, the Inquisition consumed, shattered, and degraded so many human lives.

CHAPTER 8

Remarkable Stories: Where Their Roads Led

*Truth and lies are faced alike; their port, taste, and proceedings are
the same, and we look upon them with the same eye.*
　　　　—Montaigne, *Essais* (book 3, chap. 11, "Of Cripples")

*Historians are more interested in testimonies than in witnesses from
witchcraft trials, and they thus deprive themselves of one of the phenomenon's social dimensions.*
　　　　—Robert Muchembled, *"Sorcières du Cambrésis"*

Maria Barbosa, Manuel João, Luzia da Silva Soares, Luzia Pinta, Salvador
Carvalho Serra, and Adrião Pereira de Faria would never be remembered at
the dawn of this third millennium had they escaped the clutches of the Inquisition. The first woman was poor and of ill repute, while the other two were
black slaves; one of the men was a barber, another a carpenter, and the third—
a bit more fortunate—a militia sergeant in Vila da Vigia. Their relations with
the powers-that-be were defined by submission: it would appear that Maria
Barbosa performed sexual favors for governor Diogo de Menezes, and Luzia
da Silva Soares was slave to a man who owned tracts of land rich in gold. No
matter how poorly he may have governed, Diogo de Menezes—like his enemy Dom Constantino Barradas, bishop of Brazil—would have gone down
in history, if only as a name on a long roster of colonial administrators. But
what record might have been left of Maria Barbosa?

Even when society's subaltern classes are not ignored by historians, they
seem condemned to silence. Yet there are times when sources allow us to
reconstruct "not only indistinct masses but also individual personalities";
when—to borrow Carlo Ginzburg's formulation—it becomes possible to make
out faces in the crowd, to "extend the historical concept of 'individual' in
the direction of the lower classes." This is indeed an innovative approach:
lending identity to the anonymous and affording them the same treatment
granted only to members of the ruling classes until a very short while ago.

Such an exercise, however, must be wary of the risks of becoming paternalistic or anecdotal. The "history of the vanquished"—to use an expression
very much in fashion—is not justified merely by the qualifier but rather by
the noun: it is *history,* and for this reason deserving of our attention. Corre-
spondingly, a given individual biography is placed in the limelight not to
survey facts but to probe within them for the microcosm that reveals an

entire social stratum. That these are nearly anonymous biographies, at first glance merely average and unimportant, is precisely what makes them so representative.[1]

The remarkable stories of these obscure colonists reveal the relationship between metropolis and colony, power apparatuses and individuals, elite culture and popular culture, the real and the imaginary. Knowing their stories helps us better understand what the colony's social formation was all about. It also helps us remember that beneath the single face of Clio lies a hidden mosaic of individual adventures, which may be recovered. Finally, this knowledge is paramount to maintaining our ability to feel dismayed and outraged in the face of iniquity.

Maria Barbosa

Maria Barbosa was a *parda* from Évora, where she had married the goldsmith João da Cruz.[2] According to the witnesses who accused her, in her native land she had been condemned as a sorceress and *encarochada*. Her sentence must have been banishment to Angola, where she met another *parda*, Marta Fernandes. While in Africa, "in an earthen basin [she] showed the wife of the governor [illegible] da Silveira Pereira tilling with a plow, sewing dressed in green." Back then she used to wear the bone of a hanged man about her neck. In other words, she had not given up her habits, and she was publicly flogged as a sorceress and procuress. She then went to Pernambuco, where again "they were about to make her wear a witch's hat, but out of respect for her husband, they did not." "She traveled about many parts of the world since they sent her away from every place that she went, from Pernambuco as well as from Rio Grande, and from the island of Fernão de Noronha, and from Angola, and from the town of Évora." "Never was she in a land where she did not follow the wicked path," always resuming her sorcery. In 1610 she had been in Bahia for some time. That year Bishop Dom Constantino Barradas led a Visit to the city and forwarded his findings to the Kingdom.[3] Among those accused was Maria Barbosa.

Numerous witnesses had denounced her. "Maria Barbosa leads a most wicked life, and is a poor example, harmful to other people, debauched, and in the habit of cursing many serious curses, . . . much more than any other woman," stated the local authorities, intent on cleansing the social body of the pernicious fellowship of the sorceress and on punishing this lost sheep. "She does not attend mass, nor listen to preaching; nor is she willing to abjure her sins," but works on Sundays and on saints' days. They emphasized that she was a troublesome citizen and poor Christian and then went on to a detailed list of her offenses, which were simultaneously cause and consequence of her marginalized social position. "Being married, she is mistress to many men" (which was tantamount to saying she was a prostitute);

"she is a sorceress and procuress, and for so being she has already been *encarochada* and banished to the island of Fernão de Noronha and other parts."

In the stereotype, sorceress and prostitute were inseparable. At the same time that the defendant's acts of sorcery were described, her acts of indecency were enumerated: she turned her home into a bawdyhouse; procured women for men; spent the whole night with them, eating, drinking, and offending God. She dishonored her husband, "calling him a cuckold, and making him stay at the foot of the cot, and sleeping with men in front of him," saying that "she wants to sleep with whomever she so desires." "With her fingers she makes horn-like gestures on his head," threatening to strangle him to death. She kicked her spouse out so she could live "more at her will" and surrender herself to a series of romantic adventures. "Most of the time, the said Maria Barbosa was someone's paramour, and destroyed many men." Apparently resigned to his situation, her husband lived under her yoke: although he was "[f]ormerly a goldsmith, now his wife has made him a fish buyer, and sends him to Tapagipe, where he stays the entire week, and from there he sends her fish." He occasionally would complain to his neighbors that "his wife [did] not want to join him in bed." Sometimes he went about "as if witless," while Maria Barbosa paid him little heed and called him a "royal parrot." According to one of the witnesses, "she pays him no more mind than if he were her Negro."

Prostitute and sorceress, Maria Barbosa posed a threat to the community by her mere existence and also by the example she set. People believed that women like her worked to win over followers. She sometimes put up other women in her house, as she once did with an ugly, cross-eyed woman that "they also say is a sorceress." But the disciple whose name appeared most often in the accusations was Isabel Roiz, a "fine-looking young woman." Like the colonial Celestina, Isabel preferred to live by herself and had already been initiated into the secrets of Eros. After being widowed, she and her elderly mother came from Cape Verde and went straight to live in the procuress's house.

As soon as it became public knowledge that Isabel was living at Maria Barbosa's, the keepers of the faith and guardians of good morals made it their job to rescue the new arrival from the clutches of the veteran sorceress. Francisco Pereira and Francisco Soares, both brothers of the Casa de Misericórdia (Almshouse), went to Barbosa's to get the novice, "for they said that it was dangerous in her house." But Barbosa also demonstrated ascendancy over her female disciple. She called her aside "and he, the Witness, does not know what she said, but he knows because he was present that the young woman disappeared behind some straw mats after the said Barbosa spoke to her, and now at present it is rumored that she keeps her at her house and that she gives her out."

Isabel's mentor often took her to the homes of male clients. Her elderly mother was scandalized: "She saw some things that seemed very wicked, as when the said Maria Barbosa adorned her daughter with tails in her hair, something she never wore, and put paint on her cheeks." Her protests were useless, for "the said Barbosa would respond that she had to adorn her." Isabel would receive gold earrings from the men who sought her favors. Her mentor would applaud and tell her that "the men of Brazil gave much." Fearful that her daughter would catch a venereal disease, Isabel's disconsolate mother would protest, claiming that Barbosa "would cover her daughter with lesions."

The Visitation of the bishop ruled that Maria Barbosa should pay public penance and be banished for two years to Brazil's southern captaincies. She was accused of being "notoriously the most harmful and scandalous woman to be found in these parts, where there are many wicked ones." But Barbosa had famous friends. One who protected her was Governor Dom Diogo de Menezes; he spoke "with her publicly at the window" and kept her in hiding for a while. Furious, the archbishop of Brazil excommunicated her, resorted to his prerogatives as a Visitor for the Holy Office, and only calmed down when he had managed to get Barbosa thrown in jail and have her offenses sent to the Inquisition in Lisbon. It was 1611.

Maria Barbosa gained renown among the other prisoners for her spells using herbal powders, which she used to bind the heart of one of her lovers (Diogo Castanho). She bragged that she knew many spells and magical prayers, one of which invoked a curious "sea devil." She had ties with an African sorcerer who would go to the jail in person with the herbs Maria needed for her sorcery. She handed out recipes for spells, was debauched in her speech, did not hide her knowledge of witchcraft, and boasted that she was powerful enough to "bring the devil into jail to remove her from it." In their description of Barbosa's behavior, her cellmates reinforced the image of sorceress, procuress, and prostitute that the community had already constructed around her. This collective construction is evident in her trial records, which constantly highlight one or another of the three inseparable facets. One series of witnesses stresses her whorish traits, while the next group lists her characteristics of a procuress who leads young girls astray, and yet another recounts behavior that reminds us of a loathsome, menacing witch.

In 1613 the trial records referred to Barbosa as a "defendant imprisoned by the Holy Office." Archbishop Dom Constantino's fury had found echoes in the inquisitorial "zeal," and the reexamination of witnesses commenced. This time around, they were unanimous in emphasizing her traits as a sorceress, and her spells and witcheries began weighing more heavily than the practice of prostitution. But in order to judge her a sorceress, it had first been necessary to blaze the incriminating trail that made Maria Barbosa into an "easy woman."

Barbosa's journey to Lisbon was one of many adventures. Her ship fell into the hands of pirates at the latitude of the Cape of Espichel, and the unlucky woman was first taken captive and then abandoned in Gibraltar. She reached Lisbon on her own and along the way was aided by the Casa de

Misericórdia, curiously enough the same institution up in arms against her in Bahia some years earlier. Half-naked, she asked the inquisitors to "favor her with a cloak with which to cover herself, inasmuch as she was an honest woman." Finally, in 1614, in accordance with an elliptical verdict that emphasized solely that she had been excommunicated for a long time and had not lived as a good Christian, she was ordered to appear in person at a public auto-da-fé "with a lighted candle in her hand" and to abjure *de levi.* The ruling also prohibited her from returning to Bahia, thus guarding against the "scandal" she caused in the community, based on her three-pronged guilt as sorceress, procuress, and prostitute.

Manuel João

When he left his native Maranhão and journeyed to Belém, the young Manuel João was just learning the barber trade.[4] He went to the new city in the company of two retired ensigns and his uncle, a Mercedarian friar by the name of Manuel. He stayed a while with one of his traveling companions and then left for the farm of his grandfather, Manuel Fernandes Soródio. This was the first time that Soródio had heard of his grandson, introduced to him by his son the friar. Even much later, Manuel Soródio did not want to accept Manuel João as his descendant. Despite the cleric's confirmation, the grandfather "did not recognize him as such" but did agree to take "him into his house with this title."

Right from the start, Manuel João was an outsider in the family circle. His father, Francisco João, was a blacksmith from Loures, Portugal; his mother, a Luso-Brazilian born in São Luís, was the daughter of Manuel Soródio. Considering the grandfather's reservations, it would appear that Manuel João had been born out of wedlock. Manuel Soródio did not know the boy and perhaps knew nothing of his own daughter's whereabouts, her relationship with any man, and most certainly nothing of the fruit of this union. The young barber was then just sixteen, and the year 1668 was dawning. He had been in Belém only three months, and already there were signs he had brought strife and conflict with him. He made friends with his aunt Guiomar Serodia (a year younger than he was), who was irked over a quarrel with her father. She taught Manuel João a recipe for living in constant harmony with Soródio: to sit across from him at meals and send him *figas* [gestures to ward off the evil eye] under the table. Despite their bond of friendship, years later the aunt would testify against her nephew, likewise expressing doubt about their alleged family ties: he "called her aunt, but she did not know if he was [her nephew]."

About six months after arriving in Pará, Manuel João saw his reputation besmirched by the people of Belém. More than thirty witnesses testified against him before the *ouvidor,* accusing him of being a superstitious sorcerer who invoked the devil with words that "greatly offended Christian ears." They were unanimous in blaming him for the specters that had vexed the residents in his grandfather's house ever since his arrival. In an attempt to put an end to the disorder reigning in his home, the grandfather sent his grandson and other relatives and dependents to Nossa Senhora das Mercês Convent, hopeful that the church could settle the problem through exorcism. But "much as the said clergy investigated, they could not discover anything, nor cure the evils that they suffered." Still, suspicions of a demonic pact hung in the air. Bringing pressure to bear on the lad, the priest discovered a written paper containing strange paintings and the names of what were supposedly two devils: Sorro and Oroto.

In May 1668 the *ouvidor* had the boy arrested. They described him then as "a beardless young man, with sparse hair, said to be 17 years of age, and dressed in black cotton breeches and a black gaberdine, with clogs." The bailiff seized a mandinga pouch that Manuel wore about his neck, containing the usual: a paper with prayers on it, strange drawings, twigs of rue, broken bits of an Agnus Dei, a bone that appeared to be from a fresh corpse. When questioned, the young barber began to recount his version of the events at his grandfather's house.

While he did not deny the truth of a number of extraordinary facts, Manuel João believed that many of the testimonies against him were based on hatred sown by his uncle Gaspar Baleeiro. He said that shortly after his arrival, he had taken a liking to an Indian woman named Isabel, a slave in his grandfather's house. The romance infuriated his uncle, perhaps because he too was fond of the young woman and therefore jealous. With the backing of Manuel Soródio, the uncle broke Manuel João's arm, cut off his hair, humiliated him. A deposition by the retired captain Mateus de Carvalho confirmed the boy's mistreatment, even justifying the subsequent sorceries and saying that Manuel had resorted to them, "offended by the blows his uncle Gaspar Baleeiro had given him."

The first of a series of amazing events had involved a fishing expedition. "A Negro by the name of Carlos had gone fishing, and had thrown his spear at a manatee, and had not pierced it, and the manatee had escaped from his sight without his being able to reach it." When they had told another black man, Dionísio, what had happened, he "had jeered at this and had gone fishing another day, and at the river he said he was going to swim underwater to the other bank, and after he dived under, . . . some unknown thing had taken hold of his feet on the river bottom; and with chills and trembling he had returned home, where he had remained some days in a fright."

The second extraordinary fact occurred after the burning of some haunted houses where "black shadows" were tormenting people. Gaspar Baleeiro had ordered his nephew and a black man to raze the structures, and he went along with them. On the way back home, Manuel João started to feel that "someone was striking blows against his legs, without seeing who was doing it," and he fell on the ground. That night a huge beetle appeared to him, passing over his head and going into "a corner from whence it told him that he should order them immediately to cover the rooftops they had burned, or otherwise it would not leave him alone."

Following the manatee and then the beetle, the devil's third appearance was "in the form and figure of St. Michael the Angel" but with very black feet in shackles. He ordered the barber to pray three chaplets and fast two Fridays and two Saturdays. He also taught him some inverted Hail Marys, where instead of "children of God" he should say "we are" and instead of "children of Eve" he should say "we shall be." Finally, "Amen, Jesus" should be omitted from the prayer. The young man taught this to his aunts, who also fasted and followed the angel's orders. The vision appeared quite often and said they should give him a something written with their blood if they wanted to know what those prayers were for. Manuel João refused, but he "then understood that the vision was the devil." The figure next began appearing to other people in Manuel Soródio's house, teaching ballads and practices. This is when Manuel João's alarmed grandfather decided to ask the Mercedarians to perform exorcisms.

Despite his confession, the barber was taken away to the fort of Belém and kept prisoner there while a good share of the community testified against him before the *ouvidor*. Some witnesses made clear that they felt a mixture of repugnance and attraction to the young man. One Dona Inácia told how she had met him at the home of Dona Maria Medina, a relative of Manuel Soródio's, with whom Manuel João had stayed during the exorcisms. The friend had told Dona Inácia about these specters and Manuel João's purported powers, which she termed "talents." Half-terrified, half-fascinated, Dona Inácia asked to meet him. She was surprised "to see him so young and with the reputation of having such abilities." Responding to the women's curiosity, the lad gave wings to his imagination, telling how he had been initiated into the secrets of sorcery by the "Pernambucana do Maranhão" [a nonsensical nickname: "the Pernambucan woman from Maranhão"] and how he had learned to harden water, move basins through the air, divine things. Introjecting the inquisitorial perspective, a scandalized Dona Inácia said that "it was not possible to do such things without superstitious words and diabolic art."

Other witnesses provided details on the specters and the barber's participation in them. They told how he prided himself on knowing how to conjure up demons with words, although he did not know how to make them go away. The deponents stated that "the said Manuel João was the reason the people in his house were haunted by specters, for [he is] a sorcerer and knows words that invoke the devil." "He had the gall to fill that house with devils, but not to put them out, for he did not know how to do the opposite." Those testifying also told how the young man would sometimes show up with hair ties around his feet, which he claimed to be the work of the Pernambucana do Maranhão, who had the ability to appear before him in the company of some Tapanhunos. On one occasion he had buried a howler monkey, saying it would be reborn. At other times, he ran about the house like an enraged madman and scaled to high places, on top of cupboards, "where he could not climb in so short time without the help or order of the devil, and seated there he laughed and threw a pillow at them." Taunting them, he said the devil had given him the pillow.

Witnesses were heard throughout the months of May, June, and July. Meanwhile, Manuel João remained a prisoner in the fort, where he frightened the soldiers with his divinations and dubious behavior: he would go up and down stairs despite the shackles on his feet; he would dance with them on, as if free and unchained; he would unleash high winds and heavy rains. He eventually managed to escape and, according to his own deposition, "spent two or three years sleeping about in forests and villages." He reached Maranhão with the help of the Jesuits, but he was arrested again at the order of the local *ouvidor* and held prisoner for another year.

In early 1672 João Álvares Correia, *ouvidor* and *auditor-geral* of the state, sent the prisoner to Lisbon, along with the Devassas listing his offenses. Although his crimes had been recorded in civil court, they were then transferred to the jurisdiction of the Holy Office. Manuel João was handed over to the boatswain of a brigantine, who ended up leaving him at the port of Angra on the Azorean island of Terceira, where he had no way of proceeding on his journey. The barber was once more put into prison, where he awaited the arrival of another brigantine to transport him to the capital of the Kingdom. On June 11, 1672, he was finally delivered to the jailer of the inquisitorial prisons, who found on him 210 réis, which were turned over to the treasurer of the Holy Office. It had been four years since his first arrest, and he no longer looked the same: "nineteen years, thereabouts, hair on his head all cut and dark brown in color, pale face, small eyes, no beard, hair on his upper lip, with the mark of a knife cut in the corner of his forehead and another knife mark on his face, both on the right half."

Manuel João reached Lisbon already bearing the stigma of being a sorcerer. He himself admitted this: when his questioning started all over—this time by the Inquisition—"he said that while he was on his grandfather's farm and in the town of Pará, he was taken to be a sorcerer." The Holy Office ordered that a new inquiry be held in Belém, this time to be headed by the Ecclesiastical Court. It commenced in March 1673. Given the amount of time that had elapsed, many witnesses no longer remembered what they had declared, others had passed away, and some had gone to live in the *sertão* and were too far away to be interrogated. By July, from all indications, the new Devassa had reached Lisbon. Based on it and on the previous one, the Inquisition summarized the defendant's offenses, called for his detention in its prisons, and charged him with a presumed pact, "for that which had occurred in the house [illegible] of his grandfather and uncle was not a natural thing, and it is very likely that the same demon intervened . . . in virtue of said pact, *principally because he had confessed that he was the cause of it all.*"[5]

In November 1673 the long arm of the Inquisition discovered among the residents of Lisbon two of the former witnesses who had helped build the case of sorcery against the defendant. They had been living in Belém at the time of the specters and remembered everything, attesting to how important this episode had been in the city's everyday life. The authorities who had investigated the case and arrested the accused, as well as the deponents and participants in the events themselves, certainly constituted a significant portion of Belém do Pará's population. By word of mouth, the story of these astonishing events went round—the visions, the aunts' and slaves' fainting spells, the barber's feats, the uncle's and the grandfather's wrath.

When interrogated by the Holy Office, the defendant narrated in greater detail what he had felt during the appearance of the specters. "His eyes were closed and he saw nothing, however he very well heard the people who were present speak, and by their speech he knew them quite well, and he was as if outside himself, unable to rise up." The visions came to him in shadows and "they were shapeless." Right from the angel's first appearance, to Manuel João he seemed "to be an evil angel, and the demon, *for he was not worthy or deserving that the angel St. Michael should appear before him.*"[6]

As always, the inquisitors endeavored to confound the defendant, hurling at him the dreadful logic of argumentation used in Holy Office interrogations. They first tried to unearth a pact, insistently asking if he had given the devil something so that he would appear, since the demon was not in the habit of doing so before Catholic people, nor was he given to harassing them with no profit in exchange. The inquisitors moved next to intimidation, asking "[i]f he knows or has heard tell that hell is the dwelling place of the demons, and that there they are suffering eternal penances to which they were condemned for their offenses?"

In November 1673 the Bill of Indictment ruled that there was presumptive evidence of a pact and underscored the defendant's unwillingness to confess to his true offenses: "The Defendant, using poor counsel, did not wish to do so, but instead, being blind and stubborn, he denies and deceitfully conceals [his offenses], as he is a sorcerer and has a pact, dealings, and communication with the demon." It also stressed the barber's lack of repentance—he did not regret his friendship with the devil—and insisted that the full force of justice be brought against him.

Manuel João was assigned an attorney, which meant practically nothing within the peculiar functioning of inquisitorial trials. His lawyer's arguments were extremely timid; he said that the defendant had always been a God-fearing man and had observed the church's precepts. His client was aware that "the devil is a condemned thorn" and had always fled from communication with him. The lawyer vacillated: "The Defendant has provided a complete and truthful declaration of the temptations that the devil offered him, to which he did not consent; by no means did he do any one thing to which the devil persuaded him. And therefore it should not be held against him that he has declared in the same confession that he had said he gave a writing to the devil, for he said this when importuned by the one who had asked him."

Manuel João raised doubts about some of the witnesses and called others to testify, including "Manuel Biquimão, sugar planter living in the town of Maranhão," and "Tomás Biquimão, his brother." On April 25, 1675, witnesses underwent a new round of questioning in the Carmo Convent, in São Luís. Manuel *Beckman* (the original spelling of "Biquimão") did not show up to testify, but his brother did. He stated that he was married, a resident of São Luís, the son of Tomás Biquimão and of Leonarda das Neves. He was thirty-one years old and had met the barber when they were in prison together. It seemed to him that the lad was a fine, God-fearing person. When commenting on the reasons behind his former prison mate's arrest, Tomás revealed the bias of a rich man who identified with the metropolitan mentality on many points: "It appeared to him that if [Manuel João] had committed some offense in the said crime, *he had done so out of ignorance, for being born in the State of Maranhão and not having the experience that the children of other countries have, to know good and turn away from evil.*"[7] Tomás's stay in prison was not yet related to the rebellion against the Jesuits that was to take place nine years later, when the rich *fazendeiro* would be arrested in Portugal (where he had gone as Representative of the People of Maranhão) and sent back to São Luís—exactly the opposite of what happened to the simple barber one decade earlier.

On October 27, 1676, a decision was made to send Manuel João to torture. It is not clear whether he was subjected to it then or six years later. The description that follows in fact applies to the torments he suffered on April 3, 1682. They ordered him to finish confessing in the house of torture, with the instruments readied before him. "He said that he had never been a sorcerer, that he had committed no offenses." The physicians decided he would not be able to withstand the pulley, perhaps because he had been debilitated by ten years in captivity—"at which the gentlemen ordered him put on the rack." The defendant called out "continually in the name of Jesus, saying that he had not been a sorcerer." The torture lasted a quarter of an hour.

On May 10, 1682, before the prince, the inquisitors, and all the nobility, Manuel João appeared in a public auto-da-fé in the Terreiro do Paço. He held a candle in his hand, and they flogged him until the blood flowed profusely. He abjured *de vehementi* and heard the public reading of his verdict before the curious, pitying, irritated eyes of the crowd. Ten days later, he signed the *Termo de ida e penitência*, a document stating where he would be sent and what his penance would be. He was obliged to go to confession on the Assumption of Our Lady, Christmas, and Easter; say a chaplet to the Virgin every week; and on Fridays say five Our Fathers and five Hail Marys, for the five wounds of Christ. His sentence was five years in His Majesty's galleys, "where he shall work the oars, without pay, at the discretion of the Inquisition." In punishing the sorcerer, church and state worked together.

Here all trace is lost of Manuel João, son of the blacksmith Francisco João and of a daughter of Manuel Soródio. Fourteen years had passed, and the beardless young boy had become a mature, 30-year-old man.

Luzia da Silva Soares

Manuel Freire Batalha was a Commissary of the Holy Office and had headed lengthy Inquiries throughout the interior of Minas Gerais before the first bishopric had been established in that captaincy, in 1745. In April 1742 he wrote to the Inquisition in Lisbon to report on his accomplishments as a keeper of the faith and also on suspicions that one of Domingos de Carvalho's female slaves had made a pact with the devil. The woman in question was Luzia da Silva Soares, a 40-year-old black woman who resided in the *arraial* known as Antonio Pereira, in the parish of Nossa Senhora da Conceição.[8] Years before, when he had started the Devassa, the Visitor had issued an official opinion stating that the slave should be detained in the town jail in Ribeirão do Carmo (today the city of Mariana), located in the same district. Following her arrest, around 1739, she had been taken to the prison in Rio de Janeiro, where she awaited both ratification of the witnesses who had testified against her and a decision on her voyage to Lisbon. She ended up going, and on December 18, 1742, she reached the capital.

Luzia was born near Olinda, "where they call it the village of São Bento," on the sugar plantation of one João Soares, where his mother lived as well. But the master had gambled away all his slaves, and Luzia was sold to Maria Gomes, in whose house she lived until the age of six. From then on she changed masters several times. She eventually came to belong to Manuel da Silva Preto, who lived in the parish of Antonio Dias das Minas Gerais. He died shortly thereafter, and the slave was left to his brother, José da Silva. Although she had a series of masters, Luzia enjoyed moments of freedom and adventure too and had even wandered about the woods with *calhambolas* [fugitive slaves, also known as *quilombolas*]. At the time of her capture, she was married to a Benguela slave by the name of Bartolomeu.

Luzia had always been treated well, "with much love, in the houses she had been in before becoming slave to the said sergeant-major José da Silva, so much so that the said Maria Gomes laid her down to sleep in her bed and she slept with her the whole time she was in her house, as if she were her daughter." Even in the home of Domingos de Carvalho, José da Silva's son-in-law, Luzia had been treated with great consideration—until they began to think she was a sorceress.

The first accusations against Luzia date to 1738. On that occasion her mistress had gone to the slave quarters to punish the young woman but could not get the door open, as she was overcome by a sudden sharp pain in her arm. A series of amazing events took place from that point on, each one involving Luzia. Whenever her mistress saw Luzia, she would be struck by an excruciating headache. After exploring the matter, it was discovered the headaches were triggered by pots of boiling water prepared by the slave; when the water boiled, her mistress's mouth would burn in terrible pain. If she tried to punish Luzia in despair, by striking her with the soles of her slippers, her arm would ache and go limp. Once, acting on her suspicions, she took a knife and cut some embroidery flosses wound about the young girl's neck. Her pain went away.

To verify Luzia's offenses, her masters bound and tortured her. Under this vicious torment, the slave began to superimpose her masters' beliefs on her own and to include the transgressions attributed to her in her confessions. Later, in Lisbon, she reported that "if she had denied doing these *maleficia,* they would soon punish her, so that she had seen herself forced, to escape punishment, to confess that she had done them, this not being the truth." To save herself from torture "and the pain and affliction that it caused her," she said that "she had done that which she never had."

When Luzia confessed to an initiation that perhaps never really took place, she fell back on a deep-seated African belief, common to European populations as well. She said that she had been initiated into demoniacal society by a black man named Mateus, who had persuaded her to talk to the devil at a crossroads. On that occasion, she had smelled "a stench like a goat" and heard someone snorting. A voice asked who she was. She replied that her name was Luzia, to which the devil retorted: "You are mine." Henceforth, the slave called him "her king Barbado." Mateus had hexed a child and carried its withered remains about in a leather bag that also contained gold dust and some papers, along "with other powders made of different feathers." During one of her torture sessions, Luzia confessed to having used some of these powders to make her mistress, Josefa Maria, fall ill.

Another significant stage of Luzia's confessions under torture was her admission to a pact. She said she had made a compact with the devil and had promised to be his. She had given him her blood, taking it from her ribs, belly, legs, and feet. By means of this contract as well as superstitious words, she caused maladies and also removed them when so desired. Years later, in Lisbon, she made clear that she had confessed to the pact in terror of the "mighty punishment that they gave her so that she would thus confess, and not because she had in truth done anything." Slave-masters also acted as hounds on the trail of diabolic pacts.

Luzia further confessed to having put many roots and white powders all around the house, provoking different kinds of pain, colds, and lack of appetite. She had buried pots containing roots, powders, frogs, animals, human nail parings, and hair from the white people in the house, all with the intent of causing harm. It was later necessary to dig more than one hundred holes to disinter these *maleficia.* But when her masters ordered the sorcery pots burned, everyone in the house again caught a cold.

The accusations listed in Manuel Freire Batalha's *Devassa* also blamed Luzia for the deaths of little children. She had killed her masters' daughter by sucking on the baby, "for she was a witch." The infant had been born weak and was baptized at home. Four or five days later, the child began to suffer very acute pain, and within twenty days she was dead. Her father noticed that there was a sort of bite next to her mouth and nose. It was there—as Luzia would later confess—that the slave had sucked out the baby's blood, entering the bedroom "through a hole in a window, in the figure or form of a butterfly, like the witch that she was." Family members interred the infant, but Luzia dug it up and used its arms, legs, and innards to concoct sorceries. She buried its arms and legs in the slave quarters' oven. She placed its innards in a jar and used them to make a porridge that would be administered to the mother's child, Josefa Maria. She burned the afterbirth and buried it under the doorsill. Filled with hatred, according to her masters' accusations, Luzia wanted to make her mistress even more miserable; she wanted her masters' marriage to go badly and to this end buried three handfuls of rooster tail next to the cot where her mistress slept. Like European sorceresses, so too was Luzia able to provoke sexual impotence.[9]

The accusations charged Luzia with casting spells in all directions. To do harm to her mistress's father, she had buried a rag doll with a needle stuck "into its heart." Along pathways and at crossroads she would bury powders, frogs, and various creatures that would cause the plantation slaves' feet to swell and also give them stomachaches and headaches. Two black slaves had died as a result of these *maleficia*. Luzia targeted the labor force as well, annihilating it.

These confessions and accusations attest to the existence of conflict. Luzia claimed that her mistress did not like her because the woman suspected her husband was sleeping with the slave. The black man Francisco, famed for his ability to see inside people, had denounced Luzia to their masters because he could not talk her into having sex. Tensions and conflicts were also apparent in her masters' fear of this simple slave woman's extraordinary powers. The denunciation lodged by her boss, the contractor Domingos Rodrigues de Carvalho, provides a fine example of how the master stratum lived in constant paranoia in the slave-based colony. According to Domingos, Luzia's motivation for performing "the said spell was to kill him, his father-in-law, and his wife, and become mistress of the *fazenda* where they lived." Until she achieved this goal, the slave would cast spells so the mines would yield no gold. Although the slave system formed the backdrop of this story, the fear of Luzia's *maleficia* harked back to the European roots of the witch stereotype; in Europe people likewise believed in these individuals' inordinate power to influence the means of subsistence and instruments of work.[10]

In Lisbon, Luzia's confessions took on a new light. The slave reported that Josefa Maria had once fallen ill and nothing could improve her condition, stirring the suspicion that the sickness was the result of *maleficia*. The masters had then summoned the black man Francisco Ferreira, the one who wanted to sleep with Luzia. He was quick to say that the author of the *maleficia* was Luzia, and this meant that only she could undo them. Her mistress ordered her to do so, under the threat of punishment. Luzia denied the accusations, insisting that they were all lies and that she had never cast spells and did not even know what they were.

Infuriated, Josefa Maria reported this to her father and husband. Together, the three decided to punish Luzia so that she would confess to her wrongdoings. They bound and tortured her with unprecedented brutality. Over a heap of fiery embers they heated "a large pair of blacksmith's tongs, which, after they were red hot," were pressed against the poor wretch's naked body, leaving it covered with open sores and raw flesh. Out of her senses, and in an attempt to escape further torture, Luzia confessed her responsibility for the *maleficia*. But since the mistress's health did not improve, her owners resumed the torments. They pinched her tongue and stuck a needle with four threads through it. They tied her to a ladder and set a fire next to it. Singed all over and passing out time and again, Luzia confessed to everything her masters wanted to hear: that she had made a pact with the demon and on the occasion had been surrounded by lights, circling about her; that she had hexed the child and killed it.

Irrespective of her admission to a pact, the torture continued, since Dona Josefa Maria failed to recover her good health. They used a slender cord to squeeze Luzia's head tightly; they punched her; they threw dippers of cold water at her; they stuck the tips of her toes on the firing pin of a shotgun and snapped the hammer shut, "most painfully breaking her bones when it struck." They dripped hot sealing-wax on her genital region; they put her in the stocks, leaving her irreparably disjointed—since that time, "she never again had good health, nor the strength to work, nor to do that which was necessary for her." With a sharp stick they pierced around her left eye; it came out of its socket and she lost sight in it. They beat her with an unsheathed sword until they broke her right shoulder bone. In despair, "many times she wanted to kill herself with a clasp-knife, from which God Our Lord saw fit to save her." But the worst torture she suffered was being flogged by black slaves with bunches of switches, leaving her covered in blood. They then left her tied out under the sun, where the flies bit her and creatures gnawed her flesh down to the bone. She would have died if other slaves had not taken pity and come to her rescue, washing her wounds.[11]

After this torture, her masters handed Luzia over to the law so that she could be further punished; they denounced her *"without malice or slander, but in the service of God Our Lord."*[12] At the plantation manor, her confessions had all been recorded by the priest José de Andrade, uncle to her mistress, Josefa Maria.

After all she had been through, Luzia was paraded in chains about the *arraial* for everyone to see. Years later, people still commented that she had been sent "imprisoned to Portugal by the Holy Office."

Luzia's confession to the Inquisition in Lisbon left a deep impression on the inquisitors. They ordered the reexamination of the witnesses called by the defendant, those whom she identified as having knowledge of the inflicted cruelties; this was done in 1744. Many confirmed the slave's claims, that is, that her masters had ordered her flogged solely to obtain her confession to a pact and that they had meted out "most serious treatment" and "most harsh lashings."

Luzia da Silva Soares did not end up in the secret prisons. The inquisitors were convinced that her offenses were minor and did not trust either her masters' accusations or the records of Father José de Andrade.

> It appeared by all votes that she should not be imprisoned, nor tried for the offenses for which she had been ordered into the custody of the penitential prisons to be examined, as she indeed had been; not only because of what these same examinations state, but also because the witnesses of the summary proceeding are very close kin, and people from the same home, and of whom the Defendant was a slave, and because they testified without any other grounds for believing that she used *maleficia* and had made a pact with the demon other than the fact that she had so confessed, which she did solely to escape the most harsh punishments that the same witnesses gave her, as stated in the summary proceeding that was later ordered at the instruction of this board, to better investigate the matter; where it is further stated that in the act of judicial questioning of the Defendant, carried out by the vicar Manuel Freire Batalha, present at all times was the priest José de Andrade de Morais, relative of the same witnesses, and the same person who had brought her in under arrest and handed her over to the said vicar, and for this reason she had not wished to deny that which she had already confessed, dreading and fearing that she would again be handed over to her masters, and that the latter would again punish her with the same severity and excess with which they had done so already, so many times. *And therefore she should be set free, and sent in peace to wherever it be well for her.*[13]

This remarkable document is dated May 20, 1745. The Holy Office was calling into question its own usual methods, namely, the practice of hunting down pacts and judging them based on the defendant's confessions and on depositions by witnesses who were not always reputable or unbiased. This apparently was progress. But after Luzia's trial came others, where those accused of sorcery were dealt with most harshly. More than complaisance on the part of the Holy Office, what this story may reveal is that the tribunal felt a certain irritation toward a power that had *preempted* it. After all, these torments at the masters' hands occurred before the beginning of the episcopal Inquiries, which, as seen in the last chapter, did not employ torture. Moreover, this other power, wielded by the master stratum, had vested itself with authority that should belong solely to the Holy Office. In essence, the Inquisition did not disapprove of the procedure that Luzia's masters had adopted on their plantation. But finding itself caught in the uncomfortable position of acting as its own judge, the tribunal felt compelled to take a more lenient stand with a view to reaffirming the full scope of its powers, which a given social stratum could not be allowed to usurp—otherwise, how could it justify its own existence?

It was possible to free Luzia and deem her innocent because she had already been sufficiently cleansed of her superstitious practices. On May 31, 1745, a judicial instruction closed the books on her case. The Inquisition defiantly *set a captive free*.

Luzia's trial had lasted seven years, and during its course multiple concepts were woven together. Luzia's beliefs (her apprenticeship with the slave Mateus, the practice of typically African *maleficia,* the knowledge of medicinal herbs used for such specific purposes as ceasing menstruation or causing bellies to swell) were interwoven with her masters' beliefs, more typically European and revolving around the stereotype of the witch: brewer of potions made of cadaver parts, someone capable of penetrating cracks in doors and windows, causing sexual impotence, destroying the source of daily sustenance, and, finally, entering into pacts with the devil. When Luzia was detained in the Inquisition's prisons in Portugal, a third discourse became intertwined with the first two: the inquisitorial. During her interrogations, she was asked whether she had ever used an altar stone or similar objects "for illicit ends." Luzia had never heard of such things.

Luzia Pinta

Luzia Pinta or Luiza Pinta—the two forms appear interchangeably throughout her trial—was an unmarried black freedwoman from Angola who lived in Vila de Sabará, Minas Gerais.[14] She had been brought from Africa sometime around the early 1720s. She was arrested on March 16, 1742, under Manuel Freire Batalha's Devassas. From all indications, when the Visitor reached Minas, denunciations had already been lodged against the woman in the Bishopric of Rio de Janeiro, under whose jurisdiction the gold-mining region fell. These denunciations were followed by the interrogation of witnesses, pursuant to the norms laid out by the Inquisition in Lisbon. According to standard practice, denunciations and the depositions of witnesses formed the body of accusations against the defendant and constituted the legal matter underlying the inquisitorial interrogations.

On December 18, 1742, eight months after her arrest by the Devassa, Luzia/Luiza reached Lisbon, where the Inquisition began interrogating her. Her first confession came on March 18 of the following year, when she was still in the public prison. One month later she was transferred to the private or "secret" prison, due to the gravity of her offenses. The inquisitors considered Luiza/Luzia recalcitrant, and on July 10 the prosecutor's Bill of Indictment was entered; on August 12 they began torturing her. Convicted of minor heresy, she appeared in the public auto-da-fé held on June 20, 1744, where she heard the verdict announced and abjured *de levi*. On August 4, 1744, Luzia/Luiza reached the *couto* of Castro Marim, in Algarve, to which she was banished for four years. The scribe typified her as a woman of "fifty years of age, thereabouts, *preta baça* [pale black], tall and stout, with a mark quite close to her forehead and one on each cheek [marks that suggest ritual wounds]."

Compared to other trials, Luzia Pinta's progressed rapidly. But this did not mean it was not traumatic. The mighty tribunal took Luzia/Luiza—already torn from her native land by the slave trade—and cast her to the outskirts of the very metropolis that had made her a captive in its most important colony. She watched as the African rites to which she had remained faithful were metamorphosed into an inadmissible, condemnable breach of the law. This simple story consequently bears the marks of Africa, Brazil, and Portugal, the triangle of lands that buttressed the colonial system and that the humble Luzia had trodden in great suffering.

Of what had Luzia/Luiza Pinta been accused? What grave error had led to her arrest, depriving her of her hard-won freedom?

Luzia was publicly known as a *calundureira*. People living in her *arraial* would ask her to perform divinations, shed light on the whereabouts of stolen oitavas-de-ouro, and heal the sick.

Whenever Luzia intervened in these minor problems of daily life, it was through a nocturnal ceremony: the *calundu*. She would dress up in peculiar costumes—"inventions," as the trial records state—and her head would be covered with garlands or a turban. She danced to the sound of African musical instruments, like the *atabaque* drum; she went into a trance—"great tremblings"—and provided the desired answers to questions. She was assisted by other black men and women, who danced and sang along with her. After drinking some wine, the "winds of divination would come." Sometimes she carried a rapier in her hand and would prescribe wild leaves for her patients. She sat in a tall chair, like a throne, and would leap over people lying face down on the floor, who had come in hopes of finding a cure. Some witnesses said Luzia would bray like a donkey and that at a given point she would untie a belt from round her waist and make strange gestures with it. She would sniff people's heads to tell whether they had been bewitched and would give them potions to make them vomit. According to others, there were rattlesnakes wrapped around her legs and arms, and she claimed that the winds of divination blew into her ears.

One of the witnesses, Manuel Pereira da Costa, said he knew Luzia to be a *calundureira* "because it was public knowledge." He emphasized, however, that "it was not known if she [was] a sorceress." This was precisely the doubt the Inquisition sought to silence, endeavoring instead to link one activity to the other and setting out on a foreordained hunt for confirmation of the infamous "diabolic compact"—the certificate of witch-hood, according to demonological manuals and treatises.

Most likely having been advised how the Holy Office operated, Luzia omitted any reference to the figure of the demon in her confession of March 18, 1743. She admitted to relying on mushes made from herbs and roots for healing purposes but denied the use of divinations and said that she had never entered into a pact with the devil. When questioned about her background, she declared that she was a baptized, confirmed Christian who observed religious precepts, confessed and went to mass regularly, and knew how to recite her prayers satisfactorily.

As the pressure of the interrogations intensified, Luzia broadened her confessions. On June 7, 1743, she stated that during the *calundu* ceremonies described earlier she would lose her senses. She began speaking of the medicines administered and how to go about it, all of which she did "by the destiny that God gave her." On July 3, still under pressure, Luzia went even further. She defined the *calundu* as a "contagious disease"—"it passes from one person to another"—that she had suddenly caught one day and said that the only way to deal with it was as she had described, through those ceremonies, playing instruments. She told how at times she would go places while her body would stay where it was, remaining behind as if abandoned, dead— an experience Luzia attributed to God. It was also by heavenly intervention that the words rose to her mouth, involuntarily, she knew not how, while divining and healing.

Her omission of a pact did Luzia no good. She was found guilty in an auto-da-fé held in the São Domingos Convent. The large crowd in attendance included Dom João V, the future Dom José I, and the inquisitors. Behind the story of a humble black colonist, ex-inhabitant of African lands, ex-slave, transformed into an accomplice of the devil by the will and grace of the Holy Office, lies a case study of the archaeology of African religions in Brazil. Acceding to the needs of assimilation, African colonists, or colonists of African descent, found a way to preserve their cultural universe in the form of the *calundu*. The clothes Luzia wore resembled those used by today's Baianas [Afro-Brazilian women who wear traditional white turbans, peasant style blouses, and long, layered skirts edged with lace] and most probably have Muslim roots—the "diverse inventions in the *Turkish* style" alluded to in Luzia's trial. The rattlesnakes wound about her arms and legs are found in many religious expressions common to African civilizations. Bastide offers an in-depth discussion of these serpents' role in the rites and suggests possible kinships, for example, with the Dahomans and Congolese. He settles on a broader interpretation of the serpent complex, where he perceives two different groups of magic: that of the black snake charmer, probably of Muslim or Arabic origin, and that of the black healer of snakebites, a specific case within a vaster realm of curative magic.[15] The regurgitations induced by the *calundureira* from Sabará were not unique to the African cultural universe; the indigenous peoples likewise believed they could rid a bewitched body of spells, along the lines emphasized by Evans-Pritchard—that witchcraft was a physically detectable *organic* evil.

From a land of the Bantu language—Portuguese Angola—Luzia, *calundureira,* was the cultural predecessor of contemporary Brazil's *mães-de-santo* [priestesses of Afro-Brazilian religions]. Like them, she believed that fate had granted her preordained talents, that predestination exists and it is up to each person to develop her or his gifts, such as receiving spirits. Appearing before the Holy Office, Luzia made it a point to accentuate a syncretism that was indeed there: she cited the Virgin Mary as patroness of her healing and God as responsible for her ability to divine; her successful cures had earned her two *oitavas-de-ouro*, which she had spent on masses for St. Anthony and St. Gonzalo, the ones truly responsible for her achievements. It is hard to tell whether this was more a device to dupe the enemy than a manifestation of full-fledged syncretism. Perhaps it would be more accurate to say that in response to inquisitorial pressures, expressions of Catholicism rose to the surface and encroached upon African religious traditions, moving into the voids left open when the material bases of the African slaves' universe had collapsed and elements of their own religion had been lost. These expressions could lie dormant as long as the *calundu* had free rein in the distant corners of Minas. But under the pressure of the tribunal, they emerged and assumed the role of defense mechanisms.

Clinging desperately to these markers of Catholicism, Luzia intuitively knew that she should keep her distance from any activity suggestive of a diabolic pact. "Asked if she at any time had believed in the demon and had worshipped him as she worshipped God, thinking that he be worthy of adoration and veneration, and powerful enough to save souls," she responded in the negative. She likewise denied having at any time relinquished "God Our Lord as lord of all goods, both spiritual and temporal" or having been involved with the devil or spoken with him. Finally, they asked her "if she, the Deponent, had made a pact with the demon by herself, or through an intermediary person, in what form she had made it, which words they had used, and what they had promised each other." "She said that she had never made a pact with the demon." In response to her denial, the Inquisition tried to demonize her work as a healer, claiming that it was ridiculous to rely on one single medicine to cure a variety of sicknesses. "Asked if she used the said medicine believing that in it there be a tacit, or express, pact with the devil, by means of which it would be possible to improve the health of the people on whom it was used, . . . she said that she never believed that in this medicine there was a pact or any intervention by the demon."

The inquisitor then tried to rout the devil from the *calundu* ceremony, asking Luzia if she perceived it as natural or supernatural. In reply the tribunal heard that "she, the Deponent, believes that the said sickness is supernatural, because when it comes, she remains still, her eyes turned toward the heavens for some length of time, at the end of which she bows her head and looks at once at the ill and then knows which are to live and have a cure for their ailment, and also those which have none, which for this reason she does not accept as her patients, but has them taken away by the people who brought them." This was just what the inquisitor had been waiting for: "What reason does she have for believing that all such extraordinary feats are born of the virtue God hath granted her, and not of diabolic influx, which must more naturally apply?"

The inquisitor struck another blow when Luzia confessed that sometimes her body would be passed out on the ground, and yet she would go other places: such feats could only be possible through diabolic intervention, and therefore she must have entered into a pact. Luzia replied in the negative and repeated that she had nothing to do with the devil, "nor did she rely on him for the said feats, and she instead believes that all is the work and destiny of God, who hath wanted to grant this to her." Her adversary was annoyed: "If she knows full well that these are customarily wrought through the intervention of the devil, how does she therefore intend falsely to attribute them to destiny and to her own virtue, the said facts being wholly opposed and offensive to this virtue, with which she intends to excuse herself?" Cold and calculating, the inquisitor insisted it was impossible to reconcile her virtue— the ability to cure—with her "extraordinary inventions," to wit, the extravagant clothes she wore when healing. "She said that she cannot do the healing without wearing the said inventions, *and that only God Our Lord understands the reason, because she, as a sinner, does not know how to understand it.*"[16] The inquisitor was exasperated: "Why does she attempt to excuse herself with frivolous, indecisive replies, if, from her same confession, it is known with all evidence that she achieved the aforesaid by means of a pact made with the demon, and not by destiny or her own virtue, to which she in pretense and falseness attempts to attribute it?" Luzia answered in kind: "She knows full well that she has no pact with the demon, and that God Our Lord knows how she has stated the whole truth before this board." The inquisitor tried in turn to demonize the winds of divination, the words Luzia uttered during the ceremony, and her method of healing. In the end, he charged her with the infamous pact, based on presumptive evidence.

Luzia's recourse to the Catholic substratum of her religious universe was ultimately defeated by the Inquisition's unbending logic, and she was convicted. Her efforts could not even save her from the rigors of torture: "Being bound perfectly at all eight points, she was given all the torment to which she was judged, and during it she cried out for St. Anthony, and a quarter hour was spent on it, all of which in truth came to pass."

Salvador Carvalho Serra

In December 1757 the fleet from Rio de Janeiro arrived in Lisbon, carrying the saddler Salvador Carvalho Serra.[17] He was a poor *mulato*, born to a man from Minas and the black slave he had freed, and grandson to Congolese slaves. He had left Minas Gerais and his native colony because he had fallen into the clutches of the metropolitan Inquisition. Salvador had always lived in the gold-mining *arraiais,* and the only thing he knew of Rio de Janeiro was the jail where he had been temporarily detained. Baptized and confirmed, he could recite the prayers and commandments of the Holy Mother Church. He could also read and write—in all probability quite poorly—and even though he was not married, he had two small children by a *parda* woman, who was also single.

His great misfortune had begun some five years earlier, when he had traveled to the *arraial* of Nossa Senhora da Conceição de Mato Dentro to serve as godfather at the baptism of his nephew, born to his brother Antonio, a shoemaker by trade. Recounting what happened back then, Salvador tells two different stories. Inscribed between the two is the violent pressure that inquisitorial mechanisms exerted on their accused.

Salvador's first confession is dated September 22, 1758. In it he states that at the time of the baptism he and his brother had received a paper containing fragments of communion wafer from a Congo slave owned by the painter Antonio Correia. The two brothers talked it over, wondering whether or not the hosts were consecrated. Deciding they were indeed, the two men gathered them all in one piece of paper, and Salvador put them away in a pocket. Not long after, he took the pieces out—there must have been about seven—and ate them. Some six weeks went by, and then one day the parish priest from the *arraial* of Conceição came to his house in the company of the sexton, the painter's slave, and two more black men. The cleric set about searching both Salvador and his belongings, examining even the scapulars and pouches of relics that he and his brother Antonio wore about their necks. This done, the priest left without offering any explanation. But Salvador remembered the hosts he had eaten and figured that they were the cause of the unexpected search. Tortured by his conscience, he began asking if anyone had noticed hosts missing from the sacristy. He felt somewhat relieved when he learned that the parish priest had conducted the search after receiving a written denunciation against Antonio Carvalho Serra, who had allegedly received consecrated hosts from the hands of the painter's slave. Salvador's peace of mind was, however, short-lived. He, his brother, and the painter's slave were arrested and imprisoned for nearly three years, after which Salvador was sent to the Inquisition in Lisbon.

The second narrative differs from the first on some points and adds several new bits of information. Salvador says that he was at his brother's house when the painter's slave appeared, wanting to talk to Antonio Serra. Since he was not at home, the black man gave Salvador a small paper bundle, "saying that he had brought some relics for his said brother" and that he was giving these to him. Opening the packet, Salvador saw that it contained a "whole host," lying in a wad of cotton; according to what the black man had told him, it had been consecrated. While the painter's slave went off to look for his brother, Salvador put the paper away in a pocket. Antonio got home later with a similar packet, but he did not want to keep it "because those were things of Negroes." He gave it to Salvador, who quickly placed it in his pocket with the other one.

Three or four days later, when the two brothers had already forgotten the incident, they went off to Paraúna, from there continuing on to Tapanhuacanga, where Salvador lived. Upon their arrival, the saddler found his home occupied by *capitães-do-mato*. Instead of going into his house, Salvador went with his brother to take refuge at the home of Gonçalo de Viveiros. Gonçalo informed them that the *capitães-do-mato* were looking for Antonio Carvalho Serra, who quickly headed back to his home in Conceição. Salvador stayed on at Gonçalo de Viveiros's, once in a while going out to some fields of his, always most cautiously. But then came a "day of precept and believing that the said *capitães-do-mato* were gone, he decided to go to mass in the *arraial;* and as he entered it on horseback, a man he did not know called to him from the house of Francisco da Silva Leal, saying he wanted a word with him; and, dismounting, he, the Confessor, went into the house where the said man was, who was a *capitão-do-mato* by the name of João Gaia, who straight away seized him, aided by three *caboclo* soldiers that he had brought with him." Salvador was taken inside, where they searched him and discovered a knife on his person. Since it was necessary to record this finding, the *capitão-do-mato* asked him for some paper to write on. The terrified Salvador then remembered that he had the wrapped hosts on him. He took out a blank sheet of paper, handed it to his jailer, and asked to go into the other room, where "he ate the said hosts so that they would not be found." He managed to convince the *capitão-do-mato* to let him escape for the price of twelve *oitavas-de-ouro*. It was after this that he had been arrested, in the circumstances described in his first narrative.

What the Inquisition demanded of Salvador Carvalho Serra was that he carry all his offenses with him in his memory "to make a complete and truthful confession of them," stating "the pure truth" so that his soul might be saved. Following the tribunal's standard practice, at each confession they reiterated that he should better examine his conscience, probe it deeply, and unveil his most hidden intentions.

From the viewpoint of the Holy Office, Salvador had attacked the Catholic faith—and more specifically the Most Holy Sacrament of the Eucharist—and had failed in his due observance of the "irrefutable doctrine" of the church. Christ had instituted the sacraments to heal and save souls, and for this reason no one should show them "any contempt, nor even the slightest irreverence." But the defendant, "forgetting his obligation and the utmost respect that he should pay to the Most Holy Sacrament of the Eucharist, without any fear of God, nor of Justice, to the bane of his conscience and harm of his soul," had carried two consecrated hosts in his pocket.

As penalty and penance for his offenses, Salvador was ordered to appear in a public auto-da-fé, hear the verdict read, and abjure *de levi*. This occurred on September 20, 1761, in the cloisters of the São Domingos Convent. Before being sent to the *couto* of Castro Marim, in Algarve, where he was to remain banished for two years, he would be "instructed in the mysteries of our Holy Catholic Faith necessary for the salvation of his soul" and would also fulfill all other penalties and penances and pay the costs of the court trial, which came to 2:961 réis.

Salvador spent almost four years in the Inquisition's jails in Lisbon and, according to his confessions, spent another three imprisoned in the colony—a total of seven years of incarceration for eating two communion wafers. The long arm of the Holy Office had snatched him from his native *arraial* in the heart of eighteenth-century Minas, thrown him into a dungeon in Lisbon, and ultimately exiled him to Castro Marim, where he meekly presented himself to the authorities on October 23, 1761.

Together with this shift in geography came another, greater one—one that had disturbed his beliefs, religiosity, and worldview. In signing the form stating that he abjured *de levi* (in the eighteenth century, the Inquisition printed these forms to attach to the trial records), Salvador had converted himself into a Christian stereotype, anathematizing and divorcing himself from all heresy that might be committed against the Holy Catholic Faith and promising henceforth to serve as a true soldier of Christ, persecutor and discoverer of heretics, denouncer to the inquisitors and church prelates of any deviant practice.

Left behind was another religiosity, the living religiosity that was part of people's daily lives in Minas. The bond between this living religion and everyday life pulsates in Salvador's story: his references to the parish priest, to the Familiars of the Holy Office, to hosts, and to baptism accompany references to everyday events like field chores, a trip to the tavern, journeys around the gold-rich *arraiais,* incidents involving *capitães-do-mato,* mention of various artisans living in the mining region, expressions of ties of solidarity and friendship (reliance on Gonçalo de Viveiros's hospitality, for instance), along with manifestations of prejudice and a sentiment of caste (carrying about hosts is something "Negroes" do, says Antonio Carvalho Serra, who, as Salvador's brother, was quite likely a *mulato* as well).

In the first narrative, Salvador ate the hosts for no particular reason. He states quite simply that he did not know whether they were consecrated or not and speculates that they might have been just scraps of wafers. And even if they were consecrated, what was wrong with that? He got the urge to eat them, and that is what he did.

In the second narrative, Salvador travels with his brother after swallowing the hosts; life goes on as normal, and neither of them talks about the episode, which they in fact forget. It is imprisonment that revives Salvador's memory: the violence of the *capitães-do-mato* occupying his house and pursuing his brother (why?), characteristic signs of the violence that raged actively or bubbled below the surface in Brazil's eighteenth-century mining zones. Here the host was not eaten by happenstance; rather, it was an act of self-defense meant to elude the clutches of ecclesiastical justice into which the *capitães-do-mato* would hand him. Or might the act have been a nonconfessed impulse to resort to the host as an amulet that would seal his body and defend Salvador from physical danger, considering its virtues as the Body of Christ? In any case, to him it seemed normal to carry a communion wafer all that time. After all, he wore relics and scapulars around his neck, and the church endorsed and approved such practices; they belonged to the universe of permissible religiosity. Nothing indicates that Salvador thought it out of the ordinary to carry hosts in his pocket, although his brother viewed these as "things of Negroes"—and with this discourse pointed up the syncretism more common among slaves.[18]

Something else in this second narrative is interesting: it is the action of repressive forces (in this case, led by *capitães-do-mato*, a secular rather than ecclesiastical power) that displaces an acceptable act to the universe of wrongdoing. Salvador is afraid of being denounced to other agents of repression—this time ecclesiastical—and he eats the hosts. But he remembers them only because he is seized, and only when frightened does he associate the act of carrying hosts in his pocket with wrongdoing. In other words, even when temporal, this repression has the effect of uprooting a practice common to his everyday universe and casting it into the universe of wrongdoing, dominated by the church's elite discourse.

From this path there would be no return. Once in jail, Salvador, Antonio, and the painter's slave "agreed among themselves, already knowing that they were ordered to come before the Holy Office, that they would state in this Tribunal that the said Antonio Carvalho Serra had asked the said Negro Antonio Correia for some scraps of host to seal letters, and the latter had given him some and they had remained in the hands of him, the Confessor, thus concealing that what the Negro had brought were whole wafers, since being scraps it could not be presumed that they were consecrated." Their imprisonment did away once and for all with any idea that possessing communion wafers was something routine, and together the three men constructed a third narrative, a false one intended to cover up what had really happened. Even before they were interrogated, they thus armed themselves for their confrontation with the tribunal, for by that time it was clear to them what the Holy Office signified and what it meant to stand accused before it.

The longer their stay in the inquisitorial prisons, the hazier the story gets; its sense grows muddled, its meaning changes, and hence room is open for multiple narratives, mirroring the fragmentation suffered by Salvador's original religiosity. If it was impossible to explain why the consecrated hosts had been eaten, it was useless to tell the story. The only way out was to abjure, embracing the strict religion of the metropolitan's inquisitors.

Adrião Pereira de Faria

It was April of 1754 when Adrião Pereira de Faria momentarily had to leave Vila da Vigia, in Grão-Pará, on the heels of some runaway slaves.[19] He was the administrator of his stepfather's sugarcane *aguardente* distillery but was undertaking this pursuit in his capacity as militia sergeant. Adrião was about nineteen and had been abandoned by his wife, who had run off to Maranhão with a fellow by the name of Anacleto de Sousa Magalhães. To make haste in the matter of the fugitive slaves, Adrião left some trousers at the home of a friend, Manuel Pacheco Bitancur, a 52-year-old man who was part of the town's public administration. Adrião's Calvary commenced when Manuel Pacheco picked up the trousers, and out fell a paper with some strange signs and drawings on it. Looking closer, he saw that the words were "contrary to our Holy Catholic Faith" and decided to hand the paper over to the town's *juiz ordinário* [justice of the peace], not really knowing quite what to do with it. The judge, Bernardino de Carvalho, noticed that the words "seemed to have a pact with the devil" and that the drawings represented swords and knives etched in black ink. The two decided to make sure the writing on the paper was really Adrião's, so they sought the help of Marcos Gonçalves Correia, the town's notary public. He recognized the signature as indeed belonging to the young man.

As soon as he got back, Adrião picked up his trousers and noticed that the paper was missing. He panicked. Anticipating disaster and already sensing the long arm of the Holy Office upon him, he went out, saying he had lost a very important document about a large amount of money owed him; he said that "the missing paper would be cause for him to move to a new land." He hurried to tell the blacksmith Crescêncio Escobar what had happened, because he was the one who had transcribed the paper for Adrião and advised him to carry it at all times so that he would be lucky in love and fare well in fights. Crescêncio also saw trouble ahead; he got mad at his friend and told him "he did not know how to keep anything." On the afternoon of that same day, Adrião was arrested on the order of the local vicar and was detained in Vigia's jail. He would later travel to Belém, where he stayed in the guard unit on the bishop's order.

The accusation hanging over his head was that he had signed a pact with the devil. The piece of paper stood as hard evidence and was difficult to refute. Nonetheless, Adrião tried to convince the Commissaries who interrogated him that he had signed the paper ignorant of its contents, for Crescêncio had not read it to him and he himself was unable to. But even when he had been back in the town jail, the community had already begun discriminating against him, treating him as a marginal man. One day he was playing with the jail-keeper's sword, when the Eucharist was carried down the street in the form of a viaticum for someone on their deathbed. Adrião joined those around him in kneeling down, but the sword remained in his hand. This was enough for him to be accused of disrespect. Once he arrived in Belém, his reputation as a sorcerer grew. There he relied on the services of a *mulata* named Maria Barata "for that which he needed." She would often go up to the jail bars to talk to him. But a man steered her away from Adrião, saying that the prisoner was a "great sorcerer" accustomed to going in and out between the bars—just as witches in Europe were said to do.

After a year in prison, Adrião managed to arrange a meeting with the bishop, who acceded to the accused man's pleas and released him for a time.

During his period of freedom, Adrião ran into an old girlfriend and nourished dreams of a new marriage, hopeful that his wife had died in Maranhão. While he endeavored to verify her death, he appeased his new lover's guilt feelings by promising to give her land in the town if he was unable to marry her. He even went to the church, where he arranged for the banns and asked the bishop for advice. But he was arrested yet again, this time by the Familiars of the Holy Office—it had been decided his offenses fell within the jurisdiction of that tribunal.

In November his brother wrote to the vicar of Vigia, entreating him to have mercy on Adrião, who was in prison for offenses against the Holy Office, while Crescêncio, the true culprit, remained free—all in vain. By this time, things were already in place for Adrião's voyage to Lisbon. On November 21 the Familiars Joaquim Resende Leitão and Lázaro Fernandes Borges explained that he should have a "bed, and all else for his use, as well as 60,000 réis for his support, to which he replied that he was a poor man, and that he had nothing of his own." The Commissary Caetano Eleutério Bastos sought information on the defendant's true financial situation and was informed by the superior at Vigia's monastery that indeed "that which he had inherited from his parents he had consumed and that he had no goods." Three days later, they handed him over to the captain of the *Senhora Santa Ana,* who was on his way to the metropolis. In early July of the following year, the Holy Office began to interrogate Adrião.

While Adrião had been imprisoned and while he had nurtured dreams of wedding Eugênia Maria da Costa during his fleeting period of liberty, the local Commissaries of the Holy Office and the metropolitan authorities had exchanged extensive information about him by letter, tracing the lines of the unfortunate man's fate. In August 1755 the Commissary Lourenço Álvares Roxo (who died shortly thereafter and was replaced by the aforementioned Caetano Eleutério) had forwarded a list of his offenses and the written pact to the Inquisition in Lisbon. Seven months later, the Commissary received instructions from the Inquisition to requestion the witnesses who had testified in civil court, this time pursuant to the norms of the Holy Office. But these efforts were hampered by a smallpox epidemic that raged through Belém, leaving inhabitants in nearby towns terrified of catching the disease. The epidemic was followed by other obstacles: one of the witnesses was unavailable because she herself was facing charges in secular court; another, confined to her small farm, could be contacted in a few days but was so poor that she might not be able to come "as quickly as the case required"; Bernardino de Carvalho offered this justification for not testifying: he was old, infirm, and "had a chronic urine ailment." Finally, when epidemics no longer blocked the entry of ships into the port of Belém, the great distances to be traveled created another set of problems. Canoe trips could take days: "I can only tell Your Honor that it took the bailiff three days with four Indians and a canoe on his first endeavor; and another journey took a little over one-half day, with two Indians."

When the Inquisition commenced its interrogations in Lisbon, it was already convinced of Adrião's guilt. In October it decided to place him in the secret prisons and prosecute him. Functionaries of the Holy Office had classified him as a "poor, lustful man" hungry to "have and take advantage of the female sex," to which end he sought the devil's aid. Adrião gradually realized he would need to adhere to inquisitorial concepts and admit his guilt. He began by "remembering" that he had known from the outset what was on the paper. He then went on to admit that "he knew very well that it was sinful and diabolical" and that he had accepted and used it "in hopes of benefiting from its good results." He attributed his behavior to having been "blinded by his appetite" at the time but stressed that he had been motivated by "libidinous spirit only" and not by any "heretical" purpose.

Adrião displayed an acute intelligence during the interrogations, through his concepts illustrating the struggle between good and evil, heaven and hell— the obsessions of the mentality of the era. He did not expect the devil to protect him from injuries, for this was a thing of God, who gave life. But in his sinful stubbornness to win over a given woman, he could rely only on the demon. "He solely desired from him to vanquish the will of the woman that he intended so he could gratify his lasciviousness, and it seemed to him, since the end was sinful, that the devil could and would contribute to satisfying his desires." He recognized that he had sinned but saw the sin as within the realm of Christian offense: "His weakness and lasciviousness had caused him to fall into this error, and he had always hoped to redeem himself through the sacrament of penance, *as a true Catholic, although a sinner.*"[20] Having relations "with the women of others, stealing, killing, and not going to confession in disobedience of Lent" were sinful acts, but it was up to each and every individual to decide what path to follow: "He always knew in part when he did good or evil."

Adrião longed for a God who would be less unforgiving and more benevolant toward human faults and errors and for a more democratic religion, more open to popular participation, less marked by rites and ceremonies. He judged that "to be a Christian, it was enough to be baptized, make the sign of the cross, and know the substance of confession." His mother had forced him to follow the religion of mass and obligations, at a time when his concerns lay elsewhere: "He went to mass when his mother ordered, because at that time he, the Defendant, thought only about playing and passing time, but he believed that he was a Christian, although it seemed to him that to be a saint and just, it was necessary to be of more noble birth, concurring that he could not be so because of his lowly birth." "He was not totally unaware that the lowly and humble who labored under the law of God could go to Heaven, and that it only seemed to him that to be a bishop, pontiff, and saint venerated by the Church, it was necessary to be of lofty birth, but he was not unaware that all good men could be saved."

From the very beginning of his interrogations, Adrião is thus heard making statements that echo the singular popular religiosity explored by Ginzburg in his study of Menocchio's trial. God and the devil were not wholly indivisible: "He well knew that the devil was God's enemy, but he was unawares that to follow one, it was necessary to abandon the other." He believed that it would at least be licit to make recourse to the demon for dark motives—for example, to sleep with women. Adrião gradually began to embrace the inquisitorial perspective, wherein God and the devil lived at war, eternally engaged in endless battle with each other. During the days when he had taken up his belief in the devil, the defendant had quit going to mass and prayed only to him, placing his hands beneath his arms. He would go up to the church door but would not enter. Sometimes he would have his doubts. Then he would invoke the devil, who would rail at him for vacillating: "How dost thou wish that I succor thee, if thou still hast love of another thing? Cast it out of thyself, believe in me, and thou shalt enjoy all that thou ask of me, and shalt find that I succor thee." The devil wanted Adrião to stop wearing the beads around his neck, and he quickly obeyed. He began to revere the devil as he had formerly revered God and Jesus.

The inquisitorial discourse ultimately displaced many of Adrião's statements to a context where God and the devil appear to be irreconcilable. Referring to the time when he believed in the demon—"the time of his errors"—the Holy Office declared that Adrião "did not believe in the mystery of the Most Holy Trinity, nor in Christ Our Lord, since he held only the demon as his God, to whom he directed and made his petitions." The Sessão de Crença [session during which the Inquisition interrogated the accused about his or her religious beliefs], held on May 31, 1758, provides a fine illustration of how the inquisitors skillfully set about "demonizing" the defendant's discourse.[21] They asked him whether he knew that the soul was eternal and that once the body had passed away, the soul "remains forever and that it receives its punishment or reward according to the evil or good works" carried out during one's lifetime. Adrião replied that he had believed at that time that "the soul ended together with the body, and that death occurred because medicine had no cure, for he was a stupid man who had no education whatsoever." They then asked him what he thought heaven, hell, and purgatory were. "He believed Heaven was glory, where God was, and there would the just go, and Hell the place where the devils are and there would the damned go," that is, "those who offended God." The relentless inquisitorial logic began browbeating him: if he said the damned would go to hell, this was because he knew there was a soul; when he had denied this earlier, he had been fooling the Inquisition and had tacitly concealed that he had given his own soul to the devil. Adrião tried to get himself off the hook by blaming it on the coercion of interrogation, which led him to confuse things and fail to express himself properly, causing him to stumble into con-traditions. His affirmation that the soul perished along with the body "was a lapse born of the disturbed state in which he found himself before this Board."

Unyielding, the Inquisition wanted his confession to a pact. They sent him off to torture, employing the standard practice of first intimidating him with the sight of the instruments to be used. "By the house in which he was, and the instruments he saw therein, he could easily understand how severe would be the zeal that would be used on him, which he could avoid *if he wished to finish confessing to his offenses* and his true intent of committing them, *affirming the pact that, according to the law, it is presumed he has made with the demon.*"[22] They tied him to the rack, warned him that if he died it was solely his own fault, and began to tighten it, giving it a half-turn. Adrião interrupted his torment by asking for a hearing and then confessed he had signed the paper and "had purposefully agreed to deliver his soul to the demon, wanting and intending to be his slave till he had taken advantage of a certain woman he intended, and that with this perverse spirit he had carried the paper on his person, believing and hoping that this same demon would assist him in his endeavor, the which he invoked several times with the said writing, desiring that he aid him, and he believed in him till the time when he was arrested by the *juiz ordinário* in the city of Pará." He had not made a full confession earlier for fear they would kill him.

On July 5, 1758, the Holy Office decided that from all this "resulted presumptive evidence that he, the Defendant, had made an express pact with the devil." The verdict to be read in public underscored the defendant's humble roots, in a pejorative tone: "As a *rustic* overwrought by the burning passion of his *inordinate* appetite," he had found himself grappling with violent instincts "out of his *ignorance and stupidity.*"[23] His "poverty and weakness" had led him to persuade himself that "the demon would help him in his appetite." Adrião's poverty, irrationality ("inordinate appetite"), and subjugation to his sexual instincts are thus linked to another characteristic, just as negative but somehow hidden in the text: Adrião's colonial condition.

At the end of August, the colonist from Pará—son of a Bahian man who "made his living by going into the *sertão* to hunt down Indians" and of an indigenous woman named Florência Gomes—appeared in an auto-da-fé held at the São Domingos Convent. Humiliated by the terms of the verdict, he was also made to don a witch's hat bearing the label "sorcerer." He abjured *in forma* and was sentenced to imprisonment and to wear a *sanbenito* at all times. Finally, he was forced to spend five years in banishment, serving in His Majesty's galleys.

The sly Adrião did not give up easily. While still in Pará, when the bishop had decided to release him following his first arrest, he had changed his name from Faria to Simões. In justifying this act, he said that he had been prompted by his "disdain and hatred" for "the evil he had done"—that is, walking about with a paper wherein he had made a compact with the devil. But everything suggests that he was really attempting to escape the clutches of the Holy Office. Just one month after he began serving his sentence in the galleys, he decided to lodge a petition with the board, asking that his sentence be changed so that he could serve out his banishment "where he could live with his wife, alleging that she was destitute in his absence and wretched imprisonment, and in danger without his company." The inquisitors were not taken in and remembered that the defendant himself had confessed that his wife did not live with him but in Maranhão, where she had run away in the company of another man. They also remembered that he "had been taking measures to be wed a second time," to Eugênia Maria, and that his allegations were therefore groundless. Finally, they brought up his need to be cleansed, something that could not yet be established, "only one month having passed since he commenced the banishment that he is now serving, after committing the terrible crime of idolatry, so that as an example he must be well punished."

Apparently resigned, Adrião fulfilled his Christian obligations, going to confession and mass on the four holy feasts, as the curate from the São Julião parish, in Lisbon, attested one year later. But he was back at it in 1760, again asking that his sentence be altered, this time because he was ill and could not recuperate in prison. His request was accompanied by a physician's statement that emphasized the offender's grievous condition: "He is in a miserable state, afflicted by many illnesses, for throughout most of his imprisonment he has been in the infirmary, his body all leprous, which has left him lame in one leg, which is almost immobile and incurable owing to the incommodiousness of the place, *as he the petitioner was raised in America,* and according to his repeated complaints, near to losing his life in the most underground prison where he is."[24] The Holy Office's doctor certified that Adrião suffered from universal dropsy, "a most grave and chronic ailment" and hard to cure, especially in the place where he was, which was highly favorable to this infirmity.

Everything suggests that the tribunal decided Adrião had adequately purged his errors. The trial closes with the information that he left Évora in 1765, embarking on a ship back to Pará, where the next year found him serving as a soldier.[25]

Adrião's is the most complete story of which I have knowledge and the only one that provides information on the offender's return to the colony. After all that had transpired, after the many years he had lost in the inquisitorial prisons, it appears that Adrião had the energy to make a new life for himself and find a place in society again. But cases like this must not have been common. In a way, Adrião embodies all that has been said throughout this book: he lived torn between the idea of good and evil, of heaven and hell, struggling with his own concepts of religion and seeking to make it closer and more accessible to him. He resorted to magical practices and gave himself to the devil under a pact so that he might solve problems in his daily life, like brawls and love troubles. Finally, under the pressure of interrogation and torture, he refashioned his former concepts and ultimately internalized the demonization forced upon him. Even if atypical, his return to his homeland has a symbolic significance: persecuted, mortified, broken, reduced to subhuman conditions, the colonists oftentimes persevered in their own beliefs and dreamed of returning to that land in America where they had been born. The contours of these beliefs were gaining clearer form and proving not to be reducible to the metropolitan mold.

Sabbats and *Calundus*

Indeed, the little soul that remained disconsolate and aimless after having been obliged, still so callow and helpless, to leave Warrant Officer Brandão Galvão's body was not a Brazilian soul originally, because it is very unlikely that souls are destined to be born to only one nationality, whatever it may be, nor are they likely to become attached to one.
— João Ubaldo Ribeiro, *An Invincible Memory*

An agonizing, turbulent world began falling apart in the fourteenth century. In its struggle to find ways to restructure economic, political, and social life, this world sent discoverers in search of new markets—an endeavor that found its protagonists caught between attraction to and panic before the unknown. The new universe unfolding before the Old World's eyes was at times portrayed as positive (edenic), at times as negative (diabolic). Understanding these negative images within the imagination of the discoverers—soon to become the colonizers of these new territories—is of utmost importance if we are to gain a better understanding of how they reacted to diabolic magical practices or how they yielded to them.

The European of the late Middle Ages and Early Modern age believed monstrous humanities inhabited the ends of the known world. When the New World took its place on Europe's maps, a shift occurred in the universe of the imagination, and these monstrous humanities became associated with the inhabitants of American lands; but contrary to what happened in Europe, they became demonized. Sixteenth-century accounts like those of Jean de Léry and André Thevet searched for a common thread linking the sabbat to indigenous ceremonies. As Michel de Certeau observed, the explorer/missionary was thought to serve as an exorcist of the American demons.

Sorcery in colonial Brazil was superimposed on an inviable humanity, further demonizing its members, who were already viewed with disdain. The relationship between sorcery and this inviable humanity was characteristic of the colonial dimension of the phenomenon, lending it singularity. Ever since the Middle Ages, Europe had the habit of animalizing its subaltern classes. "Masterless men" were often seen as beasts, with this resemblance between men and animals limited to one social sector, excluding society's ruling strata. In Brazil this view applied initially to indigenous peoples but was soon extended to blacks as well, eventually encompassing all the colonists. It is true that "good men" were labeled as such in opposition to "wicked men," who were members of the less privileged social sectors; however, eighteenth-century discourses such as the Count of Assumar's suggest that animal-like, diabolical traits were meant first and foremost to qualify the *colonial condition* of the colonist rather than any one social stratum. When this official referred to the colonists as a "race of demons," he was not thinking just of the "wicked men" (slaves and the dispossessed) but also of the great potentates who risked standing up to metropolitan taxation, perpetually inciting infernal rebellion.

At the same time that the colony underwent this process of "infernalization," it was shaped to fit the Europeans' edenic myths. In the colonizer's view, heaven alternated with hell—an outlook that gradually became shared by the colonists as well and that left space where purgatory could intrude. The process of colonization thus saw the forging of an ideological justification, anchored in faith and its negation, using and reworking images of heaven, hell, and purgatory. In a chronicler like Jaboatão, the alternation of Good and Evil is transparent; this history of the settler's attachment to the land and confrontation with indigenous peoples relies heavily on the images of heaven and hell. Antonil, on the other hand, poses the idea of the colony as a purgatory of penances and of sugar, Brazil's main export, refined and whitened through human effort.

Heaven, hell, and purgatory thus continually traded places with each other during the shaping of the colonial system. In the relationship between metropolis and colony, it oftentimes fell to the colony to purge the metropolis of its social ills. It was the dungeon of its delinquents and the place where slavery was reinvented, standing in sharp contrast to the incipient wage labor system then taking root in metropolitan centers. So while slavery flourished in Brazil—and colonial exploitation itself was based on it—in the metropolis the general trend was to pay the labor force in wages. At this historical turning point, the ruling strata transformed the paradisiacal vision, an integral part of the culture of so many peoples, into a tool for enticing settlers and into a constituent element of colonizing ideology. Populating the colony also meant purging the metropolis, not only of its "sick" human elements but also of forced forms of labor exploitation. Europe gradually abandoned the gradations of servile labor—foundation of the feudal system—adopting instead wage labor—cornerstone of factory and industry. In return, colonial lands became crowded with slaves. After long imaginary pilgrimages, the European imagination had relocated the Promised Land, the Eldorado of legend, the Earthly Paradise, to America, which also began to harbor the hell of slavery.

It was thus that the reinvention of slavery—or, more precisely put, the birth of early modern slavery—fostered the exploration and exploitation of the paradisiacal American land and in its wake, and as its prerequisite, brought hell for the wretched slaves. Exploiting to its very limits the forced labor of these damned beings, the white settlers saw themselves destined to dwell in purgatory, enjoying the riches they did not create themselves and for this very reason having to pay the penalty, living out the horrible being-and-not-being of white people in the land of blacks, free in a land of captives, Christians in a land of heathens. As it emerges in Antonil's writings, the white people's purgatory would appear to be this need constantly to take stock of oneself in the face of the awful contradiction of the colony's everyday life.

There were times when one theme or the other predominated: infernalization or edenic invention. Sérgio Buarque de Holanda pointed out that the polemic surrounding the New World in fact heightened in the eighteenth century, when the initial rose-colored view was fading and the colonies' "damned" aspect began to emerge: marshy, inhospitable lands inhabited by degenerate men and animals, carriers of the germs of revolt. Between the paradisiacal vision and its antithesis, two centuries had passed, centuries that had seen establishment of the slave trade and the unbridled exploitation of black Africans as slave labor. Slavery would contribute decisively to endowing the New World with its negative character, damned and hellish. This was not only because the Europeans who lived off overseas exploitation suffered the pangs of guilt and were constantly compelled to justify the act of enslaving their fellow humans—hence the negative side of the polemic, the inferiority of the American lands, so often visible in the authors used by Gerbi. It was also because the multitudes of black slaves posed an imminent danger to the established order and to perpetuation of colonial domination. From the eighteenth century come Assumar's heated texts, denying the humanity of the mestizo colonist and the black slave. From the eighteenth century comes the Inconfidência Mineira, when the colonists' newfound consciousness of their colonial condition skirted the issue of slavery and in a way "saved" the status quo of the slave system. For the rebels, the heart of the question was their dependence on the metropolis and not the exploitation of slave labor. As of the eighteenth century, no more Portuguese sorceresses were banished to Brazil. Perhaps Portugal was rethinking the purging role of the colony, which more than ever before had begun to resemble a giant Inferno.

In the early modern imagination, heaven and hell were binary elements. Within the colony's popular religiosity, the sacred and the profane would become conflated and then move apart, like the popular dragon analyzed by Le Goff. It was the kingdom of ambiguity, of the blurred, of the multifaceted, with syncretism suffusing religious life and seeping into the gaps left open by the Jesuits' catechizing efforts. Within this context, the Inquisitorial Visitations and Inquiries constituted dire moments when a deep fissure exposed the disparity between two irreconcilable worlds: that of the Inquisition and that of popular religiosity. How could the metropolitan religion, prisoner of the Catholic Reformation's formalism, find an echo within the colonial population's unpredictable, chaotic daily life, pervaded by indigenous and African rites? How could conflict be avoided between the Portuguese Inquisition's prevailing religious rigor and the reality of colonial Catholicism?

As so clearly manifested in the documentation of the Visitations to Brazil, the colony's popular beliefs and singular religiosity were characterized by a greater familiarity with the sphere of the divine, by a more natural relation to the world of sex, and—already under the sign of the Reformed Church— by an identification between sex and evil, which may have been an indication of the rupture prompted by Christian morals. There was a great need to blaspheme, to theorize freely about matters of religion, as Menocchio did, in an effort to keep the Catholic God from becoming cold, absent, distant, and unreachable. Understanding each one's attitudes and reactions from the perspective of the singular, multifaceted, syncretic religiosity of the colony is more important than knowing whether a certain colonist lashed a crucifix because he was a Jew, or whether another doubted the existence of purgatory because she was a Calvinist. In the eyes of this popular religiosity, punishing St. Anthony by hanging him upside down and behind a door was a normal thing to do, and bringing purgatory into this world—"next to that tree and along that path"—simply foreshadowed the discourse a soldier of Christ would create two centuries later: the Jesuit Antonil, for whom the colony was hell for blacks, paradise for *mulatos,* and purgatory for whites like him.

Here was a world that desacralized religion; that reinvented slave labor; that dwelled each day with the Otherness of the black, of the indigenous, and—from their perspective—with the Otherness of the colonizing white; and that sporadically fell under the sharp eye of the metropolitan Inquisition, eager to bring its opposites together and homogenize their differences. This was the world of colonial sorcery.

Like the European discoverer's imagination and like the popular religiosity of which it was part, colonial sorcery was diverse and heterogeneous, comprising essentially two parts that made up one whole: a backdrop of magical practices characteristic of so-called primitive cultures (African and indigenous) and a backdrop of magical practices characteristic of European populations, heavily imbued with a secular paganism still pulsating beneath a recent, "imperfect" Christianization. From one moment to the next, this binary nature of colonial sorcery shifts the focus of analysis from an emphasis on what is common to magical practices and sorcery to an emphasis on the singularities of colonial reality.

Melding a gamut of conceptions and beliefs, sorcery and popular religiosity were thus extremely heterogeneous. This complexity developed during the process of colonization, ultimately forging a specifically colonial character. There were times when both were tolerated: Fernão Cabral and the Santidade, Antonil and his complaisance toward the slaves' syncretic Catholicism. But the overriding tone was one of intolerance and repudiation of singularly colonial magical and religious practices. The heights of this repudiation and intolerance were the Visitations, the Inquiries, and the persecution unleashed by the Holy Office's Commissaries and Familiars on Brazilian land.

Colonial sorcery dovetailed with the population's everyday life, especially among the poorest. It could be seen in neighbors who would denounce each other, peering over their clotheslines or through a fence into the yard next door, pressing their ears against a wall, gleaning information from the day's conversations at a shop, in the church, down at the corner, through a window. People went to sorceresses for love potions, to learn magic words that would bind a lover forever, to uncover secrets, to foresee the future, to bring ships lost in the seas of India or of Africa back on course, to heal wounds, to close sores, to bless animals afflicted by maggots. The community poured out its inner demons, its anxieties, doubts, and uncertainties, upon these women and men. Their testimonies unveil an important part of the collective unconsciousness and of each person's dreams. In the erotic ravings that the tortured black slave José Francisco Pereira bared before his inquisitors, the devil who possesses him and is possessed by him always appears in the form of a white man or woman. Since he found himself compelled to confess to ghastly sins, at least his partner would be someone from the dominant race, thereby avenging his misfortune. Ugly, a midget, a slave, Catarina Maria said she was the devil's lover; he had deflowered her and always came to her in the form of a black man, redeeming her from the contempt probably shown by men of her own status. When the *caboclo* and indigenous populations in the state of Grão-Pará participated in secret ceremonies, it was through these autochthonous magical practices that they endeavored to achieve affirmation in their communities, rather than crumbling beneath the impact of Portuguese culture.

On a concrete level, sorcery became an integral part of daily life. The repression and repudiation of these practices, however, are signs of the great rupture that occurred at the close of the Middle Ages, which helps clarify the elites' reaction to what had been common practice until that point. As a result, the elite sectors began rejecting the popular universe, and it was within this context that the witch-hunt gained great impetus. Europe's religious reformations and the consolidation of early modern power apparatuses helped deepen the fissure; they were, at one and the same time, indicators and triggers of the rift that occurred between the hegemonic culture and the subaltern culture, to use Gramsci's terms. The Middle Ages had seen popular currents that were highly favorable to religious tolerance; in the Early Modern age, these were buried by the Wars of Religion and by the bonfires that burned witches, Jews, and heretics. A violent rift had occurred, and the town sorceress to whom everyone had turned and with whom everyone had fearlessly coexisted on a daily basis became an enemy to be wiped out.

Focusing on this rupture, one can ponder how the repressive discourse began detaching the figure of the demon from the heart of magical practices and folklore (in short, from the culture of the popular sectors), isolating him and modifying his significance. Under these new circumstances, it was as if the only thing seen of the devil was his venom, the only thing stressed was the negative. Early modern sorcery was to emerge as a product of this imbalance—of the way in which elite thought began placing emphasis on the figure of the devil, to the detriment of his relationship with magical practices as a whole. This statement does not constitute an unrestricted endorsement of Mandrou's thesis, according to which sorcery is defined by the elite stratum that represses it, theorizes on its repression, or omits such theorizing. This statement goes further: it raises the possibility that the profound changes under way at the dawn of the Early Modern age undermined both elite and popular thought and that this set off simultaneous, complex interactions at the different levels.

Taking place within this context, the Portuguese Inquisition and the catechizing effort to discipline European and colonial populations constituted the upper strata's responses to these upheavals, where the subaltern classes were protagonists as well. To better homogenize these strata, it was necessary to haunt them with the threat of the catechism's negation and of the dangerous power that worked stealthily and steadily against it. Perhaps this is why the definition of witchcraft rested on the existence of a diabolic pact.

Even if one believes that the rift in magical practices was first opened by the ruling class's attitudes, there are nuances to be accounted for. If it is first affirmed that the sixteenth century was the moment of rupture between elite culture and popular culture, it can be stated that as part of this break elite thought removed the demon from his previous context and distorted his significance, discarding the former connections. It must then be taken into account that if elite thought "demonized" magic in the Early Modern age and distorted the inner dynamics formerly inherent in the universe of magic, this very demonization eventually determined how magical practices were exercised and caused its practitioners to begin endorsing the ideology espoused by the repressors.

The colonists' everyday demon wore a number of different faces. At times he displayed archaic traits, which the colonial condition perhaps helped perpetuate, while in Europe these began giving way to other, more dramatic traits. In the Brazilian colony, the devil still bore the familiar marks of folkloric tradition, the ambiguity peculiar to popular culture. Devils could be invoked at any moment, to help out in a card game or to offer their friendly collusion when someone needed to let off steam verbally. Still linked to the magic of conjuration, these archaic traits joined the new reality—colonial reality—and acquired a new shape: they ceased to be *medieval* and in their new context were reconfigured and became *colonial*. They coexisted with other traits, like early modern passiveness toward the devil, which reflected echoes of demonological formulations and theorizations about compacts—and so the elite level ended up permeating the popular level. The zeniths of demonic virulence are found precisely within the realm of intertwined discourses: that is, in the trials, when colonists abandoned their long-standing familiarity with the demon and revealed themselves to be subjugated to him.

The colonists' fear of repressive apparatuses and their awareness of the Holy Office's edicts, which were read in the towns at the time of the Visitations, contributed decisively to the modernization of these archaic traits and to turning the devil into the horrendous creature of the papal bulls, of Sprenger and Kramer's *Malleus,* and of Bodin's *De la démonomanie.* Just as the Jesuits had played a demonizing role during the sixteenth century, reading sabbats into indigenous ceremonies, it was the culture of the elites that helped the devil acquire his virulent dimension within colonists' daily lives. In the eighteenth century, Nuno Marques Pereira—dreadful moralist that he was—would see sabbats in the colonial *calundus.*

By the eighteenth century, learned knowledge already had a conceived notion about magical-religious expressions in the colony. By that time, the colonial population had established singular forms of magic and sorcery: mandingas, *calundus, catimbós.* Of the twenty cases of mandinga pouches identified in the colonial period, nineteen occurred during that century. All trials or denunciations involving *calundus* or *catimbós* also took place during the eighteenth century.

Thus it was in the interweaving of different concepts and discourses that a colonial sorcery took shape. It was both the object of a complex collage and the genesis of new syntheses: today the Maria Padilha of eighteenth-century conjuration prayers is Umbanda's *pomba-gira* [female entity of ambiguous morality, tending toward prostitution and evil]. In the realm of magic and religion, syncretism would ultimately prove itself uncontainable and ineradicable; it would forever bear the ambiguous mark of popular culture, which mixed the sacred and the profane. Leaving behind it a trail of death and horrific suffering, the long process of acculturation eventually merged sabbats, masses, and *calundus.* In Salvador, in 1983, I listened as a young woman working for the Bahia state tourist agency gave the following answer to a French visitor curious as to whether the ritual washing of the steps of the Church of Bonfim was a religious festival: "It's religious, and it's also profane." I never saw the tourist again, but I can imagine his expression, caught between bewilderment and awe, as he gazed upon the deafening carnival unfolding on the steps of the most venerated church in Bahia.

Appendix: Tables

TABLE I

Type	OFFENSE	Number*	GREATEST INCIDENCE Period	Locale	Color	TOTAL
Material Survival	Divination	23	1590–1625	Bahia and Pernambuco	white (14)	
	Healing	25	1590–1625	Bahia	black (13)	
	Superstitious Blessings	2	1591 and 1733	Bahia/ Minas	white (2)	
	The Overseas Universe	14	1590–1625	Bahia	white (11)	64
Onset of Conflicts	Infanticide	4	1590–1625	Bahia	white (2)	
	Various Conflicts	16	1750–75	Minas Gerais	black (8)	
	Tensions between Master and Slave	10	1725–50	Minas Gerais	black (8)	
	Mandinga Pouches	19	1750–75	Grão-Pará/Maranhão	black (6)	51
Maintain Bonds of Affection	*Cartas de tocar*	6	1725–50	Grão-Pará/Maranhão	white (4)	
	Prayers	9	1750–75	Grão-Pará/Maranhão	white (6)	
	Sortilege	17	1750–75	Bahia	white (8)	32
Communicating with the Supernatural	Metamorphoses	8	1590–1625, 1725–50	Bahia	white (5)	
	Pacts and Invocation of Demons	24	1590–1625, 1750–75	Minas Gerais	white (2)	
	Possession	2	1668–1738	Grão-Pará/ Maranhão; Bahia	white (2)	
	Calundus	9 (all 18th c.)	1725–50	Minas Gerais	black (9)	
	Catimbós	6 (all 18th c.)	1750–75	Grão-Pará/Maranhão	indigenous (4)	58
TOTAL						205

* The number of offenses has been extrapolated from the number of cases and is therefore greater.

Table 2. Brazil: Number Accused during Period under Study (1590–1780)

Total Number of Cases	Predominant Region	Predominant Ethnicity
35.3	Minas Gerais	black (21)
34	Bahia	white (20)
30	Grão-Pará/Maranhão	white (10)
16.5	Pernambuco	white (13)
3.3	Rio de Janeiro	black (3.3)
TOTAL: 119		

Table 3. Brazil: Number Accused by Region for Each 25-Year Period

Number of Cases	Period	Predominant Region	Predominant Ethnicity
32	1590–1625	Bahia (26)	white (21)
	1625–50		
1	1650–75	Maranhão (1)	white (1)
	1675–1700		
5	1700–25	Minas Gerais (3)	black (3)
29	1725–50	Minas Gerais (13.3)	black (16)
48	1750–75	Grão-Pará/Maranhão (27)	black (17)
4	1775–1800	Minas Gerais (3)	mestizo (3)
TOTAL: 119			

Notes

Abbreviations

AEABH
  Arquivo Eclesiástico da Arquidiocese de Belo Horizonte
AEAM
  Arquivo Eclesiástico da Arquidiocese de Mariana
AGCRJ
  Arquivo Geral da Cidade do Rio de Janeiro
HAHR
  Hispanic American Historical Review
IANTT
  Instituto Arquivos Nacionais Torre do Tombo, Lisbon

Chapter 1. The New World between God and the Devil

1. See Tzvetan Todorov, *La conquête de l'Amérique: La question de l'autre,* p. 14; *The Conquest of America: The Question of the Other,* trans. Richard Howard, p. 5.

2. Jean-Paul Roux, *Les explorateurs au Moyen-Âge.*

3. In this aspect, Columbus is exemplary: "At sea, all the signs indicate land's proximity, since that is Columbus's desire. On land, all the signs reveal the presence of gold: here, too, his conviction is determined far in advance. . . . [H]e believes these lands are rich, for he greatly desires that they be so; his conviction is always anterior to the experience" (Todorov, *La conquête de l'Amérique,* pp. 27–28; *The Conquest of America,* p. 20).

4. In "O homem do século XVI," *Revista de História* 1 (1950), L. Febvre underscored the primacy of the less intellectual of the senses during the sixteenth century. See also L. Febvre, *Le problème de l'incroyance au XVIᵉ siècle: La religion de Rabelais,* pp. 467ff. Along the same line, Mandrou demonstrated how narratives at that time "nourished thoughts and the imagination"; people preferred to listen rather than see, "with all the disturbing imprecision that this

enduring preference entails" (*Introduction à la France Moderne—1500–1640*, pp. 76, 77).

5. "Of the discovery of this 'enormous unknown land' . . . all we can say is that it has made the world small, destroying an entire supra-world of enchanting dreams and lovely imaginations—'sogni leggiardi,' 'belle immaginazioni'—and of 'sommamente poetiche' geographical illusions, and the presence of America thus presents a dire threat to poetry" (cited in Antonello Gerbi, *La disputa del nuevo mundo: Historia de una polémica—1750–1900*, p. 350).

6. According to Todorov, "one might say that Columbus has undertaken it all in order to be able to tell unheard-of stories, like Ulysses; but is not a travel narrative itself the point of departure . . . of a new voyage?" (*La conquête de l'Amérique*, p. 21; *The Conquest of America*, p. 13).

7. Michel Lequenne has this to say about Columbus's ambiguous personality: "A man of more modern intellectual structure than Columbus, having at hand the most advanced cosmographic data available in the late fifteenth century, would have judged the crossing from Europe to Asia very long and dangerous; a wholly medieval spirit would have judged it too fraught with dangers for other reasons. It is precisely because he blended a medieval thinker with an intrepid adventurer of the new times that Columbus could be the necessary man" (introduction to Columbus, *La découverte de l'Amérique: I. Journal de bord, 1492–1493*, p. 23).

8. On the "vertigo of curiosity" and the "eye at the service of the discovery of the world," see Michel de Certeau, "Etno-graphie: L'oralité, ou l'espace de l'autre: Léry," in Certeau, *L'Écriture de l'histoire*, p. 242.

9. See Giuseppe Gatto, "Le voyage au Paradis: La christianisation des traditions folkloriques au Moyen-Âge," *Annales, E.S.C.*, 34th year, no. 5 (September–October 1979): 929–42. Jacques Le Goff examines many of these voyages in his work on purgatory, where he points particularly to the importance that one of these—the *Purgatory of St. Patrick*—had in constructing the image of the Christian purgatory. See *La naissance du Purgatoire*.

10. Claude Lecouteux, "Paganisme, christianisme et merveilleux," *Annales, E.S.C.*, 37th year, no. 4 (July–August 1982): 700–716.

11. Giulia Lanciani, *Os relatos de naufrágios na literatura portuguesa dos séculos XVI e XVII*, p. 52.

12. "The most pertinent of observations appears alongside improbabilities, as if the marvelous were inherent to every description of the Asian world" (Claude Sutto, "L'image du monde connu à la fin du Moyen-Âge," in Guy H. Allard, ed., *Aspects de la marginalité au Moyen-Âge*, p. 63). See also Jean Delumeau, *A civilização do Renascimento*, vol. 1, pp. 49ff.

13. Carlo Ginzburg, *Le fromage et les vers: L'univers d'un meunier au XVIᵉ siècle*, p. 80; *The Cheese and the Worms: The Cosmos of a Sixteenth-Century Miller*, trans. John Tedeschi and Anne Tedeschi, p. 42.

14. Sutto, "L'Image du monde."

15. Jacques Le Goff, "L'Occident médiéval et l'Océan Indien: Un horizon onirique," in Le Goff, *Pour un autre Moyen-Âge: Temps, travail et culture en Occident*, p. 290; *Time, Work, and Culture in the Middle Ages*, trans. Arthur Goldhammer, p. 195.

16. "Thus the oneiric horizon reflects the psychological repercussions of the very structure of medieval trade; for the West was an importer of precious

products from far-off places, which it thought of in part as real, in part fantastic, in part commercial" (Le Goff, *Pour un autre Moyen-Âge,* p. 292; *Time, Work, and Culture,* p. 196).

17. Writing of the animal species that inhabited far-off regions—like asps, dragons, and basilisks—Sérgio Buarque de Holanda states that these wonders "remained solely in India, above all, and in Ethiopia, which continued to be the two vivaria of all marvels, *primarily before discovery of the new continent*" (*Visão do Paraíso: Os motivos edênicos no descobrimento e colonização do Brasil,* p. 198; emphasis added).

18. Accounts of travels to Paradise often included news about Prester John's kingdom: "An anonymous Spanish friar, contemporary of Fazio, and who claimed to have visited all parts of the world, also offers us his vision of Paradise, but this time—accompanying the itinerary of the mysterious Prester John, who, once the great Asian sovereign, begins blending with the Christian potentate of Abyssinia— he places it over by Nubia and Ethiopia" (*Visão do Paraíso,* p. 165).

19. I refer to this book's main epigraph. See Friar Vicente do Salvador, *História do Brasil—1500–1627,* p. 15.

20. Buarque de Holanda, *Visão do Paraíso,* p. 140.

21. "Foreshadowed by pagan tradition's Islands of the Blessed [Afortunadas] and the Garden of the Hesperides, and in some fashion fertilized by these, the transfer of such marvelous settings to the Atlantic had already gained its own impetus when these traditions began intermingling with Celtic mythology, mainly Irish and Gaelic" (Buarque de Holanda, *Visão do Paraíso,* p. 166).

22. Ibid., p. 167.

23. Capistrano de Abreu, *O descobrimento do Brasil pelos portugueses,* p. 48.

24. K. Kretschmer, *Die Entdeckung Amerikas in ihrer Bedeutung für die Geschichte des Weltbildes* (Berlin, 1892), cited in Abreu, *O descobrimento do Brasil,* p. 49. In the city of Angra, on Terceira island, is a Mount Brasil; in Ireland, there is a shoal known as Brasil Rock (ibid., p. 50).

25. Antonio de Santa Maria Jaboatão, *Novo orbe seráfico brasílico ou Crônica dos frades menores da Província do Brasil* (1761), vol. 2, pp. 8–9.

26. Todorov, *La conquête de l'Amérique,* p. 22.

27. J. Servier, *Histoire de l'Utopie* (Paris: Gallimard, 1967); cited in Jean Delumeau, *Le péché et la peur: La culpabilisation en Occident—XIIIᵉ–XVIIIᵉ siècles,* p. 141.

28. If scholars have been unanimous in underscoring Léry's importance in this matter, the same cannot be said about Thevet. Charles-André Julien, however, deems him "undeniably the father of the 'noble savage,' for it was in *Les singularitez de la France Antarctique* that Ronsard found the golden age of which he dreamed." See the introduction to André Thevet, *Les français en Amérique pendant la deuxième moitié du XVIᵉ siècle,* p. v. Regarding Gandavo, Capistrano de Abreu says, "His project consists solely of revealing the land's riches and the natural and social resources found there, in order to incite the poor to come people it: his books are immigration propaganda" (bibliographic note to *Tratado da terra do Brasil* by Pero de Magalhães Gandavo, p. 18).

29. André Thevet, *Les singularitez de la France Antarctique* (1558), ed. Paul Gaffarel, p. lv (emphasis added).

30. Jean de Léry, *Histoire d'un voyage faict en la terre du Brésil,* intro. and

notes by Paul Gaffarel, vol. 1, p. 73; *History of a Voyage to the Land of Brazil,* trans. and intro. by Janet Whatley, p. 25. If fear of the sea is fear of the unknown, beings that come from the world of navigation may bring danger. This is what the tradition of medieval *tempestários* seems to tell us. During the late Middle Ages, Europe's rural populations were terrified of the evils wrought by these beings who sailed ships through the air during storms, stealing crops. Agobard had this to say about peasants: "They believe and hold that there exists a country called Magonia, where ships come through the clouds." Agobard called them "sailors of the air." See Oronzo Giordano, *Religiosidad popular en la Alta Edad Media,* pp. 142, 278.

31. Lanciani, *Os relatos de naufrágios na literatura portuguesa,* pp. 130–31.

32. Salvador, *História do Brasil,* p. 51.

33. Pe. Fernão Cardim, *Tratados da terra e gente do Brasil,* p. 66.

34. Gerbi, *La disputa del nuevo mundo,* p. 143.

35. On the twofold character of expansion, see Luís Filipe Baeta Neves, *O combate dos Soldados de Cristo na terra dos papagaios: Colonialismo e repressão cultural,* p. 28.

36. Caminha's letter in Carlos Malheiro Dias (ed.), *História da colonização portuguesa do Brasil,* vol. 2, p. 99 (emphasis in original).

37. "Regimento de Tomé de Souza, 17-12-1548," in Malheiro Dias, *História da colonização portuguesa do Brasil,* vol. 3, p. 347.

38. See, among other works by Jean Delumeau, the superb initial pages of *Naissance et affirmation de la Réforme,* pp. 47–57.

39. Vieira cited in Eduardo Hoornaert, *A igreja no Brasil Colônia, 1550–1800,* p. 40.

40. Ibid., p. 41. Hoornaert states that theological Messianism, centered on the king of Portugal, is the interpretative key to Vieira's discourse.

41. Sebastião da Rocha Pitta, *História da América portuguesa desde o ano de mil e quinhentos do seu descobrimento até o de mil e setecentos e vinte e quatro* (1730), pp. 27, 29.

42. Salvador, *História do Brasil,* p. 51.

43. Pero de Magalhães Gandavo, *História da Província de Santa Cruz* (1576), pp. 119–20.

44. Hoornaert, *A igreja no Brasil Colônia,* pp. 68–69. The excerpts from Simão de Vasconcellos are found in *Crônica da Companhia de Jesus no Brasil* (p. 1663).

45. Rocha Pitta, *História da América portuguesa,* p. 15.

46. Thevet, *Les français en Amérique,* p. 166.

47. Léry, *Histoire d'un voyage,* vol. 2, pp. 27–28; *History of a Voyage,* p. 111. "O Lord, how manifold are your works! In wisdom you have made them all; the earth is full of your creatures": Psalm 104:24 (*The New Oxford Annotated Bible* [New York: Oxford University Press, 1989]).

48. "The process of transposition began from the very moment that Columbus first set eyes on the Caribbean islands. The various connotations of Paradise and the Golden Age were present from the first. Innocence, simplicity, fertility, and abundance—all of them qualities for which Renaissance Europe hankered, and which seemed so unattainable—made their appearance in the reports

of Columbus and Vespucci" (John Huxtable Elliott, *The Old World and the New: 1492–1650*, p. 25).

49. Columbus, "Journal," October 21, 1492, cited in Todorov, *La conquête de l'Amérique*, p. 31; *The Conquest of America*, p. 23. On page 31 (*Conquest*, p. 24), Todorov further quotes the explorer: "There rises from the earth a fragrance so good and so sweet, from the flowers or the trees, that it was the fairest thing in the world." On page 39 (*Conquest*, p. 33), the author observes in Columbus a "preference for land over men." These humans are seen as part of the landscape (*Conquête*, p. 40; *Conquest*, p. 34). On page 33 (*Conquest*, p. 26) there are allusions to Columbus "the evangelizer and the colonizer."

50. See Claude Kappler, *Monstres, démons et merveilles à la fin du Moyen-Âge*, pp. 92ff.

51. It is again Sérgio Buarque de Holanda—to whom these reflections of mine owe so much—who most eloquently analyzes the recovery of the idea of the Earthly Paradise initiated in the Early Modern age (*Visão do Paraíso*, pp. 181–83).

52. Salvador, *História do Brasil*, p. 37.

53. "Carta de Pero Vaz de Caminha," in Malheiro Dias, *História da colonização portuguesa do Brasil*, vol. 2, p. 99.

54. Rocha Pitta, *História da América Portuguesa*, pp. 1, 2.

55. Ibid., p. 2 (emphasis added).

56. Jaboatão, *Novo orbe seráfico brasílico*, vol. 2, pp. 3–6.

57. In "Notícias curiosas e necessárias das coisas do Brasil," which opens the *Crônica da Companhia de Jesus,* Father Simão de Vasconcellos stated that the Earthly Paradise was to be found in America, more precisely, in Brazil. As a result, the copies of his work were confiscated. Following discussion by a number of scholars, who were "unanimous in sustaining that there was nothing in them contrary to the Holy Catholic Faith," this passage was purged. See Buarque de Holanda, *Visão do Paraíso*, pp. xxii, xxiii.

58. Jaboatão, *Novo orbe seráfico brasílico*, vol. 1, p. 149 (emphasis added). Perhaps what may be detected in Jaboatão's hesitations and timidity is what Sérgio Buarque de Holanda saw as a Portuguese near-incapacity to edenize. In a similar stance, J. S. da Silva Dias recognizes the Portuguese contribution to the revival of the myth of the Golden Age but relativizes that contribution: "Fundamental responsibility for the myth's renewed prestige does not fall to them. This responsibility falls to the Spaniards from the time of Charles V and, above all, to the French who wrote after the first quarter of the century" ("A revolução dos mitos e dos conceitos," in *Os descobrimentos e a problemática cultural do século XVI,* p. 189).

59. Anthony Knivet, *Vária fortuna e estranhos fados de Anthony Knivet, que foi com Tomás Cavendish, em sua segunda viagem, para o Mar do Sul, no ano de 1591*, pp. 82, 145 ("The Admirable Adventures and Strange Fortunes of Master Anthonie Knivet, Which Went with Master Thomas Ca[ve]ndish in His Second Voyage to the South Sea, 1591," in Samuel Purchas, *Hakluytus Posthumus or Purchas His Pilgrimes: Containing a History of the World in Sea Voyages and Lande Travells by Englishmen and Others, Vol. 16*, pp. 220, 262 [emphasis added]).

60. Gandavo, *História da Província de Santa Cruz*, pp. 82, 148–50. On the

moderate climate—a constant theme in formulations of the Earthly Paradise—see the noteworthy chapter *"non ibi aestus"* in Buarque de Holanda, *Visão do Paraíso,* pp. 277–303. In his opinion, Gandavo basically incorporated climatic considerations concerning the Earthly Paradise from the European imagination, recalling Isidore of Seville in the medieval version of *Orto do esposo:* Gandavo's edenic vision is "corrected and attenuated to the limits of what is plausible" (p. 295).

61. Gandavo, *História da Província de Santa Cruz,* p. 81.

62. Gandavo, *Tratado da terra do Brasil,* p. 41; and *História da Província de Santa Cruz,* p. 75.

63. Ambrósio Fernandes Brandão, *Diálogo das grandezas do Brasil* (1618), p. 96.

64. Ibid., p. 200.

65. Ibid., p. 45.

66. Ibid., p. 138.

67. Jaboatão, *Novo orbe seráfico brasílico,* vol. 2, p. 4.

68. "Jaboatão was a member of the Academia Brasílica dos Renascidos [Brazilian Academy of the Reborn], where he revealed his character as a flatterer, writing some *décimas* in homage to the all powerful Marquis de Pombal, the Academy's Maecenas" (José Honório Rodrigues, *História da história do Brasil, 1ª parte: Historiografia colonial,* p. 303).

69. Gerbi, *La disputa del nuevo mundo.*

70. "America was not as they imagined it; and even the most enthusiastic of [the humanists] had to accept from an early stage that the inhabitants of this idyllic world could also be vicious and bellicose, and sometimes ate each other" (Elliott, *The Old World and the New,* p. 27). Elliott speaks of the "uncertain impact" of America on Europe (pp. 1–27).

71. "From the beginnings of classical thought, there were two opposite opinions regarding man's life in days of yore: 'soft,' or positive, primitivism, formulated by Hesiod, described the primitive form of existence as a 'golden age,' in comparison with which later phases were no more than successive stages of one long ruin; 'hard,' or negative, primitivism depicted the primitive form of existence as a truly bestial state, which humanity had overcome thanks to technical and intellectual progress." The latter tendency traces its origins especially to Vitruvius (E. Panofsky, "Les origines de l'histoire humaine: Deux cycles de tableaux par Piero di Cosimo," in *Essais d'iconologie: Les thèmes humanistes dans l'art de la Renaissance* [1939], p. 59).

72. Delumeau, *Le péché et la peur,* pp. 138, 189; *Sin and Fear: The Emergence of a Western Guilt Culture,* pp. 123, 168.

73. E. Garin, "L'attesa dell'età nuova e la 'renovatio,'" in *L'attesa dell'età nuova nella spiritualità della fine del Madioevo,* Convegni del Centro di Studi sulla spiritualità medievale, held in October 1960, Todi, Italy; published in 1962, vol. 3, pp. 16–19 (cited in Delumeau, *Le péché et la peur,* p. 140; *Sin and Fear,* p. 125).

74. Budé cited in Delumeau, *Le péché et la peur,* p. 157; *Sin and Fear,* p. 140 (emphasis added).

75. "In some cases, and particularly regarding the New World, a counter-movement to this mythification of the discovered lands could be sensed from early on, triggered perhaps by the news of many colonizers' negative experi-

ences. Perhaps originating from the thesis that Indians are half beasts (in contrast with their idealization by a Las Casas or a Montaigne)—a thesis much debated among sixteenth-century thinkers and theologians—this movement would two centuries later feed into the anti-American polemic of those who argued that . . . nature in this hemisphere was infirm and degenerate" (Buarque de Holanda, *Visão do Paraíso,* p. 274).

76. Gandavo, *Tratado da terra do Brasil,* p. 42. The idea of poisonous rains and winds must have been common in the sixteenth century. When addressing the dangers of navigation near the equinoctial line, Léry alludes to this sort of precipitation: "Furthermore, the rain that falls in the region of this line not only stinks, but it is so pestilent that if it falls on the flesh, it raises pustules and big blisters, and even stains and spoils garments" (*Histoire d'un voyage,* vol. 1, p. 67; *History of a Voyage,* p. 20).

77. Gandavo, *História da Província de Santa Cruz,* p. 109 (emphasis added).

78. Cardim, *Tratados da terra e gente do Brasil,* pp. 33–34. Cardim is the author of a delightful description of the sloth: "It is an animal worth seeing; it resembles a shaggy dog, the setters; they are most ugly, and the face seems that of a woman with untidy hair" (ibid., pp. 30–31).

79. Ibid., p. 68.

80. Knivet, *Vária fortuna,* p. 132; "Admirable Adventures and Strange Fortunes," p. 252.

81. Léry, *Histoire d'un voyage,* vol. 1, p. 157; *History of a Voyage,* p. 78.

82. Cited in Gerbi, *La disputa del nuevo mundo,* p. 197.

83. "Carta de São Vicente, 12-6-1561," in Serafim Leite, ed., *Novas cartas jesuíticas: De Nóbrega a Vieira,* p. 112.

84. Jerônimo Rodrigues, "A missão dos carijós—1605–1607," in Leite, *Novas cartas jesuíticas,* p. 237.

85. Rodrigues in Leite, *Novas cartas jesuíticas,* p. 239.

86. Ibid., p. 238. One cannot help but see the analogy with Manuel de Mesquita Perestrelo's report on the wreck of the *São Bento,* which took place off the coast of Africa in 1553. Among those who had been shipwrecked there raged a plague of lice "that took the lives of some, and threatened to take the lives of all." With their clothing in rags, the men's bodies were left exposed to these creatures. "There grew so many, visibly eating us, that we could not succor ourselves, and though we scalded our garments very often, and picked the fleas every three or four days . . . when we thought we had killed them all, in a short while there were again so many that we gathered them from our garments with a splinter of wood, and carried them off to burn or bury." About four men "did so much digging about their backs and heads that they clearly died of this" (cited in Lanciani, *Os relatos de naufrágios na literatura portuguesa,* p. 141).

87. Cited in Gerbi, *La disputa del nuevo mundo,* p. 7, note 15.

88. Cited in ibid., p. 37.

89. Cited in ibid., p. 8, note 20.

90. Ibid., p. 11.

91. The image of the cowardly lion comes from Voltaire: "Mexico and Peru have lions, but they are small and without any mane; and what is stranger, the lion of these climates is a cowardly animal" (cited in ibid., p. 42, note 38).

92. Cited in ibid., p. 51, note 12.

93. These are the "geographic marginals" of which Bruno Roy writes. See

"En marge du monde connu: Les races de monstres," in Allard, *Aspects de la marginalité au Moyen-Âge*, pp. 71–81. Regarding general aspects of European teratology, I have relied on this most interesting article. On monsters, see Kappler, *Monstres, démons et merveilles à la fin du Moyen-Âge*. On the relations between teratology and science, including an analysis of the relations between popular and elite culture, see Katharine Park and Lorraine J. Daston, "Unnatural Conceptions: The Study of Monsters in France and England," *Past and Present* 92 (August 1981): 20–54.

94. Roy, "En marge du monde connu," p. 76. Solinus, Pliny, and especially Isidore of Seville were well known throughout the Iberian peninsula. See Silva Dias, "A revolução dos mitos," in *Os descobrimentos e a problemática cultural*, p. 195.

95. "The fear of the geographical unknown, of which monsters are the embodiment, is nothing but a reflection of man's countless inner fears: fear of forfeiting his bodily integrity, fear of an imminent punishment for certain behaviors, fear of the collapse of the fragile social edifice. Their abnormality defines the norm, affirms it, and puts an end to the fear" (Roy, "En marge du monde connu," p. 79).

96. Cited in Silva Dias, *Os descobrimentos e a problemática cultural*, p. 193.

97. Todorov, *La conquête de l'Amérique*, p. 23; *The Conquest of America*, pp. 15–16.

98. Cited in Delumeau, *Le péché et la peur*, p. 155; *Sin and Fear*, p. 138.

99. Park and Daston, "Unnatural Conceptions," p. 37.

100. Cited in Lanciani, *Os relatos de naufrágios na literatura portuguesa*, pp. 23, 56–57. "They only looked like men in their faces; on their heads they had no hair but an armature, as like a ram, twisted about in two turns; their ears were larger than those of a burro, the color was dark gray, their noses had four nostrils, a single eye in the middle of their foreheads, their mouths stretching from ear to ear and two kinds of teeth, hands like a howling monkey, feet like an ox, and their bodies covered with scales, harder than shells" (p. 57).

101. Knivet, *Vária fortuna*, pp. 37–38; "Admirable Adventures and Strange Fortunes," pp. 192–93.

102. Gabriel Soares de Souza, *Notícia do Brasil* (1587?), vol. 2 (São Paulo: Martins, n.d.), p. 190. The *upupiara* probably comes from indigenous folklore.

103. Gandavo, *História da Província de Santa Cruz,*, pp. 120–23.

104. Jaboatão, *Novo orbe seráfico brasílico*, vol. 1, pp. 118–19.

105. Gandavo, *História da Província de Santa Cruz*, p. 57.

106. Léry, *Histoire d'un voyage*, vol. 1, pp. 164–65; *History of a Voyage*, p. 83.

107. See Delumeau, *Le péché et la peur*, p. 156; *Sin and Fear*, p. 138.

108. Park and Daston, "Unnatural Conceptions," p. 20.

109. Ibid., p. 22.

110. Tant de sectes nouvelles
. . . Tant de monstres difformes,
Les pieds à haut, la teste contre-bas,
Enfants, morts-nez, chiens, veaux, aigneaux et chats
A double corps, trois yeux et cinq oreilles.
(cited in Delumeau, *Le péché et la peur*, pp. 156–57)

(So many new sects
. . . So many deformed monsters,
Their feet on top, their heads below,
Stillborn children, dogs, calves, sheep, and cats
With double bodies, three eyes and five ears.
(Delumeau, *Sin and Fear*)

111. Kappler, *Monstres, démons et merveilles,* p. 294.

112. The idea that monsters ceded their place to the Wild Man following the discoveries is defended by François Gagnon in the article "Le thème médiéval de l'homme sauvage dans les premières représentations des Indiens d'Amérique," in Allard, *Aspects de la marginalité au Moyen-Âge,* pp. 83–89. Shaken by millennialist movements that preached a return to the Golden Age, and convinced that historical progress transpired through rebirths (returns to an innocent primitivism), the Middle Ages had prepared the way for reception of the noble savage. It was, however, the discovery of America that lent content to the myth. See Jacques Le Goff, "L'historien et l'homme quotidien," in *L'Historien entre l'éthnologue et le futurologue,* p. 240.

113. Silva Dias, "A revolução dos mitos," in *Os descobrimentos e a problemática cultural,* p. 202.

114. In relation to the sexuality of indigenous peoples, European or Europeanized attitudes are extremely contradictory. Coeval sources, such as Jesuit letters, were scandalized by the indigenous peoples' sexual exuberance. Based on these and on the Visitations of the Holy Office, Paulo Prado built an entire theory of Brazilian lust in *Retrato do Brasil: Ensaio sobre a tristeza brasileira.* At the same time, the sexual impotence and lack of virility of the American Indian were touchstones in the seventeenth- and eighteenth-century polemics of detraction (Gerbi, *La disputa del nuevo mundo*).

115. Gerbi, *La disputa del nuevo mundo,* p. 67.

116. Ibid., p. 67. In the late eighteenth century *The Magic Flute*'s Papageno illustrated the convergence and contamination of the symbolic figures of the Wild Man and the Amerindian: the feather-covered body had replaced the hairy body (ibid., p. 67).

117. "They were fierce creatures, rugged and hairy, lewd like fauns, which inhabited the thickest woods and cavernous lairs; they were most certainly subhuman creatures, but quite different from monkeys and other beasts" (Gerbi, *La disputa del nuevo mundo,* p. 67).

118. Gagnon, "Le thème médiéval de l'homme sauvage," in Allard, *Aspects de la marginalité au Moyen-Âge,* p. 86.

119. Salvador, *História do Brasil,* p. 52 (emphasis added).

120. Ibid., p. 52.

121. Rocha Pitta, *História da América Portuguesa,* pp. 26–27.

122. Gandavo, *Tratado da terra do Brasil,* pp. 48–53. The observation about the absence of the letters *f, l,* and *r* in the indigenous tongue and the consequent explanation are repeated by numerous chroniclers and historians of the early days of the colony. Three centuries later, Arthur Schopenhauer was to say that when "the force of life was made manifest in the Western Hemisphere, it felt very serpentine and volatile, not very mammiferous and *absolutely not at all human*" (cited in Gerbi, *La disputa del nuevo mundo,* p. 422 [emphasis added]).

123. Gandavo, *Tratado da terra do Brasil,* p. 38.

124. Ibid., p. 39.
125. Gandavo, *História da Província de Santa Cruz,* p. 125.
126. Gaspar Barleus, *História dos feitos recentemente praticados durante oito anos no Brasil e noutras partes sob o governo do ilustríssimo João Maurício Conde de Nassau etc.,* trans. Cláudio Brandão, p. 64.
127. Thevet, *Les singularitez,* p. 140.
128. Thevet, *Les français en Amérique,* p. 67.
129. Thevet, *Les singularitez,* p. 233.
130. Ibid., pp. 134–35.
131. Ibid., pp. 151–52.
132. Regarding the dispute over hegemony in Europe and control of the colonies, see Fernando A. Novais, *Portugal e Brasil na crise do antigo sistema colonial, 1777–1808,* especially chapter 1, "Política de neutralidade."
133. Knivet, *Vária fortuna,* pp. 55, 56–67; "Admirable Adventures and Strange Fortunes," p. 203.
134. Knivet, *Vária fortuna,* pp. 58–59; "Admirable Adventures and Strange Fortunes," p. 206.
135. Jaboatão, *Novo orbe seráfico brasílico,* vol. 1, pp. 105–6.
136. Ibid., pp. 106, 107, 108.
137. Ibid., p. 110.
138. Ibid., p. 114.
139. "Carta do Pe. João de Azpilcueta Navarro aos irmãos de Coimbra; Porto Seguro, 19 de setembro de 1553," in Leite, *Novas cartas jesuíticas,* p. 158.
140. "Ao padre Simão Rodrigues, Provincial de Portugal, Bahia, 10-7-1552," in Leite, *Novas cartas jesuíticas,* p. 26.
141. Knivet, *Vária fortuna,* p. 84; "Admirable Adventures and Strange Fortunes," p. 222.
142. Jaboatão, *Novo orbe seráfico brasílico,* vol. 1, pp. 13–14.
143. "Carta de 19-9-1553," in Leite, *Novas cartas jesuíticas,* p. 156.
144. Rodrigues, "A missão dos carijós," in Leite, *Novas cartas jesuíticas,* p. 232. One of the colonial era's most famous practitioners of incest was João Ramalho. See Nóbrega's letter, "Ao padre Simão Rodrigues," in Leite, *Novas cartas jesuíticas,* p. 46.
145. Prado, *Retrato do Brasil,* p. 166.
146. Rodrigues, "A missão dos carijós," in Leite, *Novas cartas jesuíticas,* pp. 230, 239. On pages 226–27, there is an anthological passage on the poor education of indigenous children and on sloth.
147. Knivet, *Vária fortuna,* p. 142; "Admirable Adventures and Strange Fortunes," p. 259. In the eighteenth century De Pauw would say the Wild Men were weaker than civilized peoples because they did not work, and work strengthens the nerves (cited in Gerbi, *La disputa del nuevo mundo,* p. 62, note 54).
148. Serafim Leite, "Antonio Rodrigues, soldado, viajante e jesuíta português na América do Sul, no século XVI," *Anais da Biblioteca Nacional do Rio de Janeiro* 49 (1927): 55–73.
149. "Their similarity to animality or to disorder precludes the formation of a permanent *unanimity of opinion* regarding the possibility of conversion. Is indigenous man capable of understanding the Christian message? Does he possess *Reason? Is he Human?"* (Neves, *O combate dos Soldados de Cristo,* p. 58). Questioning the human condition of the indigenous peoples, the Jesuits also

questioned their efforts at catechism: "Are the Jesuits falling into the sin of pride in setting for themselves a task that God would not have proposed for Himself? Or had God reserved this mission to test the valor of his undisputed children?" (ibid., p. 61).

150. Cited in Gerbi, *La disputa del nuevo mundo,* p. 113. Galiani also stated that, like Wild Men, cats too could be educated and civilized; it was merely a question of time. Cats took forty to fifty thousand years to learn what they know today. "It is therefore just that Californians and Australians, who are three or four thousand years old, are still beasts" (cited in Gerbi, *La disputa del nuevo mundo,* p. 113, note 209).

151. "A pensive melancholy animal," "a serious melancholy animal" (cited in Gerbi, *La disputa del nuevo mundo,* p. 152, note 44).

152. Cited in ibid., p. 303.

153. Buarque de Holanda, *Visão do Paraíso,* pp. 298–99, 303. "Repudiation of indigenous people—of their animality—centers on three types of behavior that are classified as abhorrent and that are common to all 'natives.' These are *incest, cannibalism,* and *nudity*" (Neves, *O combate dos Soldados de Cristo,* p. 56).

154. "Carta de Pero Vaz de Caminha," in Malheiro Dias, *História da colonização portuguesa do Brasil,* vol. 2, p. 94.

155. Buarque de Holanda, *Visão do Paraíso,* p. 303; José de Anchieta, *Cartas, informações, fragmentos históricos e sermões* (Rio de Janeiro, 1933), p. 186 (emphasis added).

156. J. S. da Silva Dias, "Os portugueses e o mito do 'bom selvagem,' " in *Os descobrimentos e a problemática cultural,* p. 296.

157. Manuel da Nóbrega, *Diálogo sobre a conversão do gentio,* (1556–59?), intro. and notes by Pe. Serafim Leite, p. 54.

158. Manuel da Nóbrega, "Ao Pe. Miguel de Torres, Provincial de Portugal, 2-9-1557," in Leite, *Novas cartas jesuíticas,* p. 68.

159. On the "contagion" of animality: "The evil came first from a neighboring colony, where Portuguese blood had mixed greatly with that of the Indians. The contagion of this bad example quickly reached São Paulo, and from this mixture there resulted a perverse generation" (Charlevoix, cited in Friar Gaspar da Madre de Deus, *Memórias para a história da Capitania de São Vicente,* p. 230).

160. Barleus, *História dos feitos recentemente praticados,* p. 64 (emphasis added).

161. Manuel da Nóbrega, "Apontamento de coisas do Brasil," in Leite, *Novas cartas jesuíticas,* pp. 76, 77 (emphasis added). "The Jesuit's analysis is, as one can see, foreign to the legend of the Indian's paradisiacal goodness and lacks indications that would suggest the moral or 'cultural' superiority of their customs" (Silva Dias, "Os portugueses e o mito do 'bom selvagem,' " in *Os descobrimentos e a problemática cultural,* pp. 297–98). This author defends the thesis that the myth of the noble savage was "marginal" in Portuguese culture. In the Jesuit letters, he contends, the traits of the evil savage are "more accentuated and by far more abundant" than those of the noble savage (p. 294). On the principle of subjugation and obedience in Nóbrega, see pages 328 and 329.

162. Rodrigues, "A missão dos carijós," in Leite, *Novas cartas jesuíticas,* p. 236.

163. Gandavo, *História da Província de Santa Cruz*, p. 137 (emphasis added).
164. Salvador, *História do Brasil*, p. 377.
165. Madre de Deus, *Memórias para a história da Capitania de São Vicente*, p. 147.
166. "Prone to *melancholy*, they seek to ease it with ditties and musical instruments, of which they have their own" (Barleus, *História dos feitos recentemente praticados*, p. 24).
167. Ibid., pp. 260–61.
168. Jaboatão, *Novo orbe seráfico brasílico*, vol. 2, pp. 4, 7.
169. Thevet, *Les français en Amérique*, p. 40.
170. Léry, *Histoire d'un voyage*, vol. 2, p. 81; *History of a Voyage,*, p. 150.
171. Léry, *Histoire d'un voyage*, vol. 1, p. 122; *History of a Voyage,*, p. 56.
172. "The dialectic winds of the Fathers of Jesus, from whatever direction we approach them, blow contrary to Montaigne and Rousseau. Far from nourishing the notions of natural morals, of natural religion, of natural society, they endorse the ideals of the Christian civilization established in Europe" (Silva Dias, "Os portugueses e o mito do 'bom selvagem,'" in *Os descobrimentos e a problemática cultural*, p. 339).
173. André João Antonil, *Cultura e opulência do Brasil por suas drogas e minas*, intro. and notes by Alice P. Canabrava, p. 169 (emphasis added).
174. The demonization of American indigenous people moved forward with expansion. "The confrontation of reality and legend advanced with appreciable speed; and as penetration into the territories progressed, the revelations of missionaries and explorers brought to light non-paradisiacal realms, sometimes even deemed diabolical, within American man's 'primitive' humanity" (Silva Dias, "A revolução dos mitos," in *Os descobrimentos e a problemática cultural*, pp. 190–91).
175. Neves, *O combate dos Soldados de Cristo*, p. 63. On pages 30–33, the author offers an eloquent analysis of the discovery as the reencounter with secret regions ruled by the devil: "Are not the abysses, monsters, and seas mere obstacles, tests that must be passed—so that the 'fallen' regions might be reconquered?" (p. 31).
176. "Carta do Padre Luís da Grã a Santo Inácio, 27-12-1553," in Leite, *Novas cartas jesuíticas*, p. 163.
177. Cardim, *Tratados da terra e gente do Brasil*, pp. 185–86. In another felicitous analysis, Neves characterizes this passage as "a series of astonishments" in reaction to indigenous "disproportion." For Europeans, norms and equilibrium would be introduced with Jesuit settlement (*O combate dos Soldados de Cristo*, pp. 124–30).
178. Rodrigues, "A missão dos carijós," in Leite, *Novas cartas jesuíticas*, p. 123.
179. Ibid., pp. 214–15.
180. Ibid., p. 220.
181. "Carta de Pero Correia, 18-7-1554," in Leite, *Novas cartas jesuíticas*, p. 174.
182. "It is astonishing that, though they are not rational, these poor men, because they are deprived of the use of true reason and of knowledge of God, are subject to any number of fantastic illusions and persecutions of the evil spirit. We have said that here something similar happened prior to the advent of Our

Lord; for the evil spirit only endeavors to seduce and deprave those creatures who have no knowledge of God" (Thevet, *Les singularitez,* p. 168).

183. Ibid., p. 172.

184. Léry, *Histoire d'un voyage,* p. 71.

185. Certeau, *L'Écriture de l'histoire,* pp. 243–44.

186. Antonil, *Cultura e opulência do Brasil,* pp. 163, 164.

187. Cited in Sylvio de Vasconcellos, *Mineiridade: Ensaio de caracterização,* p. 25 (emphasis added).

188. Neves, *O combate dos Soldados de Cristo,* pp. 134, 58.

189. Gandavo, *História da Província de Santa Cruz,* p. 131.

190. "Carta de Dom João III, Évora, 21-1-1535," cited in Madre de Deus, *Memórias para a história da Capitania de São Vicente,* pp. 258–72.

191. IANTT, Inquisição de Lisboa, Caderno do Promotor, no. 126, p. 413. It was the historian Luiz Mott who discovered this passage—"a real gem," as he wrote me. I am indebted to him for kindly bringing it to my attention.

192. In this regard, see my chapter "Minas Gerais, a síntese da colônia," in Laura Vergueiro, *Opulência e miséria de Minas Gerais,* pp. 75–79.

193. This is the position taken by Le Goff in *La naissance du Purgatoire.* On pages 404–5, he makes it clear that the penalties for magical practices will be cleansed in purgatory, this new geographical space whose birth guaranteed the masses a place in the great Beyond.

194. Delumeau, *Le péché et la peur,* p. 143; *Sin and Fear,* pp. 128, 130.

195. Michel Foucault, *Histoire de la folie à l'Âge Classique,* p. 18; *Madness and Civilization: A History of Insanity in the Age of Reason,* trans. Richard Howard, p. 7.

196. Foucault, *Histoire de la folie,* p. 19; *A History of Insanity,* p. 8.

197. Foucault, *Histoire de la folie,* p. 20; *A History of Insanity,* p. 9.

198 Foucault, *Histoire de la folie,* p. 22; *A History of Insanity,* p. 11.

199. Foucault, *Histoire de la folie,* p. 22; *A History of Insanity,* p. 11. Léry has an exemplary passage in this regard: "Indeed, since we had been tossing and afloat on the sea almost four months without putting into port, it had often occurred to us that *we were in exile out there,* and it seemed as though we would never escape it" (*Histoire d'un voyage,* vol. 1, p. 73; *History of a Voyage,* p. 25 [emphasis added]).

200. Foucault, *Histoire de la folie,* p. 23; *A History of Insanity,* p. 12. A further comment on De Lancre's ideas: "It is not surprising that seamen should be treacherous, inconstant, and unpredictable. The people of Labourd, bad tillers of the ground and worse craftsmen, had little love for their country, their wives and children, and since they were neither French nor Spanish, they had no established pattern of behavior to follow" (Julio Caro Baroja, *Les sorcières et leur monde,* p. 185; *The World of the Witches,* trans. Nigel Glendinning, p. 158). On the persecution in Labourd, see Roland Villeneuve, *Le fléau des sorciers: Histoire de la diablerie basque au XVIIᵉ siècle.*

201. Antonio Sérgio, "As duas políticas nacionais," in *Ensaios II,* p. 63.

202. A. de Souza Silva Costa Lobo, *História da sociedade em Portugal: No século XV,* p. 49. The historian says: "For Portugal, its overseas possessions were always the dungeon of its delinquents."

203. Columbus stated: "Gold is the treasure, and he who possesses it holds all that he needs in this world, as he also holds the way of redeeming souls from

Purgatory and calling them to Paradise" (cited in Delumeau, *Naissance et affirmation de la Réforme*, p. 54).

204. *Relaçam do naufrágio da nao Santiago e itinerário da gente que dele se salvou*, written by Manuel Godinho Cardoso with the permission of the Holy Inquisition in Lisbon; printed by Pedro Crasbeeck, year MDCII (cited in Lanciani, *Os relatos de naufrágios na literatura portuguesa*, p. 137). On page 18, Lanciani says there is another account of the same shipwreck by another passenger, the Jesuit priest Pedro Martins, dated Goa, December 9, 1586, thus confirming this earlier year for the shipwreck.

205. Buarque de Holanda, *Visão do Paraíso*, pp. 253–54.

206. Salvador, *História do Brasil*, p. 496 (emphasis added).

207. Knivet, *Vária fortuna*, p. 86; "Admirable Adventures and Strange Fortunes," p. 224 (emphasis added).

208. Knivet, *Vária fortuna*, p. 72; "Admirable Adventures and Strange Fortunes," pp. 214–15.

209. Knivet, *Vária fortuna*, p. 153; "Admirable Adventures and Strange Fortunes," p. 267.

210. Leite, "Antonio Rodrigues, soldado, viajante e jesuíta," pp. 64, 69.

211. "Carta do Pe. João de Azpilcueta Navarro aos irmãos de Coimbra; Porto Seguro, 19 de setembro de 1553," in Leite, *Novas cartas jesuíticas*, p. 155. The first three paragraphs of this letter are particularly noteworthy.

212. "Ao Pe. Geral, Diogo Láinez, São Vicente, 12-6-1561," in Leite, *Novas cartas jesuíticas*, p. 109 (emphasis added).

213. Nóbrega, "Ao Pe. Mestre Simão Rodrigues, São Vicente, 12-2-1553," in Leite, *Novas cartas jesuíticas*, p. 35.

214. Antonil, *Cultura e opulência do Brasil*, p. 203.

215. Ibid., pp. 217–19.

216. Hoornaert, *A igreja no Brasil Colônia*, pp. 75–76. On page 76, the author cites Vieira, explaining the Jesuit's words in parentheses: "I am already convinced beyond doubt that the bondage of the first transmigration (from Africa to Brazil) has been ordained by His Mercy for the liberty of the second (from Brazil to . . . heaven)." Vieira preached this sermon to members of the brotherhood of the Rosário dos Pretos (Rosary of the Blacks), in the Recôncavo Baiano, in 1663.

217. Antonil, *Cultura e opulência do Brasil*, p. 160.

218. The metropolis might seem like paradise but it was not. The author of *A nova gazeta alemã* wrote: "The lower deck of the ship is loaded with brazilwood, and below filled with slaves, young girls and boys. They cost the Portuguese little, for most of them were given of free will, because the people there think their children are going to the Promised Land" (*A nova gazeta alemã—O valor etnográfico da Newen Zeytung Auss Presillo Landt*, ed. Joaquim Ribeiro, p. 50).

219. Madre de Deus, *Memórias para a história da Capitania de São Vicente*, p. 361. "If therefore at the time of 1580 João Ramalho already had some 90 years of residence in Brazil, it follows that he arrived here in 1490, more or less thereabouts."

220. "Carta de Pero Vaz de Caminha," in Malheiro Dias, *História da colonização portuguesa do Brasil*, vol. 2, p. 90. Another reference to Afonso Ribeiro can be found on pages 94–95.

221. Malheiro Dias, *História da colonização portuguesa do Brasil,* vol. 2, p. 97.

222. Ibid., p. 99.

223. Abreu, *O descobrimento do Brasil,* p. 29; Prado, *Retrato do Brasil,* p. 159.

224. The outline of a serious study appears in Emília Viotti da Costa, "Primeiros povoadores do Brasil," *Revista de História* (São Paulo) 13, no. 17 (1956): 3–22.

225. Prado, *Retrato do Brasil,* p. 155.

226. Ibid., p. 194.

227. Ibid., p. 198.

228. Todorov, *La conquête de l'Amérique,* pp. 25–26; *The Conquest of America,* p. 18.

229. "Any misappropriation of tobacco, in any part of Brazil, left out of records and journals, under which all is dispatched, shall carry the penalty of seizure of this tobacco and of the vessel on which it is found and in addition five years of banishment to Angola for the author of the crime" (Antonil, *Cultura e opulência do Brasil,* p. 252).

230. Since this topic will be the subject of a later chapter, I will leave further commentary aside for now, as well as references to the trials on which this hypothesis is based.

231. "A Santo Inácio de Loyola, carta de Nóbrega de São Vicente, 25-3-1555," cited in Leite, *Novas cartas jesuíticas,* p. 60.

232. Jaboatão, *Novo orbe seráfico brasílico,* vol. 1, p. 75.

233. Brandão, *Diálogo das grandezas do Brasil,* p. 155.

234. "Carta do Conde ao Príncipe de Orange," cited in Barleus, *História dos feitos recentemente praticados,* pp. 45–46.

235. I address the issue of the onus and usefulness of the socially dispossessed strata in "As metamorfoses do ônus e da utilidade," in Laura de Mello e Souza, *Desclassificados do ouro: A pobreza mineira no século XVIII,* pp. 215–19. In another article, I begin to explore the relation between perception of this metamorphism and capitalist consciousness. See "Notas sobre os vadios na literatura colonial do século XVIII," in Roberto Schwarz (ed.), *Os pobres na literatura brasileira,* pp. 9–12.

Chapter 2. Popular Religiosity in the Colony

1. The spirit of organization was an early modern novelty in the realm of Christian history and apostleship, with St. Ignatius being one of its greatest "theoreticians." See Jean Delumeau, *Le catholicisme entre Luther et Voltaire,* pp. 103–4. In a fine formulation, Delumeau characterized St. Vincent de Paul's later activities as "the spirit of organization placed at the service of love" (p. 108); *Catholicism between Luther and Voltaire: A New View of the Counter-Reformation,* trans. Jeremy Moiser, pp. 56, 59.

2. See Charles R. Boxer, *A igreja e a expansão ibérica, 1440–1770,* p. 99; Fortunato de Almeida, *História da igreja em Portugal,* ed. Damião Peres, vol. 1, pp. 367ff.

3. Hoornaert, *A igreja no Brasil Colônia,* pp. 35–36.

4. "The council was ecumenical *de jure* and not *de facto.* It primarily rep-

resented Europe's southern Christianity" (Delumeau, *Le catholicisme entre Luther et Voltaire,* p. 67).

5. Boxer, *A igreja e a expansão ibérica,* p. 101.

6. Delumeau, *Le catholicisme entre Luther et Voltaire,* pp. 138–39; Hoornaert, *A igreja no Brasil Colônia,* p. 35; Boxer, *A igreja e a expansão ibérica,* p. 104.

7. Gilberto Freyre, *Casa Grande e Senzala: Formação da família brasileira sob regime de economia patriarcal,* p. xxxvii; *The Masters and the Slaves: A Study in the Development of Brazilian Civilization,* trans. Samuel Putnam, p. xxxiii. The testimony of the slave Joana, arrested in Belém by the Visitation of 1764–68 for practicing sorcery, casts doubt on the alleged influence wielded by plantation chaplains: "When she was in this town, she always attended mass on prescribed days and on Saturdays of Our Lady; however, after moving to the *engenho,* only very rarely did she attend mass, for she had no opportunity except when her masters went" (IANTT, Inquisição de Lisboa, Processo no. 2.691, "Processo de Joana preta crioula").

8. Hoornaert, *A igreja no Brasil Colônia,* pp. 12–13.

9. Eduardo Hoornaert, "A cristandade durante a primeira época colonial," in Eduardo Hoornaert, Riolando Azzi, Klaus Van Der Grijp, and Benno Brod (eds.), *História da igreja no Brasil: Primeira época,* pp. 248–49.

10. Ibid., pp. 355–56.

11. John Bossy, "The Counter-Reformation and the People of Catholic Europe," *Past and Present* 47 (May 1970): 59.

12. Jean-Marie Goulemot, "Démons, merveilles et philosophie à l'Âge Classique," *Annales, E.S.C.,* 35th year, no. 6 (November–December 1980): 1226.

13. Ibid., p. 1226. See Lucien Febvre, "Sorcellerie: Sottise ou révolution mentale?" *Annales, E.S.C.,* year 3, no. 1 (January–March 1948); and Robert Mandrou, *Magistrats et sorciers en France au XVIIe siècle.*

14. Goulemot, "Démons, merveilles et philosophie," p. 1236.

15. Jean Delumeau, "Les chrétiens au temps de la Réforme," in *Un chemin d'histoire: Chrétienté et christianisation,* p. 18.

16. Delumeau, *Le catholicisme entre Luther et Voltaire,* p. 233; *Catholicism between Luther and Voltaire,* p. 159.

17. Giordano, *Religiosidad popular en la Alta Edad Media,* p. 183.

18. Jean Delumeau, "Ignorance religieuse, mentalité magique et christianisation," in *Un chemin d'histoire,* p. 120.

19. Ibid., p. 117.

20. Jean Delumeau, "Les réformateurs et la superstition," in *Un chemin d'histoire,* p. 79.

21. Keith Thomas, *Religion and the Decline of Magic: Studies in Popular Beliefs in Sixteenth and Seventeenth Century England,* p. 169. See chapter 6, "Religion and the People," pp. 151–73.

22. Sônia A. Siqueira, *A Inquisição portuguesa e a sociedade colonial,* p. 87.

23. Ibid., pp. 65, 253.

24. Delumeau, *Naissance et affirmation de la Réforme,* p. 76: "The two enemy Reformations represented the same startling of Christian conscience." In another work he states: "The two Reformations judged themselves hostile to

each other when at heart they were carrying out the same work" (Delumeau, "Les réformateurs et la superstition," in *Un chemin d'histoire*, p. 79).

25. Delumeau, "Les réformateurs et la superstition," in *Un chemin d'histoire*, p. 72.

26. Delumeau, *Un chemin d'histoire*, preface, p. 4.

27. Cited in Delumeau, "Les réformateurs et la superstition," in *Un chemin d'histoire*, p. 72 ("Luther's Small Catechism with Preface," in Robert Colb and Timothy J. Wengert (eds.), *Book of Concord: Confessions of the ELCA*, [Minneapolis: Fortress Press, 2000], pp. 347–48).

28. Robert Muchembled, "Sorcellerie, culture populaire et christianisme," *Annales, E.S.C.*, 28th year, no. 1 (January–February 1973): 268.

29. Delumeau, "Ignorance religieuse," in *Un chemin d'histoire*, p. 122.

30. Giordano, *Religiosidad popular en la Alta Edad Media*, p. 19.

31. A. H. de Oliveira Marques, *A sociedade medieval portuguesa*, p. 170; *Daily Life in Portugal in the Late Middle Ages*, trans. S. S. Wyatt, p. 226.

32. Oliveira Marques, *A sociedade medieval portuguesa*, p. 170; *Daily Life in Portugal*, p. 226.

33. These authors include José Ferreira Carrato: "This Portuguese faith excels in its externalist religiosity, which will be more accentuated here" (*Igreja, iluminismo e escolas mineiras coloniais*, p. 29).

34. Oliveira Marques, *A sociedade medieval portuguesa*, pp. 156–57.

35. Carrato, *Igreja, iluminismo e escolas mineiras coloniais*, p. 45. "The Christianization of older days was both narrower in scope and shallower than has been supposed" (Delumeau, *Un chemin d'histoire*, preface, p. 8).

36. Jorge Benci, *Economia cristã dos senhores no governo dos escravos* (1700), pp. 93–94, 95–96 (emphasis added).

37. Antonil, *Cultura e opulência do Brasil*, p. 161.

38. Ibid., p. 164.

39. Roger Bastide, *Les religions africaines au Brésil: Vers une sociologie des interprétations de civilisations*, p. 157; *The African Religions of Brazil: Toward a Sociology of the Interpenetration of Civilizations*, trans. Helen Sebba, p. 113.

40. "Syncretism is symptomatic of one of the conditions of slave societies: the mixing of races and peoples, the cohabitation of the most diverse ethnic groups in one place, and the creation, at a level above the self-centered 'nations,' of a new form of solidarity in suffering, a solidarity of color" (Bastide, *Les religions africaines au Brésil*, p. 260; *The African Religions of Brazil*, p. 187).

41. Bastide, *Les religions africaines au Brésil*, p. 79; *The African Religions of Brazil*, p. 58.

42. Bastide, *Les religions africaines au Brésil*, p. 26; *The African Religions of Brazil*, p. 19.

43. Bastide, *Les religions africaines au Brésil*, p. 91; *The African Religions of Brazil*, p. 66. The first scholar to identify the syncretic relationships between Catholic saints and African *orixás* was Nina Rodrigues. Today, the main *pais-de-santo* and *mães-de-santo* of Bahian Candomblé—especially those of Ketu lineage—repudiate this notion of equivalences, seeking instead a religious purism.

44. Bastide, *Les religions africaines au Brésil*, p. 91; *The African Religions of Brazil*, p. 66.

45. *Primeira Visitação do Santo Ofício às partes do Brasil pelo licenciado*

Heitor Furtado de Mendonça—Denunciações da Bahia, 1591–1593, intro. by Capistrano de Abreu, p. 277.

46. Ibid., p. 321.

47. Ibid., p. 346.

48. Ibid., p. 473.

49. Ibid., p. 266.

50. Ibid., p. 383.

51. Ibid., p. 454 (emphasis added). Hoornaert says the Santidades were indigenous Messianic movements that were a reaction against the missionaries. In the Jesuit provinces of the south, a number of Messianic Santidade movements are also said to have existed (Hoornaert, "A cristandade," in Hoornaert et al., *História da igreja no Brasil*, p. 393).

52. Freyre, *Casa Grande e Senzala*, vol. 1, p. 379 (emphasis added).

53. José Gonçalves Salvador, *Cristãos-novos, Jesuítas e Inquisição*, p. 187; see also p. 159.   João Lúcio de Azevedo, *História dos cristãos-novos portugueses*: "Livorno, Bordeaux, and Amsterdam were ports of preference sought by the Jewish Portuguese who went into exile. Nowhere else, however, did they find refuge as felicitous as that in Holland" (p. 387). Eduardo d'Oliveira França points out the coming and going of New Christians from Bahia to Holland and from Holland to Bahia (*Segunda Visitação do Santo Ofício às partes do Brasil pelo inquisidor e visitador o licenciado Marcos Teixeira: Livro das confissões e ratificações da Bahia, 1618–1620*, intro. by Eduardo d'Oliveira França and Sônia A. Siqueira, *Anais do Museu Paulista* 17: 158).

54. "Of the 83 clerics who in 1656 held posts in the prelateship, at least 12 were of Jewish lineage, which gives us a percentage of almost 15%, and with regards to the captaincies of Rio de Janeiro and of São Vicente, we list 46 priests and 14 friars of [Jewish] lineage, and almost all native to this land" (Gonçalves Salvador, *Cristãos-novos, Jesuítas e Inquisição*, p. 189). "The convents were at that time crowded with clergy of Jewish descent, many of whom were sincere Catholics" (Anita Novinsky, *Cristãos-novos na Bahia, 1624–1654*, p. 52).

55. Novinsky, *Cristãos-novos na Bahia*, p. 161.

56. Sônia Siqueira's position seems untenable to me. "In the externalization of their faith, the Jews reaffirmed themselves daily, emphasizing their difference from Christian generality and individualizing themselves collectively" (*A Inquisição portuguesa e a sociedade colonial*, p. 68).

57. Novinsky, *Cristãos-novos na Bahia*, p. 162.

58. André Vauchez, *La spiritualité du Moyen-Âge occidental, VIIIᵉ–XIIᵉ siècles*, p. 24; *Spirituality of the Medieval West: From the Eighth to the Twelfth Century*, p. 25.

59. Vauchez, *La spiritualité du Moyen-Âge occidental*, p. 26; *Spirituality of the Medieval West*, p. 27. One of the finest analyses of the incorporation of folk elements by Christianity—which has inspired almost all subsequent analyses—is offered by Jacques Le Goff in "Culture cléricale et traditions folkloriques dans la civilisation mérovingienne," in *Pour un autre Moyen-Âge*. The same author addresses the institution of worship of the dead by the monks of Cluny in *La naissance du Purgatoire*. Analyzing medieval literature on voyages to the great Beyond, Giuseppe Gatto points to a trend toward Christianizing folk traditions by incorporating elements of oral tradition into the universe of written tradition ("Le voyage au Paradis," p. 938).

60. I do not feel Oronzo Giordano is correct in his formulation: "that slow and complex phenomenon of osmosis or, if you prefer, of religious syncretism, understood as an encounter, an often inverted adaptation, a merger of diverse experiences and of natural attitudes of man before the sacred" (*Religiosidad popular en la Alta Edad Media,* p. 138).

61. "Indeed, a folk feature may maintain its own consistency and reality, alongside and independent of a religious feature, so long as it is not absorbed by it. . . . However, these both become an element of popular religion as soon as they take on a religious connotation, for some reason or in some way. In certain cases, it may even happen that one of these elements, after having been admitted into the world of popular religion, becomes merely a popular tradition, devoid of any component of a spiritual nature" (Raoul Manselli, *La religion populaire au Moyen-Âge: Problèmes de méthode et d'histoire,* p. 37).

62. "The theory of 'survivals' of paganism has become obsolete: nothing 'survives' in a culture; everything is living, or it is not" (Jean-Claude Schmitt, "'Religion populaire' et culture folklorique," *Annales, E.S.C.,* 31st year, no. 5 [September–October 1976]: 946).

63. Regarding medieval Christianity, Manselli says that it "lives . . . in constant tension, endeavoring to incorporate from what it receives whatever is acceptable and striving to do away with whatever disfigures it or threatens its structuring forces" (*La religion populaire au Moyen-Âge,* p. 41).

64. Delumeau, *Le catholicisme entre Luther et Voltaire,* p. 145; *Catholicism between Luther and Voltaire,* p. 89. On religious syncretism in Mexico, see Jacques Lafaye, *Quetzacóatl et Guadalupe: La formation de la conscience nationale au Méxique.* See also Robert Ricard, *The Spiritual Conquest of Mexico: An Essay on the Apostolate and the Evangelizing Methods of the Mendicant Orders in New Spain, 1523–1572,* trans. Lesley Byrd Simpson, pp. 264–82. On the study of indigenous survivals in Peru despite the church's efforts to suppress them, see Pierre Duviols, *La lutte contre les religions autochtones dans le Pérou colonial: L'extirpation de l'idolatrie entre 1532 et 1660.*

65. Leila Mezan Algranti, "O feitor ausente: Estudo sobre a escravidão urbana no Rio de Janeiro (1808–1821)."

66. Nuno Marques Pereira, *Compêndio narrativo do peregrino da América* (1728), vol. 1, pp. 111, 113.

67. Hoornaert, "A cristandade," in Hoornaert et al., *História da igreja no Brasil,* p. 388.

68. Bastide, *Les religions africaines au Brésil,* p. 173; *The African Religions of Brazil,* pp. 124–25.

69. On the joyful masses of the sixteenth century, see Hoornaert et al., *História da igreja no Brasil,* p. 297. The baroque festivals have been described by authors of that era, among them Simão Ferreira Machado. See Afonso Ávila's *Resíduos seiscentistas em minas: Textos do século do ouro e as projeções do mundo barroco,* where both the *Triunfo eucarístico* and the *Áureo trono episcopal* are published and commented on.

70. *Primeira Visitação, Denunciações da Bahia,* p. 267.

71. Anita Novinsky, "A gente das bandas do sul," *Suplemento Literário de O Estado de S. Paulo,* April 15, 1967; cited in Gonçalves Salvador, *Cristãos-novos, Jesuítas e Inquisição,* p. 113.

72. Gonçalves Salvador, *Cristãos-novos, Jesuítas e Inquisição,* p. 84. The

people of the Iberian peninsula likewise hated the Holy Office. "A tailor from Pontevedra [Spain] is denounced in 1565 for stating that he holds the Holy Office in as much esteem as the tail of a dog" (Carmelo Lisón-Tolosana, *Brujería, estructura social y simbolismo en Galicia*, p. 28).

73. *Primeira Visitação do Santo Ofício às partes do Brasil: Confissões de Pernambuco*, ed. J. A. Gonsalves de Mello, p. 138.

74. *Segunda Visitação do Santo Ofício às partes do Brasil: Denunciações da Bahia (1618—Marcos Teixeira)*, intro. by Rodolfo Garcia, *Anais da Biblioteca Nacional do Rio de Janeiro* 49 (1927): 136.

75. *Primeira Visitação: Denunciações da Bahia*, p. 287. Friar Vicente do Salvador alludes to the Calvinist "João Bouller," who arrived among the first French accompanying Nicolas Durand de Villegaignon to Rio. The Portuguese from São Vicente—where Bouller fled—saw him "sometimes prick the authority of the Supreme Pontiff, the use of the sacraments, the value of indulgences, and the worship of images." Denounced to the bishop, he was obstinate and did not want to recant; he ended up dying at the hands of an executioner (*História do Brasil*, p. 193). Capistrano de Abreu tells a different story: after being tried by the Holy Office of 1560 to 1564 and released, João Bolés had gone to India, where he disappeared. See Capistrano de Abreu, "João Cointa, Senhor de Bolés," in *Ensaios e estudos (Crítica e história)*, pp. 11–30. See also "Processo de João de Bolés e justificação requerida pelo mesmo (1560–1564)," in *Anais da Biblioteca Nacional do Rio de Janeiro* 25 (1903): 215–308.

76. IANTT, Inquisição de Lisboa, Processo no. 2.289, "Processo de Isidoro da Silva cordoeiro filho de Antonio da Silva lavrador de mandioca e natural e morador na cidade da Bahia." As was the case of nearly all the trials I consulted, the pages are not numbered.

77. Ginzburg, *Le fromage et les vers*, p. 56; *The Cheese and the Worms*, pp. 20–21.

78. *Primeira Visitação do Santo Ofício às partes do Brasil pelo Licenciado Heitor Furtado de Mendonça: Denunciações de Pernambuco, 1593–1595*, intro. by Rodolfo Garcia, p. 426.

79. *Primeira Visitação: Confissões de Pernambuco*, p. 34.

80. Ibid., p. 24.

81. Ibid., p. 27. Arriving in Rome in the eighteenth century, Giacomo Casanova observed that in no other Catholic city did people pay so little heed to religion. Women went to mass in clothing not at all modest: their heads covered by a thin gauze, their eyes uncovered, always staring at the men (Maurice Andrieux, *La vie quotidienne dans la Rome Pontificale au XVIIIe siècle*, pp. 143, 153). Widespread prostitution in the two main cities of the Italian Renaissance, Rome and Venice, engendered a veritable "myth of the Italian Renaissance courtesan," which, according to Paul Larivaille, was a fallacy (*La vie quotidienne des courtisanes en Italie au temps de la Renaissance*, pp. 195–201).

82. "The conjugal state cannot be preferred to the state of virginity or of celibacy," the assembly of Trent affirmed. "To the contrary, it is better or more blessed to remain in virginity or celibacy than to be joined in matrimony" (Delumeau, *Le catholicisme entre Luther et Voltaire*, p. 94; *Catholicism between Luther and Voltaire*, p. 13).

83. *Primeira Visitação: Denunciações de Pernambuco,* p. 89 (emphasis added).

84. Ibid., p. 43.

85. Ibid., p. 57.

86. Ibid., pp. 90–91.

87. See Souza, *Desclassificados do ouro,* pp. 174–77.

88. IANTT, Inquisição de Lisboa, Manuscritos da Livraria, no. 959.

89. Ibid.

90. IANTT, Inquisição de Lisboa, Processo no. 3.723, "Processo de frei Luís de Nazareth religioso professo de Nossa Senhora do Carmo Colado da Província da Bahia e morador na mesma cidade."

91. IANTT, Inquisição de Lisboa, Manuscritos da Livraria, no. 959.

92. *Segunda Visitação: Denunciações da Bahia,* p. 148.

93. See Jean Delumeau, *La peur en Occident, XIVe–XVIIIe siècles,* pp. 305–45; see also *A civilização do Renascimento,* vol. 2, p. 125.

94. With regard to the obscene and erotic backdrop of popular festivals, see Giordano, *Religiosidad popular en la Alta Edad Media,* pp. 103–4. On the topic of the country of Cockaigne, see Ginzburg, *Le fromage et les vers,* p. 128; *The Cheese and the Worms,* p. 83. See also Jean Delumeau (ed.), *La mort des Pays de Cocagne: Comportements collectifs de la Renaissance à l'âge classique*; and Mikail Bakhtine, *L'oeuvre de François Rabelais et la culture populaire au Moyen-Âge et sous la Renaissance.*

95. "Baltazar Fonseca, stonemason, who was 35 years old in 1594, was accused of not believing in the Cross and in saints such as Peter, Paul, and John, but only in God" (Arnold Wiznitzer, *Os judeus no Brasil colonial,* p. 22).

96. *Primeira Visitação: Denunciações de Pernambuco,* p. 188.

97. *Primeira Visitação: Denunciações da Bahia,* p. 351. On popular Catholicism in Brazil, Artur Ramos says: "God, as a monotheistic abstraction, is an incomprehensible entity, existing solely in the play of words. For the common man to stop and think about Him, He must be *configured and represented* in a concrete symbol. And so thus we see the Eternal Father transformed into a bearded old man, with a heavy scowl and a gruff and thunderous voice. Legacy of ancient paganisms" (*O folclore negro no Brasil,* p. 17 [emphasis in the original]).

98. *Primeira Visitação do Santo Ofício às partes do Brasil pelo Licenciado Heitor Furtado de Mendonça: Confissões da Bahia 1591–1592,* preface by Capistrano de Abreu, p. 58.

99. *Primeira Visitação: Denunciações da Bahia,* pp. 385–86.

100. *Primeira Visitação: Confissões da Bahia,* p. 128.

101. In medieval times there was one current of elite thought that saw God as unattainable, cloistered in a far-off universe, which only revelation (and never reason) could reach: the system of the English Franciscan William of Ockham (1270–1347). It lies at the base of the violent Protestant reaction against the everyday familiarity with which God was treated. One proverb went: "Laissez faire Dieu, qui est homme d'aage." Jean Froissart stated: "Pour si hault homme qui Dieu est" (Delumeau, *Naissance et affirmation de la Réforme,* pp. 58, 60).

102. Delumeau, "Ignorance religieuse," in *Un chemin d'histoire,* p. 131. Black influence was to reinforce this barter aspect of popular religiosity. For Fernando

Ortiz, the black "theoanthropic economy" differed greatly from one of "long-term credit." To the contrary, it was "a religion of immediate consumption, of barter rites, without credit or accumulated interest" (cited by Bastide, *Les religions africaines au Brésil*, p. 196; *The African Religions of Brazil*, p. 141).

103. *Primeira Visitação: Confissões de Pernambuco*, pp. 135, 117.

104. Ibid., p. 32.

105. Ibid., pp. 76, 77.

106. *Segunda Visitação: Confissões da Bahia*, p. 451.

107. Ibid., p. 506.

108. *Livro da Visitação do Santo Ofício da Inquisição ao Estado do Grão-Pará, 1763–1769*, intro. by José Roberto Amaral Lapa, pp. 198–99.

109. IANTT, Inquisição de Lisboa, no. 145-6-180A.

110. I owe this observation to Hilário Franco, Jr.

111. *Segunda Visitação: Denunciações da Bahia*, p. 160.

112. *Primeira Visitação: Confissões de Pernambuco*, p. 24.

113. *Segunda Visitação: Denunciações da Bahia*, p. 370. Menocchio said Jesus was a man like any other, only "with more dignity" (Ginzburg, *Le fromage et les vers*, p. 39; *The Cheese and the Worms*, p. 6).

114. *Segunda Visitação: Denunciações da Bahia*, p. 105.

115. Ibid., p. 159.

116. Ibid., pp. 152, 153, 182, 195. The quotation is found on page 195.

117. *Livro da Visitação: Estado do Grão-Pará*, pp. 228–29.

118. *Primeira Visitação: Denunciações de Pernambuco*, p. 124.

119. Ibid., p. 34.

120. Ibid., p. 124.

121. Ibid., pp. 91–92. Lashing crucifixes was quite a common practice among colonists. Around 1628 an Old Christian who lived in Vila de São Paulo was accused of lashing a crucifix (Gonçalves Salvador, *Cristãos-novos, Jesuítas e Inquisição*, p. 109).

122. *Primeira Visitação: Denunciações de Pernambuco*, pp. 300–6.

123. Norman Cohn, *Los demonios familiares de Europa*, p. 125; *Europe's Inner Demons*, p. 92.

124. Emmanuel Le Roy Ladurie, *Montaillou, village occitan, de 1294 à 1324*, p. 479; *Montaillou: The Promised Land of Error*, trans. Barbara Bray, p. 302.

125. Le Roy Ladurie, *Montaillou, village occitan*, p. 479; *Montaillou: The Promised Land of Error*, p. 302.

126. *Primeira Visitação: Denunciações de Pernambuco*, p. 20.

127. Boxer, *A igreja e a expansão ibérica*, p. 132; *The Church Militant and Iberian Expansion, 1440–1770*, p. 108.

128. Hoornaert et al., *História da igreja no Brasil*, p. 345.

129. Georges Balandier, *La vie quotidienne au Royaume du Kongo du XVIᵉ au XVIIIᵉ siècle*, cited in Muchembled, "Sorcellerie, culture populaire et christianisme," p. 278.

130. Gonçalves Fernandes, *O folclore mágico do Nordeste: Usos, costumes, crenças e ofícios mágicos das populações nordestinas*, p. 119.

131. Ginzburg, *Le fromage et les vers*, p. 56; *The Cheese and the Worms*, pp. 20–21. During the eighteenth-century Visitation to northern Brazil, an entire family was accused of disrespecting the image of Christ: "They would back away from the Altar and, unbuttoning their trousers, would raise their shirts behind

and turn this part toward the said images and opening their buttocks they would show them to the images, at the same time looking with a contorted face and base posture at the said image of the Lord" (*Livro da Visitação: Estado do Grão-Pará*, p. 220).

132. Delumeau, *Naissance et affirmation de la Réforme*, p. 53.

133. Delumeau, "Les réformateurs et la superstition," in *Un chemin d'histoire*, p. 67; J. Huizinga, *El otoño de la Edad Média* (Buenos Aires: *Revista de Ocidente Argentina*, 1947), p. 214.

134. Hoornaert et al., *História da igreja no Brasil*, p. 347. Concerning the episode involving Nossa Senhora da Graça and the spouses Caramuru-Paraguaçu, see Jaboatão, *Novo orbe seráfico brasílico*, vol. 1, p. 51; Rocha Pitta, *História da América Portuguesa*, p. 31.

135. Jaboatão, *Novo orbe seráfico brasílico*, vol. 1, pp. 88–91.

136. Hoornaert et al., *História da igreja no Brasil*, p. 346.

137. *Primeira Visitação: Denunciações de Pernambuco*, p. 43. In Portugal as well it was common to introduce the Virgin into profane contexts, carnivalizing her role: "Hickey was scandalized when he saw the Holy Virgin in a silver dress, covered in jewels, dancing a fandango with Our Lord, hair powdered" (Suzanne Chantal, *A vida quotidiana em Portugal ao tempo do terremoto*, p. 179).

138. *Primeira Visitação: Denunciações de Pernambuco*, p. 43.

139. *Primeira Visitação: Denunciações da Bahia*, pp. 511–12.

140. *Segunda Visitação: Denunciações da Bahia*, p. 103.

141. IANTT, Inquisição de Lisboa: Manuscritos da Livraria, no. 959.

142. *Segunda Visitação: Confissões da Bahia*, p. 360.

143. Le Roy Ladurie, *Montaillou, village occitan*, pp. 288, 493.

144. Ibid., p. 528; *Montaillou: The Promised Land of Error*, pp. 320–21.

145. Ginzburg, *Le fromage et les vers*, p. 38; *The Cheese and the Worms*, p. 4.

146. *Segunda Visitação: Denunciações de Pernambuco*, p. 175; see also pp. 114–15.

147. *Primeira Visitação: Denunciações da Bahia*, p. 550; Antonio Baião, "A Inquisição no Brasil—Extractos d'alguns livros de denúncias," *Revista de História* (Sociedade Portuguesa de Estudos Históricos, Lisbon) 1 (January–March 1912): 194.

148. AEAM, Devassas—1747–1748, p. 32.

149. IANTT, Inquisição de Lisboa: Caderno do Promotor, no. 128, 1762; cited in Luiz Mott, "Acotundá: Raízes setecentistas do sincretismo religioso afro-brasileiro," p. 7.

150. Freyre, *Casa Grande e Senzala*, vol. 1, p. 343.

151. Ibid., pp. 342–43.

152. Ibid., p. 312.

153. Ibid., p. 313.

154. Ibid., p. 343.

155. Freyre noted "the erotic vibrancy, the procreative tension, which the country of necessity sought to maintain in the fervent era of Imperial colonization" (*Casa Grande e Senzala*, vol. 1, pp. 346–47; *The Masters and the Slaves*, pp. 259–60).

156. Delumeau, *Naissance et affirmation de la Réforme*, p. 54.

157. Vauchez, *La spiritualité du Moyen-Âge occidental*, p. 26; *Spirituality of*

the Medieval West, p. 27: "The faithful felt unprotected before God, the far-away and yet Omnipresent Judge. They experienced the need to resort to go-betweens."

158. Wicked powers were attributed to the saints, and at Berry people spoke of saints being "jealous" (Delumeau, *Le catholicisme entre Luther et Voltaire*, p. 246; *Catholicism between Luther and Voltaire*, p. 168). In his *Peregrinatio colloquium*, Desiderius Erasmus poked fun at the groundless fears the saints provoked in simple folk: "Peter may close the gates to heaven; Paul is armed with a sword; Bartholomew, with a knife; William, with the lance. The holy fire is at Anthony's beck and call. Francis of Assisi himself, after he went to heaven, may blind or make mad those who do not respect him. Poorly worshipped saints unleash terrible diseases" (cited in Delumeau, "Les réformateurs et la superstition," in *Un chemin d'histoire*, p. 68).

159. *Segunda Visitação: Denunciações da Bahia*, p. 109.

160. *Segunda Visitação: Confissões da Bahia*, p. 367.

161. *Segunda Visitação: Denunciações da Bahia*, p. 170.

162. Ibid., p. 166; see also p. 121.

163. Ibid., p. 178.

164. *Primeira Visitação: Denunciações da Bahia*, p. 170.

165. Ibid., pp. 350–51.

166. Ibid., p. 544.

167. *Segunda Visitação: Confissões da Bahia*, p. 390.

168. *Primeira Visitação: Denunciações da Bahia*, p. 288.

169. *Primeira Visitação: Confissões de Pernambuco*, p. 129.

170. IANTT, Inquisição de Lisboa: Processo no. 4.491, "Processo de José de Jesus Maria que dantes se chamava José de Moura que tem parte de cristão-novo solteiro, ermitão filho de Manuel d'Oliveira tratante, natural de Montemor e novo residente nesta cidade de Lisboa. Réu preso nos cárceres da Inquisição dela." I am indebted to Professor Anita Novinsky for referring me to this trial.

171. *Primeira Visitação: Confissões de Pernambuco*, p. 138. Suzanne Chantal provides examples of wrath directed against saints in eighteenth-century Lisbon. After various threats against the image of St. Anthony, boatmen who were rowing against the current on the Tagus and had not seen their supplications answered pulled out their knives and yelled in fury: "Son of a . . . if not out of respect for this bastard you carry on your lap, I would cut off your . . ." (*A vida cotidiana em Portugal*, p. 175).

172. *Primeira Visitação: Confissões de Pernambuco*, p. 50.

173. "[The New Christian] calls into question society's values, Catholic dogma, and the morals imposed by this dogma" (Novinsky, *Cristãos-novos na Bahia*, p. 162).

174. *Segunda Visitação: Denunciações da Bahia*, p. 145.

175. *Segunda Visitação: Confissões da Bahia*, p. 360.

176. *Primeira Visitação: Denunciações de Pernambuco*, pp. 433–34.

177. *Primeira Visitação: Confissões de Pernambuco*, p. 143. Vauchez points out that as part of the process of desacralization of the world and the rise of laicism, the dogma of the Holy Trinity was even discussed at crossroads (*La spiritualité du Moyen-Âge occidental*, p. 79; *Spirituality of the Medieval West*, pp. 78–79).

178. *Primeira Visitação: Denunciações da Bahia*, p. 395.

179. *Segunda Visitação: Denunciações da Bahia,* p. 192.
180. *Segunda Visitação: Confissões da Bahia,* p. 403.
181. Manselli, *La religion populaire au Moyen-Âge,* p. 115.
182. Ginzburg, *Le fromage et les vers,* p. 179; *The Cheese and the Worms,* p. 128.
183. *Primeira Visitação: Confissões de Pernambuco,* p. 26.
184. *Primeira Visitação: Denunciações de Pernambuco,* p. 91.
185. Ibid., p. 95; see also pp. 39–40.
186. Ibid., pp. 396–97.
187. Ibid., pp. 420–22.
188. Aaron J. Gurevich, "Au Moyen-Âge: Conscience individuelle et image de l'au-delà," *Annales E.S.C.,* 37th year, no. 2 (March–April 1982): 272–73.
189. I refer again to the notable book by Jacques Le Goff, *La naissance du Purgatoire.*
190. *Primeira Visitação: Confissões de Pernambuco,* pp. 139–40.
191. *Primeira Visitação: Denunciações de Pernambuco,* p. 167.
192. Ibid., p. 165.
193. Ibid., p. 141.
194. *Primeira Visitação: Confissões de Pernambuco,* pp. 110–11.
195. *Livro da Visitação, Estado do Grão-Pará,* pp. 225–26. Menocchio had this to say about fetuses: "When we are in the mother's womb we are just like nothing, dead flesh" (Ginzburg, *Le fromage et les vers,* p. 139; *The Cheese and the Worms,* p. 93).
196. *Segunda Visitação: Denunciações da Bahia,* p. 168.
197. *Primeira Visitação: Denunciações de Pernambuco,* pp. 435–36.
198. Ibid., p. 140.
199. Ibid., p. 190.
200. *Primeira Visitação: Confissões de Pernambuco,* p. 77.
201. Ibid., p. 48.
202. Ibid., p. 144.
203. Ibid., p. 90.
204. Ibid., p. 91.
205. Manselli, *La religion populaire au Moyen-Âge,* p. 97.
206. *Primeira Visitação: Denunciações da Bahia,* p. 367.
207. Andrieux, *La vie quotidienne dans la Rome Pontificale,* p. 156.
208. *Primeira Visitação: Confissões de Pernambuco,* p. 147.
209. Fighting with the indigenous slave Catarina, Isabel Fernandes said that "she did not believe in the oil she had received if it was not paid for" (ibid., p. 119). Jerônima Baracha repeated practically the same blasphemy: "Fighting with one of her female slaves, vexed, she said that she would rub off the oil and chrism if the Negro woman did not pay" (ibid., p. 104).
210. Ibid., p. 98.
211. *Segunda Visitação: Denunciações da Bahia,* p. 140.
212. Ibid., p. 173.
213. Ibid., p. 182.
214. Hoornaert contends that the liberating aspect of the sacramental system was demoralized because the society was a repressive slave system. "The imperatives of concrete life in Brazil, above all the imperative of slavery and the consequent perversion of human relationships in this country, stripped the liber-

ating sacraments like baptism and confession of any and all salvational force they are meant to signify, at the risk of reducing them to empty symbols" ("A cristandade," in Hoornaert et al., *História da igreja no Brasil,* p. 312).

215. Cited in Delumeau, "L'histoire de la christianisation," in *Un chemin d'histoire,* p. 146.

216. Because they refer more directly to magic, issues involving theft of hosts and altar stones will be discussed in the next chapter.

217. *Primeira Visitação: Confissões da Bahia,* p. 49.

218. Ibid., p. 61.

219. *Primeira Visitação: Denunciações da Bahia,* p. 488.

220. IANTT, Inquisição de Lisboa, Processo no. 12.925, "Processo de Violante Carneira cristã-velha viúva moradora nesta cidade."

221. Menocchio thought he was hurting no one with his blaspheming (Ginzburg, *Le fromage et les vers,* p. 104; *The Cheese and the Worms,* p. 62). "Everybody has his calling, some to plow, some to hoe, and I have mine, which is to blaspheme" (*Le fromage et les vers,* p. 37; *The Cheese and the Worms,* p. 4). There was an entire set of laws against blasphemers. Delumeau states that starting in the sixteenth century throughout western and central Europe—"with amazing unanimity"—authorities had the impression "that their contemporaries swore and blasphemed greatly, and much more so than in the past." This was perhaps a result of the period's instability, which had people swinging from one extreme to the other, from violence to regret, denoting "superficial Christianization" and heretical and atheistic sympathies ("L'histoire de la christianisation," in *Un chemin d'histoire,* p. 152). Title 2 of the Philippine Ordinances is called "Concerning those who renounce, or blaspheme against God, or against the Saints." See *Código Filipino ou ordenações e leis do Reino de Portugal,* ed. Cândido Mendes de Almeida. At the time of Dom Dinis, there was a law that those who blasphemed should have their tongues yanked out and their bodies burned. "Under Afonso V, it apparently became impossible to fulfill the law to the letter, perhaps because blaspheming and disbelief had become generalized" (Oliveira Marques, *A sociedade medieval portuguesa,* p. 172).

222. *Livro da Visitação: Estado do Grão-Pará,* p. 163.

223. Ibid., pp. 233, 234. João de Sousa Tavares was another irreverent blasphemer. In 1775, in the town of Minas do Paracatu, he said that "Christ was not in the host, that Catholics were beasts of burden for Jesus Christ, that the apple of paradise was the privy parts of Eve and that God had forbidden the eating of it" (IANTT, Cadernos do Promotor, nos. 129 and 130; cited in Mott, "Acotundá," p. 10).

224. *Livro da Visitação: Estado do Grão-Pará,* pp. 275–76.

225. Notice again the merger of religiosity and daily life: discussions of matters of faith mixed with wagers involving chickens!

226. *Primeira Visitação: Confissões de Pernambuco,* pp. 110–14.

227. Although part of everyday life, the world of the demons was unsettling, and recourse to it grew increasingly illicit. See Françoise Bonney, "Autour de Jean Gerson: Opinions de théologiens sur les superstitions et la sorcellerie au début du XVe siècle," *Le Moyen-Age—Revue d'Histoire et de Philologie* 77, 4th series, vol. 26, no. 1 (1971): 89.

228. The first two decades of the seventeenth century represented the time of greatest risk of inquisitorial intervention in the colony (Gonçalves Salvador, *Cristãos-novos, Jesuítas e Inquisição*, pp. 114–15).

229. Cohn, *Los demonios familiares*, pp. 90–94, 100–7.

230. Delumeau, *La peur en Occident*, p. 232.

231. Thomas, *Religion and the Decline of Magic*, p. 470.

232. Philippe Erlanger, *La vie quotidienne sous Henri IV*, pp. 19, 31.

233. Ibid., p. 32. In the fifteenth century, Johannes Tinctoris listed the feats the devil could and could not perform (Muchembled, "Sorcellerie, culture populaire et christianisme," p. 280).

234. Delumeau, *Le catholicisme entre Luther et Voltaire*, p. 248; *Catholicism between Luther and Voltaire*, p. 170.

235. Cohn, *Los demonios familiares*, p. 294.

236. *Primeira Visitação: Confissões da Bahia*, p. 61.

237. Muchembled, "Sorcellerie, culture populaire et christianisme," p. 280. Delumeau states that within the collective mentality there often was no difference in nature between a saint—or God—and the devil. See "Les réformateurs et la superstition," in *Un chemin d'histoire*, p. 69. Demons are a sort of "saints of evil" (Manselli, *La religion populaire au Moyen-Âge*, p. 76).

238. Manselli, *La religion populaire au Moyen-Âge*, p. 76.

239. Muchembled, "Sorcellerie, culture populaire et christianisme," p. 269.

240. Delumeau, *Le catholicisme entre Luther et Voltaire*, p. 253; *Catholicism between Luther and Voltaire*, p. 173.

241. For Jean Bodin, no earthly power could resist the force of Satan, "Prince of this world." Pierre de Bérulle would later say that the demon was lord of the earth following the advent of original sin: "Satan, who before had no rights over the world or any power over man, has despoiled him victoriously of his kingdom and arrogated to himself the power and empire of the world, which had been man's from his birth" (cited in Delumeau, *Le catholicisme entre Luther et Voltaire*, pp. 253–54; *Catholicism between Luther and Voltaire*, p. 173).

242. "Ao Pe. Luís Gonçalves da Câmara, 15-6-1553," in Leite, *Novas cartas jesuíticas*, p. 41.

243. "Carta de Pero Correia," in Leite, *Novas cartas jesuíticas*, p. 71.

244. Leite, *Novas cartas jesuíticas*, pp. 174, 175. The devil thus sanctioned and legitimized Christian orthodoxy, both Catholic and Protestant. The primitive Christian church had seen demons in gods and pagans; the bellicose religious sects of the sixteenth and seventeenth centuries alleged that their opponents worshipped Satan: "This was said by Protestants of Catholics, by Catholics of Protestants, and by Christians of the Red Indians and other primitive peoples" (Thomas, *Religion and the Decline of Magic*, p. 477).

245. Rodrigues, "A missão dos Carijós," in Leite, *Novas cartas jesuíticas*, p. 216.

246. Cited in Delumeau, *Le catholicisme entre Luther et Voltaire*, p. 253; *Catholicism between Luther and Voltaire*, p. 173. English quotation from "Luther's Large Catechism," in *Book of Concord: The Symbols of the Evangelical Lutheran Church* (St. Louis: Concordia Publishing House, 1952), p. 204.

247. Delumeau, *Le catholicisme entre Luther et Voltaire*, p. 60.

248. Cited in Delumeau, *La peur en Occident,* p. 245; see also pp. 240 and 246.

249. On the role of spirits among indigenous peoples, see A. Métraux, *A religião dos Tupinambás,* trans. Estévão Pinto, p. 137.

250. " . . . and so great is the fear they have of him that in but imagining him they die, as has occurred many times already" (Cardim, *Tratados da terra e gente do Brasil,* p. 102).

251. "Carta dos meninos do Colégio de Jesus na Bahia ao Pe. Pedro Domenech, 5-8-1552," in Leite, *Novas cartas jesuíticas,* p. 150.

252. Hoornaert, *A igreja no Brasil Colônia,* p. 65.

253. Delumeau, "Les réformateurs et la superstition," in *Un chemin d'histoire,* p. 68.

254. *Primeira Visitação: Denunciações da Bahia,* p. 366.

255. *Primeira Visitação: Denunciações de Pernambuco,* p. 168.

256. *Primeira Visitação: Denunciações da Bahia,* p. 367.

257. Ibid., p. 544.

258. Ibid., pp. 508–9.

259. *Primeira Visitação: Confissões da Bahia,* p. 126.

260. *Primeira Visitação: Denunciações da Bahia,* p. 470.

261. Ibid., pp. 270, 273.

262. Ibid., pp. 508–9.

263. *Primeira Visitação: Denunciações de Pernambuco,* pp. 59–60.

264. *Primeira Visitação: Denunciações da Bahia,* p. 348.

265. Ibid., pp. 398–99.

266. *Primeira Visitação: Confissões de Pernambuco,* p. 24.

267. *Primeira Visitação: Confissões da Bahia,* p. 68.

268. *Primeira Visitação: Denunciações da Bahia,* p. 395.

269. Ibid., p. 351.

270. Cohn, *Los demonios familiares,* p. 294.

271. Giordano, *Religiosidad popular en la Alta Edad Media,* p. 153.

272. Jorge Benci, *Economia cristã dos senhores no governo dos escravos,* p. 120.

273. Pereira, *Compêndio narrativo do peregrino da América,* p. 133.

274. Ibid.

275. Ibid., p. 125. For Ronaldo Vainfas, what is notable about the Pilgrim's account is "the consciousness of the contradictions between the *Christian version* and the *pragmatic version* of slavery: what was a 'horrendous clamor' for the 'pilgrim' was 'sonorous' and 'peaceful' for the slave master" ("Idéias escravistas no Brasil Colonial," p. 134).

276. See chapter 1 of this book.

277. Pereira, *Compêndio narrativo do peregrino da América,* p. 259.

278. Sílvia Hunold Lara, "Campos da violência."

279. IANTT, Inquisição de Lisboa: Processo no. 12.231, cited in Siqueira, *A Inquisição Portuguesa e a sociedade colonial,* p. 223.

280. Siqueira, *A Inquisição Portuguesa e a sociedade colonial,* p. 223.

281. *Primeira Visitação: Denunciações da Bahia,* p. 282.

282. Ibid., p. 283.

283. Ibid., p. 331.

284. Ibid., p. 338.

285. "Also associated with the Mendes family was the Crypto-Jew Fernão Roiz, a blasphemer, sugar master by trade. He was married to one of the daughters of Tristão, named Esperança" (Gonçalves Salvador, *Cristãos-novos, Jesuítas e Inquisição,* p. 179).

286. Antonil, *Cultura e opulência do Brasil,* p. 232.

287. Ibid., p. 233.

288. Ibid., p. 234.

289. Ibid.

290. Vainfas offers a fine analysis of this section of text, from a different perspective. For him, there is an analogy between the slave and Jesus, and purgatory is the slave trade ("Idéias escravistas no Brasil Colonial," p. 173).

291. *Primeira Visitação: Denunciações de Pernambuco,* p. 80.

292. These words were pronounced by a freed *mulato* slave, Antonio Dias, to the young man Arnal de Holanda, son of his boss, Cristóvão Lins (ibid., p. 423).

293. This eloquent phrase is taken from José Saramago's *Memorial do convento* (São Paulo: DIFEL, 1983), p. 50.

Part II. Sorcery, Magical Practices, and Daily Life

1. See Caro Baroja, *Les sorcières et leur monde,.* See also Carlo Ginzburg, "Présomptions sur le sabbat," *Annales, E.S.C.,* 39th year, no. 2 (March–April 1984): 341–54. Ginzburg goes further than Dumézil. For the latter, the existence of a mythical complex shared by different peoples can be explained by a common genetic source, while Ginzburg stresses the issue of a dissemination based on linguistic parallelism and borrowings between Indo-European and non-Indo-European tongues (p. 346).

2. Caro Baroja, *Les sorcières et leur monde,* p. 32.

3. Cohn, *Los demonios familiares,* pp. 253 and 194, respectively.

4. Gustav Henningsen, *El abogado de las brujas: Brujería vasca e Inquisición española,* trans. Marisa Ray-Henningsen.

5. Edward Evans-Pritchard, *Witchcraft, Oracles and Magic among the Azande,* 405.

6. Robert Rowland, "Anthropology, Witchcraft, Inquisition," p. 16.

7. Mandrou, *Magistrats et sorciers,* p. 78.

8. Thomas, *Religion and the Decline of Magic,* pp. 464–65. For an analysis of the controversy surrounding this topic, see also Carlos Roberto Figueiredo Nogueira, "Universo mágico e realidade: Aspectos de um contexto cultural (Castela na modernidade)," pp. 9–36.

Chapter 3. Material Survival

1. Cohn, *Los demonios familiares,* p. 227; *Europe's Inner Demons,* p. 113.

2. *Código Filipino ou ordenações e leis do Reino de Portugal,* book 5, vol. 3, t. 33 § 2. In 1612 it was stated in *Confessional,* written by Brittany's Evzen Gueguen, that divination by art or intelligence of the Enemy, such as using the

song or flight of birds, was a deadly sin, as was the use of divinations entailing "a manifest or occult pact with the Enemy, as charmers make" (cited in Delumeau, "Ignorance religieuse," in *Un chemin d'histoire,* p. 125).

3. Francisco Bethencourt, "Astrologia e sociedade no século XVI: Uma primeira abordagem," reprint from *Revista de História Econômica e Social* (Lisbon, 1982): 63.

4. *Primeira Visitação: Denunciações de Pernambuco,* p. 187.

5. IANTT, Inquisição de Lisboa: Processo no. 1.377, "Processo de Antonia Maria casada com Vasco Janeiro natural e moradora da cidade de Beja."

6. IANTT, Inquisição de Lisboa, Processo no. 1.565. This is in point of fact a denunciation.

7. IANTT, Inquisição de Lisboa, Processo no. 210, "Sumário contra Maria Francisca preta escrava de Mateus Alves Martins moradora na rua Formosa da cidade do Pará." This indictment, which includes a number of denunciations lodged during the Visitation of Geraldo José de Abranches, is not found in Amaral Lapa's *Livro da Visitação: Estado do Grão-Pará* (nor are a number of other documents, as will be seen later). Perhaps the complete work has yet to be published.

8. IANTT, Inquisição de Lisboa, Processo no. 2.697, "Apresentação e confissão de Manuel Pacheco Madureira natural desta cidade viúvo de Dona Claudina Maria Pinheira." Amaral Lapa transcribes only the confession (*Livro da Visitação: Estado do Grão-Pará,* pp. 236–39).

9. *Livro da Visitação: Estado do Grão-Pará,* p. 157.

10. Yvonne Cunha Rego (ed.), *Feiticeiros, profetas, visionários: Textos antigos portugueses,* p. 167. Casting sieves was deemed a serious offense under the Philippine Ordinances, bringing a penalty of public flogging and a fine of two mil-réis. In this divination, the names of suspected wrongdoers were written on the rind of a sieve (*Código Filipino,* book 5, vol. 3, p. 1151).

11. "Stick a pair of shears in the rind of a sieve and let two persons set the top of each of their forefingers upon the upper part of the shears holding it with the sieve up from the ground steadily; and ask Peter and Paul whether A, B, or C hath stolen the thing lost; and at the nomination of the guilty person the sieve will turn round" (Thomas, *Religion and the Decline of Magic,* p. 213).

12. See Thomas's observations in ibid., pp. 213–14.

13. *Segunda Visitação: Confissões da Bahia,* pp. 447, 449, 450.

14. Giordano, *Religiosidad popular en la Alta Edad Media,* p. 170; see also p. 169. The church actually went backward: in the *Confessional* from Brittany, cited earlier, it had been stated that using Bible verses to find lost objects was a mortal sin (Delumeau, "Ignorance réligieuse," in *Un chemin d'histoire,* pp. 125–26).

15. Thomas, *Religion and the Decline of Magic,* p. 214.

16. Ibid., p. 214.

17. IANTT, Inquisição de Lisboa, mº 27-20, Novos Maços.

18. IANTT, Inquisição de Lisboa, Processo no. 1.377.

19. IANTT, Inquisição de Lisboa, mº 27-20, Novos Maços.

20. Ibid. This divination greatly resembles another, employed by Dona Paula Tereza de Miranda Souto Maior for matters of the heart. Tried by the Inquisition in Lisbon for sorcery during the first quarter of the eighteenth century, she

was a good friend of Dom João V. She "would light two candles and in between them place a urinal almost wholly filled with water, and inside she would place nine straw rushes and would pronounce the words that the sorceress had taught her; and in the said urinal she would see the church of a friars' convent and in it the said person whom she desired to wed" (Rego, *Feiticeiros, profetas, visionários,* p. 79).

21. *Livro da Visitação: Estado do Grão-Pará,* pp. 184–85. Water and mirrors seem to do the same job: reflect the criminal's image. Le Roy Ladurie speaks of the "art of St. George" employed in the village of Aix-les-Thermes, where a young girl would read a mirror to find the trail or traces of stolen goods (*Montaillou, village occitan,* p. 580).

22. Almeida, *História da igreja em Portugal,* vol. 1, p. 403.

23. Lisón-Tolosana, *Brujería, estructura social y simbolismo en Galícia,* p. 23.

24. Thomas, *Religion and the Decline of Magic,* p. 234.

25. Robert Mandrou, *Possession et sorcellerie au XVIIᵉ siècle: Textes inédits,* p. 112. In 1624 the curé of Brazey, in the diocese of Autun, conjured demons in order to find a treasure hidden in Brandon castle, said to date to the time when the English occupied a large part of French territory (i.e., the One Hundred Years War). He was hanged and burned (ibid., pp. 115–20).

26. IANTT, Inquisição de Évora, mᵒ 803, no. 7.759. After having searched for this trial as part of the Inquisition at Lisbon (since the accused was listed as Brazilian), I was eventually able to locate it as part of the Inquisition at Évora, thanks to the assistance of Francisco Bethencourt, who provided me with invaluable information.

27. Francisco Barbosa was a sorcerer known as "the uncle of Massarelos." He was garroted following an auto-da-fé held in Lisbon on July 24, 1735. He boasted of discovering treasures guarded by twelve male and twelve female Moors, all richly dressed (Rego, *Feiticeiros, profetas, visionários,* p. 90).

28. *Primeira Visitação: Denunciações da Bahia,* p. 295.

29. *Segunda Visitação: Confissões da Bahia,* p. 452.

30. Ibid., p. 448.

31. AEAM, Livro de Devassas—Comarca do Serro do Frio, 1734, pp. 52–52v.

32. Robert Muchembled, "Sorcières du Cambrésis: L'acculturation du monde rural aux XVIᵉ et XVIIᵉ siècles," in Marie-Sylvie Dupont-Bouchat, Willem Frijhoff, and Robert Muchembled, *Prophètes et sorciers dans les Pays-Bas, XVIᵉ–XVIIᵉ siècles,* pp. 180–81.

33. Métraux, *A religião dos Tupinambás,* p. 153.

34. Brandão, *Diálogo das grandezas do Brasil,* pp. 167–68. Disapproval of magical practices continued in the early eighteenth century. For Antonil, sorcerers and word healers were "deserving of abomination," as were those who resorted to them, "abandoning God" (*Cultura e opulência do Brasil,* p. 149).

35. Thomas, *Religion and the Decline of Magic,* p. 536.

36. François Lebrun, *Médecins, saints et sorciers au XVIIᵉ et XVIIIᵉ siècles,* pp. 94, 97, 99, 103.

37. Thomas, *Religion and the Decline of Magic,* p. 14.

38. Ibid., pp. 5, 12.

39. For the Azande in the Southern Sudan, witchcraft is to blame for practically all maladies. See Evans-Pritchard, *Witchcraft, Oracles and Magic among the Azande,* p. 404.

40. AEAM, Devassas—janeiro 1767–maio 1778, p. 21; cited in Luciano Raposo de Almeida Figueiredo, "O avesso da memória: Estudo do papel, participação e condição social da mulher no século XVIII mineiro," p. 134.

41. *Primeira Visitação: Denunciações da Bahia,* pp. 319, 318.

42. AEAM, Devassas—1721–1735, p. 79.

43. Lisón-Tolosana, *Brujería, estructura social y simbolismo en Galicia,* p. 49. "Como curaba, las gentes de envidia empezaron a decir que era hechicera [since she could heal, some envious people started to say she was a witch]," one of the accused women stated.

44. *Segunda Visitação: Confissões da Bahia,* p. 447.

45. AEAM, Livro de Devassas—Comarca do Serro do Frio, 1734, p. 17.

46. Claude d'Abbeville, *História da missão dos padres capuchinhos na ilha do Maranhão,* p. 253.

47. Métraux, *A religião dos Tupinambás,* p. 163.

48. In the Ursuline convent in Aix, Gaufridy followed the devil's orders to blow on women to seduce them (Mandrou, *Magistrats et sorciers,* p. 201). Around the same time, in Gascony, Marie Barast's breath had the power to kill little children (Emmanuel Le Roy Ladurie, *La sorcière de Jasmin,* p. 48).

49. Rego, *Feiticeiros, profetas, visionários,* pp. 176–77.

50. *Primeira Visitação: Denunciações da Bahia,* p. 536.

51. IANTT, Inquisição de Lisboa, Processo no. 252, m° 26.

52. AEAM, Devassas—1721–1735, p. 47.

53. IANTT, Inquisição de Lisboa, Processo no. 212, "Sumário contra José preto escravo de Manuel de Souza natural da Costa da Mina e morador na rua de São Vicente na Cidade do Pará." Amaral Lapa published part of the indictment, except the inquisitor's final provisions regarding the defendant. See *Livro da Visitação: Estado do Grão-Pará,* pp. 137–40, 153–54.

54. IANTT, Inquisição de Lisboa, Processo no. 1.377, "Processo de Antonia Maria casada com Vasco Janeiro natural e moradora da cidade de Beja."

55. *Segunda Visitação: Confissões da Bahia,* p. 448.

56. Delumeau, *Le catholicisme entre Luther et Voltaire,* p. 243; *Catholicism between Luther and Voltaire,* p. 166.

57. The Cathars kept the deceased's nail parings and hair precisely because they embodied vital energy (Le Roy Ladurie, *Montaillou, village occitan,* p. 60).

58. IANTT, Inquisição de Lisboa, Processo no. 17.771, "Auto sumário que mandou fazer o reverendo vigário da vara João de Barros Leal sobre o que adiante se segue." These accusations are not found in Amaral Lapa's *Livro da Visitação: Estado do Grão-Pará* and do not seem to be a part of it, although they took place during the Visitation, in 1767.

59. IANTT, Inquisição de Lisboa, Processo no. 17.771.

60. IANTT, Inquisição de Lisboa, Processo no. 212. See Amaral Lapa, *Livro da Visitação: Estado do Grão-Pará,* pp. 137–38.

61. *Livro da Visitação: Estado do Grão-Pará,* p. 166.

62. Ibid., p. 172.

63. Ibid., pp. 172–73.

64. Ibid., pp. 267–68.

65. Ibid., p. 268.

66. Fernandes, *O folclore mágico do Nordeste,* pp. 96–97.

67. Abbeville, *História da missão dos padres capuchinhos,* p. 253.

68. Rego, *Feiticeiros, profetas, visionários,* pp. 49–50.

69. Philippe Ariès, *Essais sur l'histoire de la mort en Occident: Du Moyen-Âge à nos jours,* pp. 17–45. "In traditional societies—that is, in the early Middle Ages but also in all folk and oral cultures as well—man resigned himself without great suffering to the idea that we are all mortal" (p. 45).

70. IANTT, Inquisição de Lisboa, Processo no. 15.559, "Segunda via de uma denunciação acerca de um preto tido, e havido por feiticeiro."

71. IANTT, Inquisição de Évora, mç. 803, no. 7.759. The term "stone malady" could refer to either kidney stones or gallstones. The problem was quite common in sixteenth- and seventeenth-century England, where it became known as the Stuart malady (Thomas, *Religion and the Decline of Magic,* pp. 6–7).

72. *Livro da Visitação: Estado do Grão-Pará,* p. 152.

73. Ibid., p. 153.

74. Fernandes, *O folclore mágico do Nordeste,* pp. 37–38.

75. Delumeau, "Ignorance religieuse," in *Un chemin d'histoire,* p. 126. In England, an individual with a toothache was supposed to set down the following verse three times on a little paper: "Jesus Christ for mercy sake / Take away this toothache" (Thomas, *Religion and the Decline of Magic,* p. 180).

76. *Segunda Visitação: Confissões da Bahia,* p. 457. On curative prayers mixing the sacred and occultism, see Robert Mandrou, *De la culture populaire en France aux XVIIᵉ et XVIIIᵉ siècles,* p. 72.

77. Thomas, *Religion and the Decline of Magic,* p. 178. Lebrun lists a number of prayers meant for curative purposes (*Médecins, saints et sorciers,* pp. 110–11).

78. AEAM, Devassas—maio–dezembro 1753, p. 21v; cited in Figueiredo, "O avesso da memória," p. 134.

79. *Quebranto* could be diagnosed by these symptoms: paleness, sleepiness, lassitude, a glazed look. See Artur Ramos, *O negro brasileiro,* p. 195.

80. *Livro da Visitação: Estado do Grão-Pará,* pp. 151–52.

81. IANTT, Inquisição de Lisboa, Processo no. 2.705, "Apresentação da índia Domingas Gomes da Ressurreição." See also *Livro da Visitação: Estado do Grão-Pará,* pp. 179–82, where the Genealogy and Verdict handed down by the Visitor are of course not to be found.

82. IANTT, Inquisição de Lisboa, Processo no. 2.706. In Spain, visiting foreigners were surprised by the custom of placing numerous amulets on children to ward off the evil eye. Julio Caro Baroja, "La magia en Castilla," in *Algunos mitos españoles,* p. 265.

83. IANTT, Inquisição de Lisboa, Processo no. 2.706. See also *Livro da Visitação: Estado do Grão-Pará,* p. 152.

84. IANTT, Inquisição de Lisboa, Processo no. 2.705. See also *Livro da Visitação: Estado do Grão-Pará,* p. 180. Amaral Lapa transcribes this prayer in a slightly different fashion, attributable to the fact that he and I consulted different copies.

85. Fernandes, *O folclore mágico do Nordeste,* p. 43. Amulets, scapulars,

signs of the cross, and mysterious powders were ways of warding off the evil eye in the late Middle Ages. See Giordano, *Religiosidad popular en la Alta Edad Media*, p. 126.

86. IANTT, Inquisição de Lisboa, Processo no. 3.723, "Processo de Frei Luís de Nazaré, religioso professo de Nossa Senhora do Carmo Colado da Província da Bahia e morador na mesma cidade."

87. Lebrun, *Médecins, saints et sorciers*, p. 96.

88. Delumeau, *Le catholicisme entre Luther et Voltaire*, p. 243; *Catholicism between Luther and Voltaire*, p. 166.

89. IANTT, Inquisição de Lisboa, Processo no. 3.723 (emphasis added). Concerning this trial, see my study "O padre e as feiticeiras: Notas sobre a sexualidade no Brasil Colonial," in Ronaldo Vainfas (ed.), *História e sexualidade no Brasil*.

90. Giordano, *Religiosidad popular en la Alta Edad Media*, p. 246.

91. Le Roy Ladurie, *Montaillou, village occitan*, p. 332.

92. Lecouteux, "Paganisme, christianisme et merveilleux," pp. 706–7.

93. Almeida, *História da igreja em Portugal*, vol. 2, p. 365.

94. *Código Filipino*, book 5, vol. 4, p. 1152.

95. Fernandes, *O folclore mágico do Nordeste*, p. 40.

96. *Primeira Visitação: Confissões da Bahia*, p. 121.

97. AEAM, Devassas—1733, p. 32v.

98. Lanciani, *Os relatos de naufrágios na literatura portuguesa*, p. 32.

99. "La peur en mer," in Delumeau, *La mort des Pays de Cocagne*, p. 91.

100. Delumeau, "Ignorance religieuse," in *Un chemin d'histoire*, p. 120.

101. Cited in Henningsen, *El abogado de las brujas*, p. 23.

102. Cited in Caro Baroja, *Les sorcières et leur monde*, p. 224; *The World of the Witches*, p. 197. *Relación que hizo el Doctor don lope de ysasti presbytero y beneficiado de leço, que es en guipuzcoa acerca de las meleficas de Cantabria por mandado del Sor Inquisidor Campofrio en Madrid*, 1618, MSS 2031, Biblioteca Nacional, Madrid, pp. 133 r–136 v.

103. Among Trobriand Islanders, only men could avail themselves of the protective magic of mist (*kayga'u*). See B. Malinowski, *La vie sexuelle des sauvages du Nord-Ouest de la Mélanésie*, trans. Dr. S. Jankelevitch, p. 58.

104. IANTT, Inquisição de Lisboa, Processo no. 2.704, "Apresentação e confissão de Maria Joana, solteira."

105. IANTT, Inquisição de Lisboa, Processo no. 3.382.

106. B. Malinowski, *Los argonautas del Pacífico Occidental*, pp. 239–48.

107. Cohn, *Los demonios familiares*, p. 220.

108. *Primeira Visitação: Denunciações da Bahia*, p. 432.

109. Ibid., p. 385.

110. *Primeira Visitação: Confissões da Bahia*, p. 61.

111. IANTT, Inquisição de Évora, m° 803, no. 7.759.

112. IANTT, Inquisição de Lisboa, Processo no. 10.181, "Processo de Manuel João barbeiro solteiro filho de Francisco João ferreiro natural e morador da cidade de São Luís do Maranhão preso nos cárceres da Inquisição de Lisboa."

113. IANTT, Inquisição de Lisboa, Processo no. 9.972, "Processo de Manuel da Piedade homem preto escravo do capitão Gaspar de Valadares, natural da cidade da Bahia e morador nesta de Lisboa." I am indebted to Professor Anita Novinsky for referring me to this trial.

114. *Primeira Visitação: Denunciações da Bahia*, p. 343.

115. Ibid., p. 412.

116. IANTT, Inquisição de Lisboa, Processo no. 5.180, "Processo de Isabel Maria de Oliveira, solteira, filha de Roque de Oliveira, lavrador, natural da Vila de Cantanhede [*sic*], Bispado de Coimbra e moradora na cidade de Belém do Grão-Pará."

117. *Primeira Visitação: Denunciações de Pernambuco*, pp. 98–99.

118. IANTT, Inquisição de Lisboa, Processo no. 3.382, "Processo de Maria Barbosa mulher parda casada com João da Cruz ourives natural da cidade de Évora moradora na Bahia de Todos os Santos partes do Brasil presa no cárcere da Inquisição desta cidade de Lisboa."

119. *Primeira Visitação: Denunciações de Pernambuco*, pp. 121–22.

120. *Livro da Visitação: Estado do Grão-Pará*, p. 185.

121. Rego, *Feiticeiros, profetas, visionários*, pp. 171–72.

122. Ibid., pp. 132–33.

123. Ibid., p. 79.

124. Lisón-Tolosana, *Brujería, estructura social y simbolismo en Galícia*, p. 24. This is probably a reference to the disaster at Alcazarquivir.

125. This compilation was drawn up from lists of autos-da-fé: IANTT, Inquisição de Lisboa, Novos Maços, m° 6-1; Novos Maços, m° 5-4; Manuscrito da Livraria, no. 732; Manuscrito da Livraria, no. 959; Livros 144-2-41; Livros 145-6-180A; 159/6/862; 149-6-671. On Maria da Silva, see IANTT, Inquisição de Lisboa, Processo no. 7.020.

126. Although the Inquisition banished these individuals to Brazil, some of them appealed and had their sentences reduced to exile in Portuguese *coutos*: Úrsula Maria, for example, who claimed to suffer from gout and who never reached Brazil (AF May 10, 1682), and Paula de Moura, who served out her sentence in Algarve (AF December 10, 1673). See, respectively, IANTT, Inquisição de Lisboa, Processo no. 4.912; and OANTT, Inquisição de Lisboa, Processo no. 5.723. In addition to the lists of autos-da-fé cited above, this compilation also included the following trials: IANTT, Inquisição de Coimbra, Processo no. 4.501 and Processo no. 6.823; IANTT, Inquisição de Lisboa, Processos nos. 1.063; 4.744; 6.308; 7.579; 12.616; 11.242; 11.358; 7.095; 834; 6.005: 7.611; 7.840; and 74.

127. IANTT, Inquisição de Lisboa, Manuscrito da Livraria, Processo no. 959 and Processo no. 557 (for Joana da Cruz).

Chapter 4. The Onset of Conflict

1. Caro Baroja, *Les sorcières et leur monde*, p. 66.

2. IANTT, Inquisição de Lisboa, m° 27-20, Novos Maços.

3. AEAM, Livro de Devassas—7 janeiro 1767–1777, p. 34v.

4. AEAM, Devassas—1763–1764, pp. 17–17v.

5. Sorceresses have traditionally held the bones of the dead in great esteem. In the late Middle Ages, Incmar de Reims referred to them in his *De divortio Lotharii et Tetbergae*. See Giordano, *Religiosidad popular en la Alta Edad Media*, p. 287. The sorceresses in Logroño used the bones of the dead to make poisonous water (Rego, *Feiticeiros, profetas, visionários*, p. 55). In "Galán Castrucho," by Lope de Vega, reference is made to the bones of hanged men that

witches used in their sortilege: "que a la horca / vas de noche con candelas / y las muelas / quitas a los ahorcados / que aún muertos no están seguros / de conjuros / y de maldades que haces" (cited in Caro Baroja, "La magia en Castilla," in *Algunos mitos españoles,* p. 231). As seen earlier, malice could be done using hair, fingernail parings, and human excrement, which contained a person's vital spirit. See also Thomas, *Religion and the Decline of Magic,* p. 438.

6. *Primeira Visitação: Denunciações da Bahia,* p. 385.

7. IANTT, Inquisição de Lisboa, Processo no. 3.382, "Processo de Maria Barbosa mulher parda casada com João Cruz ourives natural da cidade de Évora moradora na da Bahía de Todos os Santos partes do Brasil presa no cárcere da Inquisição desta cidade de Lisboa."

8. AEAM, Devassas—janeiro 1767–maio 1778, p. 65. See also Figueiredo, "O avesso da memória," pp. 135–36. Figueiredo states: "In Pitangui, a sorceress threatened to kill a number of people in the community. She engendered tremendous insecurity among the local population, feared as she was" (p. 135).

9. IANTT, Inquisição de Lisboa, Processo no. 11.163, "Processo de Luzia da Sila Soares, preta."

10. Mandrou, *Magistrats et sorciers,* p. 96.

11. Marie-Sylvie Dupont-Bouchat, "La répression de la sorcellerie dans le duché de Luxembourg au XVIᵉ et XVIIᵉ siècles," in Dupont-Bouchat, Frijhoff, and Muchembled, *Prophètes et sorciers dans les Pays-Bas,* pp. 57–58.

12. Le Roy Ladurie, *La sorcière de Jasmin,* pp. 15–69: "Trois sorcières gasconnes."

13. On sorcery and neighborly relations, see Lisón-Tolosana, *Brujería, estructura social y simbolismo en Galicia,* p. 49.

14. IANTT, Inquisição de Lisboa, Processo no. 1377, "Processo de Antonia Maria casada com Vasco Janeiro natural e moradora da cidade de Beja." Years later, in Portugal, Domingas Maria learned similar prayers to keep a woman's husband from killing her. Pieces of cloth, a pigeon heart, rosemary, a new cross, and a palm of new broom straw were boiled together. The prayer went: "By Barabbas, Satan, and Caiaphas and Maria Padilha and her whole company, warm the heart of the said prisoner, etc." (Rego, *Feiticeiros, profetas, visionários,* p. 170). Another supplicative prayer was: "Good Jesus, give me succor as the sea flows, the wind blows, the heavens shine with stars, in like manner flow, blow, and shine, that so and so can do me no evil" (ibid., p. 172).

15. Thomas, *Religion and the Decline of Magic,* p. 179. He offers as typical of this category of prayer one employed in the early eighteenth century to stop bleeding: "There was a man born in Bethlehem of Judaea whose name was called Christ. Baptized in the River Jordan in the water of flood; and the Child also was meek and good; and as the water stood so I desire thee the blood of (such a person or beast) to stand in their body, in the name of the Father, Son and Holy Ghost" (p. 180).

On the thaumaturge kings, see Marc Bloch, *Les rois thaumaturges.* Delumeau transcribes prayers that invoke such real-life saints as Abelard as well as fictitious ones, like St. Bouleverse: "O grand Saint Bouleverse, vous qui avez le pouvoir de bouleverser la terre, vous êtes un saint et moi un pécheur, je vous invoque et vous prend pour mon singulier défenseur, partez, partez, je vous envoie chez (un tel), bouleversez sa tête, bouleversez son esprit, bouleversez son coeur, chavirez, tournez pour moi sa tête, brisez tous ses membres, faites éclater la foudre et déchaînez la tempête et la discorde chez (un tel)" ("Ignorance religieuse," in *Un chemin d'histoire*, p. 115).

16. "Hallowed be thou Vervain, as thou growest on the ground / For in the mount of Calvary there thou was first found . . . , etc." (Thomas, *Religion and the Decline of Magic*, p. 181).

17. IANTT, Inquisição de Lisboa, Processo no. 1.377, "Processo de Antonia Maria casada com Vasco Janeiro natural e moradora da cidade de Beja."

18. Le Roy Ladurie, *La sorcière de Jasmin*, p. 42.

19. Henningsen, *El abogado de las brujas*, p. 25.

20. Rego, *Feiticeiros, profetas, visionários*, p. 15.

21. Dupont-Bouchat, "La répression de la sorcellerie," pp. 53–54.

22. The seventeenth century—when the madness of the witch-hunts had perhaps entered its death throes—was a time of tremendous crisis. See Eric J. Hobsbawm's classic work, "La crisis general de la economía europea en el siglo XVII," in *En torno a los orígenes de la revolución industrial*, pp. 7–70.

23. Almeida, *História da igreja em Portugal*, vol. 3, p. 357.

24. Júlio Dantas, "Bruxedos de amor," in *O amor em Portugal no século XVIII*, pp. 275–76.

25. This was the most widely employed law in the world of magic. By stirring the waters of a marsh, a sorceress could unleash storms, etc. (Delumeau, *Le catholicisme entre Luther et Voltaire*, pp. 240–41; *Catholicism between Luther and Voltaire*, p. 164).

26. *Primeira Visitação: Denunciações da Bahia*, p. 303.

27. Lisón-Tolosana, *Brujería, estructura social y simbolismo en Galícia*, p. 49. The poem by Lope de Vega cited earlier alludes to acts of malice against nursing children: "Abre, hechicera bruja, / la que estruja / cuantos niños hay de teta" (cited in Baroja, "La magia en Castilla," in *Algunos mitos españoles*, p. 230).

28. *Primeira Visitação: Denunciações de Pernambuco*, pp. 24–26.

29. Le Roy Ladurie, *La sorcière de Jasmin*, p. 58.

30. Rego, *Feiticeiros, profetas, visionários*, p. 19.

31. Ibid., p. 52.

32. Geoffrey Parrinder, *La brujería*, pp. 168–69.

33. Cited in Francisco Vidal Luna, "A vida quotidiana em julgamento: Devassas em Minas Gerais," in Francisco Vidal Luna and Iraci del Nero da Costa, *Minas colonial: Economia e sociedade*, p. 83.

34. IANTT, Inquisição de Lisboa, Processo no. 11.163. I am indebted to Professor Anita Novinsky for referring me to this trial.

35. Lady Alice Kyteler, a fourteenth-century Irish sorceress, was accused of making "love charms with the brains of an unbaptized child" (Parrinder, *La brujería*, p. 109; *Witchcraft: European and African*, p. 89). Canidia, Horace's witch, performed *maleficia* using a child's liver and marrow (Caro Baroja, *Les sorcières et leur monde*, p. 51; *The World of the Witches*, p. 33).

36. Bastide, *Les religions africaines au Brésil*, p. 92; *The African Religions of Brazil*, p. 67.

37. Thomas, *Religion and the Decline of Magic*, p. 531.

38. Brandão, *Diálogo das grandezas do Brasil*, pp. 167–68.

39. IANTT, Inquisição de Lisboa, mº 27-20, Novos Maços.

40. IANTT, Inquisição de Lisboa, Processo no. 11.767, "Processo de José

Francisco Pereira homem preto escravo de João Francisco Pedroso natural de Judá na Costa da Mina e morador nesta cidade de Lisboa."
41. IANTT, Inquisição de Lisboa, Processo no. 11.163.
42. Ibid.
43. IANTT, Inquisição de Lisboa, Processo no. 9.972, "Processo de Manuel da Piedade homem preto escravo do capitão Gaspar de Valadares, natural da cidade da Bahia e morador nesta de Lisboa."
44. IANTT, Inquisição de Lisboa, Processo no. 631, "Processo de Marcelina Maria mulher preta filha de Antonio e Luzia pretos escravos, natural do Rio de Janeiro e moradora nesta cidade em casa de seu senhor João Eufrásio de Figueiroa."
45. Lisón-Tolosana, *Brujería, estructura social y simbolismo en Galícia,* p. 39.
46. Lebrun, *Médecins, saints et sorciers,* p. 107.
47. IANTT, Inquisição de Lisboa, Processo no. 3.723.
48. IANTT, Inquisição de Lisboa, Processo no. 11.767.
49. AEAM, Devassas—julho 1762–dezembro 1769 (cited in Figueiredo, "O avesso da memória," p. 135).
50. IANTT, Inquisição de Lisboa, Processo no. 2.691, "Processo de Joana preta crioula." Amaral Lapa publishes only one of the denunciations against the slave (*Livro da Visitação: Estado do Grão-Pará,* pp. 191–94).
51. IANTT, Inquisição de Lisboa, Processo no. 11.163. In sixteenth-century England, sorcery sometimes reflected a conflict between neighborliness and a growing sense of private property (Thomas, *Religion and the Decline of Magic,* p. 556). In late seventeenth-century France, magical practices masked conflicts between shepherds and herd owners (Mandrou, *Magistrats et sorciers,* p. 504).
52. Antonil, *Cultura e opulência do Brasil,* pp. 163–64.
53. Cited in Figueiredo, "O avesso da memória," p. 135. This procedure was also employed to subdue someone to your will, and Joana used it on her husband for this purpose (IANTT, Inquisição de Lisboa, Processo no. 2.691).
54. AEAM, Devassas—1748–1749, p. 15v.
55. AEAM, Devassas—julho 1762–dezembro 1769.
56. Roberto Borges Martins believes that nineteenth-century Minas, along with the U.S. antebellum South, was the greatest slave system the Americas ever saw. See "Slavery in a Non-Export Economy: Nineteenth-Century Minas Gerais Revisited," in collaboration with Amílcar Martins Filho (*HAHR* 63, no. 3 [1983]: 537–68).
57. Waldemar de Almeida Barbosa, *Negros e quilombos em Minas Gerais.*
58. Luís dos Santos Vilhena, *Recopilação de notícias soteropolitanas e brasílicas,* notes by Brás do Amaral.
59. IANTT, Inquisição de Lisboa, Processo no. 10.181.
60. Giordano, *Religiosidad popular en la Alta Edad Media,* p. 268.
61. Lecouteux, "Paganisme, christianisme et merveilleux," p. 707. The *Homilia de sacrilegiis* had the following to say about amulets: "Quicumque salomoniacas scripturas facit et qui caracteri in carta sive in bergamena, sive in laminas aereas, ferreas, plumbeas vel in quacumque christum vel scribi hominibus vel animalibus multis ad collum alligat, iste non christianus, sed paganus est" (ibid.).
62. Muchembled, "Sorcellerie, culture populaire et christianisme," p. 279.

63. Goulemot, "Démons, merveilles et philosophie," p. 1249.

64. Thomas, *Religion and the Decline of Magic,* p. 232.

65. Mandrou, *De la culture populaire en France,* p. 71.

66. Lebrun, *Médecins, saints et sorciers,* p. 126. Even today, people in Spain use the *kutun,* which is a kind of pouch containing ashes, chicken manure, powdered umbilical cord, bay leaves, olives, rue, etc. (Caro Baroja, "La magia en Castilla," in *Algunos mitos españoles,* p. 264).

67. Cited in Delumeau, *Le catholicisme entre Luther et Voltaire,* p. 240.

68. Bastide, *Les religions africaines au Brésil,* pp. 199, 210.

69. Ibid., p. 209.

70. IANTT, Inquisição de Lisboa, Processo no. 1.377.

71. IANTT, Inquisição de Lisboa, m° 27-20, Novos Maços.

72. I am grateful to Luiz Mott—who possesses a vast knowledge of religious matters and popular religiosity—for this invaluable information on the altar stone (including the reference found in the *Constituições primeiras*) and on purificators.

73. Lecouteux, "Paganisme, christianisme et merveilleux," p. 706. I refer to *Tugendsteine,* a secularized form of ancient beliefs. On sacred Roman stones, see Giordano, *Religiosidad popular en la Alta Edad Media,* p. 63.

74. Rego, *Feiticeiros, profetas, visionários,* p. 80.

75. In 1604 a priest from Château-Landon was hanged in Nemours because he consecrated the *corpus domini* with a piece of paper, using it for the purpose of divination (Mandrou, *Magistrats et sorciers,* p. 82).

76. In the late Middle Ages, it was not uncommon for clerics and even bishops to pass themselves off as prophets and to practice pagan rites using sacred objects and ornaments (Giordano, *Religiosidad popular en la Alta Edad Media,*, p. 184).

77. IANTT, Inquisição de Lisboa, m° 27-20, Novos Maços.

78. Bethencourt, "Astrologia e sociedade no século XVI," p. 62.

79. On the Solomonic tradition and ritual magic, see Cohn, *Los demonios familiares,* p. 259; *Europe's Inner Demons,* p. 104.

80. Giordano, *Religiosidad popular en la Alta Edad Media,*, pp. 157–58.

81. For all these cases, see IANTT, Inquisição de Lisboa, 145-6-180A.

82. IANTT, Inquisição de Lisboa, Processo no. 16.722.

83. IANTT, Inquisição de Lisboa, Processo no. 9.972, "Processo de Manuel da Piedade, homem preto escravo do capitão Gaspar de Valadares, natural da cidade da Bahia e morador nesta de Lisboa."

"The hiding of different objects beneath the altar ornaments and the recitation of certain prayers *in petto* at the moment of consecration represent a regular repertoire in this reclaiming of the rite for demoniacal ends: some of the supernatural powers unleashed by the Church during mass are thus subjugated and deviated from their purpose, for the sake of Satanic works" (Mandrou, *Magistrats et sorciers,* p. 82).

84. IANTT, Inquisição de Lisboa, Processo no. 11.774, "Processo de José Francisco Pedroso homem preto solteiro escravo de Domingos Francisco Pedroso homem de negócios natural de Judá na Costa da Mina e morador nesta cidade de Lisboa Ocidental."

85. IANTT, Inquisição de Lisboa, Processo no. 11.767, "Processo de José Francisco Pereira homem preto escravo de João Francisco Pedroso natural de

Judá na Costa da Mina e morador nesta cidade de Lisboa." I am indebted to Professor Anita Novinsky for referring me to this trial.

86. IANTT, Inquisição de Lisboa, Processo no. 11.774.

87. IANTT, Inquisição de Lisboa, Processo no. 11.767.

88. IANTT, Inquisição de Lisboa, Processo no. 254.

89. IANTT, Inquisição de Lisboa, Processo no. 1.562.

90. IANTT, Inquisição de Lisboa, Processo no. 508, "Processo de José Martins, homem preto, e livre, natural e morador do sítio do Riachão, termo da Vila de Jacobina, Arcebispado da Bahia, preso nos cárceres do Santo Ofício."

91. IANTT, Inquisição de Lisboa, Processo no. 1.131, "Processo de Mateus Pereira Machado, escravo de Veríssimo Pereira, mineiro, solteiro, filho de José de Castro, natural da freguesia de São José da Peroroca [*sic*], limite da Vila de Cachoeira, morador nos campos da mesma vila, e assistente na de Santo Antonio da Jacobina, tudo Arcebispado da Bahia, preso nos cárceres do Santo Ofício."

92. IANTT, Inquisição de Lisboa, Processo no. 1.134, "Processo de Luís Pereira de Almeida, escravo de Dona Antonia Pereira de Almeida natural da Vila de Jacobina e morador no sítio do Riachão, Arcebispado da Bahia."

93. IANTT, Inquisição de Lisboa, Processo no. 508.

94. IANTT, Inquisição de Lisboa, Processo no. 8.909, "Processo de José Fernandes homem pardo carpinteiro natural e morador na Vila de Nossa Senhora da Abadia, Arcebispado da Bahia."

95. Giordano, *Religiosidad popular en la Alta Edad Media,* p. 57.

96. Lecouteux, "Paganisme, christianisme et merveilleux," p. 706.

97. Parrinder, *La brujería,* p. 109; *Witchcraft,* p. 89.

98. Oliveira Marques, *A sociedade medieval portuguesa,* p. 171.

99. "Cera del cirio-pascual / Y trébol de cuatro hojas, / Et simiente de granojas / Et pie de gato negral, / Agua de fuente perenal, / Con la sangre del cabrón / Y el ala del dragón / Pergamino virginal" (cited in Caro Baroja, "La magia en Castilla," in *Algunos mitos españoles,* p. 242).

100. Mandrou, *Magistrats et sorciers,* p. 148.

101. Dupont-Bouchat, "La répression de la sorcellerie," p. 65.

102. IANTT, Inquisição de Lisboa, Processo no. 4.684, "Processo de Salvador Carvalho Serra, homem pardo, seleiro, solteiro, filho de Manuel Carvalho Serra, lavrador, natural do sítio de Brumado, Freguesia do Sumidouro, e morador no arraial do Itambé, termo da Vila do Príncipe, Bispado de Mariana" (information contained on the cover page contradicts the facts found in the records); IANTT, Inquisição de Lisboa, Processo no. 1.078. I am once again indebted to Luiz Mott, who referred me to this trial, for both his friendship and kindness.

103. Vauchez, *La spiritualité du Moyen-Âge occidental,* p. 18; *Spirituality of the Medieval West,* p. 19.

104. IANTT, Inquisição de Lisboa, Processo no. 213, "Processo de Anselmo da Costa índio carpinteiro solteiro filho de Atanásio da Silva natural e morador no lugar da freguesia de Nossa Senhora da Conceição de Benfica Bispado do Grão-Pará." Amaral Lapa published the vicar's denunciation (*Livro da Visitação: Estado do Grão-Pará,* pp. 214–18).

105. IANTT, Inquisição de Lisboa, Processo no. 218, "Processo de Joaquim Pedro índio sem ofício natural do lugar de Azevedo termo de Vila Viçosa de Cametá e morador na vila de Beja Bispado do Pará sacristão da igreja desta

vila." Amaral Lapa published one of the denunciations from this trial, that of Raimundo José Bittancur (*Livro da Visitação: Estado do Grão-Pará*, pp. 203ff.).

106. On the role of altar stones in indigenous and black cultures, see Fernandes, *O folclore mágico do Nordeste*, pp. 16–18. Pages 44, 45, and 99 contain prayers still in use today to protect from injury caused by sharp objects, knives, bullets, and snakebite.

107. Here I am borrowing some of Goulemot's thoughts on popular mentality and the magical universe. See "Démons, merveilles et philosophie," pp. 1237–38.

Chapter 5. Maintaining Bonds of Affection

1. Caro Baroja, *Les sorcières et leur monde*, pp. 50–52; *The World of the Witches*, pp. 32–34.

2. Caro Baroja, *Les sorcières et leur monde*, p. 118; *The World of the Witches*, p. 101. In his "Comedia de las burlas de amor," Lope de Vega says: "Este amaba a una ramera, / a quien trató muchos años, / mujer de mal trato y fiera, / remediadora de daños / y por extremo hechicera" (cited in Caro Baroja, "La magia en Castilla," in *Algunos mitos españoles*, p. 236).

3. Dupont-Bouchat, "La répression de la sorcellerie," pp. 142–43.

4. Thomas, *Religion and the Decline of Magic*, p. 568.

5. Freyre, *Casa Grande e Senzala*, vol. 2, pp. 450–51; this translation is based in part on *The Masters and the Slaves*, p. 333.

6. Rego, *Feiticeiros, profetas, visionários*, p. 19 (emphasis added).

7. Caro Baroja, "La magia en Castilla," in *Algunos mitos españoles*, pp. 229-30.

8. Rego, *Feiticeiros, profetas, visionários*, p. 78.

9. *Primeira Visitação: Denunciações da Bahia*, p. 433.

10. In the words of John Gaule (*Select Cases of Conscience Touching–Witches*, p. 1646), the stereotype of a witch was an "old woman with a wrinkled face, a furr'd brow, a hairy lip, a gobber tooth, a squint eye, a squeaking voice, or a scolding tongue" (cited in Thomas, *Religion and the Decline of Magic*, p. 567).

11. *Primeira Visitação: Confissões da Bahia*, p. 49.

12. AEAM, Devassas—fevereiro–maio 1731, p. 4 (cited in Figueiredo, "O avesso da memória," p. 136).

13. IANTT, Inquisição de Lisboa, m° 27-20, Novos Maços.

14. IANTT, Inquisição de Lisboa, Processo no. 11.767.

15. IANTT, Inquisição de Lisboa, Processo no. 1.894, "Processo de Adrião Pereira de Faria aliás Adrião Pereira de Passos sargento dos auxiliares natural da Vila da Vigia e morador no Engenho de Tapariuassu Bispado do Grão-Pará."

16. IANTT, Inquisição de Lisboa, Processo no. 2.696, "Apresentação de Crescêncio Escobar mameluco que tem ofício de ferreiro casado com Deodata Vitória da Cunha morador na Vila da Vigia."

17. Cohn, *Los demonios familiares*, pp. 220–21; *Europe's Inner Demons*, pp. 107–8.

18. Delumeau, "Ignorance religieuse," in *Un chemin d'histoire*, p. 125.

19. *Primeira Visitação: Confissões da Bahia*, p. 61.

20. *Livro da Visitação: Estado do Grão-Pará*, p. 201.

21. IANTT, Inquisição de Lisboa, Processo no. 2.704, "Apresentação e confissão de Maria Joana, solteira." See also *Livro da Visitação: Estado do Grão-Pará*, pp. 254–58, where parts of the trial have been published.

22. IANTT, Inquisição de Lisboa, Processo no. 1.377.

23. IANTT, Inquisição de Lisboa, Processo no. 2.704.

24. *Livro da Visitação: Estado do Grão-Pará*, pp. 254–55. See "Feitiço do Amor Fiel," in *Grande livro de São Cipriano ou Tesouros do feiticeiro*, p. 203.

25. IANTT, Inquisição de Lisboa, Processo no. 2.697, "Apresentação e confissão de Manuel Pacheco Madureira natural desta cidade viúvo de Dona Claudina Maria Pinheira." See also *Livro da Visitação: Estado do Grão-Pará*, p. 238.

26. *Livro da Visitação: Estado do Grão-Pará*, pp. 132–34.

27. IANTT, Inquisição de Lisboa, Processo no. 2.702, "Apresentação e confissão de Manuel Nunes da Silva natural da Vila da Vigia." See *Livro da Visitação: Estado do Grão-Pará*, p. 240, where Amaral Lapa transcribes the prayer somewhat differently. See also IANTT, Inquisição de Lisboa, Processo no. 2.704 (for Maria Joana); IANTT, Inquisição de Lisboa, Processo no. 2.697 (for Manuel P. Madureira); and *Livro da Visitação: Estado do Grão-Pará*, p. 201 (for Manuel José da Maia).

28. IANTT, Inquisição de Lisboa, Processo no. 5.180 (emphasis added).

29. I refer again to Thomas, *Religion and the Decline of Magic*, pp. 181–82.

30. IANTT, Inquisição de Lisboa, Processo no. 2.704; *Livro da Visitação: Estado do Grão-Pará*, p. 252.

31. See Julio Caro Baroja, "El toro de San Marcos—A: Exposición," in *Ritos y mitos equívocos*.

32. Julio Caro Baroja, "El toro de San Marcos—B: Comparaciones," in *Ritos y mitos equívocos*, pp. 104, 105, 107.

33. IANTT, Inquisição de Lisboa, Processo no. 1.894.

34. IANTT, Inquisição de Lisboa, Processo no. 3.382.

35. IANTT, Inquisição de Lisboa, Processo no. 1.377. Madre Paula, lover to Dom João V, knew a similar spell, which she used some two decades later: "I cast this salt so that my master shall come fetch me, speak to me, love me; may he come and not tarry, by Barabbas, by Caiaphas, and at these signs, may the dogs howl, the flocks graze, the cats leap"; cited in Chantal, *A vida cotidiana em Portugal*, p. 182. In "Galán Castrucho," by Lope de Vega, the procuress Teodora is described as "Caiaphas's cook" (Caro Baroja, "La magia en Castilla," in *Algunos mitos españoles*, p. 230).

36. IANTT, Inquisição de Lisboa, Processo no. 2.697; *Livro da Visitação: Estado do Grão-Pará*, p. 238.

37. *Livro da Visitação: Estado do Grão-Pará*, p. 257; Inquisição de Lisboa, Processo no. 2.704. Comparing the two versions, I have filled in some of the blanks left by Amaral Lapa.

38. "Conjúrote estrella, la más alta y la más bella, como conjuro la una, conjuro las dos, y como conjuro las dos, conjuro las tres . . . [repeating till reaching nine stars] todas nuebe os juntad y a Fulano combate le dad, y en la

huerta de moysen entrad, y nueve varetas de amor le cortad, y en la fragua de berzebú, barrabás, satanás y lucifer entrad, y nueve rejones amolad y al diablo coxuelo los dad que se los baya a lançar a fulano por mitad del coraçon que no le dexen reposar, hasta que conmigo venga a estar."

"Je te saue mille fois ô étoile plus resplendissante que la Lune. Je te conjure d'aller trouver Bellzebuth . . . & lui dire qu'il m'envoye trois esprits, Alpha, Rello, Jalderichel, & le Bossu du Mont Gibel . . . afin qu'ils aillent trouver N. fille de N. . . . Et que pour l'amour de moi ils lui ôtent le jeu, & le ris de bouche, & fassent qu'elle ne puisse ni aller, ni reposer, ni manger, ni boire, jusqu'à se qu'elle soit venue accomplir la volonté de moi N; fils de N. & c." (Caro Baroja, "La magia en Castilla," in *Algunos mitos españoles,* pp. 250–51).

39. All references to Maria Joana are taken from "Apresentação e confissão de Maria Joana solteira," IANTT, Inquisição de Lisboa, Processo no. 2.704. Amaral Lapa publishes part of her confessions (*Livro da Visitação: Estado do Grão-Pará,* pp. 250–58).

40. *Livro da Visitação: Estado do Grão-Pará,* p. 209. Among Trobriand Islanders, young men would wash themselves with leaves when they wanted to capture a woman's heart. This is what Malinowski called "ablution magic" (*La vie sexuelle des sauvages,* pp. 345–48).

41. *Primeira Visitação: Confissões da Bahia,* p. 59.

42. Ibid., p. 60.

43. IANTT, Inquisição de Lisboa, Processo no. 2.691.

44. IANTT, Inquisição de Lisboa, Processo no. 631. Chapter 3 talks about belief in the magical power of urine, sperm, blood, and hair, which were often used in making philters. See Delumeau, *Le catholicisme entre Luther et Voltaire,* p. 243; *Catholicism between Luther and Voltaire,* p. 166. The Cathars believed that the first menstrual blood could be used as a love potion (Le Roy Ladurie, *Montaillou, village occitan,* pp. 62, 275).

45. *Primeira Visitação: Denunciações da Bahia,* p. 300.

46. *Primeira Visitação: Confissões da Bahia,* pp. 53–54. Innumerable types of sortilege involving the soles of shoes were used in Europe. To counter spells, one was supposed to spit in one's right shoe before putting it on (Lebrun, *Médecins, saints et sorciers,* p. 107). To be rid of a lover, the eminent Dr. Curvo Semedo recommended spreading his or her feces on the inner sole (Dantas, *O amor em Portugal no século XVIII,* pp. 274–75). See also "Mágica da palmilha do pé esquerdo," in *Grande livro de São Cipriano,* p. 197.

47. IANTT, Inquisição de Lisboa, Processo no. 3.382.

48. IANTT, Inquisição de Lisboa, Processo no. 5.180.

49. IANTT, Inquisição de Lisboa, Processo no. 9.972.

50. IANTT, Inquisição de Lisboa, mᵒ 27-20, Novos Maços.

51. IANTT, Inquisição de Lisboa, Processo no. 3.382.

52. Cited in Figueiredo, "O avesso da memória," p. 83.

53. AEAM, Livro de Devassas, 7 janeiro 1767–1777, p. 67v. See AEAM, Devassas—maio–dezembro 1753, p. 67, which talks about Josefa Doce, from the parish of Carijós, who used a variety of ingredients and superstitions so that men would like her.

54. IANTT, Inquisição de Lisboa, Processo no. 5.180.

55. AEAM, Livro de Devassas, 7 janeiro 1767–1777, p. 47.
56. Rowland, "Anthropology, Witchcraft, Inquisition," p. 10.
57. Lucy Mair, cited in ibid., p. 11.

Chapter 6. Communicating with the Supernatural

1. IANTT, Inquisição de Lisboa, Processo no. 252, m° 26, "Processo de Luzia Pinta preta forra filha de Manuel da Graça natural da cidade de Angola e moradora na Vila do Sabará Bispado do Rio de Janeiro." Once again, I am indebted to Professor Anita Novinsky for her generosity in referring me to this trial.

2. See Gatto, "Le voyage au Paradis," pp. 929–42.

3. On the comparison of God to a colonial Brazilian master, see Hoornaert, "A instituição eclesiástica," in Hoornaert et al., *História da igreja no Brasil*, p. 342.

4. "Apresentação a confissão de Maria Joana de Azevedo," in *Livro da Visitação: Estado do Grão-Pará*, pp. 255–57.

5. See Arnold Hauser, *História social da literatura e da arte*, vol. 1, pp. 569–70.

6. Many present-day African societies believe that people can metamorphose into animals (Parrinder, *La brujería*, pp. 188–89; *Witchcraft*, pp. 145–47).

7. Caro Baroja, *Les sorcières et leur monde*, pp. 55–56; *The World of the Witches*, pp. 36–37.

8. Caro Baroja, *Les sorcières et leur monde*, p. 63; *The World of the Witches*, p. 44.

9. Ginzburg, "Présomptions sur le sabbat," p. 344.

10. Rego, *Feiticeiros, profetas, visionários*, p. 17.

11. Métraux, *A religião dos Tupinambás*, p. 158. The sorcerers' favorite form to take was that of a tiger.

12. *Primeira Visitação: Denunciações da Bahia*, p. 540.

13. Ibid., pp. 349–50. In colonial Mexico, Martín Ucelo, or Ocelotl, was accused of transforming himself into a tiger, lion, dog, and cat. See Ricard, *The Spiritual Conquest of Mexico*, p. 271.

14. *Primeira Visitação: Denunciações da Bahia*, p. 342. The custom of hiding children or warning them about the dangers of witches made its way into folktales. The Seven Dwarves, for example, advised Snow White not to open the door to her witch-stepmother.

15. IANTT, Inquisição de Lisboa, Processo no. 11.163.

16. Parrinder, *La brujería*, p. 184; *Witchcraft*, p. 146.

17. Delumeau, *Le catholicisme entre Luther et Voltaire*, p. 96; *Catholicism between Luther and Voltaire*, p. 50.

18. Ramos, *O folclore negro no Brasil*, p. 119.

19. IANTT, Inquisição de Lisboa, Processo no. 508.

20. IANTT, Inquisição de Lisboa, Processo no. 10.181.

21. IANTT, Inquisição de Lisboa, Processo no. 1.377.

22. IANTT, Inquisição de Lisboa, Processo no. 11.163.

23. IANTT, Inquisição de Lisboa, Processo no. 9.972.

24. IANTT, Inquisição de Lisboa, Processo no. 11.767.

25. Caesarius, a German monk from the monastery of Heisterbach, believed it was not uncommon for demons to appear as Moriscos or black Moors (Cohn, *Los demonios familiares,* pp. 102–3; *Europe's Inner Demons,* pp. 25–26).

26. Here I am borrowing from Germain Bazin's evocative analysis: "Formes démoniaques," in Germain Bazin et al., *Satan,* p. 508. In the same collection, see the many forms the devil takes in dreams, in Dr. Jolande Jacobi, "Les démons du rêve," p. 454.

27. Cited in Thomas, *Religion and the Decline of Magic,* p. 469.

28. Ibid., p. 476.

29. Ibid., p. 477.

30. Cited in Erlanger, *La vie quotidienne sous Henri IV,* p. 65.

31. Cited in Thomas, *Religion and the Decline of Magic,* p. 475, note 3 (emphasis added). On Escoto and *The Discovery of Witchcraft,* see Rossell Hope Robbins, *The Encyclopedia of Witchcraft and Demonology,* p. 453.

32. *Primeira Visitação: Denunciações da Bahia,* pp. 299, 319; *Primeira Visitação: Denunciações de Pernambuco,* pp. 121–22, 187; AEAM, Devassas—maio 1730–abril 1731, p. 17.

33. AEAM, Livro de Devassas—7 janeiro 1767–1777, p. 67v.

34. IANTT, Inquisição de Lisboa, Processo no. 5.180.

35. AEAM, Devassas—maio–dezembro 1753, p. 58v; cited in Figueiredo, "O avesso da memória," p. 133.

36. Thomas, *Religion and the Decline of Magic,* p. 446.

37. Rego, *Feiticeiros, profetas, visionários,* p. 37. On the nursing of familiars by witches, see Parrinder, *La brujería,* pp. 116–17.

38. Caro Baroja, *Les sorcières et leur monde,* p. 90; *The World of the Witches,* pp. 71–72. At the cathedral of Notre Dame in Semur-en-Auxois, two animals resembling toads and birds of prey hang from a woman's breasts. See Roland Villeneuve, *Le diable: Érotologie de Satan,* p. 68.

39. Thomas, *Religion and the Decline of Magic,* p. 446. On Hopkins's fight against animal familiars, see also Parrinder, *La brujería,* p. 113. The Zulu and Lovedu of contemporary Africa have also been said to believe in animal familiars (Parrinder, *La brujería,* p. 184; *Witchcraft,* p. 146).

40. *Primeira Visitação: Confissões da Bahia,* pp. 61–62.

41. Ibid., p. 62. The name of Lady Alice's familiar was Robert Artisson (Parrinder, *La brujería,* p. 109). In the sixteenth century, Margerey Barnes had three familiars: Paygne, a rat; Russoll, a cat; and Dunsott, a dog (ibid., p. 111).

42. *Primeira Visitação: Confissões da Bahia,* p. 61.

43. Cohn, *Los demonios familiares,* p. 245.

44. Cohn, *Los demonios familiares,* p. 228; *Europe's Inner Demons,* p. 114.

45. Cited in Delumeau, "Ignorance religieuse," in *Un chemin d'histoire,* p. 125.

46. Cohn, *Los demonios familiares,* p. 219; *Europe's Inner Demons,* p. 106. Laden with magical significance, Uriel, Raguel, Tibuel, Adinus, Tubuel, Sabaoc, and Simiel were among the names of Jewish origin given to angels (Giordano, *Religiosidad popular en la Alta Edad Media,* p. 137).

47. *Primeira Visitação: Denunciações de Pernambuco,* p. 108.

48. Thomas, *Religion and the Decline of Magic,* p. 445.

49. Evans-Pritchard, *Witchcraft, Oracles and Magic among the Azande,* p. 22.

50. IANTT, Inquisição de Lisboa, Processo no. 1.377.

51. IANTT, Inquisição de Lisboa, Processo no. 5.180; *Livro da Visitação: Estado do Grão-Pará,* pp. 182–83. In 1748 the devil appeared as a little black boy to Sister Maria do Rosário (cited in Rego, *Feiticeiros, profetas, visionários,* p. 124).

52. Excerpt from Yves d'Évreux, transcribed by Métraux, *A religião dos Tupinambás,* pp. 159–60.

53. See the introduction to part II.

54. Thomas, *Religion and the Decline of Magic,* pp. 539, 474.

55. *Primeira Visitação: Denunciações da Bahia,* p. 527.

56. *Primeira Visitação: Confissões da Bahia,* p. 59.

57. Ibid., pp. 61–62.

58. *Primeira Visitação: Denunciações da Bahia,* pp. 425, 567–68.

59. IANTT, Inquisição de Lisboa, Processo no. 1.377.

60. IANTT, Inquisição de Lisboa, m° 27-20, Novos Maços.

61. AEAM, Livro de Devassas—Comarca do Serro do Frio, 1734, pp. 75, 84, 88, 88v, 89.

62. AEAM, Devassas—1756–1757, pp. 50, 50v, 51, 51v, 52.

63. Caro Baroja, *Les sorcières et leur monde,* p. 91; *The World of the Witches,* p. 73.

64. Thomas, *Religion and the Decline of Magic,* p. 470. The devil brought about high winds and storms in a world that did not yet know technology or have scientific explanations for natural events.

65. Evans-Pritchard, *Witchcraft, Oracles and Magic among the Azande,* pp. 21–50; Ramos, *O folclore negro no Brasil,* pp. 24–25. Caesarius of Heisterbach believed it possible for devils to take up residence in a human's bowels, amidst excrement (Cohn, *Los demonios familiares,* p. 104; *Europe's Inner Demons,* p. 26).

66. In their youth, Erasmus and Luther, among others, were devotees of St. Anne (Delumeau, *Naissance et affirmation de la Réforme,* p. 54). On St. Anne as a symbol of the mansion house, see Hoornaert, "A cristandade," in Hoornaert et al., *História da igreja no Brasil,* p. 370.

67. The legend of Theophilus had long been known to the Anglo-Saxons as well, according to Thomas (*Religion and the Decline of Magic,* p. 439). On Theophilus, see Caro Baroja, *Les sorcières et leur monde,* pp. 91–92; *The World of the Witches,* p. 73. See also P. M. Palmer and R. P. More, *The Sources of the Faust Tradition* (New York: Oxford University Press, 1936), where the story of Theophilus appears on pages 58–77.

68. See Jacques Solé, *L'amour en Occident à l'Époque Moderne,* pp. 132–33. See also Hugh R. Trevor-Roper, "A obsessão das bruxas na Europa dos séculos XVI e XVII," in *Religião, reforma e transformação social,* p. 98; *The European Witch-Craze of the Sixteenth and Seventeenth Centuries.*

69. IANTT, Inquisição de Lisboa, Processo no. 631.

70. Mandrou, *Magistrats et sorciers,* p. 399.

71. See, among others, Margareth Murray, *El culto de la brujería en Europa Occidental;* and Jules Michelet, *La sorcière.* The idea of the sabbat as an intel-

lectual construct is defended by Cohn in *Los demonios familiares de Europa.* (*Europe's Inner Demons*) and by Henningsen in *El abogado de las brujas.*

72. IANTT, Inquisição de Lisboa, Processo no. 9.972.

73. Rego, *Feiticeiros, profetas, visionários,* p. 15.

74. IANTT, Inquisição de Lisboa, Processo no. 11.774, "Processo de José Francisco homem preto solteiro escravo de Domingos Francisco Pedroso homem de negócios natural de Judá na Costa da Mina e morador nesta cidade de Lisboa Ocidental."

75. Mircea Éliade, "Quelques observations sur la sorcellerie européenne," in *Occultisme, sorcellerie et modes culturelles,* p. 123.

76. Rowland, "Anthropology, Witchcraft, Inquisition," p. 6.

77. Éliade, "Quelques observations," in *Occultisme, sorcellerie et modes culturelles,* p. 121.

78. IANTT, Inquisição de Lisboa, Processo no. 11.767, "Processo de José Francisco Pereira homem preto escravo de João Francisco Pedroso natural de Judá na Costa da Mina e morador nesta cidade de Lisboa."

79. IANTT, Inquisição de Lisboa, Processo no. 10.181.

80. Cohn, *Los demonios familiares,* p. 99. See also Giordano, *Religiosidad popular en la Alta Edad Media,* pp. 132–33.

81. Thomas, *Religion and the Decline of Magic,* p. 478.

82. IANTT, Inquisição de Lisboa, Processo no. 3.723.

83. Ibid. (emphasis added).

84. IANTT, Inquisição de Évora, m° 803, Processo no. 7.759.

85. AGCRJ, 45-1-15, "Autos de um processo de injúria a mulher casada intentado por Ana Maria da Conceição e seu marido contra Rita Sebastiana," pp. 30v–31. I am indebted to Sílvia H. Lara for referring me to this document.

86. Bastide, *Les religions africaines au Brésil,* p. 78; *The African Religions of Brazil,* p. 57: "The African religions are closer to their origins, purer and richer, in the big cities than in the country."

87. Bastide, *Les religions africaines au Brésil,* p. 91; *The African Religions of Brazil,* p. 66.

88. Bastide, *Les religions africaines au Brésil,* p. 126; *The African Religions of Brazil,* p. 90.

89. AEAM, Devassas—1756–1757, pp. 96–96v.

90. AEAM, Devassas—julho 1762–dezembro 1769, p. 49.

91. Ibid., p. 114.

92. AEAM, Livro de Devassas—Comarca do Serro do Frio, 1734, p. 97.

93. AEABH, Visitas Pastorais—Paróquia de Sabará, 1734, p. 52v; cited in Figueiredo, "O avesso da memória," p. 133.

94. Ibid.

95. AEAM, Devassas—maio–dezembro 1753, p. 101v; cited in Figueiredo, "O avesso da memória," p. 134.

96. Pereira, *Compêndio narrativo do peregrino da América,* p. 123.

97. Ibid., p. 125; the English translation of this quotation is from Bastide, *The African Religions of Brazil,* p. 137.

98. Bastide, *Les religions africaines au Brésil,* p. 216; *The African Religions of Brazil,* p. 156.

99. See Mott, "Acotundá."

100. Pereira, *Compêndio narrativo do peregrino da América,* p. 125 (emphasis added).

101. IANTT, Inquisição de Lisboa, Processo no. 252, m° 26, "Processo de Luzia Pinta preta forra filha de Manuel da Graça natural da cidade de Angola e moradora na Vila do Sabará Bispado do Rio de Janeiro."

102. Bastide, *Les religions africaines au Brésil,* p. 334; *The African Religions of Brazil,* p. 240.

103. Bastide, *Les religions africaines au Brésil,* pp. 222–23; *The African Religions of Brazil,* p. 161.

104. The old *calundu* was able "to survive in spite of miscegenation. Its new members, however, were not recruited exclusively from one people, since peoples no longer existed. Recruitment was governed by other laws—neighborhood factors or the prestige of the cult leaders or personal friendships" (Bastide, *Les religions africaines au Brésil,* p. 234; *The African Religions of Brazil,* p. 168).

105. Mott, "Acotundá," pp. 1–2.

106. Ibid., p. 4.

107. Ibid., pp. 10–11.

108. Simão Ferreira Machado, "Prévia alocutória" to the *Triunfo eucarístico,* in Ávila, *Resíduos seiscentistas em Minas,* vol. 1, p. 25.

109. IANTT, Inquisição de Lisboa, Processo no. 17.771, "Auto sumário que mandou fazer o reverendo viário da vara João de Barros Leal sobre o que adiante se segue."

110. The magical power of the snakehead can also be found in European sortilege. See "O poder da cabeça de víbora para fazer o bem e o mal," in *Grande livro de São Cipriano,* p. 235.

111. *Livro da Visitação: Estado do Grão-Pará,* pp. 176–77.

112. Ibid., pp. 211–12.

113. Ibid., p. 173.

114. Ibid., pp. 222–23.

115. The song went like this: "Tu eyró, Tu ey vyro—Atipondi, pondira, atipondi pondi, ipondira uzemio pondira, nari, nari, natequata su ma im me eresari." IANTT, Inquisição de Lisboa, Processo no. 2.701, "Confissão do índio Marçal Agostinho."

116. Ibid.

Chapter 7. Intertwined Discourses

1. See especially *Naissance et affirmation de la Réforme,* pp. 48–57; *La peur en Occident;* and *Le péché et la peur.*

2. On the colonial system, see Novais's classic work *Portugal e Brasil na crise do antigo sistema colonial;* as well as Immanuel Wallerstein, *El moderno sistema mundial: La agricultura capitalista y los orígenes de la economía-mundo europea en el siglo XVI.*

3. The image of the fiery cross is drawn from Robert Muchembled, "Satan ou les hommes?: La chasse aux sorcières et ses causes," in Dupont-Bouchat, Frijhoff, and Muchembled, *Prophètes et sorciers dans les Pays-Bas,* p. 15.

4. Trevor-Roper, "A obsessão das bruxas"; and Franco Cardini, *Magia, stregoneria, superstizioni nell'Occidente medievale.* On page 90, Cardini says: "Insofar as it intended to restore Christianity to its purest and solely Evangelical

sources, the Reformation repudiated the climate of syncretism under which Europe had been Christianized in the Middle Ages, and in so doing mortally wounded popular religion." See also Delumeau, *La peur en Occident,* pp. 359, 352.

5. On more general aspects of the medieval Inquisition, see Jean Guiraud, *L'Inquisition médiévale.*

6. See Norman Cohn's enlightening study *Los demonios familiares de Europa (Europe's Inner Demons),* cited repeatedly in this book, especially chapter 3, "La demonización de los herejes medievales (II)," pp. 55–89.

7. Le Goff, "Culture cléricale et traditions folkloriques," in *Pour un autre Moyen-Âge,* pp. 223–35; *Time, Work, and Culture,* pp. 153–58.

8. Le Goff, *La naissance du Purgatoire.*

9. Cardini, *Magia, stregoneria, superstizioni,* p. 60.

10. Ibid., p. 63.

11. "From a world filled with figures evocative of gothic gargoyles or drawings by Bosch, we move into another, where there is no room for irony or humorous images" (Julio Caro Baroja, *Inquisición, brujería y criptojudaísmo*).

12. See Dupont-Bouchat, "La répression de la sorcellerie," p. 72.

13. Adopted by a good share of historians who have written on sorcery, this chronological framework is questioned by Émile Brouette, who defends the hypothesis that repression of sorcery was as bloody from the close of the fifteenth century to the first half of the sixteenth as from 1560 to 1630. His assertion is grounded primarily on Flemish cases. See "La civilisation chrétienne du XVIᵉ siècle devant le problème satanique," in Bazin et al., *Satan,* p. 376.

14. See the table in Muchembled's "Satan ou les hommes?" (p. 17).

15. See Caro Baroja, *Les sorcières et leur monde,* pp. 197–216; *The World of the Witches,* pp. 171–89; and Henningsen, *El abogado de las brujas.* In his book, Henningsen pays homage to Salazar Frias, a judge who was ahead of the French magistracy in altering the attitude toward the crime of sorcery.

16. Robbins tells us that counties in the northern part of England were panic-stricken after this trial, which traced out guidelines and anticipated the *razzia* inaugurated thirty years later by Hopkins. See *The Encyclopedia of Witchcraft and Demonology,* pp. 296–98.

17. Mandrou, *Magistrats et sorciers.* See also Michel de Certeau, *La possession de Loudun.*

18. See Paul Boyer and Stephen Nissenbaum, *Salem Possessed: The Social Origins of Witchcraft.* See also Chadwick Hansen, *Sorcellerie à Salem (Witchcraft at Salem).*

19. Dupont-Bouchat, "La répression de la sorcellerie," pp. 118–19.

20. Muchembled developed these ideas in a number of works. See especially "Satan ou les hommes?" (p. 32) and "Sorcières du Cambrésis" (p. 160); and "L'autre côté du miroir: Mythes sataniques et réalités culturelles aux XVIᵉ et XVIIᵉ siècles," *Annales, E.S.C.,* 40th year, no. 2 (March–April 1985): 299.

21. See Dupont-Bouchat, "La répression de la sorcellerie," pp. 153–54. She does not actually link sorcery to pauperism but does venture the hypothesis that the impoverished dispossessed were scapegoats who drew the attention of early modern European authorities in place of the sorceress.

22. Delumeau, *La peur en Occident,* p. 352.

23. Oliveira Marques, *A sociedade medieval portuguesa,* p. 171.

24. Maria Tereza Campos Rodrigues, "Aspectos da administração munici-

pal de Lisboa no século XV" (reprint of nos. 101 to 109 of the *Revista Municipal* [Lisbon]).

25. Almeida, *História da igreja em Portugal,* vol. 1, p. 403.

26. James IV (James I as king of England) considered himself well versed in the subject and in 1597 wrote *Demonology* in refutation of Escoto's positions. In 1603 he had all copies of *Discovery of Witchcraft* burned. See Robbins, *The Encyclopedia of Witchcraft and Demonology,* pp. 277–78.

27. Trevor-Roper, "A obsessão das bruxas," p. 137.

28. Cardini, *Magia, stregoneria, superstizioni,* pp. 88–89. Ulrico Molitor, *De las brujas y adivinas;* Heinrich Kramer and James Sprenger, *Malleus maleficarum,* English trans. Montague Summers.

29. Cardini, *Magia, stregoneria, superstizioni,* pp. 88–89.

30. Ibid., p. 89.

31. Ibid., p. 90.

32. Delumeau, *La peur en Occident,* p. 240.

33. Ibid., pp. 353, 358.

34. Febvre, "Sorcellerie, sottise ou révolution mentale?" p. 13.

35. Bartolomé Bennassar, "Le pouvoir inquisitorial," in *L'Inquisition espagnole,* p. 75; and Antonio José Saraiva, *Inquisição e cristãos-novos,* p. 15.

36. Saraiva, *Inquisição e cristãos-novos,* p. 237.

37. To cite just a few examples of slaves incarcerated for many years: Luzia da Silva Soares, Domingos Álvares, Luís Pereira de Almeida, Mateus Pereira Machado—all arrested in the mid-eighteenth century. See, respectively, IANTT, Inquisição de Lisboa, Processo no. 11.163; IANTT, Inquisição de Évora, m° 803, Processo no. 7.759; IANTT, Inquisição de Lisboa, Processo no. 1.134; IANTT, Inquisição de Lisboa, Processo no. 1.131.

38. The situation in Gaul could be likened to that in Portugal: most charges brought before the Inquisition involved denunciations of Judaism, and more than 50 percent of those accused were merchants. Next came offenses typical to the post-Tridentine context: blasphemy and bigamy. See Jaime Contreras, *El Santo Ofício de la Inquisición de Galícia: Poder, sociedad y cultura,* p. 588. In Valencia, by contrast, the greatest number accused were Moors. See Ricardo García Cárcel, *Herejía y sociedad en el siglo XVI: La Inquisición de Valencia, 1530–1609.*

39. Boxer, *A igreja e a expansão ibérica,* p. 107; *The Church Militant,* pp. 85–86. On pages 107–8, however, Boxer falls into a contradiction, stating that "those unfortunate enough to have had experience of both institutions" regarded the Portuguese as "more rigorous and cruel" (quoted from *The Church Militant,* p. 86). In any case, the kind of treatment given to the witches of Zugarramurdi by the tribunal at Logroño was not customary in Spain, where magical practices were viewed with greater complaisance than other crimes.

40. Nogueira, "Universo mágico e realidade: Aspectos de um contexto cultural," pp. 182–84.

41. Anita Novinsky defends the thesis that the New Christian bourgeoisie was the favorite target of the Portuguese Inquisition. See *Cristãos-novos na Bahia* and *Inquisição: Inventário de bens confiscados a cristãos-novos.*

42. Wiznitzer, *Os judeus no Brasil colonial,* pp. 29–31.

43. Novinsky, *Cristãos-novos na Bahia,* pp. 107–9. The number of arrests

by the Inquisition rose sharply under Philip IV (p. 105).

44. Solange Behocary Alberro, "Inquisition et société: Rivalités de pouvoirs à Tepeaca (1656–1660)," *Annales, E.S.C.,* 36th year, no. 5 (September–October 1981): 758–84. Fearing the consequences of Dom Marcos Teixeira's Visitation to Bahia, many New Christians fled to Buenos Aires in 1618. See Gonçalves Salvador, *Cristãos-novos, Jesuítas e Inquisição,* p. 103.

45. The inquisitorial tribunals were not able to handle many cases a year: "fifty trials per year was a usual average" (Henningsen, *El abogado de las brujas,* p. 45). Alberro speaks of "usual slowness and meticulousness" ("Inquisition et société: Rivalités de pouvoirs à Tepeaca," p. 779).

46. See Salvador, *Cristãos-novos, Jesuítas e Inquisição,* p. 85; and Novinsky, *Cristãos-novos na Bahia,* p. 21. Novinsky was the first to write about the Grande Inquirição [Great Inquiry] held in Bahia by the Jesuits, in 1646, under the orders of Bishop Dom Pedro da Silva (see pp. 72, 73, 124–25, 128–29). Gonçalves Salvador raises the hypothesis that the Holy Office had a presence in Rio de Janeiro prior to 1619 in the form of a commissary (*Cristãos-novos, Jesuítas e Inquisição,* pp. 95–96). In 1627 two visiting commissaries reportedly traveled to the northeast and to the south of Brazil: Antonio Rosado and Luís Pires da Veiga, respectively (pp. 105–7). Pires da Veiga also visited Angola, in service as a deputy of the Holy Office. To date, I have no knowledge of any records (*Livros de assento*) of these Visitations, even though it seems practically certain they took place. On Pires da Veiga's visitation to Africa, see José Lourenço D. de Mendonça and Antonio Joaquim Moreira, *História dos principais actos e procedimentos da Inquisição em Portugal,* p. 142.

47. Almeida, *História da igreja em Portugal,* vol. 2, pp. 406–7.

48. The Holy Office had five sets of Instructions: two in the sixteenth century, two in the seventeenth, and one in the eighteenth, the last under Pombal, which restrained the inquisitors. The fourth, in 1640, was the most important and usually serves as the basis for analyses of the tribunal's workings. See Mendonça and Moreira, *História dos principais actos,* p. 124.

49. One example is the trial of Maria Gonçalves Cajada—or Arde-lhe-o-rabo—during the First Visitation. See IANTT, Inquisição de Lisboa, Processo no. 10.748.

50. IANTT, Inquisição de Lisboa, Processo no. 1.377.

51. IANTT, Inquisição de Lisboa, Processo no. 5.180 (emphasis added).

52. Amaral Lapa was not aware of these trial records and says nothing about events prior to the Visitation to Grão-Pará. See the introduction to *Livro da Visitação: Estado do Grão-Pará,* pp. 19–79.

53. See Marcos Carneiro de Mendonça (ed.), *A Amazônia na era Pombalina: Correspondência inédita do governador e capitão-general do Estado do Grão-Pará e Maranhão Francisco Xavier de Mendonça Furtado, 1751–1759.*

54. Novinsky, *Cristãos-novos na Bahia,* p. 111.

55. On the Inquisition's voracious confiscation of goods, see ibid., p. 65.

56. See Laura de Mello e Souza, "As devassas eclesiásticas da Arquidiocese de Mariana: Fonte primária para a história das mentalidades," *Anais do Museu Paulista* (São Paulo) 33 (1984): 65–73.

57. Luiz Mott published the Bahian Inquiry: "Os pecados da família na Bahia de Todos os Santos," *Centro de Estudos Baianos* (Salvador) (1972). The

Inquiry in Mato Grosso was recently discovered by the Colombian historian Fernando Torres Londoño, who has since written on the topic. See "O crime do amor," in *Amor e família no Brasil,* ed. Maria Angela d'Incao; as well as *A outra família: concubinato, igreja e escândalo na colônia.*

58. Following this same line of interpretation but focusing specifically on Minas, see my analysis of the "normatizing" efforts of eighteenth-century colonial authorities: *Desclassificados do ouro,* chap. 3, "Nas redes do poder," pp. 91–140.

59. Siqueira, *A Inquisição portuguesa e a sociedade colonial,* p. 187. She also states that it was the Inquisition's job more to persuade than to punish: "In principle, to love, not to hate" (p. 267). Such observations do not seem fitting to me, as readily gleaned from the interpretative stance put forward in this book.

60. Cited in Bastide, *Les religions africaines au Brésil,* p. 77; *The African Religions of Brazil,* p. 56.

61. Bastide, *Les religions africaines au Brésil,* pp. 188–89; *The African Religions of Brazil,* pp. 135–36.

62. Trevor-Roper, "A obsessão das bruxas"; *The European Witch-Craze of the Sixteenth and Seventeenth Centuries.*

63. Thomas, *Religion and the Decline of Magic.*

64. Delumeau, *Un chemin d'histoire;* see also *La peur en Occident.*

65. Muchembled, "Sorcières du Cambrésis," p. 161; and "L'autre côté du miroir," p. 298.

66. Muchembled, "Sorcières du Cambrésis," p. 196; Le Roy Ladurie, *La sorcière de Jasmin,* p. 67. Ladurie underscores the blending of popular and elite elements. Muchembled states that the stereotype came from the top down (p. 161).

67. Mandrou, *Magistrats et sorciers,* p. 83.

68. Muchembled, "L'autre côté du miroir," p. 302.

69. Delumeau, *La peur en Occident,* pp. 384, 385, 388; Dupont-Bouchat, "La répression de la sorcellerie," p. 93.

70. Muchembled, "L'autre côté du miroir," pp. 294, 288.

71. This expression is used by Delumeau in *La peur en Occident* (p. 243).

72. Thomas, *Religion and the Decline of Magic,* p. 449.

73. Ibid., p. 461.

74. Cohn, *Los demonios familiares,* pp. 207, 214.

75. Rowland, "Anthropology, Witchcraft, Inquisition," pp. 20–21.

76. Thomas, *Religion and the Decline of Magic,* p. 455; Cohn, *Los demonios familiares,* p. 320.

77. Rowland, "Anthropology, Witchcraft, Inquisition," p. 32.

78. Henningsen, *El abogado de las brujas,* pp. 349, 346, 343.

79. Ginzburg, *Le fromage et les vers; The Cheese and the Worms.*

80. Henningsen, *El abogado de las brujas,* p. 345.

81. Michel de Montaigne, *Essais,* notes and text established by Albert Thibaudet, book 3, chap. 11.

82. Mandrou, *Magistrats et sorciers,* pp. 539–40.

83. "Après tout, c'est mettre ses conjectures à bien haut pris que d'en faire cuire um homme tout vif" (Montaigne, *Essais,* p. 1003).

84. See Cohn, *Los demonios familiares,* p. 81.

85. Salvador, *Cristãos-novos, Jesuítas e Inquisição,* pp. 119–20.

86. Mendonça and Moreira, in *História dos principais actos,* pp. 283ff.

87. Wiznitzer, *Os judeus no Brasil colonial,* p. 13. The *Livros de Visitações* often contain denunciations of people who were already deceased but who during their lives had conducted themselves contrary to what the Inquisition held to be correct.

88. Saraiva, *Inquisição e cristãos-novos,* p. 80.

89. Caro Baroja, *Les sorcières et leur monde,* pp. 138, 193; *The World of the Witches,* pp. 118, 167.

90. Saraiva, *Inquisição e cristãos-novos,* p. 79 (quotation); Muchembled, "Sorcières du Cambrésis," p. 169.

91. Saraiva, *Inquisição e cristãos-novos,* p. 84.

92. Caro Baroja, *Inquisición, brujería y criptojudaísmo,* p. 280.

93. Bartolomé Bennassar, "L'Inquisition, ou la pédagogie de la peur," in *L'Inquisition espagnole,* pp. 123–24.

94. Saraiva, *Inquisição e cristãos-novos,* pp. 100–101.

95. IANTT, Inquisição de Lisboa, Processo no. 11.767, "Publicação da Prova da Justiça."

96. IANTT, Inquisição de Lisboa, Processo no. 1.377, verdict from the second trial.

97. Mendonça and Moreira, *História dos principais actos,* p. 133. For Sônia Siqueira, who fails to go as far as the Portuguese historiography mentioned above, mutual accusations between members of the same family were a demonstration of the strength of Christian ties, which outweighed those of the family institution (A Inquisição portuguesa e a sociedade colonial, p. 257). On the use of means of persuasion, see Francisco Bethencourt, "Campo religioso e Inquisição em Portugal no século XVI."

98. For another context, see Muchembled, "L'autre côté du miroir," p. 290.

99. Bennassar, "Le pouvoir inquisitorial," in *L'Inquisition espagnole,* p. 96.

100. *Primeira Visitação: Denunciações de Pernambuco,* pp. 108–10.

101. IANTT, Inquisição de Lisboa, Processo no. 1.131; see also Processos nos. 508 and 1.134.

102. IANTT, Inquisição de Lisboa, Processos nos. 11.774 and 11.767.

103. IANTT, Inquisição de Lisboa, Processo no. 8.909.

104. IANTT, Inquisição de Lisboa, Processo no. 2.691.

105. IANTT, Inquisição de Lisboa, Processo no. 12.925, "Processo de Violante Carneira cristã-velha moradora nesta cidade"; IANTT, Inquisição de Lisboa, Processo no. 10.748, "Processo de Maria Gonçalves Cajada, cristãvelha."

106. Accompanying a list of offenses sent in 1728 from Recife to Lisbon, where they were to be examined by the Council General of the Inquisition, there was a short letter, probably written by a Commissary of the Holy Office. The document speaks to this matter: "I send these things and diverse notes that I have taken from diverse people who came to me to denounce what they knew about some persons, obliged by scruple or sent by their confessors" (IANTT, Inquisição de Lisboa, mº 27-20, Novos Maços; emphasis added).

107. IANTT, Inquisição de Lisboa, Processo no. 1.078.

108. IANTT, Inquisição de Lisboa, Processo no. 1.377, contestation of the second trial.

109. Pereira, *Compêndio narrativo do peregrino da América,* p. 134 (emphases added).

110. Bennassar believes that after first murdering a great number of people, the Inquisition eased up somewhat. The terror, however, hung on. See "L'Inquisition, ou la pédagogie de la peur," in *L'Inquisition espagnole*, p. 119.

111. Lisón-Tolosana, *Brujería, estructura social y simbolismo en Galícia*, p. 31; see also p. 30.

112. See Dupont-Bouchat, "La répression de la sorcellerie," p. 110; Rowland, "Anthropology, Witchcraft, Inquisition," p. 22.

113. *Manual dos Inquisidores para uso das Inquisições de Espanha e Portugal* (chap. 1, p. 4), cited in Mendonça and Moreira, *História dos principais actos*, p. 304. See also Nicolas Eymeric and Francisco Peña, *Le manuel des inquisiteurs*, intro., trans., and notes by Louis Sala-Molins, 3rd part. The expression "fanatical about detail" is Le Roy Ladurie's (*Montaillou, village occitan*, p. 14; *Montaillou: The Promised Land of Error*, p. xiii).

114. Michel Foucault, *Histoire de la séxualité, 1: La volonté de savoir*, pp. 82–83; *The History of Sexuality, Volume 1: An Introduction*, trans. Robert Hurley, p. 61; see also pp. 78–80.

115. IANTT, Inquisição de Lisboa, Processo no. 3.723.

116. IANTT, Inquisição de Lisboa, Processo no. 2.704.

117. See Cardini's analysis in *Magia, stregoneria, superstizioni*, pp. 90–91.

118. See Delumeau, *La peur en Occident*, p. 380; and Rowland, "Anthropology, Witchcraft, Inquisition," p. 4.

119. *Primeira Visitação: Confissões de Pernambuco*, p. 43.

120. Ibid., p. 54.

121. In addition, this episode reflects movements of convergence and divergence in sacramental and inquisitorial confessions. I am indebted to Ronaldo Vainfas for this observation.

122. *Primeira Visitação: Confissões de Pernambuco*, p. 114.

123. *Primeira Visitação: Denunciações de Pernambuco*, p. 281 (emphasis added).

124. " . . . and that it seems to him that the said Pero Gonçalves had pronounced the said words in jest, for he is a jester and talker, and he holds him to be a good Christian man, and for this reason he had not thought ill when he had heard them" (ibid., p. 436).

125. Ibid., pp. 435–36 (emphasis added).

126. *Primeira Visitação: Confissões de Pernambuco*, pp. 36–37.

127. IANTT, Inquisição de Lisboa, Processo no. 4.684.

128. IANTT, Inquisição de Lisboa, Processo no. 2.696.

129. *Primeira Visitação: Confissões de Pernambuco*, pp. 100–1.

130. *Primeira Visitação: Denunciações de Pernambuco*, p. 280.

131. IANTT, Inquisição de Lisboa, Processo no. 2.706.

132. IANTT, Inquisição de Lisboa, Processo no. 2.705.

133. Suzanne Chantal alludes to the burning of the Inquisition palace as a result of the fire that followed the earthquake (in *A vida quotidiana em Portugal ao tempo do terremoto*, pp. 21–22*).*

134. IANTT, Inquisição de Lisboa, Processo no. 1.131 (emphasis added).

135. Dominican cleric Maria do Rosário, accused of sorcery and a diabolic pact, tried to run away at the time of the earthquake but ended up back in the clutches of the Inquisition (Rego, *Feiticeiros, profetas, visionários*, pp. 139–40). Rebellions broke out in Andalusia in 1652 in response to a terrible rise in

prices, hunger, and poverty. Prisoners were set free and looting ensued, but no one dared touch the Inquisition's jails (Bennassar, "L'Inquisition, ou la pédagogie de la peur," in *L'Inquisition espagnole*, p. 105).

136. Cardini, *Magia, stregoneria, superstizioni*, p. 76.

137. Ibid.

138. García Cárcel, *Herejía y sociedad en el siglo XVI*, p. 248; and Cohn, *Los demonios familiares*, pp. 220–21; *Europe's Inner Demons*, pp. 107–8.

139. Muchembled, "L'autre côté du miroir," pp. 288–89, 294.

140. Ginzburg, "Présomptions sur le sabbat," pp. 341–54.

141. Lisón-Tolosana, *Brujería, estructura social y simbolismo en Galícia*, p. 32.

142. IANTT, Inquisição de Lisboa, Processo no. 1.377 (emphasis added).

143. IANTT, Inquisição de Lisboa, Processo no. 10.748 (emphasis added). The inquisitor insisted that she "declare the truth, by which she had done and said all the aforementioned things . . . because it could not be presumed that all were tricks as she says."

144. IANTT, Inquisição de Lisboa, Processo no. 5.180 (emphasis added).

145. IANTT, Inquisição de Lisboa, Processo no. 2.691 (emphasis added).

146. IANTT, Inquisição de Lisboa, Processo no. 2.704.

147. IANTT, Inquisição de Lisboa, Processo no. 2.702.

148. IANTT, Inquisição de Lisboa, Processo no. 2.697.

149. IANTT, Inquisição de Lisboa, Processo no. 9.972 (emphasis added).

150. Foucault, *Histoire de la sexualité*, pp. 92–93; *The History of Sexuality*, p. 69. All other quotations in the previous two paragraphs and in the following paragraphs concerning José Francisco are taken from IANTT, Inquisição de Lisboa, Processo no. 11.767.

151. Luiz Mott has studied this process in "Etno-demonologia: Aspectos da vida sexual do diabo no mundo ibero-americano (séculos XVI ao XVIII)."

152. Del Río cited in Maurice Garçon and Jean Vinchon, *Le diable: Étude historique, critique et médicale*, p. 123.

153. I refer the reader again to Éliade's analysis "Quelques observations," in *Occultisme, sorcellerie et modes culturelles*, p. 121. He affirms that Judeo-Christian tradition has demonized sexuality.

154. Joseph Turmel, *Histoire du diable*, 174.

155. Ibid., p. 178; and Caro Baroja, *Les sorcières et leur monde*, p. 69; *The World of the Witches*, p. 50.

156. Cohn, *Los demonios familiares*, pp. 226–27; *Europe's Inner Demons*, pp. 112–13.

157. Erlanger, *La vie quotidienne sous Henri IV*, pp. 66–67. The idea that sexual intercourse with the devil is ice-cold appeared as early as the thirteenth century, when Gregory IX issued the papal bull *Vox in Rama* (see Cohn, *Los demonios familiares*, pp. 52–33).

158. See Thomas's excellent analysis in *Religion and the Decline of Magic*, p. 519.

159. Carlo Ginzburg, *I Benandanti: Stregoneria e culti agrari tra Cinquecento e Seicento*.

160. Lisón-Tolosana, *Brujería, estructura social y simbolismo en Galícia*, p. 37.

161. See Rowland, "Anthropology, Witchcraft, Inquisition," p. 23.

162. IANTT, Inquisição de Lisboa, Processo no. 9.972 (emphasis added).
163. IANTT, Inquisição de Lisboa, Processo no. 3.723 (emphasis added).
164. IANTT, Inquisição de Lisboa, Processo no. 11.774 (emphasis added).
165. IANTT, Inquisição de Lisboa, Processo no. 15.559.
166. Muchembled, "L'autre côté du miroir," p. 296. He makes mention of popular festivals that were punished as expressions of sorcery. See also, by the same author, *Culture populaire et culture des élites* (*XVᵉ–XVIIIᵉ siècles*).
167. See especially the first two chapters of this book.
168. See Bastide, *Les religions africaines au Brésil*, p. 315.
169. Pereira, *Compêndio narrativo do peregrino da América*, p. 114.
170. Dupont-Bouchat, "La répression de la sorcellerie," p. 93.
171. Amaral Lapa, introduction to *Livro da Visitação: Estado do Grão-Pará*, p. 27.
172. See IANTT, Inquisição de Lisboa, Processos nos 1.131, 1.134, 508, 1.078, and 4.684.
173. Almost the same thing was said of Joaquim Pedro: "For the use he made of the altar stone was not for superstitious ends, that would imply a pact or the suspicion of one; nor can one presume from this fact an abandonment of religion, but rather, as much as befits the capacity of the Accused, he desired from the same sacred thing the greater effects that would help to preserve his life" (IANTT, Inquisição de Lisboa, Processo no. 218).
174. IANTT, Inquisição de Lisboa, Processo no. 213.
175. IANTT, Inquisição de Lisboa, Processo no. 210.
176. IANTT, Inquisição de Lisboa, Processo no. 212.
177. Mandrou, *Magistrats et sorciers*, pp. 540, 556–57, 560–61.
178. Mendonça and Moreira, *História dos principais actos*, p. 124. "This Regimento [Instruction] was the work of the Marquis de Pombal; in a manner of speaking, it broke the inquisitors' arms, and from then on, however much they wanted, they could do little."
179. I refer readers to the chapter "Os problemas da colonização portuguesa," in Novais, *Portugal e Brasil na crise do antigo sistema colonial*, pp. 117–211.
180. IANTT, Inquisição de Lisboa, Processo no. 218.
181. Speech by Tiradentes, cited in Souza, *Desclassificados do ouro*, p. 41.
182. Mandrou, *Magistrats et sorciers*, pp. 454–55.
183. This analysis is based on the thoughts of Goulemot found in "Démons, merveilles et philosophie," pp. 1223–50.
184. Countless sorceresses appeared in an auto-da-fé in Lisbon in 1714; but contrary to what had occurred in the previous century, none of them was banished to Brazil (IANTT, Inquisição de Lisboa, Processo no. 145-6-180A).
185. Bartolomé Bennassar states that the Spanish Inquisition "bequeathed the Monarchical State a homogenous people of resigned beliefs and reflections" ("Le Royaume de la conformité," in *L'Inquisition espagnole*, pp. 391–92).
186. See IANTT, Inquisição de Lisboa, Processo no. 1.894.
187. Mendonça and Moreira, *História dos principais actos*, p. 313.
188. Henry Kamen, *A Inquisição na Espanha*, trans. Leônidas Gontijo de Carvalho, p. 214.
189. Vieira cited in Mendonça and Moreira, *História dos principais actos*, pp. 383–86.
190. *Regimento do Santo Ofício da Inquisição dos Reinos de Portugal*, pp.

329–30. See also Mendonça and Moreira, *História dos principais actos*, p. 337.

191. Salvador, *Cristãos-novos, Jesuítas e Inquisição*, p. 108.

192. IANTT, Inquisição de Lisboa, Processo no. 1.131.

193. IANTT, Inquisição de Lisboa, Processo no. 1.078. This trial was brought to my attention by my friend Luiz Mott, who generously made his notes available to me.

194. Mendonça and Moreira, *História dos principais actos*, p. 329.

195. IANTT, Inquisição de Lisboa, Processo no. 9.972.

196. IANTT, Inquisição de Lisboa, Processo no. 1.131.

197. IANTT, Inquisição de Lisboa, Processo no. 8.909.

198. These autos-da-fé in Brazil took place on May 30, 1592; January 24, 1593; and early 1595, according to Gonçalves Salvador, *Cristãos-novos, Jesuítas e Inquisição*, pp. 87–88; and on January 26, 1592; August 23, 1592; January 24, 1593; August 15, 1593 (all in Bahia); October 9, 1594; September 17, 1595; and September 10, 1595 (all in Olinda), according to Siqueira, *A Inquisição portuguesa e a sociedade colonial*, pp. 298–99.

199. IANTT, Inquisição de Lisboa, Processo no. 10.748.

200. Ana Martins was "relaxed" as a sorceress in an auto-da-fé held in 1694; Francisco Barbosa, Massarelos's uncle, had his turn in 1735; and in 1744, when countless sorceresses appeared in an auto-da-fé, Mécia da Costa, known as Borrachoa, was relaxed. These are just some examples. See IANTT, Inquisição de Lisboa, Manuscritos da Livraria, no. 959.

201. IANTT, Inquisição de Lisboa, Processo no. 11.767.

202. IANTT, Inquisição de Lisboa, Processo nos. 9.972, 8.909, and 508.

203. IANTT, Inquisição de Lisboa, Processo nos. 9.972, 8.909, 508, 1.131, and 1.377.

204. Wiznitzer, *Os judeus no Brasil colonial*, p. 26.

205. Salvador, *Cristãos-novos, Jesuítas e Inquisição*, pp. 81–82.

206. See, among others, Bennassar, "L'Inquisition, ou la pédagogie de la peur," in *L'Inquisition espagnole*, p. 122.

207. Almeida, *História da igreja em Portugal*, vol. 2, p. 426 (emphasis added).

208. Siqueira, *A Inquisição portuguesa e a sociedade colonial*, p. 297 (emphasis added).

209. D. Luís da Cunha, *Testamento político*, preface and notes by Manuel Mendes, p. 75: "And may Your Highness be certain that whenever there is a private tribunal to punish certain crimes, criminals will always be found." See also Cavaleiro de Oliveira, *Opúsculos contra o Santo Ofício*, ed. A. Gonçalves Rodrigues.

210. "Might it be because there were no men with the strength of mind to accompany the impetus of *quinhentismo* [the sixteenth-century universe of ideas]. Unlikely. The reason is otherwise, and we must seek it in another light: in the light of the bonfires of the Inquisition" (Antonio Sérgio, "O Reino Cadaveroso, ou o problema da cultura em Portugal," in *Ensaios II*, p. 42).

211. "The European myth of the witch . . . finds no strict equivalence in our country. If the inquisitors reveal an awareness of the myth in their interrogations of prisoners, . . . the accused very rarely confess to their attendance at sabbats (and even then, one of the constituent elements of the myth—the night-flight—is generally missing), and not often do they confess to a pact, although they frequently mention communication with the demon and with souls" (Bethencourt,

"Campo religioso e Inquisição em Portugal no século XVI," p. 5).

212. IANTT, Inquisição de Lisboa, Processo no. 1.377; and ANTT, Inquisição de Évora, m° 803, no. 7.759.

Chapter 8. Remarkable Stories: Where Their Roads Led

1. Quotations from Ginzburg, *Le fromage et les vers,* pp. 15–16; *The Cheese and the Worms,* preface, p. xx.

2. On Maria Barbosa, see IANTT, Inquisição de Lisboa, Processo no. 3.382.

3. Anita Novinsky, *Cristãos-novos na Bahia,* p. 111.

4. IANTT, Inquisição de Lisboa, Processo no. 10.181.

5. Ibid. (emphasis added).

6. Ibid. (emphasis added).

7. Ibid. (emphasis added).

8. IANTT, Inquisição de Lisboa, Processo no. 11.163.

9. In *De vita sua,* Guibert of Nogent says that his mother remained a virgin for seven years after her wedding due to *maleficia* performed by her mother-in-law. See Giordano, *Religiosidad popular en la Alta Edad Media,* p. 203.

10. See, among others, Le Roy Ladurie, *La sorcière de Jasmin,* p. 30. The sorceress always increases her strength and wealth at the cost of others and has the power to destroy crops and livestock.

11. The savagery with which masters treated their slaves was proven once more when the historian Luiz Mott discovered a remarkable document at the Arquivo Nacional in Lisbon's Torre do Tombo entitled "A tortura dos escravos na Casa da Torre: Um documento inédito dos Arquivos da Inquisição."

12. IANTT, Inquisição de Lisboa, Processo no. 11.163 (emphasis added).

13. Ibid. (emphasis added).

14. IANTT, Inquisição de Lisboa, Processo no. 252, m° 26.

15. Ibid. (emphasis added); Bastide, *Les religions africaines au Brésil,* pp. 185–86; *The African Religions of Brazil,* pp. 133–34.

16. IANTT, Inquisição de Lisboa, Processo no. 252, m° 26 (emphasis added).

17. IANTT, Inquisição de Lisboa, Processo no. 4.684.

18. For people in medieval Europe, the communion wafer held supernatural powers. In the eleventh century, peasants would bury consecrated hosts in the ground in order to increase its fertility. See Vauchez, *La spiritualité du Moyen-Âge occidental,* p. 18; *Spirituality of the Medieval West,* p. 19.

19. IANTT, Inquisição de Lisboa, Processo no. 1.894.

20. Ibid. (emphasis added).

21. Questions might include whether the person was Catholic, baptized and confirmed, knew the sacraments, and so on. Responses were considered part of the deponent's confession.

22. Ibid. (emphasis added).

23. Ibid. (emphasis added).

24. Ibid. (emphasis added).

25. When he presented himself before the Holy Office in 1763, Crescêncio Escobar believed that Adrião was already residing in Maranhão: "and at present he does not know where he lives, and has only heard it said that he lives in the city of Maranhão, where he had gone after being given penance by the Holy Office" (*Livro da Visitação: Estado do Grão-Pará,* p. 130).

Glossary

abjuração de levi; in forma; de vehementi: When an accused was given penance by the Inquisition, she or he had to swear that the error would not be repeated. Abjuration *de levi* was applicable in the case of minor offenses, followed by *in forma* and the more serious *de vehementi*. One who had abjured *de vehmenti* ran the risk of much harsher punishment if charged a second time.

arraial (plural *arraiais*): 1. A settlement that lacked either civil or ecclesiastical independence, with no Municipal Council or independent parish. 2. A fortified camp.

atabaque: An Afro-Brazilian percussion instrument.

auditor-geral: An official who conducted quarterly inquiries and reported any misuse of war prizes to the military's general accounting office in Portugal.

auto-da-fé: A public ceremony where those tried by the Inquisition heard their sentences read; those condemned to the stake were handed over to the secular power, which would carry out the sentence as part of the ceremony.

beata: A woman devoted to religious life, but not necessarily a member of any official order.

bentinhos: Scapulars, or small cloth squares with religious images worn on a ribbon around the neck.

bolsa de mandinga: See "mandinga."

caboclo/cabocla: 1. A male/female of mixed indigenous and white blood. 2. A peasant from northern or northeastern Brazil, usually with copper-colored skin.

cafuzo/cafuza: A male/female of mixed indigenous and black blood.

calundu: These ceremonies were in a certain way the colonial precursors of today's Afro-Brazilian Candomblé.

calunduzeiro/calunduzeira: Man/woman who performs *calundu* rites.

Candomblé: 1. A syncretic Afro-Brazilian religion originating in Bahia; its gods, the *orixás,* trace their roots to Yoruba deities. 2. The ceremonies practiced by this religion.

capitães-do-mato: Mercenaries hired to capture runaway slaves.

cartas de tocar (**"touch-letters"**): Probably specific only to colonial Brazil, these love charms were a kind of magical writing that achieved their effect when touched against the desired man or woman.

catimbós: Indigenous rituals of possession and sorcery.

Commissary: Someone (quite often a parish priest) who provided the Inquisition with information or other forms of assistance.

confraria: 1. A religious brotherhood. 2. A civil association organized around common professional or social interests.

converso: A Christian convert originally of Muslim or sometimes Jewish faith or one of the convert's descendants.

Coura: The Coura people (known as *courá, courano, curá, curano,* and by other terms, primarily in eighteenth-century Minas) were Sudanese, neighbors to the Minas, and from all indications belonged to the Yoruba language group.

couto: An outlying area where criminals and heretics were sent to live after their trial.

crioulo/crioula: Until the late nineteenth century, this term did not connote only skin color but designated a slave who had been born in Brazil.

Devassa: An inquiry conducted by a Brazilian bishopric to ascertain whether both clergy and faithful were following church doctrine (determined by the Council of Trent).

encarochado/encarochada: Forced to wear a conical pasteboard hat as a form of punishment, usually with writing labeling the convicted person a sorcerer or sorceress.

engenho: A sugar plantation.

Familiar: A lay official in service to the Holy Office of the Inquisition.

fazenda: 1. A cattle ranch. 2. A large farm.

fazendeiro/fazendeira: 1. A rancher. 2. A farmer who owns a relatively large estate.

Inconfidência Mineira: Late-eighteenth-century uprising in Minas Gerais.

mameluco/mameluca: A male/female of mixed white and indigenous blood.

mandinga or *bolsa de mandinga* (**mandinga pouch**): Small bag of cloth or leather containing bits of paper with prayers written on them, worn about the neck on a chain or ribbon as a powerful form of protection.

mandingueiro/mandingueira: One who made mandinga pouches.

Mina: A slave originally from the Mina coast of west Africa.

mocambo: 1. Another term for *quilombo,* i.e., a settlement of runaway slaves. 2. A hut within the settlement.

mulato/mulata: A male/female of mixed black and white blood.

orixá: A Candomblé deity.

ouvidor: An appellate judge.

pajé: An indigenous "priest" or healer.

pardo/parda: A male/female of mixed black and white blood.

quilombo: A settlement of runaway slaves.

relaxed: Since the Inquisition had no power to carry out executions, those condemned to the stake were "relaxed," or handed over to civil authorities, who would carry out the sentence.

sanbenito: A penitential robe worn as part of an inquisitional sentence, as a mark of infamy.

sertão (**plural** *sertões*): The sparsely populated Brazilian backlands; wilderness.

Sources and Bibliography

1. Archives

1.1. Arquivo Eclesiástico da Arquidiocese de Mariana, Minas Gerais

Devassas—1721–1735.
Livro de Devassas—Comarca do Serro do Frio, 1734.
Devassas—1747–1748.
Devassas—maio–dezembro 1753.
Devassas—1756–1757.
Devassas—julho 1762–dezembro 1769.
Devassas—janeiro 1767–maio 1778.
Devassas—7 janeiro 1767–1777.

1.2. Arquivo Geral da Cidade do Rio de Janeiro, Rio de Janeiro

Autos de um processo, 45-1-15.

1.3. Arquivo Nacional da Torre do Tombo, Lisbon

1.3.1. Inquisition at Coimbra

Processos nos. 08 4.501; 4.912; 5.723; 6.823.

1.3.2. Inquisition at Évora

Processo—mº 803, no. 7.759.

1.3.3. Inquisition at Lisbon

Caderno do Promotor no. 126.
mº 27-20, Novos Maços.
Lists of Autos da Fé: *Novos Maços, mº 6-1; Novos Maços, mº 5-4; Manuscritos da Livraria, no. 732; Manuscritos da Livraria, no. 959; Livros 144-2-41; Livros 145-6-180A; 159/6/862; 149-6-671.*

Processos nos 74; 210; 212; 213; 218; 252, m° 26; 254; 437; 508; 557; 631; 834; 1.063; 1.078; 1.131; 1.134; 1.377; 1.562; 1.565; 1.894; 2.289; 2.691; 2.696; 2.697; 2.701; 2.702; 2.704; 2.705; 2.706; 3.382; 3.723; 4.491; 4.684; 4.744; 4.964; 5.180; 6.005; 6.308; 7.020; 7.095; 7.579; 7.611; 7.840; 8.909; 9.972; 10.181; 10.748; 11.163; 11.242; 11.358; 11.767; 11.774; 12.616; 12.925; 15.559; 16.348; 16.722; 17.771.

2. Printed Sources

2.1. Laws and Instructions

Código Filipino ou ordenações e leis do Reino de Portugal. 14th ed. Ed. Cândido Mendes de Almeida. 3 vols. Rio de Janeiro: Tipografia do Instituto Filomático, 1870.

Eymeric, Nicolas, and Francisco Peña. *Le manuel des inquisiteurs.* Intro., trans., and notes by Louis Sala-Molins. Paris: Mouton, 1973.

Regimento do Santo Ofício da Inquisição dos Reinos de Portugal, 1640. Mimeo.

2.2. Published Correspondence and Other Documents

Baião, Antonio. "A Inquisição no Brasil—Extractos d'alguns livros de denúncias." *Revista de História* (Sociedade Portuguesa de Estudos Históricos, Lisbon) 1 (January–March 1912).

Leite, Serafim. "Antonio Rodrigues, soldado, viajante e jesuíta português na América do Sul." *Anais da Biblioteca Nacional do Rio de Janeiro* 49 (1927).

———, ed. *Novas cartas jesuíticas: De Nóbrega a Vieira.* São Paulo: Companhia Editora Nacional, 1940.

Mendonça, Marcos Carneiro de, ed. *A Amazônia na era Pombalina: Correspondência inédita do governador e capitão-general do Estado do Grão-Pará e Maranhão Francisco Xavier de Mendonça Furtado, 1751–1759.* 3 vols. N.p.: Instituto Histórico e Geográfico Brasileiro, 1963.

Novinsky, Anita. *Inquisição—Inventário de bens confiscados a cristãos-novos.* Lisbon: Imprensa Nacional Casa da Moeda Livraria Camões, n.d.

Rego, Yvonne Cunha, ed. *Feiticeiros, profetas, visionários: Textos antigos portugueses.* Lisbon: Imprensa Nacional–Casa da Moeda, 1981.

2.3. Visitations of the Holy Office

Livro da Visitação do Santo Ofício da Inquisição ao Estado do Grão-Pará, 1763– 1769. Intro. by José Roberto Amaral Lapa. Petrópolis: Vozes, 1978.

Primeira Visitação do Santo Ofício às partes do Brasil: Confissões de Pernambuco. Ed. J. A. Gonsalves de Mello. Recife: Universidade Federal de Pernambuco, 1970.

Primeira Visitação do Santo Ofício às partes do Brasil pelo licenciado Heitor Furtado de Mendonça—Confissões da Bahia, 1591–1592. Preface by Capistrano de Abreu. Rio de Janeiro: F. Briguiet, 1935.

Primeira Visitação do Santo Ofício às partes do Brasil pelo licenciado Heitor Furtado de Mendonça—Denunciações da Bahia, 1591–1593. Intro. by Capistrano de Abreu. São Paulo: Editora Paulo Prado, 1925.

Primeira Visitação do Santo Ofício às partes do Brasil pelo licenciado Heitor Furtado de Mendonça—Denunciações de Pernambuco, 1593–1595. Intro. by Rodolfo Garcia. São Paulo: Editora Paulo Prado, 1929.

Segunda Visitação do Santo Ofício às partes do Brasil: Denunciações da Bahia (1618—Marcos Teixeira). Intro. by. Rodolfo Garcia. *Anais da Biblioteca Nacional do Rio de Janeiro* 49 (1927).

Segunda Visitação do Santo Ofício às partes do Brasil pelo inquisidor e visitador o licenciado Marcos Teixeira: Livro das confissões e ratificações da Bahia, 1618–1620. Intro. by Eduardo d'Oliveira França and Sônia A. Siqueira. *Anais do Museu Paulista* 17 (1963).

2.4. Chroniclers, Demonologists, and Others

Abbeville, Claude d'. *História da missão dos padres capuchinhos na ilha do Maranhão.* Trans. Sergio Millet. São Paulo: Martins, n.d.

Antonil, André João. *Cultura e opulência do Brasil por suas drogas e minas* (1711). Intro. and notes by Alice P. Canabrava. São Paulo: Companhia Editora Nacional, n.d.

Ávila, Afonso. *Resíduos seiscentistas em Minas: Textos do século do ouro e as projeções do mundo barroco.* Belo Horizonte: Universidade Federal de Minas Gerais/Centro de Estudos Mineiros, 1967.

Barleus, Gaspar. *História dos feitos recentemente praticados durante oito anos no Brasil e noutras partes sob o governo do ilustríssimo João Maurício Conde de Nassau, etc.* Trans. Cláudio Brandão. Rio de Janeiro: Ministério da Educação, 1940.

Benci, Jorge. *Economia cristã dos senhores no governo dos escravos* (1700). São Paulo: Grijalbo, 1977.

Brandão, Ambrósio Fernandes. *Diálogo das grandezas do Brasil* (1618). Rio de Janeiro: Dois Mundos Editora, n.d.

Cardim, Pe. Fernão. *Tratados da terra e gente do Brasil.* 3rd ed. São Paulo: Companhia Editora Nacional/MEC, 1978.

Columbus, Christopher. *La découverte de l'Amérique: I. Journal de bord—1492–1493.* Paris: Maspero, 1980.

Cunha, D. Luís da. *Testamento político.* Preface and notes by Manuel Mendes. Lisbon: Seara Nova, 1943.

Deus, Friar Gaspar da Madre de. *Memórias para a história da Capitania de São Vicente.* 3rd ed. Intro. and notes by Affonso E. Taunay. São Paulo–Rio de Janeiro: Weisflog Irmãos, 1920.

Gandavo, Pero de Magalhães. *História da Província de Santa Cruz* (1576). Rio de Janeiro: Ed. Anuário do Brasil, n.d.

———. *Tratado da Terra do Brasil.* Rio de Janeiro: Ed. Anuário do Brasil, n.d.

Jaboatão, Antonio de Santa Maria. *Novo orbe seráfico brasílico ou Crônica dos frades menores da Província do Brasil* (1761). Rio de Janeiro: Tipografia Brasiliense de Maximiano Gomes Ribeiro, 1858.

Knivet, Anthony. "The Admirable Adventures and Strange Fortunes of Master Anthonie Knivet, Which Went with Master Thomas Ca[ve]ndish in His Second Voyage to the South Sea, 1591." In Samuel Purchas, *Hakluytus Posthumus or Purchas His Pilgrimes: Containing a History of the World in Sea Voyages and Lande Travells by Englishmen and Others, Vol. 16.* Glasgow: James MacLehose and Sons, 1906.

———. *Vária fortuna e estranhos fados de Anthony Knivet, que foi com Tomás Cavendish, em sua segunda viagem, para o Mar do Sul, no ano de 1591*. Trans. Guiomar de Carvalho Franco. São Paulo: Brasiliense, 1947.

Kramer, Heinrich, and James Sprenger. *Malleus Maleficarum*. Trans. Montague Summers. London: Arrow Books, 1978.

Léry, Jean de. *Histoire d'un voyage faict en la terre du Brésil*. 2 vols. Intro. and notes by Paul Gaffarel. Paris: Alphonse Lemerre Editeur, 1880.

———. *History of a Voyage to the Land of Brazil*. Trans. and intro. by Janet Whatley. Berkeley: University of California Press, 1992.

Molitor, Ulrico. *De las brujas y adivinas*. Trans. Buenos Aires: Editorial Jorge Alvarez. S.A., n.d.

Montaigne, Michel de. *Essais*. Notes and text established by Albert Thibaudet. Éditions de la Nouvelle Revue Française. Paris: Bibliothèque de la Pléiade, 1946.

Nóbrega, Manuel da. *Diálogo sobre a conversão do gentio*. Intro. and notes by Pe. Serafim Leite. Lisbon: Edição Comemorativa do IV Centenário da Fundação de São Paulo, 1954.

A Nova Gazeta Alemã—O valor etnográfico da Newen zeytung Auss Presillo Landt. Ed. Joaquim Ribeiro. Rio de Janeiro: Record, n.d.

Oliveira, Cavaleiro de. *Opúsculos contra o Santo Ofício*. Ed. A. Gonçalves Rodrigues. Coimbra: Fundo Sá Pinto da Universidade de Coimbra, 1942.

Pereira, Nuno Marques. *Compêndio narrativo do peregrino da América* (1728). 6th ed. Rio de Janeiro: Publicação da Academia Brasileira, 1939.

Rocha Pitta, Sebastião da. *História da América Portuguesa desde o ano de mil e quinhentos do seu descobrimento até o de mil e setecentos e vinte e quatro* (1730). Lisbon: Editor Francisco Artur da Silva, 1880.

Salvador, Friar Vicente do. *História do Brasil—1500–1627*. 3rd ed. Revised by Capistrano de Abreu and Rodolfo Garcia. São Paulo: Melhoramentos, n.d.

Thevet, André. *Les français en Amérique pendant la deuxième moitié du XVIe siècle*. Paris: PUF, 1953.

———. *Les singularitez de la France Antarctique*. Ed. Paul Gaffarel. Paris: Maisonneuve & Cie., 1878.

Vilhena, Luís dos Santos. *Recopilação de notícias soteropolitanas e brasílicas*. Notes by Brás do Amaral. Bahia: Imprensa Oficial do Estado, 1922.

3. Bibliography

Abreu, Capistrano de. *O descobrimento do Brasil pelos portugueses*. Rio de Janeiro: Laemmert & Co., 1900.

———. *Ensaios e estudos (Crítica e história)*. 3rd series. Rio de Janeiro: Briguiet, 1938.

Alberro, Solange Behocary. "Inquisition et société: Rivalités de pouvoirs à Tepeaca (1656–1660)." *Annales, E.S.C.*, 36th year, no. 5 (September–October 1981): 758–84.

Algranti, Leila Mezan. "O feitor ausente: Estudo sobre a escravidão urbana no Rio de Janeiro (1808–1821)." Master's thesis, Universidade de São Paulo, São Paulo, Brazil, 1983.

Almeida, Fortunato de. *História da igreja em Portugal*. Ed. Damião Peres. Porto: Portucalense Editora, 1967.

Andrieux, Maurice. *La vie quotidienne dans la Rome Pontificale au XVIIIe siècle*.

Paris: Hachette, 1962.

Ariès, Philippe. *Essais sur l'histoire de la mort en Occident: Du Moyen-Âge à nos jours*. Paris: Seuil, 1975.

Azevedo, João Lúcio de. *História dos cristãos-novos portugueses*. Lisbon: Livraria Clássica Editora, 1921.

Bakhtin, Mikail. *L'oeuvre de François Rabelais et la culture populaire au Moyen-Âge et sous la Renaissance*. Trans. A. Robel. Paris: Gallimard, 1970.

Balandier, Georges. *La vie quotidienne au Royaume du Kongo du XVIe au XVIIIe siècle*. Paris: Hachette, n.d.

Barbosa, Waldemar de Almeida. *Negros e quilombos em Minas Gerais*. Belo Horizonte: n.p., 1972.

Bastide, Roger. *The African Religions of Brazil: Toward a Sociology of the Interpenetration of Civilizations*. Trans. Helen Sebba. Baltimore/London: Johns Hopkins University Press, 1978.

————. *Les religions africaines au Brésil: Vers une sociologie des interprétations de civilisations*. Paris: PUF, 1960.

Bazin, Germain, et al. *Satan*. Études Carmelitaines series. N.p.: Desclée de Brower, 1948.

Bennassar, Bartolomé. *L'Inquisition espagnole*. Paris: Hachette, 1979.

Bethencourt, Francisco. "Astrologia e sociedade no século XVI: Uma primeira abordagem." Reprint from *Revista de História Econômica e Social* (Lisbon) (1982).

————. "Campo religioso e Inquisição em Portugal no século XVI." Paper presented at "Seminário sobre religiosidade popular," Porto, Lisbon, 1983.

Bloch, Marc. *Les rois thaumaturges*. Paris: Armand Colin, 1961.

Bonney, Françoise. "Autour de Jean Gerson: Opinions de théologiens sur les superstitions et la sorcellerie au début du XVe siècle." *Le Moyen-Age—Revue d'Histoire et de Philologie* 72, 4th series, 26, no. 1 (1971).

Bossy, John. "The Counter-Reformation and the People of Catholic Europe." *Past and Present* 47 (May 1970).

Boxer, Charles R. *The Church Militant and Iberian Expansion, 1440–1770*. Baltimore/London: Johns Hopkins University Press, 1978.

————. *A igreja e a expansão ibérica—1440–1770*. Trans. Lisbon: Edições 70, 1981.

Boyer, Paul, and Stephen Nissenbaum. *Salem Possessed: The Social Origins of Witchcraft*. Cambridge, Mass.: Harvard University Press, 1974.

Brouette, Émile. "La civilisation chrétienne du XVIe siècle devant le problème satanique." In Germain Bazin et al., *Satan*. Études Carmelitaines series. N.p.: Desclée de Brower, 1948.

Buarque de Holanda, Sérgio. *Visão do Paraíso: Os motivos edênicos no descobrimento e colonização do Brasil*. 2nd ed. São Paulo: Companhia Editora Nacional, 1969.

Cardini, Franco. *Magia, stregoneria, superstizioni nell'Occidente medievale*. Florence: La Nuova Italia Editrice, 1979.

Caro Baroja, Julio. *Algunos mitos españoles*. 3rd ed. Madrid: Ediciones del Centro, 1974.

————. *Inquisición, brujería y criptojudaísmo*. 3rd ed. Barcelona: Ariel, 1974.

————. *Ritos y mitos equívocos*. Madrid: Ediciones Istmo, 1974.

————. *Les sorcières et leur monde*. Trans. M. A. Sarrailh. Paris: Gallimard, 1972.

————. *The World of the Witches*. Trans. Nigel Glendinning. London: Phoenix Press, 2001.

Carrato, José Ferreira. *Igreja, iluminismo e escolas mineiras coloniais.* São Paulo: Companhia Editora Nacional, 1968.

Certeau, Michel de. *L'Écriture de l'histoire.* Paris: Gallimard, 1975.

———. *La possession de Loudun.* Paris: Julliard, 1970.

Chantal, Suzanne. *A vida quotidiana em Portugal ao tempo do terremoto.* Trans. Lisbon: Edição Livros do Brasil, n.d.

Cohn, Norman. *Los demonios familiares de Europa.* Trans. Madrid: Alianza, 1975.

———. *Europe's Inner Demons: The Demonization of Christians in Medieval Christendom* (1973). Rev. ed. Chicago: University of Chicago Press, 1993.

Contreras, Jaime. *El Santo Ofício de la Inquisición de Galícia: Poder, sociedad y cultura.* Madrid: Akal, 1982.

Costa, Emília Viotti da. "Primeiros povoadores do Brasil." *Revista de História* (São Paulo) 13, no. 17 (1956).

Dantas, Júlio. *O amor em Portugal no século XVIII.* Lisbon: Sociedade Editora Artur Brandão e Cia., n.d.

Delumeau, Jean. *Catholicism between Luther and Voltaire: A New View of the Counter-Reformation.* Trans. Jeremy Moiser. London: Burns & Oates; Philadelphia: Westminster Press, 1977.

———. *Le catholicisme entre Luther et Voltaire.* Paris: PUF, 1971.

———. *Un chemin d'histoire: Chrétienté et christianisation.* Paris: Fayard, 1981.

———. *A civilização do Renascimento.* 2 vols. Trans. Lisbon: Imprensa Universitária, 1984.

———. *Naissance et affirmation de la Réforme.* Paris: PUF, 1968.

———. *Le péché et la peur: La culpabilisation en Occident—XIII*ᵉ*–XVIII*ᵉ *siècles.* Paris: Fayard, 1983.

———. *La peur en Occident, XIV*ᵉ*–XVIII*ᵉ *siècles.* Paris: Fayard, 1978.

———. *Sin and Fear: The Emergence of a Western Guilt Culture, 13th–18th Centuries.* Trans. Eric Nicholson. New York: St. Martin's Press, 1990.

———, ed. *La mort des Pays de Cocagne: Comportements collectifs de la Renaissance à l'âge classique.* Paris: Publications de la Sorbonne, 1976.

Dupont-Bouchat, Marie-Sylvie. "La répression de la sorcellerie dans le duché de Luxembourg au XVIᵉ et XVIIᵉ siècles." In Marie-Sylvie Dupont-Bouchat, Willem Frijhoff, and Robert Muchembled, *Prophètes et sorciers dans les Pays-Bas, XVI*ᵉ*–XVIII*ᵉ *siècles.* Paris: Hachette, 1978.

Duviols, Pierre. *La lutte contre les religions autochtones dans le Pérou colonial: L'extirpation de l'idolatrie entre 1532 et 1660.* Paris: Institut Français d'Études Andines, 1971.

Éliade, Mircea. *Occultisme, sorcellerie et modes culturelles.* Paris: Gallimard, 1978.

Elliott, John Huxtable. *The Old World and the New: 1492–1650.* London: Cambridge University Press, 1972.

Erlanger, Philippe. *La vie quotidienne sous Henri IV.* Paris: Hachette, 1958.

Evans-Pritchard, Edward. *Witchcraft, Oracles and Magic among the Azande.* London: Oxford University Press, 1950.

Febvre, Lucien. "O homem do século XVI." *Revista de História* 1 (1950).

———. *Le problème de l'incroyance au XVI*ᵉ *siècle: La religion de Rabelais.* Paris: Albin Michel, 1947.

———. "Sorcellerie, sottise ou révolution mentale?" *Annales, E.S.C.,* year 3, no. 1 (January–March 1948).

Fernandes, Gonçalves. *O folclore mágico do Nordeste: Usos, costumes, crenças e ofícios mágicos das populações nordestinas*. Rio de Janeiro: Civilização Brasileira, 1938.

Figueiredo, Luciano Raposo de Almeida. "O avesso da memória: Estudo do papel, participação e condição social da mulher no século XVIII mineiro." Final research report for Fundação Carlos Chagas, Rio de Janeiro, May 1984.

Foucault, Michel. *Histoire de la folie à l'Âge Classique*. Paris: Gallimard, 1972.

———. *Histoire de la sexualité, 1: La volonté de savoir*. Paris: Gallimard, 1976.

———. *The History of Sexuality, Volume 1: An Introduction*. Trans. Robert Hurley. New York: Vintage Books, 1990.

———. *Madness and Civilization: A History of Insanity in the Age of Reason*. Trans. Richard Howard. New York: Vintage Books, 1988.

Freyre, Gilberto. *Casa Grande e Senzala: Formação da família brasileira sob regime de economia patriarcal*. 9th ed. 2 vols. Rio de Janeiro: José Olympio, 1958.

———. *The Masters and the Slaves: A Study in the Development of Brazilian Civilization*. Trans. Samuel Putnam. New York: Alfred A. Knopf, 1966.

García Cárcel, Ricardo. *Herejía y sociedad en el siglo XVI: La Inquisición de Valencia, 1530–1609*. Barcelona: Península, 1980.

Garçon, Maurice, and Jean Vinchon. *Le diable: Étude historique, critique et médicale*. Paris: Gallimard, 1926.

Gatto, Giuseppe. "Le voyage au Paradis: La christianisation des traditions folkloriques au Moyen-Âge." *Annales, E.S.C.*, 34th year, no. 5 (September–October 1979).

Gerbi, Antonello. *La disputa del nuevo mundo: Historia de una polémica, 1750–1900* (1955). Trans. A. Alatorre. Mexico City/Buenos Aires: Fondo de Cultura Económica, 1960.

Ginzburg, Carlo. *I Benandanti: Stregoneria i culti agrari tra Cinquecento e Seicento*. 3rd ed. Torino: Piccola-Biblioteca Einaudi, 1966.

———. *The Cheese and the Worms: The Cosmos of a Sixteenth-Century Miller*. Trans. John Tedeschi and Anne Tedeschi. Baltimore: Johns Hopkins University Press, 1992.

———. *Le fromage et les vers: L'univers d'un meunier au XVIe siècle*. Paris: Flammarion, 1980.

———. "Présomptions sur le sabbat." *Annales, E.S.C.*, 39th year, no. 2 (March–April 1984): 341–354.

Giordano, Oronzo. *Religiosidad popular en la Alta Edad Media*. Trans. Madrid: Editorial Gredos, 1983.

Gonçalves Salvador, José. *Cristãos-novos, Jesuítas e Inquisição*. São Paulo: Pioneira-Edusp, 1969.

Goulemot, Jean-Marie. "Démons, merveilles et philosophie à l'Âge Classique." *Annales, E.S.C.*, 35th year, no. 6 (November–December 1980).

Grande livro de São Cipriano ou Tesouros do feiticeiro. Lisbon: Edições Afrodite, 1971.

Guiraud, Jean. *L'Inquisition médiévale*. Paris: Jules Tallandier, 1978.

Gurevich, Aaron J. "Au Moyen-Âge: Conscience individuelle et image de l'au-delà." *Annales, E.S.C.*, 37th year, no. 2 (March–April 1982).

Hansen, Chadwick. *Sorcellerie à Salem*. Trans. Paris: Denoël, 1972.

———. *Witchcraft at Salem*. New York: G. Braziller, 1969.

Hauser, Arnold. *História social da literatura e da arte*. São Paulo: Mestre Jou, 1972.

Henningsen, Gustav. *El abogado de las brujas: Brujería vasca y Inquisición española*. Trans. Marisa Ray-Henningsen. Madrid: Alianza Editorial, 1983.

L'Historien entre l'éthnologue et le futurologue. Actes du séminaire international organisé sous les auspices de l'Association Internationale pour la Liberté de la Culture, la Fondation Giovanni Agnelli et la Fondation Giorgio Cini, Venice, Italy, April 2–8, 1971. Paris: Mouton, 1972.

Hobsbawm, Eric J. *En torno a los orígenes de la revolución industrial.* Trans. 2nd ed. Buenos Aires: Siglo XXI, 1971.

Hoornaert, Eduardo. *A igreja no Brasil Colônia, 1550–1800.* São Paulo: Brasiliense, 1982.

Hoornaert, Eduardo, Riolando Azzi, Klaus Van Der Grijp, and Benno Brod, eds. *História da igreja no Brasil: Primeira época.* Vol. 2. 2nd ed. Petrópolis: Vozes, 1979.

Kamen, Henry. *A Inquisição na Espanha.* Trans. Leônidas Gontijo de Carvalho. Rio de Janeiro: Civilização Brasileira, 1966.

Kappler, Claude. *Monstres, démons et merveilles à la fin du Moyen-Âge.* Paris: Payot, 1980.

Lafaye, Jacques. *Quetzacóatl et Guadalupe: La formation de la conscience nationale au Méxique.* Paris: Gallimard, 1974.

Lanciani, Giulia. *Os relatos de naufrágios na literatura portuguesa dos séculos XVI e XVII.* Lisbon: Instituto de Cultura Portuguesa, 1979.

Lancre, Pierre De. *Tableau de l'inconstance des mauvais anges.* Paris, 1612.

Lara, Sílvia Hunold. "Campos da violência." Dissertation, Universidade de São Paulo, São Paulo, Brazil, 1986.

Larivaille, Paul. *La vie quotidienne des courtisanes en Italie au temps de la Renaissance.* Paris: Hachette, 1975.

Lebrun, François. *Médecins, saints et sorciers au XVIIe et XVIIIe siècles.* Paris: Temps Actuels, 1983.

Lecouteux, Claude. "Paganisme, christianisme et merveilleux." *Annales, E.S.C.* 37th year, no. 4 (July–August 1982).

Le Goff, Jacques. *La naissance du Purgatoire.* Paris: Gallimard, 1981.

———. *Pour un autre Moyen-Âge: Temps, travail et culture en Occident.* Paris: Gallimard, 1977.

———. *Time, Work, and Culture in the Middle Ages.* Trans. Arthur Goldhammer. Chicago: University of Chicago Press, 1982.

Le Roy Ladurie, Emmanuel. *Montaillou: The Promised Land of Error.* Trans. Barbara Bray. New York: Vintage Books, 1979.

———. *Montaillou, village occitan, de 1294 à 1324.* Paris: Gallimard, 1975.

———. *La sorcière de Jasmin.* Paris: Seuil, 1983.

Lisón-Tolosana, Carmelo. *Brujería, estructura social y simbolismo en Galícia.* Madrid: Akal, 1983.

Lobo, A. de Souza Silva Costa. *História da sociedade em Portugal no século XV.* Lisbon: Imprensa Nacional, 1903.

Londoño, Fernando Torres. "O crime do amor." In Maria Angela d'Incao, ed., *Amor e família no Brasil.* São Paulo: Contexto, 1989.

———. *A outra família: Concubinato, igreja e escândalo na colônia.* São Paulo: Edições Loyola, 1999.

Luna, Francisco Vidal, and Iraci del Nero da Costa. *Minas colonial: Economia e sociedade.* São Paulo: FIPE-Pioneira, 1982.

Malheiro Dias, Carlos, ed. *História da colonização portuguesa do Brasil.* 4 vols. Porto: Litografia Nacional, 1923.

Malinowski, B. *Los argonautas del Pacífico Occidental.* 2nd ed. Trans. Barcelona: Península, 1975.

———. *La vie sexuelle des sauvages du Nord-Ouest de la Mélanésie.* Trans. Dr. S. Jankelevitch. Paris: Payot, 1930.

Mandrou, Robert. *De la culture populaire en France aux XVIIe et XVIIIe siècles.* Paris: Stock, 1964.

———. *Introduction à la France Moderne—1500–1640.* Paris: Albin-Michel, 1974.

———. *Magistrats et sorciers en France au XVIIe siècle.* Paris: Plon, 1968.

———. *Possession et sorcellerie au XVIIe siècle: Textes inédits.* Paris: Fayard, 1979.

Manselli, Raoul. *La religion populaire au Moyen-Âge: Problèmes de méthode et d'histoire.* Montreal-Paris: Publications de l'Institut d'Études Mediévales Albert le Grand, 1975.

Marques, A. H. de Oliveira. *Daily Life in Portugal in the Late Middle Ages.* Trans. S. S. Wyatt. Madison: University of Wisconsin Press, 1971.

———. *A sociedade medieval portuguesa.* 4th ed. Lisbon: Sá da Costa, 1981.

Mendonça, José Lourenço D. de, and Antonio Joaquim Moreira. *História dos principais actos e procedimentos da Inquisição em Portugal.* Lisbon: Imprensa Nacional–Casa da Moeda, 1980.

Métraux, A. *A religião dos Tupinambás.* Trans. Estévão Pinto São Paulo: Companhia Editora Nacional, 1950.

Michelet, Jules. *La sorcière.* Paris: Garnier-Flammarion, 1976.

Mott, Luiz. "Acotundá: Raízes setecentistas do sincretismo religioso afro-brasileiro." 1985. Mimeo.

———. "Etno-demonologia: Aspectos da vida sexual do diabo no mundo ibero-americano (séculos XVI ao XVIII)." Paper presented at the 14th Meeting of the Associação Brasileira de Antropologia.

———. "Os pecados da família na Bahia de Todos os Santos." *Centro de Estudos Baianos* (Salvador) (1972).

———. "A tortura dos escravos na Casa da Torre: Um documento inédito dos Arquivos da Inquisição." Paper presented at SECNB: Sociedade de Estudos da Cultura Negra do Brasil, Salvador, Bahia, Brazil, April 9–15, 1984.

Muchembled, Robert. "L'autre côté du miroir: Mythes sataniques et réalités culturelles aux XVIe et XVIIe siècles." *Annales, E.S.C.,* 40th year, no. 2 (March–April 1985).

———. *Culture populaire et culture des élites (XVe–XVIIIe siècles).* Paris: Flammarion, n.d.

———. "Satan ou les hommes?: La chasse aux sorcières et ses causes." In Marie-Sylvie Dupont-Bouchat, Willem Frijhoff, and Robert Muchembled, *Prophètes et sorciers dans les Pays-Bas, XVIe–XVIIIe siècles.* Paris: Hachette, 1978.

———. "Sorcellerie, culture populaire et christianisme." *Annales, E.S.C.,* 28th year, no. 1 (January–February 1973).

———. "Sorcières du Cambrésis: L'acculturation du monde rural aux XVIe et XVIIe siècles." In Marie-Sylvie Dupont-Bouchat, Willem Frijhoff, and Robert Muchembled, *Prophètes et sorciers dans les Pays-Bas, XVIe–XVIIIe siècles.* Paris: Hachette, 1978.

Murray, Margareth. *El culto de la brujería en Europa Occidental.* Trans. Barcelona: Labor, 1978.

Neves, Luís Filipe Baeta. *O combate dos soldados de Cristo na terra dos papagaios: Colonialismo e repressão cultural.* Rio de Janeiro: Forense-Universitária, 1978.

Nogueira, Carlos Roberto Figueiredo. "Universo mágico e realidade: Aspectos de um contexto cultural (Castela na modernidade)." Dissertation, Universidade de São Paulo, São Paulo, Brazil, 1980.

Novais, Fernando A. *Portugal e Brasil na crise do antigo sistema colonial, 1777–1808.* São Paulo: Hucitec, 1979.

Novinsky, Anita. *Cristãos-novos na Bahia, 1624–1654.* São Paulo: Perspectiva, 1972.

Panofsky, Erwin. *Essais d'iconologie: Les thèmes humanistes dans l'art de la Renaissance.* Trans. Paris: PUF, 1967.

Park, Katharine, and Lorraine J. Daston. "Unnatural Conceptions: The Study of Monsters in France and England." *Past and Present* 92 (August 1981).

Parrinder, Geoffrey. *La brujería.* Trans. Buenos Aires: Eudeba, 1963.

———. *Witchcraft: European and African.* London: Faber and Faber, 1963.

Prado, Paulo. *Retrato do Brasil: Ensaio sobre a tristeza brasileira.* 7th ed. Rio de Janeiro: Livraria José Olympio, 1972.

Ramos, Artur. *O folclore negro no Brasil.* Rio de Janeiro: Civilização Brasileira, 1935.

———. *O negro brasileiro.* 2nd ed. São Paulo: Companhia Editora Nacional, 1940.

Ricard, Robert. *The Spiritual Conquest of Mexico: An Essay on the Apostolate and the Evangelizing Methods of the Mendicant Orders in New Spain, 1523–1572.* Trans. Lesley Byrd Simpson. Berkeley: University of California Press, 1982.

Robbins, Rossell Hope. *The Encyclopedia of Witchcraft and Demonology.* 3rd ed. London: Peter Nevill Ltd., 1963.

Rodrigues, José Honório. *História da história do Brasil, 1ª parte: Historiografia colonial.* São Paulo: Companhia Editora Nacional, 1979.

Rodrigues, Maria Tereza Campos. *Aspectos da administração municipal de Lisboa no século XV.* Reprint of nos. 101 to 109 of the Revista Municipal (Lisbon).

Roux, Jean-Paul. *Les explorateurs au Moyen-Âge.* Paris: Seuil, 1961.

Rowland, Robert. "Anthropology, Witchcraft, Inquisition." Mimeographed article. (Published in revised form in G. Henningsen and John Tedeschi [eds.], *The Inquisition in Early Modern Europe: Studies on Sources and Methods* [De Kalb: Northern Illinois University Press, 1986].)

Roy, Bruno. "En marge du monde connu: Les races de monstres." In Guy H. Allard, ed., *Aspects de la marginalité au Moyen-Âge.* Montreal: Éditions de l'Aurore, n.d.

Saraiva, Antonio José. *Inquisição e cristãos-novos.* Porto: Editorial Inova, n.d.

Schmitt, Jean-Claude. " 'Religion populaire' et culture folklorique." *Annales, E.S.C.,* 31st year, no. 5 (September–October 1976).

Sérgio, Antonio. "O Reino Cadaveroso, ou o problema da cultura em Portugal." In *Ensaios II.* Lisbon: Sá da Costa, 1972.

Silva Dias, J. S. da. *Os descobrimentos e a problemática cultural do século XVI.* Coimbra: Publicações do Seminário de Cultura Portuguesa, 1973.

Siqueira, Sônia A. *A Inquisição portuguesa e a sociedade colonial.* São Paulo: Ática, 1978.

Solé, Jacques. *L'amour en Occident à l'époque moderne.* Paris: Albin Michel, 1976.

Souza, Laura de Mello e. *Desclassificados do ouro: A pobreza mineira no século XVIII.* Rio de Janeiro: Graal, 1982.

———. "As devassas eclesiásticas da Arquidiocese de Mariana: Fonte primária para a história das mentalidades." *Anais do Museu Paulista* (São Paulo) 33 (1984): 65–73.

———. "Notas sobre os vadios na literatura colonial do século XVIII." In Roberto Schwarz, ed., *Os pobres na literatura brasileira.* São Paulo: Brasiliense, 1983.

———. "O padre e as feiticeiras: Notas sobre a sexualidade no Brasil Colonial." In Ronaldo Vainfas, ed., *História e sexualidade no Brasil.* Rio de Janeiro: Graal, 1986.

Sutto, Claude. "L'Image du monde connu à la fin du Moyen-Âge." In Guy Allard, ed., *Aspects de la marginalité au Moyen-Âge.* Montreal: Éditions de l'Aurore, n.d.

Thomas, Keith. *Religion and the Decline of Magic: Studies in Popular Beliefs in Sixteenth and Seventeenth Century England.* 4th ed. London: Weidenfeld and Nicolson, 1980.

Todorov, Tzvetan. *The Conquest of America: The Question of the Other.* Trans. Richard Howard. Norman: University of Oklahoma Press, 1999.

———. *La conquête de l'Amérique: La question de l'autre.* Paris: Seuil, 1982.

Trevor-Roper, Hugh R. "A obsessão das bruxas na Europa dos séculos XVI e XVII." In *Religião, reforma e transformação social.* Trans. Lisbon: Editorial Presença– Martins Fontes, n.d.

———. *The European Witch-Craze of the Sixteenth and Seventeenth Centuries.* London: Penguin Books, 1967.

Turmel, Joseph. *Histoire du diable.* Paris: Les Éditions Rieder, 1931.

Vainfas, Ronaldo. "Idéias escravistas no Brasil Colonial." Master's thesis, Universidade Federal Fluminense, Rio de Janeiro, Brazil, 1983.

———, ed. *História e sexualidade no Brasil.* Rio de Janeiro: Graal, 1986.

Vasconcellos, Sylvio de. *Mineiridade: Ensaio de caracterização.* Belo Horizonte: Imprensa Oficial, 1968.

Vauchez, André. *La spiritualité du Moyen-Âge occidental—VIIIe–XIIe siècles.* Paris: PUF, 1975.

———. *Spirituality of the Medieval West: From the Eighth to the Twelfth Century.* Trans. Kalamazoo, Mich.: Cistercian Publications, 1993.

Vergueiro, Laura. *Opulência e miséria de Minas Gerais.* São Paulo: Brasiliense, 1983.

Villeneuve, Roland. *Le diable: Érotologie de Satan.* Paris: Jean-Jacques Pauvert Éditeur, 1963.

———. *Le fléau des sorciers: Histoire de la diablerie basque au XVIIe siècle.* Paris: Flammarion, 1983.

Wallerstein, Immanuel. *El moderno sistema mundial: A agricultura capitalista y los orígenes de la economía-mundo europea en el siglo XVI.* Trans. Mexico City: Siglo Veintiuno Editores, 1979.

Wiznitzer, Arnold. *Os judeus no Brasil colonial.* Trans. Olivia Krähenbühl. São Paulo: Pioneira-EDUSP, 1960.

Index